Cinematic Ghosts

Cinematic Ghosts

Haunting and Spectrality from
Silent Cinema to the Digital Era

EDITED BY MURRAY LEEDER

Bloomsbury Academic
An imprint of Bloomsbury Publishing Inc

B L O O M S B U R Y
NEW YORK · LONDON · NEW DELHI · SYDNEY

Bloomsbury Academic

An imprint of Bloomsbury Publishing Plc

1385 Broadway
New York
NY 10018
USA

50 Bedford Square
London
WC1B 3DP
UK

www.bloomsbury.com

BLOOMSBURY and the Diana logo are trademarks of Bloomsbury Publishing Plc

First published 2015

© Murray Leeder and Contributors, 2015

All rights reserved. No part of this publication may be reproduced or transmitted in any form or by any means, electronic or mechanical, including photocopying, recording, or any information storage or retrieval system, without prior permission in writing from the publishers.

No responsibility for loss caused to any individual or organization acting on or refraining from action as a result of the material in this publication can be accepted by Bloomsbury or the author.

ISBN: HB: 978-1-6289-2214-1
PB: 978-1-6289-2213-4
ePub: 978-1-6289-2216-5
ePDF: 978-1-6289-2215-8

Library of Congress Cataloging-in-Publication Data

Cinematic ghosts : haunting and spectrality from silent cinema to the digital era / edited by Murray Leeder.
  pages cm
  ISBN 978-1-62892-214-1 (hardback) – ISBN 978-1-62892-213-4 (paperback)
1. Ghosts in motion pictures. 2. Supernatural in motion pictures. I. Leeder, Murray, editor.
  PN1995.9.S8C55 2015
  791.43'657–dc23
  2015003282

Typeset by Integra Software Services Pvt. Ltd.

Contents

Acknowledgments viii

Introduction
Murray Leeder, University of Calgary 1

PART ONE Ghosts of Pre-Cinema and Silent Cinema 15

1 Phantom Images and Modern Manifestations: Spirit Photography, Magic Theater, Trick Films, and Photography's Uncanny
Tom Gunning, University of Chicago 17

2 "Visualizing the Phantoms of the Imagination": Projecting the Haunted Minds of Modernity
Murray Leeder, University of Calgary 39

3 Specters of the Mind: Ghosts, Illusion, and Exposure in Paul Leni's *The Cat and the Canary*
Simone Natale, Humbolt University 59

4 Supernatural Speech: Silent Cinema's Stake in Representing the Impossible
Robert Alford, University of California, Berkeley 77

PART TWO Cinematic Ghosts from the 1940s through the 1980s 95

5   Bad Sync: Spectral Sound and Retro-Effects
    in *Portrait of Jennie*
    René Thoreau Bruckner, University of Southern California 97

6   "Antique Chiller": Quality, Pretention, and History
    in the Critical Reception of *The Innocents* and *The Haunting*
    Mark Jancovich, University of East Anglia 115

7   Shadows of Shadows: The Undead in Ingmar
    Bergman's Cinema
    Maurizio Cinquegrani, University of Kent 129

8   Locating the Specter in Dan Curtis's *Burnt Offerings*
    Dara Downey, University College Dublin 143

9   The Bawdy Body in Two Comedy Ghost Films:
    Topper and *Beetlejuice*
    Katherine A. Fowkes, High Point University 159

PART THREE Millennial Ghosts 177

10 "I See Dead People": Visualizing Ghosts in
    the American Horror Film before the Arrival of CGI
    Steffen Hantke, Sogang University 179

11 Spectral Remainders and Transcultural Hauntings:
    (Re)iterations of the *Onryō* in Japanese Horror Cinema
    Jay McRoy, University of Wisconsin – Parkside 199

CONTENTS

12 *Painted Skin*: Romance with the Ghostly
Femme Fatale in Contemporary Chinese Cinema
Li Zeng, Illinois State University 219

13 "It's Not the House That's Haunted": Demons,
Debt, and the Family in Peril in Recent Horror Cinema
Bernice M. Murphy, Trinity College, Dublin 235

14 Glitch Gothic
Marc Olivier, Brigham Young University 253

15 Showing the Unknowable: *Uncle Boonmee
Who Can Recall His Past Lives*
Mitsuyo Wada-Marciano, Carleton University 271

Afterword: Haunted Viewers
Jeffrey Sconce, Northwestern University 290

List of Contributors 296

Index 300

Acknowledgments

First and foremost, thanks must go to the editorial staff at Bloomsbury, especially Katie Gallof, for their tireless efforts and support. I would also like to extend special thanks to Indiana University Press: Tom Gunning's "Phantom Images," which originally appeared in *Fugitive Images: From Photography to Video* (ed. Patrice Petro, Copyright © 1995, IU Press), is reprinted with permission of Indiana University Press. I would also like to thank all of the contributors for taking a shot on an unproved editor.

This project was spurred in part by conversations with André Loiselle, Simone Natale, and James Cahill, all of whom deserve special recognition for their early encouragement and advice. Other supportive parties included Pamela Thurschwell, Esther Peeren, Adam Lowenstein, Colin Davis, Annette Hill, Aviva Briefel, Bliss Cua Lim, Matthew Solomon, Drew Beard, Colin Williamson, Ryan Pierson, Adam Hart, Brian R. Hauser, Aalya Ahmad, Sean Moreland, Jeffrey Weinstock, Tara Turner, and more. I would also like to thank all of my colleagues and friends at Carleton University, the University of Manitoba, and the University of Calgary for their help and support at various stages (Daniel Sheridan and David Richler deserve to be singled out for particular tasks along the way).

I would also like to thank my wife, Alana Conway, for her patience, love, and support.

Introduction

Murray Leeder

> *"Bless my soul, I'm a spirit! I haven't a body!*
> *I haven't had one for four years. Is that clear?"*
> *"But I can see you."*
> *"All you see is an illusion. It's like a blasted lantern slide!"*
> CAPTAIN GREGG (REX HARRISON) AND LUCY MUIR
> (GENE TIERNEY) IN *THE GHOST AND MRS. MUIR* (1947)

The cinema is full of ghosts. And why not? The ghost is a powerful, versatile metaphor. It can signify the ways in which memory and history, whether traumatic, nostalgic, or both, linger on within the "living present."[1] It can be a potent representation of and figure of resistance for those who are unseen and unacknowledged, reduced to a spectral half-presence by dominant culture and official history.[2] It presents intriguing alternatives to linear conceptions of time and narrative, opening "the possibility of a

---

[1] For various examples, see Avery F. Gordon, *Ghostly Matters: Haunting and the Sociological Imagination* (Minneapolis: University of Minnesota Press, 1997), Gabriele Schwab, *Haunting Legacies: Violent Histories and Transgenerational Trauma* (New York: Columbia University Press, 2010); Arthur Redding, *Haints: American Ghosts, Millennial Passions, and Contemporary Gothic Fiction* (Tuscaloosa: The University of Alabama Press, 2011).

[2] A decidedly nonexhaustive list would include: Renée L. Bergland, *The National Uncanny: Indian Ghosts and American Subjects* (Hanover: University Press of New England, 2000); Bianca Del Villano, *Ghostly Alterities: Spectrality and Contemporary Literatures in English* (Stuttgart: Ibidem-Verlag, 2007); Marisa Parham, *Haunting and Displacement in African American Literature* (London: Routledge, 2008), Tabish Khair, *The Gothic, Postcolonialism and Otherness: Ghosts from Elsewhere* (Houndmills, Basingstoke: Palgrave Macmillan, 2009); Gerry Turcotte, *Peripheral Fear: Transformations of the Gothic in Canadian and Australian Fiction* (Brussels: Peter Lang, 2009); Katrin Althans, *Darkness Subverted: Aboriginal Gothic in Black Australian Literature and Film* (Bonn: Bonn University Press, 2010); Esther Peeren, *The Spectral Metaphor: Living Ghosts and the Agency of Invisibility* (Houndmills, Basingstoke: Palgrave Macmillan, 2014).

radicalized concept of noncontemporaneity," as Bliss Cua Lim puts it.[3] It can also be a figure for the alienating disjuncture between body and spirit wrought by modern communications technologies.[4] Kafka knew this when, at the end of his failed epistolary romance with Felice Bauer, he wrote bitterly that "Written kisses don't reach their destination, rather they are drunk on the way by the ghosts.... The ghosts won't starve, but we will perish."[5]

Of course, ghosts are more than just a metaphor: they "exist in their own right.... Ghosts have legitimate power, articulate real pains and desires, and refuse fully to be explained away as figments of diseased or troubled imaginations."[6] They are part of the worldview of billions, and the modernity has brought with it the hopes that we might document ghosts, objectively and scientifically, using modern media. Some spiritualists embraced the spirit photograph, which purportedly presented positive proof of the afterlife's reality,[7] and various early twentieth-century writers wondered about an equivalent "spirit-cinema."[8] The ghost-hunting television serials so popular today—*Most Haunted* (2002–2010), *Ghost Hunters* (2004–), etc.[9]—show us that the dream of spirit-cinema is still alive. The quest for mediated ghost-seeing (or otherwise ghost-sensing) was paralleled by attempts to contact

---

[3]Bliss Cua Lim, "Spectral Times: The Ghost Film as History Allegory," *Positions: East Asia Cultures Critique* 9.2 (Fall 2001), 288.
[4]Jeffrey Sconce, *Haunted Media: Electronic Presence from Telegraphy to Television* (Durham: Duke University Press, 2000); Emily D. Edwards, *Metaphysical Media: The Occult Experience in Popular Culture* (Carbondale: Southern Illinois University Press, 2005), esp. 3–69; Annette Hill, *Paranormal Media* (London: Routledge, 2011).
[5]Qtd. in Friedrich Kittler, *Gramophone, Film, Typewriter* (Stanford: Stanford University Press, 1999), 225, 226.
[6]Redding 6.
[7]See Martyn Jolly, *Faces of the Dead: The Belief in Spirit Photography* (London: British Library, 2006); John Harvey, *Photography and Spirit* (London: Reaktion Books, 2007); Louis Kaplan, *The Strange Case of William Mumler, Spirit Photographer* (Minneapolis: Minnesota University Press, 2008); Simone Natale, "A Short History of Superimposition," *Early Popular Visual Culture* 10.2 (2012), 125–45.
[8]Matthew Solomon, *Disappearing Tricks: Silent Film, Houdini, and the New Magic of the Twentieth Century* (Urbana: University of Illinois Press, 2010), 24–5.
[9]For sources on these, see Jessica O'Hara, "Making Their Presence Known: TV's Ghost-Hunter Phenomenon in a 'Post-'World,'" in *The Philosophy of Horror*, ed. Thomas Fahy (Lexington: University Press of Kentucky, 2010), 72–85; Alissa Burger, "*Ghost Hunters:* Simulated Participation in Televisual Hauntings," in Introduction, *Popular Ghosts: The Haunted Spaces of Everyday Culture*, eds. María del Pilar Blanco and Esther Peeren (New York: Continuum), 162–74; Karen Williams, "The Liveness of Ghosts: Haunting and Reality TV," in Introduction, *Popular Ghosts: The Haunted Spaces of Everyday Culture*, eds. María del Pilar Blanco and Esther Peeren (New York: Continuum), 149–61; Sarah Juliet Lauro and Catherine Paul, "'Make Me Believe!': Ghost-Hunting Technology and the Postmodern Fantastic," *Horror Studies* 4.2 (October 2013), 205–23; Karen J. Renner, "Negotiations of Masculinity in American Ghost-Hunting Reality Television," *Horror Studies* 4.2 (October 2013), 225–43.

the dead through radio technology,[10] and in many respects spiritualism traces back to the invention of the telegraph, its stunning new potential for new-instantaneous long-distance communication opening fresh speculations about talking with the dead. The Internet, too, has its own ghostly potential; as Trond Lundemo writes, "Cyberspace is a ghostly matter with important connections to the all-surrounding ether of modern media transmissions."[11]

Certainly, all media have their spectral dimensions. "Every new medium is machine for the production of ghosts,"[12] as John Durham Peters puts it, and his statement encapsulates much of the recent research on the role the supernatural has played in the modern world. In different ways, a number of scholars have charted the ways in which the communication and recording technologies of the last two centuries, rather than chasing the supernatural from the world, have enhanced its domain. With its ability to record and replay reality and its presentation of images that resemble the world but as intangible half-presences, cinema has been described as a haunted or ghostly medium from early on. The exchange from *The Ghost and Mrs. Muir* that opens this introduction illustrates cinema's own tendency toward reflexivity about these ghostly qualities. Captain Gregg has no body and yet we see him. We see an illusion, and yet it is *something*, and to characterize this paradox for Lucy and to us, the Captain needs to reach to a metaphor from one of cinema's ancestors, the magic lantern, itself associated with realms of the supernatural for centuries.[13]

Cinema does not need to depict ghosts to be ghostly and haunted. Deliberately or accidentally, it has become a storehouse for our dead. It may be the case that, as one reporter wrote when *La Poste* reviewing the Lumière cinematograph, "When this device is made available to the public, everyone will be able to photograph those dear to them, not just in their immobile form but in their movement, in their action, and with speech on

---

[10]See especially Sconce 59–91, as well as the film *White Noise* (2005). The classic UK television play *The Stone Tape* (1972) also deals with attempts to use modern sound technology to document the supernatural, and *The Fog* (1980) draws suggestive connections between radio, the ocean and the "etheric ocean" of telecommunications (see Murray Leeder, "Skeletons Sail an Etheric Ocean: Approaching the Ghost in John Carpenter's *The Fog*," *The Journal of Popular Film and Television* 37.2 (2009), 70–9).
[11]Trond Lundemo, "In the Kingdom of Shadows: Cinematic Movement and Its Digital Ghost," in *The YouTube Reader*, eds. Pelle Snickars and Patrick Vonderau (Stockholm: National Library of Sweden, 2009), 316. See also Sarah Walters, "Ghosting the Interface: Cyberspace and Spiritualism," *Science as Culture* 6.3 (1997), 414–43; Isabella van Efferen, "Dances with Spectres: Theorizing the Cybergothic," *Gothic Studies* 11.1 (2009), 99–112, Sconce 167–209.
[12]John Durham Peters, *Speaking into the Air: A History of the Idea of Communication* (Chicago: University of Chicago Press, 1999), 139.
[13]An appropriate reference for the film's early twentieth century setting.

their lips; then death will no longer be absolute..."[14] but this apparent immortality is also a brand of living death. In 1937, Graham Greene remarked that "One really begins to feel that the cinema has got a history when it's so full of ghosts. Miss Jean Harlow walking and speaking after death...."[15] An urban legend emerged about, of all films, *Three Men and a Baby* (1987), where an unexplained image at the back of the frame (actually a cardboard cutout, a prop from an excised subplot) became the basis for an extravagant legend about a suicidal boy who killed himself in the apartment where the film was shot.[16] It is unclear whether we are supposed to believe that the ghost was present on the set and was documented by the film's cameras, or if the ghost somehow resides within the film itself (perhaps the way Sadako lives within the tape in *Ring* (1998)), but the distinction is basically a fine one. It attests to the continuing appeal of the idea of cinema as a haunted space.

In broader view, this association goes back to cinema's beginnings.[17] Ghosts have been with cinema since its first days, finding a natural residence in the films of trick filmmakers like Georges Méliès, George Albert Smith, Edwin R. Booth, and Segundo du Chomón. Cinema's capacity for substitutions, transpositions, and other tricks enabled and motivated the production of ghost and poltergeist scenes, such as in the innumerable "haunted hotel" scenarios of a traveler comically beset by supernatural forces.[18] Furthermore, many of the media that anticipate cinema centrally involve ghosts and the supernatural as well. There were the gloomy shows of the Phantasmagoria, pioneered at the end of the late eighteenth century, which mixed magic lanterns with a gamut of tricks to display images of skeletons, devils, and ghosts. The Phantasmagoria provided an experience that tested the boundaries of the scientific and the supernatural.[19] There

---

[14] Qtd. in Jon Stratton, *The Desirable Body: Cultural Fetishism and the Erotics of Consumption* (Manchester: Manchester University Press, 1996), 83.
[15] Qtd. in Tom Ruffles, *Ghost Images: Cinema of the Afterlife* (Jefferson: McFarland, 2004), 199.
[16] "Three Men and a Ghost," *Snopes.com*, http://www.snopes.com/movies/films/3menbaby.asp January 9, 2007 (accessed April 11, 2013). The film was actually shot on a soundstage, but the legend persists to this day.
[17] For other accounts of the ghostliness of pre- and early cinema not otherwise cited here, see Lynda Nead, *The Haunted Gallery: Painting, Photography, Film c. 1900* (New Haven: Yale University Press, 2007), and Owen Davies, *The Haunted: A Social History of Ghosts* (Houndmills, Basingstoke: Palgrave Macmillan, 2007), 187–215.
[18] Méliès's *L'auberge ensorcelée* (1897) and J. Stuart Blackton's *The Haunted Hotel* (1907) are among the best examples.
[19] See Terry Castle, *The Female Thermometer: 18th Century and the Invention of the Uncanny* (New York: Oxford University Press, 1995); Laurent Mannoni, *The Great Art of Light and Shadow: The Archaeology of Cinema* (Exeter: University of Exeter Press, 2000); Mervyn Heard, *Phantasmagoria: The Secret Life of the Magic Lantern* (Hastings: The Projection Box, 2006).

INTRODUCTION 5

was the theatrical technique called "Pepper's Ghost," honed in the 1860s, that used reflections to project the "live" image of a moving, transparent specter who could interact with the actor on the stage.[20] Its evolution, the fairground "Ghost Show," would be one of the venues through which audiences first experienced moving photography.[21] Meanwhile, spirit photography provided the photographic techniques that led to cinematic double exposures, the first conventional strategy for displaying ghosts on screen.

Famously, Maxim Gorky appealed to spectral metaphors during his initial viewing of the Lumière program at Nizhni-Novgorod in 1896:

> Last night I was in the Kingdom of Shadows.
>
> If you only knew how strange it is to be here. It is a world without sound, without colour. Everything there—the earth, the trees, the people, the water and the air—is dipped in monotonous grey. Gray rays of the sun across the grey sky, grey eyes in grey faces, and the leaves of the trees are ashen grey. It is not life but its shadow, not motion but its soundless spectre.

The review continues for three pages in this mode of melancholy, in contrast to those commentators in early cinema who emphasized shock, novelty, and amazement. Of the people on the screen, Gorky states:

> the grey silhouettes of the people, as though condemned to eternal silence and
>
> cruelly punished by being deprived of all the colours of life, glide noiselessly along the grey ground.
>
> Their smiles are lifeless, even though their movements are full of living energy and are so swift as to be almost imperceptible. Their laughter is soundless, although you see the muscles contracting in their grey faces. Before you a life is surging, a life deprived of words and shorn of the living spectrum of colours—the grey, the soundless, the bleak and dismal life.

---

[20] See Dassia N. Posner, "Spectres on the New York Stage: The (Pepper's) Ghost Craze of 1863," in *Representations of Death in Nineteenth-Century U.S. Writing and Culture*, ed. Lucy Elizabeth Frank (Aldershot: Ashgate, 2007), 189–204; Helen Groth, "Reading Victorian Illusions: Dickens's *Haunted Man* and Dr. Pepper's 'Ghost'," *Victorian Studies* 5.10 (Autumn 2007), 43–65; Jeremy Brooker, "The Polytechnic Ghost: Pepper's Ghost, Metempsychosis and the Magic Lantern at the Royal Polytechnic Institution," *Early Popular Visual Culture* 5.2 (2007), 189–206.

[21] See Vanessa Toulmin, *Randall Williams: King of Showmen. From Ghost Show to Bioscope* (London: The Projection Box, 1998), Davies 209–10.

It is terrifying to see, but it is the movement of shadows, only of shadows. Curses and ghosts, the evil spirits have cast entire cities into eternal sleep, come to mind and you feel as though Merlin's vicious trick is being enacted before you.[22]

As he sat watching images that posterity would recall as exemplifying realism, Gorky clearly did not need ghostly subject matter to perceive cinema as a supernatural medium. Nor was he alone in location spectrality at the level of medium. Stephen Bottomore quotes an account of an Englishman recalling a boyhood visit to the cinema as "yet another glimpse of the supernatural in a world half shrouded in a fog of myth."[23] Likewise, spiritualists, long used to framing new developments in science as fresh evidence for the existence of the spirit world, would draw the cinematic into their rhetorical arsenal, from W.T. Stead's citation of "The Kinetiscope of Nature" and "The Kinetiscope of the Mind" in 1896[24] to spiritualist Dr. Guy Bogart visiting the set of *The Bishop of the Ozarks* (1923), a film with a pro-spiritualist theme, and becoming "convinced he saw a real spirit manifest itself on the set to complement the film's special effects."[25]

It is tempting to locate these reactions within a period of what Laura Mulvey calls a "technological uncanny," a sense of unease and anxiety associated with a new medium that eventually vanishes with familiarity.[26] And yet it seems equally possible to argue, with reference to cinema's aforementioned predecessors, that cinema's supernatural affinities stemmed as much from its continuities with previous media as its newness. The trope of film as supernatural would linger in film theory and criticism, with several scholars identifying cinema as the ideal medium for the depiction of supernatural. In 1923, reflecting on *The Phantom Carriage* (1921) and *Earthbound* (1920), Ricciotto Canudo argued that "cinema permits, and must further develop, the extraordinary and striking faculty of *representing immateriality*."[27] A year later, Béla Balázs would assert

---

[22]Maxim Gorky, "A review of the Lumière programme at the Nizhni-Novgorod Fair, as printed in the *Nizhegorodski listok*, newspaper, July 4, 1896, and signed 'I.M. Pacatus,'" Appendix to Jay Leyda, *A History of the Russian and Soviet Film* (London: Unwin House, 1960), 407.
[23]Stephen Bottomore, "The Panicking Audience? Early Cinema and the 'Train Effect,'" *Historical Journal of Film, Radio and Television* 19.2 (1999), 179.
[24]W.T. Stead, "Suggestions from Science for Psychic Students: Useful Analogies from Recent Discoveries and Inventions," *Borderland* 3.4 (1896), 400–11.
[25]Jolly, 143.
[26]Laura Mulvey, *Death 24x a Section: Stillness and the Moving Image* (London: Reaktion, 2006), 27.
[27]Ricciotto Canudo, "Reflections on the Seventh Art," in *French Film Theory and Criticism: A History/ Anthology, 1907–1939*, V1, ed. Richard Abel (Princeton: Princeton University Press, 1988), 300–1. Emphasis original.

INTRODUCTION

that "[it] is certain ... that no written or oral literature is able to express the ghostly, the demonic and the supernatural as well as the cinematic."[28] In 1945, Parker Tyler argued that

> Movie-camera trickery is of a magic-carpet kind—but here this expression not only is a figure of speech but denotes an actual vision, albeit only an image recorded by one mechanism and thrown by another onto a screen— an image as insubstantial as a ghost itself. With this power to render the human substance into mere symbolic ectoplasm, the movie camera possesses a perambulation parallel to the movements supposedly initiated in actual Ghost Land.[29]

Many decades later, the idea of cinema as ghostly would be revisited in earnest, mainly by scholars associated with the so-called spectral turn inaugurated by the publication of Jacques Derrida's controversial *Specters of Marx* (1993; English translation 1994) and the punning neologism "hauntology."[30] Some years earlier, Derrida played himself in several scenes of Ken McMullan's experimental film *Ghost Dance* (1983). In the longest of these, lead actress Pascale Ogier asks Derrida if he believes in ghosts. Derrida says:

> Here the ghost is me. Since I've been asked to play myself in a film, which is more or less improvised, I feel as if I'm letting a ghost speak through me. Curiously, instead of playing myself, without knowing it I let a ghost ventriloquize my words, or play my role ... Cinema is an art of phantoms (*phantomachia*), a battle of phantoms. I think that's what the cinema's about, when it's not boring. It's the art of letting ghosts come back ... I believe that modern developments in technology and telecommunication, instead of diminishing the realm of ghosts ... enhances the power of ghosts and their ability to haunt us ... I say, "Long live the ghosts."

---

[28] Béla Balázs, *Béla Balázs: Early Film Theory: Visible Man and The Spirit of Film* (New York: Beghahn Books, 2010).
[29] Parker Tyler, "Supernaturalism in the Movies," *Theatre Arts* 26.6 (June 1945), 343.
[30] Jacques Derrida, *Specters of Marx: The State of Debt, the Work of Mourning and the New International* (New York: Routledge, 1994). For explications of hauntology, see *Ghostly Demarcations: A Symposium on Jacques Derrida's* Specters of Marx, ed. Michael Sprinkler (London: Verso, 1999); Colin Davis, *Haunted Subjects: Deconstruction, Psychoanalysis and the Return of the Dead* (Houndmills, Basingstoke: Palgrave Macmillan, 2007); Christine Berthin, *Gothic Hauntings: Melancholy Crypts and Textual Ghosts* (Houndmills, Basingstoke: Palgrave Macmillan, 2010).

Ogier died a year after the film was released, the day before her twenty-sixth birthday, and Derrida later would describe the experience of watching the film again with the knowledge of her death:

> Suddenly I saw Pascale's face, which I know was a dead woman's face, come onto the screen. She answered my question: "Do you believe in ghost?" Practically looking me in the eye, she said to me again, on the big screen, "Yes, now I do, yes." Which now? Years later in Texas. I had the unnerving sense of the return of her specter, the specter of her specter coming back to say to me—to me, here, now: "Now…now…now, that is to say in this dark room on another continent, in another world, here, now, yes, believe me, I believe in ghost."[31]

This passage sums up several different aspects of the ghost: the overturning of time and space implicit in Hamlet's statement (much discussed by Derrida) that "The time is out of joint," the enabling of haunting by technology, and the personal, in which the ghost is associated with an individual experience of mourning. All of these links are facilitated by cinema: a haunted medium, a haunting medium, a medium that puts us in touch with ghosts.

The idea of cinema having a special relationship with the ghost, of itself being ghostly or haunted, is a powerful and widespread one. In *Dark Places: The Haunted House in Film* (2008), Barry Curtis develops the reflexive properties of haunted cinematic space at some length.[32] Decades earlier, sociologist Barry Brummett noted a set of homologies between the cinematic audience and ghosts: "At a very simple level, the movie-goers haunt the theatre like ghosts haunt their respective houses. Audiences as well as ghosts gather in the dark…audiences experience the same paradoxes of free and restricted movement encountered by characters and ghosts."[33] Brummett also noted that Baudry's statement that "if the eye which moves is no longer fettered by a body, by the laws of matter and time, if there be

---

[31] Jacques Derrida and Bernard Steigler, "Spectrographies," in *The Spectralities Reader: Ghosts and Haunting in Contemporary Cultural Theory*, eds. María del Pilar Blanco and Esther Peeren (New York: Bloomsbury, 2013), 40. For more on *Ghost Dance*, see "Derrida on Film: Staging Spectral Sincerity," in *The Rhetoric of Sincerity*, eds. Ernest van Alphen, Mieke Bal and Carel Smith (Stanford: Stanford University Press, 2009), 214–29.
[32] Barry Curtis, *Dark Places: The Haunted House in Film* (London: Reaktion, 2008).
[33] Barry Brummett, "Electric Literature as Equipment for Living: Haunted House Films," *Critical Studies in Mass Communications* 2.3 (1985), 258.

INTRODUCTION 9

no assignable limits to its displacement"[34] appears to describe a ghost but in fact describes the viewer of a film.[35]

Yet declaring "the spectre as the 'ur' figure of cinema"[36] is fraught with difficulties of its own, and opens itself to critiques common to hauntology and the spectral turn. The editors of the collection *The Victorian Supernatural* (2004) observe that "for Derrida, history is structurally and necessarily haunted, but where is the supernatural to be found in this kind of haunting? The problem is that the ghost is only one in a series of deconstructive tropes."[37] They argue that Derrida's conception of the ghost, though evocative, is necessarily an ahistorical one. It is not sensitive to how the supernatural means different things in different cultures and at different times, and is not well suited to considerations of people's actual experience of the supernatural. Likewise, Roger Luckhurst, in the article that coined the term "spectral turn," warns against the "generalizing economy of haunting" as ahistorical and limiting, producing a paradigm whereby the ghost is not a specific symptom singular to its time and place but rather is understood only within "the generalized structure of haunting [which] is symptomatically blind to its generative loci."[38]

This is part of the reason why *Cinematic Ghosts*, which casts a wide net in terms of critical methodologies, contains relatively few essays adopting the psychoanalytic and deconstructive approaches to the cinematic ghosts that have often prevailed. It is not in rejection of these critical approaches, but rather an attempt to complicate the picture and expand the field. Presenting a variety of essays assaying cinema's ghosts, this volume marks the first collection of essays specifically about cinematic ghosts. It enters a lively field of publishing about ghosts, magic, and the supernatural in the last twenty years. Books specifically about cinema and ghosts are not numerous, but those that exist (including Katherine A. Fowkes's *Giving Up the Ghost: Spirits, Ghosts and Angels in Mainstream Comedy Films* (1998), Tom Ruffles's *Ghost Images: Cinema of the Afterlife* (2004), Lee Kovacs's *The Haunted Screen: Ghosts in Literature and Film* (2005), Alice Rayner's *Ghosts: Death's Double*

---

[34] Jean-Louis Baudry, "The Ideological Effects of the Cinematic Apparatus," *Film Quarterly* 28.2 (Winter 1974–1975), 43.
[35] Brummett 252–3.
[36] Alan Cholodenko, "The Crypt, the Haunted House, of Cinema," *Cultural Studies Review* 10.2 (September 2004), 103.
[37] Nicola Brown, Carolyn Burdett and Pamela Thurschwell, "Introduction," in *The Victorian Supernatural*, eds. Nicola Brown, Carolyn Burdett and Pamela Thurschwell (Cambridge: Cambridge University Press, 2004), 12.
[38] Roger Luckhurst, "The Contemporary London Gothic and the Limits of the 'Spectral Turn,'" *Textual Practice* 16.3 (2002), 532, 528.

and the Phenomena of Theatre (2006), Mark Pizzotto's Ghosts of Theatre and Film in the Brain (2006), and Barry Curtis's aforementioned Dark Places: The Haunted House in Film (2008)) all represent useful contribution to a growing area.[39] Cinematic Ghosts hopes to build on their example. The principal focus here is on films featuring "non-figurative ghosts"—that is, ghosts supposed, at least diegetically, to be "real"—in contrast to "figurative ghosts,"[40] though certain of the films discussed herein, notably Uncle Boonmee Who Can Recall His Past Lives (2010), test the usefulness of this distinction.

* * * * *

The first section of Cinematic Ghosts is entitled "Ghosts of Pre-Cinema and Silent Cinema." It begins with a reprint of an important, often-cited, but now-out-of-print article by Tom Gunning, "Phantom Images and Modern Manifestations: Spirit Photography, Magic Theater, Trick Films, and Photography's Uncanny." Originally published in 1995, it played a significant role in the recent wave of interest in media and the modern supernatural. Its value to a great many scholars has been the links it draws between Freud's uncanny, the hope to use modern technology to overcoming death or contact the afterlife, and the technologies and practices that led to cinema. In his chapter, Murray Leeder takes these themes in a slightly different direction, exploring the uncanniness of proto-cinematic media through projection and its linkages with the haunted inner spaces of the modern subject. His article "'Visualizing the Phantoms of the Imagination': Projecting the Haunted Minds of Modernity" explores this topic through examples like Edward Bulwer-Lytton's novella "The Haunted and the Haunters," David Starr Jordan's Sympsychography Hoax and W.T. Stead's writings on the "Kinetiscope of the Mind." It then moves forward to demonstrate the persistence of the film–mind–supernatural nexus, referencing Gordon Lightfoot's song "If You Could Read My Mind" and the film Stir of Echoes (1999).

The other two essays in this section move forward from early cinema to explore ghosts in the later silent period. In "Specters of the Mind: Ghosts, Illusion, and Exposure in Paul Leni's The Cat and the Canary," Simone Natale examines the influential haunted house film The Cat and the Canary (1927).

---

[39] It would be impossible to cite all of the individual articles on cinematic ghost films not otherwise mentioned here, though I will single out Mike Wayne's "Spectres, Marx's Theory of Value, and the Horror Film," Film International 10 (2004), 4–13, and Aviva Briefel's "What Some Ghosts Don't Know: Spectral Incognizance and the Horror Film" (Narrative 17.1 (2009), 95–108 as key texts.

[40] Here I borrow María del Pilar Blanco and Esther Peeren's language (María del Pilar Blanco and Esther Peeren, Introduction, Popular Ghosts: The Haunted Spaces of Everyday Culture (New York: Continuum), x).

In Tzvetan Todorov's terms,[41] this is a "fantastic-uncanny" narrative in which supernatural possibilities eventually give way to naturalistic explanations. But Natale shows that, even as it narratively mirrors an exposé of the supernatural such as those performed by nineteenth-century magicians, *The Cat and the Canary* ultimately participates in the displacement of the supernatural into the mind described by Terry Castle in her work on the Phantasmagoria. Closing out the section, Robert Alford's "Supernatural Speech: Silent Cinema's Stake in Representing the Impossible" explores the silent cinema's interest in visualizing the supernatural by honing in "supernatural speech," something cinema can imaginatively and powerfully (and yet, safely) represent even as it cannot instantiate it. Alford argues that this is an ability that was diminished, if not lost altogether, with the conversion to sound.

The second section is entitled "Cinematic Ghosts from the 1940s through the 1980s." The Second World War saw the emergence of the group of comic and romantic ghost films that would later be referred to as *film blanc*[42] and the section begins with a new approach to one of the most beloved: William Dieterle's *Portrait of Jennie* (1948). Like Alford's paper, René Thoreau Bruckner's "Bad Sync: Spectral Sound and Retro-effects in *Portrait of Jennie*" concerns sound as a haunting element of the cinema. Here, Bruckner hones in on the desynchronizing and detemporalizing potential of "bad sync" as an unintended effect that is nonetheless appropriate to the film's themes of temporal rupture.

As *Portrait of Jennie* also shows, the ghost has tended to lend itself to "quality" depictions of the supernatural in cinema, even within the generally understood parameters of the horror film. The "quality horror film" of the first half of the 1960s, seeming to target a more adult and literate audience, included a number of prominent ghost films (generally adaptations). However, Mark Jancovich's "'Antique Chiller': Quality, Pretention, and History in the Critical Reception of *The Innocents* and *The Haunting*" shows us that these films, now considered classics, were received less warmly at the time, in part because their ambiguous position between serious cinematic art and lowbrow entertainment challenged accepted cultural categories. Taking the discussion of ghosts as a presence in "quality" cinema in another direction, Maurizio Cinquegrani's "Shadows of Shadows: The Undead in Ingmar Bergman's Cinema" explores the permutations of the traditional Swedish specters, the *draugr* or *haugbúi*, as they emerge in Swedish cinema in general

---

[41]Tzvetan Todorov, *The Fantastic: A Structural Approach to a Literary Genre* (Cleveland: Press of Case Western Reserve University, 1973).
[42]Peter L. Valenti, "The Film Blanc: Suggestions for a Variety of Fantasy, 1940–45," *Journal of Popular Film* 6.4 (1978), 294–304.

and Bergman's often-haunted films in particular. Cinquegrani works to locate Bergman's specters within gothic and pagan traditions, as well as Swedish national literature and cinema.

Dara Downey's article "Locating the Spectre in Dan Curtis's *Burnt Offerings*" deals with another adaptation, *Burnt Offerings* (1976), which Downey argues explores a classic haunted house theme in an unusually direct way: the "imprisoning and dangerous qualities of domestic space." Downey draws attention to how the film allegorizes the tyranny of domestic space over the lives of middle-class housewives in the mid-twentieth-century American culture. A different strain of domestic haunted house narrative is under consideration in Katherine A. Fowkes's "The Bawdy Body in Two Comedy Ghost Films: *Topper* and *Beetlejuice*." These two films, made a half-century apart in 1937 and 1988, respectively, are both slapstick comedies about ghost couples. "While it may seem ironic for dead characters to be used as a device to provoke a better appreciation of life," writes Fowkes, "this function seems to be one that comedy ghosts are particularly well suited to fulfill, particularly through challenging ideas about the dignity and mastery of the human body."

The third section is entitled "Millennial Ghosts," and it largely covers the fertile period that marks the transition from "Chances are, ghosts will make another comeback,"[43] the first line of one academic collection on the subject of ghosts in 1999, to "It seems that ghosts are everywhere these days,"[44] the first line of another from eleven years later. The first article of this section, Steffen Hantke's "'I See Dead People': Visualizing Ghosts in the American Horror Film before the Arrival of CGI" takes its title from the monumentally successful *The Sixth Sense* (1999), and explores the changing strategies of representations of ghosts throughout American cinema history. Hantke argues that a new strategy emerges in the digital era for the depictions of ghosts, especially in the J-horror, and found-footage cycles.

As Hantke alludes to a significant development around the millennium is the increased interest in Asian ghost films, and, in particular, the arrival of the iconic ghost of "J-Horror" onto the international stage. Jay McRoy's "Spectral Remainders and Transcultural Hauntings: (Re)iterations of the *Onryō* in Japanese Horror Cinema" chronicles the cinematic history of the *onryō*, the pallid, black-haired female ghost of Japanese tradition. McRoy explores the cinematic history of the *onryō* and then explores her

---

[43]Peter Buse and Andrew Stott, Introduction, *Ghosts: Deconstruction, Psychoanalysis, History* (New York: St. Martin's Press, 1999), 1.
[44]Blanco and Peeren, ix.

contemporary expansion onto the transnational stage through the *Ringu* and *Ju-on* cycles. In contrast, Li Zeng's essay "*Painted Skin*: Romance with the Ghostly Femme Fatale in Contemporary Chinese Cinema" discusses how Chinese cinema has done little to exploit its folklore of vengeful female ghosts. Rather, a film like *Painted Skin* (2008) turns a monstrous ghost into a romantic one. Comparing different iterations of the old story on which the story is based, the article shows that *Painted Skin* reflects the same male fear of female sexuality as the original folk tale but develops these themes differently, reflecting the cultural and social context of contemporary Chinese culture.

Bernice M. Murphy's "'It's Not the House That's Haunted': Demons, Debt, and the Family in Peril in Recent Horror Cinema" explores another new trend: the return of suburban haunted house stories in roughly the last half decade, when the American middle class have been suffering from a financial crisis that mirrors that of the 1970s and 1980s (when the last boom of suburban supernatural narratives occurred). Murphy focuses on the products of the low-budget production company Blumhouse Productions (including *Paranormal Activity* (2009), *Insidious* (2011), *Sinister* (2012), and *The Conjuring* (2013)).

Examining another breed of low-budget millennial horror film that emphasizes ghosts, Marc Olivier's "Glitch Gothic" hones in on the glitch aesthetic so common in found-footage horror films of the twenty-first century, where ghostly apparitions are associated with sudden disruptions to the flow of digital media. He argues that the "jarring spectacle of data ruins is becoming to the twenty-first century what the crumbling mansion was to Gothic literature of the nineteenth century: the privileged space for confrontations with incompatible systems, nostalgic remnants, and restless revenants."

The collection's final essay concerns perhaps the most acclaimed ghost film of recent years. In "Showing the Unknown: *Uncle Boonmee Who Can Recall His Past Lives*," Mitsuyo Wada-Marciano explores how Apichatpong Weerasethakul's *Palme d'Or*-winning masterpiece, a work finely attuned to the spectral potential of cinematic time and sound, blurs boundaries of media, genre, and such conceptual dichotomies as past/present, reality/fantasy, human/animal, and life/death.

Lastly, Jeffrey Sconce, author of the seminal *Haunted Media*, provides an afterword entitled "Haunted Viewers," exploring the cinematic ghost's survival or non-survival into digital domains.

* * * * *

No collection of this sort could be exhaustive, and *Cinematic Ghosts* certainly does not claim to be. Many key ghost films are not subjected to sustained analysis here, numerous national traditions go under- or unrepresented, and certain critical approaches go unused. The ghosts of avant-garde/experimental cinema and of documentary represent just two substantial topics unexplored here. The work is haunted, as it were, by its own gaps and omissions.

PART ONE

Ghosts of Pre-Cinema and Silent Cinema

1

Phantom Images and Modern Manifestations: Spirit Photography, Magic Theater, Trick Films, and Photography's Uncanny

Tom Gunning

> *Ghosts. Cine recordings of the vivacious doings of persons long dead.*
> KEN JACOBS ON HIS FILM *TOM, TOM THE PIPER'S SON*

> *The rest of the company, with myself, seemed not to know whether or not there is any truth in these modern manifestations.*
> SUSAN B. ANTHONY, DIARY NOTATION IN 1854, ON A DISCUSSION OF SPIRITUALISM

While western culture's valorization of the visual may be rooted in a tradition which identifies the conceivable with the visible (the idea with what one sees),[1] there is no question that in the nineteenth century

---

[1] For the original visual meaning of the terms *idea* and *eidos*, see Paul Friedlander, *Plato: An Introduction*, Trans. Hans Meyerhoff (New York: Harper, 1958), 13–16; and F.E. Peters, *Greek Philosophical Terms: A Historical Lexicon* (New York: New York University Press, 1967), 46.

we enter into a new realm of visuality, and that it is the photograph that stands as its emblem.[2] The key role of the photograph as a guarantor of a new realm of visual certainty comes from a network of interrelated aspects. First, to use (as others have)[3] the vocabulary of Charles Sanders Peirce, there is the photograph's dual identity as an icon, a bearer of resemblance, and as an index, a trace left by a past event. The idea that people, places, and objects could somehow leave behind—cause, in fact—their own images gave photography a key role as evidence, in some sense apodictic. Essential to the belief system which photography engendered was the fact that the image was created by a physical process over which human craft exerted no decisive role. Photography was therefore a scientific process, free from the unreliability of human discourse. Photography could serve as both tool of discovery and means of verification in a new worldview constructed on an investigation of actual entities explored through their visible aspects.

However, if photography emerged as the material support for a new positivism, it was also experienced as an uncanny phenomenon, one which seemed to undermine the unique identity of objects and people, endlessly reproducing the appearances of objects, creating a parallel world of phantasmatic doubles alongside the concrete world of the senses verified by positivism. While the process of photography could be thoroughly explained by chemical and physical operations, the cultural reception of the process frequently associated it with the occult and supernatural. Balzac gives a good example of this in a digression in his novel *Cousin Pons* which states that Daguerre's invention has proved "that a man or a building is incessantly and continuously represented by a picture in the atmosphere, that all existing objects project into it a kind of spectre which can be captured and perceived."[4]

Balzac's description shows his ability to defamiliarize the surfaces of reality through poetic re-description. But more than that, it testifies to a widespread understanding of photography that paralleled (without necessarily contradicting) its official role as scientific record of visual reality. At the same time that the daguerreotype recorded the visual nature of

---

[2] Perhaps the most detailed and insightful of the recent investigations of the change in visual perception in the nineteenth century is Jonathan Crary's *Techniques of the Observer: On Vision and Modernity in the Nineteenth Century* (Cambridge: MIT Press, 1990).

[3] Among the critics who have discussed the indexical aspects of photography are Peter Wollen, *Signs and Meanings in the Cinema* (Bloomington: Indiana University Press, 1969), 120–6, and Rosalind Krauss, "Tracking Nadar," *October* 5 (1978), 34. Krauss's essay, which also involves a discussion of spirit photography, was a strong influence on my essay.

[4] The similar sense of photography as an occult activity is given in Nathaniel Hawthorn's nearly contemporaneous *The House of Seven Gables* from 1851, in which the daguerreotypist Holgrave attributes visionary properties to his "sun-portraits" and is also a mesmerist.

material reality it also seemed to dematerialize it, to transform it into a ghostly double. However, before one sees in Balzac's conception a simple return to a Platonic idealism in which the *eidos* of every object seems to hover around it and photography becomes the proof of idealism, one must note the decentering implications of this description. Every object, place, and person is continuously radiating these images (a process that Balzac's friend the photographer Nadar remembered the writer describing to him as a constant shedding of an immaterial skin[5]). Rather than representing an ur-form of these objects, the only true reality as in Plato's idealism, these images are constantly cast off, like a sort of detritus. Photography simply retains some of them. This process of individual entities constantly broadcasting normally imperceptible signals, which can be received as images, exemplifies an extraordinary new mythology of modernity as it confronted technological change. Unlike official allegories which vaunted the forces of commerce and technology with desiccated images from classical mythology, this modern mythology welcomed the dissolving effects of modernity into the core of its metaphysics.

When I call this early reception of photography uncanny, I hope to summon all the resonances of this term. Thanks to Freud's English translator's decision to render his complex German term *unheimlich* by "uncanny," the specter of Freud's famous essay arises irrepressibly. Since my principal topic in this essay will be the use of photographs to document the presence of spirits, this visitation is not at all unwelcome. Among the themes that Freud relates to the experience of the uncanny is that of the double. And it is my thesis that was the uncanny ability of photography to produce a double of its subject that gave it its unique ontology as much as its existential link with its original source. This extraordinary reproductive quality now seems so familiar that it takes the defamiliarization of initial reception such as Balzac's to restore to us an original sense of amazement.

The theme from "The Uncanny" that most inflected Freud's future writing was that of repetition, which followed from his discussion of the double. It was the fascination with repetition, first broached in this essay, that led Freud to discover the compulsion to repeat and ultimately led him beyond the pleasure principle to a confrontation with the death drive and his late posing of the conflict between Eros and Thanatos.[6] Freud admits that the

---

[5]Nadar, "My Life as a Photographer," Trans. Thomas Repensek. *October* 5 (1978), 7–28.
[6]The further development of the compulsion to repeat comes in *Beyond the Pleasure Principle* (1920, *The Standard Edition of the Complete Psychological Works of Sigmund Freud*, Trans. and ed. James Strachey, Vol. 18, 1–64).

connection between repetition and the uncanny may not seem obvious at first sight. However, he adds, under certain circumstances and conditions repetition does arouse an uncanny sensation, one which recalls "the sense of helplessness experienced in some dream states." As an example he narrates an experience of his own:

> As I was walking one hot summer afternoon, through the deserted streets of a provincial town in Italy which was unknown to me, I found myself in a quarter of whose character I could not remain long in doubt. Nothing but painted women were to be seen at the windows of the small houses, and I hastened to leave the narrow street at the next turning. But after having wandered about for a time without enquiring my way, I suddenly found myself back in the same street, where my presence was now beginning to excite attention. I hurried away once more only to arrive by another detour at the same place yet a third time. Now, however, a feeling overcame me which I can only describe as uncanny, and I was glad enough to find myself back at the piazza I had left a short while before, with-out any further voyages of discovery.[7]

We could compare it to an extraordinary literary work from 1875, which chronicles a similarly obsessive and uncanny urban labyrinth. In Villiers de L'Isle-Adam's short story "The Very Image," a businessman on his way to an appointment wanders somewhat accidentally into an imposing building which rises before him "like a stone apparition" but has a curiously hospitable air about it. As Villiers describes it:

> I promptly found myself before a room with a glass roof through which a ghastly light was falling.
>
> > There were pillars on which clothes, mufflers, and hats had been hung. Marble tables were installed on all sides.
> > Some people were there with legs outstretched, heads raised, staring eyes and matter of fact expressions, who appeared to be meditating.
> > And their gaze was devoid of thought and their faces the color of the weather.
> > There were portfolios lying open and papers spread out beside each one of them.

---

[7] Sigmund Freud, "The 'Uncanny,'" *S.E.* 17 (1920), 237.

> And then I realized that the mistress of the house, on whose courteous welcome I had been counting, was none other than Death.[8]

The narrator had wandered into the Paris morgue, a site open to the public in the nineteenth century, where gawkers could gaze on unclaimed corpses laid out on stone tables beneath dripping water taps.

The narrator rushes to get a cab to keep his appointment. However, arriving at the arranged rendezvous, he:

> promptly found myself in a room into which a ghastly light was filtered through the windows.
> There were pillars on which clothes, mufflers, and hats had been hung ....[9]

And the text repeats with minuscule variations its previous description. The narrator returns home, resolving never again to do business, and shudders as he stresses that "the second glimpse is more sinister than the first."[10]

Several things are striking about this convergence of texts. First, Villiers had understood several decades before Freud the uncanny effect of repetition. Second, the confrontation with the repressed, here death and in Freud commercial illicit sex, comes through a sort of helpless surrender of the dream logic of urban topography. However timeless the effects of the unconscious may be, we see again how often in Freud they illuminate the new experiences of modernity. And finally and most importantly for my thesis, the effect of repetition, particularly in Villiers, inevitably recalls the possibilities of photography. Although Villiers evokes his capture in a closed circuit of time through repetition of a verbal text, this description summons up memories of film loops, of the uncanny possibilities of a photographic repetition of situations and actions.[11] And it is this effect of exact duplication, I believe, that makes the second glimpse, the double of the first, so sinister.

Although Freud does not cite the way photography evokes to the "constant recurrence of the same thing"[12] explicitly, it does haunt the

---

[8]Villiers de L'Isle-Adam, "The Very Image," in *Cruel Tales*, Trans. Robert Baldrick (Oxford: Oxford University Press, 1985), 103.
[9]Ibid., 104.
[10]Ibid., 105.
[11]Followers of recent horror films may recall a brilliant use of this sort of repetition in *Nightmare on Elm Street Part 4* (1988).
[12] The use of this phrase of Nietzsche's seems to be a conscious citation on Freud's part, as his editors indicate (234n).

margins (or at least the footnotes) of the essay. His discussion of the double proceeds from Otto Rank's classic essay on the theme, which—as Freud notes—began with a consideration of a film: the Hanns Heinz Ewers-Stellan Rye-Paul Wegener 1913 production of *The Student of Prague*. This early classic of the German uncanny cinema portrayed its unearthly double through the old photographic trick of multiple exposures (which was likewise essential to both the spirit photographers I shall discuss and the filmmaking of Georges Méliès).[13] While both Freud and Rank demonstrate that the double has a long lineage (from archaic beliefs in detachable souls to the romantic Doppelganger) that predates photography, nonetheless photography furnished a technology which could summon up an uncanny visual experience of doubling, as much as it was capable of presenting facts in all their positivity and uniqueness.

Balzac wrote his description of photography about a decade after Daguerre's first successful experiments. While *Cousin Pons* was being published in 1846, the United States was seized by a different sort of manifestation which led to a new worldwide metaphysical system, spiritualism. First in the small village of Hydesville, New York, and later in the city of Rochester (coincidentally to become the industrial home of both Eastman Kodak company and Xerox), a pair of young girls, the Fox sisters, were subject to a consistent rapping noise, which was eventually interpreted as a coded message from a spirit of a murdered peddler. Taken under the management of an older sister, the Fox girls soon became the center of a new movement based on communicating with the dead through séances at which rapped-out messages were received and inspired communications obtained during trances.[14] Although ideas of necromancy and other forms of intercourse with the dead are universal, the modernity of the Fox sisters and related phenomena was generally recognized and hailed by many as a new revelation. Spiritualism soon had an international following, but the sense of America as the land of the future and the home of the latest technology gave the Fox sisters' revelations an added connotation of apocalyptic modernity, and later American mediums an added authority.

---

[13] A thorough examination of the Ewers-Rye-Wegener film is offered by Heide Schülpmann ("The First German Art Film: Rye's *The Student of Prague*," in *German Literature: Adaptations and Transformations*, ed. Eric Rentschler (New York: Methuen, 1986), 9–24). Kristin Thompson supplies a valuable discussion of Wegener's ideas about film around the time of *The Student of Prague* in her essay "*Im Anfang War*," in which she quotes Wegener as indicating that he entered cinema in order to do something only film could do—create the Doppelganger effect, through double exposure ("*Im Anfang War*...: Some Links between German Fantasy Films of the Teens and Twenties," in *Before Caligari: Germany Cinema, 1895–1920*, eds. Paolo Cherchi Usai and Lorenzo Codelli (Pordenone: Edizzioni Biblioteca dell'Immagine, 1990), 142).

[14] Perceptive histories of spiritualism can be found in both Braude and Judah.

The spiritualist movement related its revelations to modern changes in technology and science, such as electricity, telegraphy, and new discoveries in chemistry and biology,[15] showing the sort of merging of pseudoscience and spirituality that Robert Darnton found surrounding mesmerism in prerevolutionary France.[16] Although this was primarily a means of endowing their new revelations with the growing authority of recent inventions,[17] there are also indications that the mentality of spiritualists and devotees of new technology had something in common. Thomas Watson, the assistant to Alexander Graham Bell in the invention of the telephone, had an interest in séances and explored the possibility that the new apparatus would be an aid in spiritual discoveries.[18] Likewise, electrical engineers delighted in creating simulacra of spiritualist manifestations through scientific means, such as the demonstration of the power of electricity given by the Edison Company in Boston in 1887 during which "[b]ells rung, drums beat, noises natural and unnatural were heard, a cabinet revolved and flashed fire, and a row of departed skulls came into view, and varied coloured lights flashed from their eyes" (Marvin 57).

In addition, this modernity manifested itself in the political positions taken by early spiritualists which were perhaps the most radical of any group in the pre–Civil War United States. Spiritualists as a rule supported abolitionism and temperance reforms, experimented with founding communistic communities, and championed a host of women's rights issues, including dress and marriage reforms, as well as suffrage. In fact, the spiritualist support of women's sexual rights in marriage led to a frequent accusation of license and "free love."[19]

It is hardly surprising that spiritualism would eventually intersect with photography. That photography could create a transparent wraith-like image (if the plate were double exposed or if the figure photographed moved before a full exposure was made) was realized by the first photographers. In 1856 Sir David Brewster in his book describing his new invention, the stereoscope, advised his readers that "[f]or the purposes of amusement the photographer might carry us even into the realm of the supernatural," since it was quite possible "to give a spectral appearance to one or more

---

[15]Ann Braude, *Radical Spirits: Spiritualism and Women's Rights in Nineteenth-Century America* (Boston: Beacon, 1983), 9.
[16]Robert Darnton, *Mesmerism and the End of the Enlightenment in France* (New York: Schocken, 1970).
[17]Ibid., 4.
[18]Avital Ronell, *The Telephone Book: Technology—Schizophrenia—Electric Speech* (Lincoln: University of Nebraska Press, 1989), 99.
[19]See Braude for a fascinating discussion of the social and political positions of early spiritualism.

of his figures and to exhibit them as 'thin air' amid the solid realities of the stereoscopic picture."[20] For Brewster, who in his 1832 work *Letters on Natural Magic*[21] had dissolved superstitions and apparently miraculous events into scientifically explainable optical illusions, such photographic phantoms were simply "philosophical toys," amusements which first amazed but then could be used to demonstrate the principles of science. But that such images could display the iconic accuracy and recognizability of photographic likenesses and at the same time the transparency and insubstantiality of ghosts seemed to demonstrate the fundamentally uncanny quality of photography, its capture of a specter-like double.

Since spiritualists saw their revelation as fundamentally modern, casting out the outmoded Calvinist beliefs in original sin and hellfire damnation, they welcomed evidence that their new revelation of the afterlife could be established "scientifically."[22] For spiritualists spirit photography was more than an amusement and could expand their new forms of spiritual manifestation. Although there may well be earlier examples, the practice gained notoriety (and, when he was tried for fraud, a legal context) with William Mumler in the early 1860s. First in Boston, then in New York City, Mumler made a commercial business of spirit photography, producing (for prices as high as $10) portraits, strictly conventional in pose and composition, in which sitters were portrayed in the company of ghosts, transparent images, frequently of famous persons (Mumler's photographs included images of Lincoln and Beethoven) usually standing behind the sitters and often embracing them. Although each spirit photographer has a slightly different style in the placement, size, and number of the spirit images that appeared as ghostly superimpositions over the more "solid reality" of the living person, Mumler seems to have set a basic iconography of spirit photography as an extension of portraiture.[23]

As I will show, the explanations offered for spirit photography were fluid and changed with different periods and different influences within spiritualism.

---

[20]David Brewster, *The Stereoscope, Its History, Theory and Construction* (London: Murray, 1956), 105.
[21]David Brewster, *Letters on Natural Magic* (New York: Harper, 1832).
[22]J. Stilson Judah, *The History and Philosophy of the Metaphysical Movements in America* (Philadelphia: Westminster, 1967), 16.
[23]All accounts of spirit photography I have examined begin with Mumler. See Paul Coates, *Photographing the Invisible* (New York: Arno, 1973), 1–21; Fred Gettings, *Ghosts in Photography: The Extraordinary Story of Spirit Photography* (New York: Harmony, 1978), 25–7; Cyril Permutt, *Photographing the Spirit World: Images from Beyond the Spectrum* (London: Aquarian, 1988), 12–16; and Eldrige Thomas Gerry ("Argument of Eldrige Thomas Gerry, Counsel for the People in the Case of William H. Mumler, "Pamphlet on File at George Eastman House", n.d.).

Most often spirit photographers (including Mumler) claimed they did not know how their photographs happened.[24] Clearly this was in part a protective statement. Since most photographs are the result of quite explainable methods of double exposure, claiming ignorance of how the effects were produced protected photographers from accusations of fraud. However, this lack of commitment about how the images were formed was also put forth by spiritualists who were devoted believers in the authenticity of spirit photography and who, not being practitioners, were immune to prosecution for fraud. There was a constant debate within spiritualist, Theosophical, and occult circles throughout the late nineteenth and early twentieth centuries about what supernatural forces actually produced these images. Although the supposition that the images were photographs of spirits of the dead was certainly the earliest and most prevalent, it was by no means universal. Most often commentators on the phenomenon simply claimed that the photographs were the product of some supernatural force, with many avowed spiritualists supposed that the spirits of the dead may actually have had little to do with them. The images that appear in these photographs were generally described with the noncommittal, but provocative, term *extras*. They were defined as presences that had not been visible, at least to the sitters, at the time the photographs were made and whose appearance first on the negative and then on the print were a surprise to the sitters and sometimes to the photographers.

The appearance of spirit photography after the Civil War coincided with transformations within spiritualism itself. The first heroic decade of the spiritualist movement (which also saw its radical social agenda) based itself primarily in auditory phenomena and the transmission of messages. Although many of these messages were of a mundane personal sort, reassuring family members of the happiness of departed relatives or giving medical and financial advice, others were of a prophetic and even political nature. As Ann Braude's fascinating study of the relation between spiritualism and the movement for women's rights reveals, the first widely attended women speakers in the United States were spiritualist trance speakers, women who spoke in public lecture halls as the mediums for supernatural spirits, frequently delivering orations in support of the social reforms that the movement supported.[25]

After the Civil War the emphasis in spiritualism shifted, moving from auditory messages to visual "manifestations," either through the actual

---

[24]Gerry, 11.
[25]Braude, 84–95.

appearances of supernatural figures, the presentation of ghostly actions (floating trumpets, transported objects, disembodied hands), ectoplasmic extrusions from mediums' bodies, or other spectacular evidences of supernatural presences. As Braude indicates, this changed the role of the medium from a vatic prophetess to a producer of nonverbal displays under conditions that tended to remove the medium from the public eye and ear.[26] Darkness and devices such as the spirit cabinet (introduced by medium performers such as the Davenport brothers) rendered the medium an invisible presence, while practices such as tying mediums up (as a guard against fraud) made them immobile, shifting the focus from the medium entirely to the manifestations. Spirit photographs are part of this new emphasis on visual evidence and movement away from a prophetic message. After the Civil War the social agenda of spiritualism also began to fade, although there were still vestiges of it into the twentieth century—for instance, Virginia Woodhull, the first woman to run for U.S. president, was also the head of an American spiritualist organization.[27] The reasons for this are undoubtedly complex, including the loss of the central social rallying point of the abolition of slavery and the general political reaction after the Reconstruction. Further, certain political movements, such as women's rights, began to distance themselves from spiritualism as the apocalyptic excitement of its first appearance faded and it was looked on less as a scientific discovery than a backwash superstition.

Although I can only touch on the fascinating cultural relation between women and spiritualism, it is important to note that the first spirit mediums were women and that the predominance of women as mediums continued throughout most of spiritualist history. As Braude points out, the conception of the medium corresponded to cultural understandings of the feminine principle. The medium was passive, but passive in a particularly dynamic way. She was receptive, sensitive, a vehicle—a medium—by which manifestation appeared. All mediums, men or women, had to be, in spiritualist parlance, feminine, or negative (borrowing again from electricity and magnetism, a technical term which also has implications for photography), in order to let the spirit world manifest itself. While one may feel the confining aspects of such gender stereotypes, it is important to stress the enormous value spiritualism placed on this feminine negativity, and therefore on feminine leadership and feminist issues in the movement. While such practices as the concealing spirit cabinet and spirit photography displaced the medium from the spotlight by the growing importance of visual manifestations, the role of the medium remained crucial.

---

[26] Ibid., 177.
[27] Ibid., 170–3.

But there is no doubt that in what we could term the second generation of spiritualists—after the Civil War—the medium becomes enframed in a sort of apparatus, and this apparatus is frequently under the control of a man. Men assumed a variety of mediatory functions, serving as business managers for women mediums[28] or show-biz masters of ceremony who mediated between audience and medium, or, as in the case of Florence Cook, the medium became a subject exposed for male investigation. In the "scientific" discourse of spiritualism, the medium became less the voice of a new revelation than a new phenomenon demanding scrutiny. Women mediums and the phenomenon of spiritualism increasingly became a spectacle presented for observation, whether displayed for a scientific investigation with circumscribed roles of experimental subject and probing scientist, or as a theme for popular entertainment, with female assistants put in a trance by a male stage magician.

The role of the mediating apparatus becomes literalized in spirit photography as the process of photography takes over the medium's role. Perhaps the most profound connection between photography and spiritualist manifestation lies in the concept of the sensitive medium. Most theorists of spirit photography claimed that the presence of a medium (though in this case male mediums are more frequent than female) was necessary for an image to be formed.[29] It was claimed that all the great spirit photographers—Mumler, Wylie, Hudson, Mrs. Deane, among others—were spirit mediums. Besides this human figure the other sine qua non was the sensitive plate. Recognizable spirit photographs were supposedly created without using either lens or camera. Both David Daguid and Madge Donohue claimed that all they did was to hold the sensitive plates in their hands, and that this contact between two sensitive, receptive mediums—one spiritual, the other photographic—was sufficient to form a latent image.[30]

While spiritualism had always had a sensational and spectacular aspect, there is no doubt that the new emphasis on manifestations led to an even greater theatricality. A second sort of spirit photography (often denied the name by some purists,[31] since such photographs merely record events which

---

[28]Ibid., 177.
[29]Paul Coates describes each spirit photographer he treats in his book as a medium.
[30]Coates describes Duguid's process (65–89). Likewise Madge Donahue claimed to achieve her "skotographs" by holding photographic plates in her hand until a series of taps "tell me that the spirit photographers wish to speak to me" (Scrapbook of spirit photographs by Madge Donohue c. 1929–1935 with notes by Ms. Donahue, preserved at Visual Studies Workshop Archive, Rochester, New York, n.p.).
[31]Coates, ix.

are visible to anyone present rather than making use of the mediumistic properties of the sensitive plate) consisted of photographs made during manifestation séances, including images of what became known as "full materializations," full-bodied figures of spirits. Materializations became celebrated with the séances at the Eddy household in Chittendon, Vermont, in the 1870s, in which the figures of the spirits John King and his daughter Katie King appeared fully visible.[32] Katie King was a particularly lovely apparition who touched and even kissed male members of the séance. Katie King became quite peripatetic and was also materialized by the medium Florence Cook in England. Cook's materializations are of particular importance in the history of spiritualism because they were investigated by William Crookes, a distinguished British scientist, discoverer of the new element thallium (essential to the later development of the cathode ray tube), and eventually president of the British Royal Society. Although Crookes's account of his investigation of Cook's materialization during 1874 doesn't exactly demonstrate a scientific scrutiny of the phenomenon, he was willing to place his considerable reputation behind the authenticity of these manifestations.[33]

The primary evidence that Crookes produced were some forty-four photographs taken during the materialization of Katie King. Crookes in later life refused to publish these photos and the negatives were apparently destroyed by heirs who wished this aspect of the scientist's career forgotten. However, a few were published at the time and a few others discovered in the 1930s. As evidence for the authenticity of the phenomenon they seem to controvert Crooke's claims that Katie King had no resemblance to her medium, Florence Cook. Comparisons of photographs of Cook and King show nearly identical features, a point which had been observed at the time by other people who attended these materializations. While Katie appeared and walked around the room, Cook was supposedly collapsed in a deep trance within the spirit cabinet. Breaking tradition, Crookes in his investigation was allowed into the cabinet and claimed both to have seen Cook's slumped-over figure (her face bundled in a scarf) and to have minutely examined the physicality of King: "I could look closely into her face, examine her features and hair, touch her hands and might even touch and examine her ears closely, which were not pierced for earrings."[34] While

---

[32]Braude, 76–7.
[33]The most thorough—and skeptical—account of the Crookes-Cook affair can be found in Trevor N. Hall, *The Medium and the Scientist: The Story of Florence Cook and William Crookes* (Buffalo: Prometheus, 1984).
[34]Gettings, 126.

Katie King's resemblance to Florence Cook may well provide evidence of fraud (and certainly calls into question Crookes's objective observational powers), it doesn't undermine the uncanny quality of these photographs. Although such images of a full materializations do not involve spirit aid in the photography itself (it simply records a supposedly supernatural event faithfully, hence its purported scientific value), the process of materialization mimes a photographic process. The woman medium retires into a dark chamber (camera obscura) and produces a double of herself which emerges into the light. The harsh glare of Crookes's magnesium-flare lighting and the exotic gown and headdress of King, as well as her somnolent eyes, give these photographs an extraordinary erotic charge, just as Crookes's record of his scrutiny of her physical features exhibits an eroticized fascination underpinning the unwavering gaze justified by his scientific stance and the purported uniqueness of the phenomenon. Crookes himself indicated that the physical beauty he found in the subject of his investigation overran the ability of photography to capture it:

> Photography is as inadequate to depict the perfect beauty of Katie's face, as words are powerless to describe her charms of manner. Photography may indeed give a map of her countenance; but how can it reproduce the brilliant purity of her complexion, or the ever varying expression of her most mobile features.[35]

Enraptured (and perhaps, as some claimed, duped) as Crookes may have been, we also see here how much the spiritual medium has become subjected to the male gaze as the source of both authentication and aesthetic approval. Florence Cook may undergo a sort of primal photographic process in emanating her double, but it is Crookes, the man of science, who fixes the image and lends it his authority while Florence remains enframed within her spirit cabinet.

While full-bodied materialization continued to play a role in mediumistic séances, séances that were photographed in the late nineteenth and early twentieth centuries placed particular emphasis on the somewhat less spectacular but possibly more uncanny ectoplasmic manifestations. *Ectoplasm* was a term given by French occultist Dr. Richet to a whitish, malleable substance that oozed from the orifices of mediums.[36] The appearance of this mucous-like substance gave séances an oddly physiological

---

[35]Qtd. in Hall, 86.
[36]For a discussion of ectoplasm, see Gettings, 115–28.

turn, as normally taboo processes—bodily orifices extruding liquefying masses—were accepted as evidence of spiritual forces. Such ectoplasmic masses were considered supernatural phenomenon and also supplied the malleable stuff from which figure manifestations such as Katie King were formed (Mrs. Marryat, a witness of Cook's séances, described Katie as disappearing like "melting wax").[37] Ectoplasm was a sort of *prima materia* which was molded by spirit forces to create manifestations. Mediums such as Eva C. claimed that the patently two-dimensional nature of some of her manifestations, rather than indicating fraud, simply showed the manifestation process in an incomplete stage, moving from two-dimensional images to fully manifested third-dimensional figures.[38]

Perhaps most uncanny are instances of ectoplasmic extrusions bearing images within them. There are several instances, primarily in the twentieth century, in which mediums produce from their orifices spirit images or photographs. Such instances led Dr. Richet to theorize that ectoplasm "may be merely an image, and not a living being."[39] This phenomenon clarifies the role images play in spiritualist manifestations, not only as representations of something otherwise not seen, but also supplying a sort of pictographic code between the visible world and the realms of the invisible. Spirits are not simply captured in pictures; they communicate by a sort of picture language.[40] The medium herself became a sort of camera, her spiritual negativity bodying forth a positive image, as the human behaves like an uncanny photomat, dispensing images from her orifices.[41]

While photographing materializations played the more conventionally scientific role of capturing in a hopefully spectacular manner the evidences of the senses, the increasingly spectacular nature of spiritualism mined a deep fascination in visual events that amazed spectators by defying conventional belief. The potential entertainment value of such visual attractions was immediately recognized. The Davenport brothers, for instance, toured Europe and the United States with a spirit cabinet show which produced phantom hands, levitating objects, musical instruments that appeared to play themselves, and other supernatural manifestations while the brothers themselves were apparently securely tied within the cabinet. During their

---

[37] Hall, 66.
[38] Gettings, 121–3.
[39] Ibid., 123.
[40] Donahue's "skotographs" include messages in a strange sort of spirit writing made of patterns of dots which she decoded.
[41] Besides the images reproduced in Gettings and Permutt, the *Proceedings for the Society for Psychic Research* July 1922 includes some extraordinary photos of Eva C. with images coming out of her mouth.

European tour in the 1860s the brothers exploited their attraction as a theatrical event, gaining support and appreciation particularly from such masters of the nineteenth-century spectacular stage as Dion Boucicault and Henry Irving. When skeptical onlookers objected to the darkness in which these performances were held, Irving leapt to the brothers' defense by citing photography: "Isn't a dark chamber essential in the process of photography?" he queried. Irving wondered how satisfying the results would be if photographers were asked to produce images outside of their camera obscuras.[42]

Inevitably, spectacular spiritualism encountered the nineteenth-century magic show and had a role in transforming it into an intensely visual theater of illusion.[43] Attending an exhibition given by the Davenport brothers, John Neville Maskelyne, a young apprentice watchmaker whose fascination with mechanical devices had led him to stage magic, recognized the possibilities of such shows when liberated from metaphysical claims. When an obscuring shade slipped for a moment during the Davenports' performance, piercing the darkness essential to their "manifestations," Maskelyne exercised the gaze of an intrigued craftsman rather than an enraptured scientist. He perceived one of the brothers, having liberated himself from his bonds, emerge from the cabinet, manipulate some object, and then reassume his position and retie his ropes. Maskelyne and his magician partner Cook undertook to figure out and reproduce the various effects the Davenports had created, and announced a spectacle that would recreate the séance "without the aid of spirits."[44]

Maskelyne made the recreation of séances one of the mainstays of his extremely successful career as a stage illusionist. A poster for Maskelyne and Cook circa 1877 announced an "exposition of spiritualism so-called Light and Dark Séance Extraordinary including the appearance of the spirit form of John King."[45] While Maskelyne was intent on exposing spiritualists

---

[42]Harry Houdini, *A Magician Among the Spirits* (New York: Harpers, 1924), 272. Accounts of the Davenport brothers' career can be found in Ibid., 20–35.
[43]The theater of magical illusions is described in Hopkins. Of course, illusionary spectacles involving ghosts and spirit manifestations preceded the modern spiritualist movement, with the most spectacular example being Robertson's Fantasmagoria of the end of the eighteenth and early nineteenth centuries. On Robertson, see Francois Levie, *Etienne-Gaspard Robertson, La vie d'un fantasmagorie* (Québec: Préamble, 1990) and Erik Barnouw, *The Magician and the Cinema* (New York: Oxford University Press, 1981), 19–27, and for exhibition of phantasmagorias in nineteenth-century America, see Theodore X. Barber, "Phantasmagorical Wonders: The Magic Lantern Ghost Show in Nineteenth Century America," *Film History* 3.3 (1989), 73–86.
[44]Jasper Maskelyne, *White Magic: The Story of the Maskelynes* (London: Paul, 1936), 21–8.
[45]Reproduction of poster in file at Billy Rose Theater Collection, Library of Performing Arts, Lincoln Center, New York.

(and even testified at the fraud trial of spiritualist slate writer Dr. Slade to explain how his phenomenon could be managed),[46] he also professed admiration for the dexterity of the Davenport brothers.[47] Spiritualists, he seemed to indicate, put on a good show, one that was so enthralling visually that it could be presented without serving as evidence for supernatural events.

Maskelyne occupies a key position in the development of modern magic. While magical illusions, even elaborate ones, are as old as stagecraft, the new technology of the nineteenth century made illusions both easier to manage and more spectacular. Advances in electricity, mechanics, and lighting ushered in a golden age of magical theater, which also fed the nineteenth-century passion for visual amusements. Jean Eugène Robert-Houdin, another former clockmaker turned conjurer, is often seen as the founder of modern magic and one of the first to use electricity for magical effects.[48] Robert-Houdin had also made the exposure of spiritualist phenomena part of his magical stock-in-trade and had presented his own re-creation of the Davenports' séances after the brothers' European tour reached Paris (Houdini 257). Robert-Houdin's technologically modern versions of supernatural phenomena also played a role in imperial France's expanding colonial policy. Napoleon III sent the conjurer to cow the Marabouts, a group of Algerian wonder-workers leading local resistance. Robert-Houdin's magic shows included feats of prestidigitation, the creation of automata, and full-blown theatrical spectacles using stagecraft to produce elaborate optical illusions. Maskelyne, particularly after he and Cook installed themselves in a permanent theater, the Egyptian Hall in London (former site of curiosities and freak shows), developed Robert-Houdin's brand of magic spectacle even further. He created a number of spectacular turns (along with the more traditional feats of prestidigitation and the display of automata that he also delighted in) frequently patterned on spiritualist phenomena. The fascination in visual entertainments and modern technology also made the Egyptian Hall a natural place for some of the first permanent English film programs, as Maskelyne added motion pictures to the bill immediately after the Lumière brothers' premiere in London.[49]

The Houdin-Maskelyne tradition of magical performers can be seen as having two direct heirs. One was Harry Houdini, the American magician and

---

[46] Maskelyne, 54.
[47] Maskelyne states this in an undated clipping from "The Playgoer" in a file under his name, Billy Rose Theater Collection, Library of Performing Arts, Lincoln Center, New York.
[48] Albert Hopkins, ed. *Magic: Stage Illusions, Special Effects and Trick Photography* (1898, New York: Dover, 1976), 11–19.
[49] Barnouw, 56–7.

escape artist born Ehrich Weiss, who named himself after the famous French conjurer. Although Houdini's escape routines basically took a different direction from the optical magic of his predecessors, he continued and extended Maskelyne's debunking of spiritualists. With Houdini the investigation of spiritualists became a personal obsession, involving his own doubts and desires concerning life after death, rather than Maskelyne's appreciation of a good show. In 1909 he did track down the surviving Davenport brother who recognized Houdini as a fellow illusionist and revealed to him many of the tricks of their trade, including the rope tricks by which they freed themselves of their bonds and the special design of their spirit cabinet.[50]

The other branch of the Houdin-Maskelyne legacy forks into a new technological medium. Georges Méliès, youngest son of a successful boot manufacturer, after being enraptured by his visits to Egyptian Hall during a stay in London, bought nearly defunct *Théâtre Robert-Houdin* (including Robert-Houdin's original automata) and turned it into a thoroughly updated theater of magical illusions. Méliès's successful illusions at the *Théâtre Robert-Houdin* included newly designed spiritualist numbers, in which devices of lighting, careful control of point of view, and an elaborate optical shutter derived from photography recreated the effects of a materialization séance.[51]

But, of course, Méliès's main claim to fame comes from grafting the nineteenth-century tradition of magic theater onto the nascent apparatus of motion pictures. First fascinated simply with the newest technological marvel in visual illusions (he is reported to have exclaimed at the preview of the Lumière brothers' invention, "That's for me, what a great trick"),[52] Méliès's first films were simple actualities. However, he soon discovered the possibilities of using the cinema's control over point of view and ability to overcome time through shooting and splicing to create magical performances which were not only endlessly repeatable but also reproducible, so that the illusions of the *Théâtre Robert-Houdin* could be seen across France and around the world.[53] A number

---

[50]Houdini, 36. Famous magician Harry Kellar actually began as an assistant to the Davenport brothers (see Hopkins, 24).

[51]Paul Hammond gives a particularly good account of Méliès's relation to the tradition of magic theater (*Marvelous Méliès* (London: Fraser, 1974), 14–26). Pierre Jenn reprints a complete description by Méliès of his "Les phénomènens des spiritisme, Un grand succès du Théâtre Robert-Houdin par. Méliès," in *Georges Méliès: Cinéaste* (Paris: Albatross, 1984), 153–68.

[52]This comment is quoted from a recorded interview in Anne-Marie Quévarain and Marie-Georges Charconnet-Melies, "Méliès et Freud: Un avenir pour les marchands d'illusons?," in *Méliès et la naissance du spectacle cinématographique*, ed. Madeleine Maltete-Méliès (Paris: Klincksieck, 1984), 235. This essay also draws provocative associations between spiritualism, hypnotism, hysteria, psychoanalysis, and the work of Méliès.

[53]I have explored Méliès's relation to magical illusions and emerging film technique in "Primitive Cinema."

of his magic films included routines inspired by spiritualism, including the film *L'Armoire des frères Davenport* (1902), which may be based on the original *Robert-Houdin* version of the brothers' séance—a film which (unfortunately like most of Méliès's work) has not survived.[54]

In the spring of 1903, a few months after completing his most famous film *A Trip to the Moon*, Méliès produced the short film *The Spiritualist Photographer*, of which a paper print deposited at the Library of Congress for copyright purposes has survived. It shows many of the aspects common to the essentially nonnarrative magic films that made up the bulk of Méliès's work. As a strong example of what I have termed *the cinema of attractions*, the film addresses an acknowledged spectator rather than creating a fictional universe. This sort of direct solicitation of the spectator through a punctual succession of magic or curious "attractions" typified much of early cinema before 1906 or so. For Méliès and other early filmmakers the purpose of a film lay more in astonishing a viewer than in creating a narrative structure based on cause and effect and character development.

The Spiritualist Photographer begins with a message addressed directly to the audience. As a magician's assistant enters, he places two inscribed placards, one in French and one in English, in the front of the set. The English text (a translation of the French) reads, "Spiritualistic photo. Dissolving effect obtained without black background. Great novelty." Through this written legend, Méliès not only directly addresses the spectator but defines his film as a technical trick, pointing out its novel aspect (the lack of a black background which was generally necessary for a solid superimposition in trick films). Although the announcement declares the effect to be a "spiritualistic photo," any claim that the effect is supernatural is undercut. Méliès invites technical amazement at a new trick rather than awe at a mystery.[55]

The magician, played by Méliès himself, enters the set, acknowledging the spectator with a wave of his hand. After placing an ornate frame on a platform and unrolling a large blank piece of paper within the frame, he brings onto the set a young woman dressed as a sailor. He places the woman in front of the paper and conjures up a mystical flame in front of her. As the flame grows, the woman seems to fade away and the paper behind her becomes imprinted with her image. After rolling the life-sized photo into a cone, the magician then unfurls it, producing from within the woman restored to life and the paper now blank.

---

[54] *158 Scénarios de Films Disparus de Georges Méliès* reprints the original description of Méliès's *L'Armoire des Frères Davenport 1902, 46–7.*
[55] A detailed description of this film can be found in *Essai de Reconstitution*, 134–5.

The series of transformations that take place involve very much the sort of masculine manipulation of the female body and image that Lucy Fischer discusses in her essay "The Vanishing Lady."[56] The woman stands passively, often needing to be physically rearranged by the male magician's hands, and his theatrical passes and active pacing around the set clearly indicate that he is the source of demiurgic powers. But the visual fascination of the trick comes exactly from the play between an apparently three-dimensional mobile woman figure and her static figure transferred to paper and initially ornately framed. While the magician directs the living model with a courtly extended hand, he can directly touch and pat her two-dimensional image.

Like the most radical spirit photographs, the magician played by Méliès obtains the woman's image without a camera. But the supernatural effect here comes from the fact that the model merges with her image, the image itself replacing her. And in the usual logic of reversible magic procedures, the image itself can also give birth to the live entity. Here is a photograph in which the living body not only emanates its light-bearing specter but also becomes replaced by it, as body melds with paper. Image and model have an interchangeable ontology here, not simply through an indexical process of tracing an image but via a mysterious process in which image replaces body and vice versa. For Méliès, spirit photography results less in communication with the dead than in an exchange of identities between image and model.

A film like Méliès's *The Spiritualist Photographer* traces a complex genealogy between the new technology of photography, a new spiritual revelation, a development of a theatrical spectacle, and then a further development of the technology of photography into motion pictures. Although the configuration of these complex intersections within visual culture is fascinating in itself, I believe that it also carries implications for our modern understanding of visual images and allows us to reexamine what meaning photography has within visual culture. In her insightful essay on Nadar, Rosalind Krauss relates photography to spiritualist and Swedenborgian

---

[56]Lucy Fischer, "The Vanishing Lady: Women, Magic and the Movies," in *Film Before Griffith*, ed. John Fell (Berkeley: University of California Press, 1983), 339–54. Perhaps even more relevant is Linda Williams's essay "Film Body: An Implantation of Perversions," in *Narrative, Apparatus, Ideology: A Film Theory Reader*, ed. Philip Rosen (New York: Columbia University Press, 1986), 507–43, which deals with both Méliès and Muybridge in terms of a subjection of the woman's body to the nascent cinematic apparatus. Williams's thesis may be extended to the general transformation of spiritualism after the Civil War in which the original feminine spiritual negativity seemed to be increasingly subjected to a male-operated apparatus. However, one should resist making this scenario too Manichean. Early spiritualism still worked within certain patriarchal assumptions, and the importance of female mediums (including spirit photographers like Mrs. Dean and Madge Donahue) continued into the twentieth century. One could similarly see Méliès's films as presenting scenarios of the evasion of control as much as domination.

phenomena through the concept of the photograph as index, as trace. Certainly all claims of spirit photography as evidence of an afterlife rest on this indexical claim: that ghosts invisible to the human eye are nonetheless picked up by the more sensitive capacity of the photograph.

However, the claims made for spirit photography, particularly as it moved into the twentieth century, were generally more complicated than this. Much of this complexity was undoubtedly the product of base rationalizations trying to cover up clear examples of fraud. Nonetheless, the attitudes such explanations reveal toward photography are as ideologically revealing as they are rationally unconvincing. It was pointed out by unconvinced investigators of spirit photography that the "extras" that appeared in such photographs were often exact duplications of existing photographs or even of other artworks.[57] While this fact all too clearly indicates the method by which most spirit photographs were made—the rephotographing of existing photographs—spiritualist apologists, unable to deny the fact of duplication, claimed that such phenomenon did not rule out supernatural occurrences.[58]

The explanation of spirit photography that became current in the early twentieth century held that the photographs were not simple records of the appearance of invisible spirits. Rather, spirit photographs were the products of unknown spiritual forces which used the images of the dead as a way of communicating their existence to the living. Paul Coates, author of the early classic work on spirit photography *Photographing the Invisible*, indicated that these spirit forces may actually need to consult existing photographs in order to create these images. After all, spiritualist doctrine indicated that spirits transformed radically after death, and existing photographs taken during a lifetime might provide the necessary model for them to "refresh their memory" and recreate their previous appearance in a spirit portrait.[59] We see here that a photograph, rather than providing indexical evidence of the appearance of a spirit, becomes a model for reduplication and the basis of recognition. A spiritualist leader, Dr. Alfred Russell Wallace, declared the spirit photograph was a creation by spiritual forces rather than a record of their appearance: "It does not follow that the form produced is the actual image of the spiritual form. It may be but a reproduction of the former mortal

---

[57]One such case of reproduction fraud is discussed in Hopkins, 435–89. The discussion of spirit photography in Hopkins's compilation is taken from Woodbury.
[58]See Coates's discussion of the "Cyprian Priestess" (84–9) and of the portrait of Empress Elizabeth of Austria (103–7). Maskelyne exposed one such reproduction in 1909, although Coates again feels the "materialist" magician has misunderstood how spirit photography really functions (109–15).
[59]Coates quotes a Mr. Blackwell who theorizes this process (160).

form with its terrestrial accompaniments for the *purpose of recognition*."[60] Coates gives spirit testimony through mediums that the process of spirit photography was a complicated procedure which marshaled the efforts of spirit chemists and spirit photographers on the "other side."[61] Instead of images of spirits, spirit photography becomes understood as a joint effort, nearly an industry, which multiplies images and sees to their distribution in order to announce the existence of spiritual forces. Photography becomes independent of its ordinary indexical references, since supernatural forces use it primarily as a process of reproduction and communication.[62]

At least one form of spirit photography dispensed with any indexical claim of spirit agency altogether, returning to Brewster's suggestions for the deliberate (and natural) production of phantom images, but using the iconographic effects of transparent phantoms for other emotional effects than entertainment. Although I have not established how widespread the practice was, spirit photographs were produced as mourning images in the nineteenth century. Photographs of dead relatives were knowingly superimposed over images of their surviving loved ones, often in watchful and protective stances.[63] Rather than claiming evidence for survival after death, such images used photography's reproductive possibility to create a convincing (or consoling) image of mourning and faith. If there is a belief embodied in these images, it would have to be translated by the acknowledgment that the subjects of photographic portraits may die, but their images are eternally reproducible. Although of a very different mood than Maskelyne and Méliès's entertainments, such images share with them a fascination with visual illusions, a fascination which may be multiplied rather than diminished when separated from claims of recording an indexical reality.

I return, then, to the aspect of photography that seemed so occult to Balzac, not simply that it captured the trace of something, but that it involved a nearly endless series of images that all objects constantly radiate. The process of mechanical reproduction does more than dissolve the aura of uniqueness that seemed to guarantee individual identity; it

---

[60] Qtd. in Glendenning (126).
[61] Coates, 199.
[62] Gettings indicates spirit communications often directed photographers on the length of exposure for a photograph (106).
[63] I am indebted to a conversation with David Francis of the Division of Motion Picture and Recorded Sound at the Library of Congress for this insight. I have found what appears to be a clear example at the George Eastman House archive, in which a phantom image is superimposed over a mantle piece bearing family photographs.

replaces the unique with a mirror play of semblages. The undermining of traditional modes of authenticity and truth that thinkers from Benjamin to Baudrillard have associated with modern image-making processes depends on this proliferation of images. As Jonathan Crary has indicated, the potentially endless mechanical reproduction that photography makes available aids the system of exchange and circulation on which modern capitalism and industrialization are founded. Photography is, in this sense, the standardization of imagery. The essential aspect of photography, its truly modern and destabilizing role, may work at cross-purpose to its identity as an index which can be traced back to a unique original. Photography as mechanical reproduction may undermine identity through its iconic power to create doubles of an unaltering similarity (identity?). For Balzac, the photograph simply confirmed an occult belief that objects radiate images. Similarly, for the spiritualists, photography seemed to give evidence to a metaphysical belief, but only because the belief itself could be adapted to a system of infinite multiplication.

The spiritualist encounter with photography reveals the uncanny aspect of this technological process, as one is confronted with doubles that can be endlessly scrutinized for their recognizable features, but whose origins remain obscure. Although mere images, photographs remain endlessly reproducible, able to survive the physical death of their originals. While serving, on the one hand, as evidence of a supernatural metaphysical existence, spirit photographs also present a uniquely modern conception of the spirit world as caught up in the endless play of image making and reproduction and the creation of simulacra. What is haunting about these images is perhaps their very lack of tangible reference, serving even within spiritualist metaphysics simply as a nostalgic reminder of how things once appeared, a *symbolon* passed between the living and the dead as a token of recognition.

In spirit photography we find an extraordinary conjunction of uncanny themes, the visual double, the "constant recurrence of the same thing," and the fascination with death and its overcoming through the technical device of mechanical reproduction. As revelatory images, evidence of an afterlife, such photographs led to byzantine conceptions of the spirit realm as engaged in the manufacture and reproduction of image doubles. As visual spectacles and entertainment, such manifestations opened the way for the enjoyment of appearances whose very fascination came from their apparent impossibility, their apparent severance from the laws of nature. Instead of a discourse of visuality that underwrites a new worldview of material certainty with apodictic clarity, we uncover a proliferating spiral of exchanges and exchanges of images, founded in a process of reproduction for which no original may ever be produced. Spooky, isn't it?

2

"Visualizing the Phantoms of the Imagination": Projecting the Haunted Minds of Modernity

Murray Leeder

> "If you could read my mind, love, what a tale
> my thoughts would tell,
> Just like an old-time movie, 'Bout a ghost from a wishing well."
>
> GORDON LIGHTFOOT, "IF YOU COULD READ MY MIND,"
> *COMPLETE GREATEST HITS*, RHINO, 2002. CD

So sings Gordon Lightfoot in the opening of his 1970 hit "If You Could Read My Mind." It is a song replete with invocations of the cinematic to convey this paradoxical interplay of embodiment and bondage, insubstantiality and invisibility, specifically within mental space. In his mind, the singer is a ghost, bound in a gothic fortress from an old-time movie, needing to be set free but cannot so long as the (presumably female) addressee of the song cannot truly see him; this image drawn from an "old-time movie" characterizes his essential vulnerability and, presumably, his consequential emotional unavailability. "If You Could Read My Mind" is a relationship song, certainly, but the metaphors it deploys unobtrusively tap into a triad with centuries of lineage: cinema (or the projected image more broadly), the ghost, and the inner spaces of the mind. The scenario the song describes echoes Plato's Cave, itself famously linked to both cinema and mental space by Jean-Louis Baudry,[1] except the singer is not the one doing the looking. Rather, he needs to be seen but cannot be. The lyrics evokes those narratives of ghosts desperate to be put to rest, going back at least to Pliny the Younger's tale of the Greek philosopher Athenodorus's investigation of a ghost that stalked an Athenian house "with fetters on his legs and chains on his wrists."[2]

Terry Castle has influentially historicized Freud's uncanny through her analysis of the Phantasmagoria, the theatrical form developed in the late eighteenth century that used magic lantern technology and a gamut of theatrical tricks to project frightening images onto screens (an older-than-old-time movie). The very term "phantasmagoria," Castle shows, moved from describing this external spectacle to

> the phantasmic imagery of the mind. This metaphoric shift bespeaks ... a very significant transformation in the human consciousness over the past two centuries ... the spectralization or "ghostifying" of mental space .... Thus in everyday conversation we affirm that our brains are filled with ghostly shapes and images, that we "see" figures and scenes in our minds, that we are "haunted" by our thoughts.[3]

Lightfoot's construction of the mind as a space that is both ghostly and cinematic plays into this persistent association of the projected image with thought and the supernatural—often both simultaneously.

Numerous sources have explored the supernatural qualities of cinema in general and early cinema in particular, especially through its links with

---

[1] Jean-Louis Baudry, "The Ideological Effects of the Basic Cinematographic Apparatus," *Film Quarterly* 28.4 (Winter 1974–1975), 42. For more, see Nathan Andersen, *Shadow Philosophy: Plato's Cave and Cinema* (Abingdon: Routledge, 2014).
[2] Pliny the Younger, *Complete Letters* (Oxford: Oxford University Press, 2006), 182. The ghost is only set free once a skeleton in chains is unearthed and properly buried.
[3] Terry Castle, *The Female Thermometer: 18th-Century Culture and the Invention of the Uncanny* (New York: Oxford University Press, 1995), 141–3. For similar explorations, see Marina Warner, *Phantasmagoria: Spirit Visions, Metaphors, and Media into the Twenty-First Century* (Oxford: Oxford University Press, 2006); Owen Davies, *The Haunted: A Social History of Ghosts* (Houndmills, Basingstoke: Palgrave, 2007), esp. 133–62; Shane McCorristine, *Spectres of the Self: Thinking about Ghosts and Ghost-Seeing in England, 1750–1920* (Cambridge: Cambridge University Press, 2010); Srdjan Smajić, *Ghost-Seers, Detectives and Spiritualists: Theories of Vision in Victorian Literature and Science* (New York: Cambridge University Press, 2010). For more on the Phantasmagoria, see Laurent Mannoni's *The Great Art of Light and Shadow: The Archaeology of Cinema* (Exeter: University of Exeter Press, 2000) and Mervyn Heard, *Phantasmagoria: The Secret Life of the Magic Lantern* (Hastings: The Projection Box, 2006).

spirit photography.[4] Indeed, the fact that the airy, half-present aesthetic of the superimposition entered cinema as a privileged means for depicting both ghosts and dreams/hallucinations illustrates the connections between the supernatural and the phantasmagorical space of the mind (one thinks of *The Avenging Conscience* (1914) or even *Sherlock Jr.* (1924), where the dreaming projectionist is initially figured as a ghostly double exposure). This article, however, focuses on several examples that highlight the ghostliness of projection as a discourse that unifies cinema and the modern construction of haunted mental space. It will thus identify early cinema's supernatural qualities as not (or not only) attributable to its newness or novelty, but to its continuities with media of projected light and shadow that carry supernatural potential since the Phantasmagoria and before.

"Unsubstantial, impalpable,—simulacra, phantasms": Bulwer-Lytton's Shadows

Cinema emerged into the late-Victorian world obsessed with magic and the supernatural. The latter half of the nineteenth century had seen the emergence of stage magic as respected middle-class entertainment; the rise of spiritualism as a modern, purportedly scientific religion; the occult revival; and the emergence of psychical research. In the United Kingdom, one of cinema's first exhibition venues was the so-called Ghost Show[5] that evolved both from the Phantasmagoria and the theatrical practice called "Pepper's Ghost" (which used bright lights and carefully positioned panes of glass to make it appear like an actor was interacting with a ghost live on stage[6]). It

---

[4] Among other sources, see Tom Gunning, "Phantom Images and Modern Manifestations: Spirit Photography, Magic Theater, Trick Films and Photography's Uncanny," in *Fugitive Images: From Photography to Video* (Bloomington: Indiana University Press, 1995), 42–71; Karen Beckman, *Vanishing Women: Magic, Film and Feminism* (Durham: Duke University Press, 2003), 72–91; Matthew Solomon, *Disappearing Tricks: Silent Film, Houdini, and the New Magic of the Twentieth Century* (Urbana: University of Illinois Press, 2010), esp. 17–19, 25–5, 104–5; Simone Natale, "A Short History of Superimposition: From Spirit Photography to Early Cinema," *Early Popular Visual Culture* 10.2 (2012): 125–45.
[5] Vanessa Toulmin, *Randall Williams: King of Showmen. From Ghost Show to Bioscope* (London: The Projection Box, 1998).
[6] See Helen Groth, "Reading Victorian Illusions: Dickens's *Haunted Man* and Dr. Pepper's Ghosts," *Victorian Studies* 5.10 (2007), 43–75; Dassia N. Posner, "Spectres on the New York Stage: The (Pepper's) Ghost Craze of 1863," in *Representations of Death in Nineteenth-Century U.S. Writing and Culture*, ed. Lucy Elizabeth Frank (Aldershot: Ashgate, 2007), 189–204.

is perhaps no surprise, then, to find early commentators using supernatural metaphors to characterize cinema's curious qualities. But the mind is never that far away, either: in the most famous of these accounts, Maxim Gorky qualifies his initial description of cinema's gray, silent netherworld with "[h]ere I shall try to explain myself, lest I be suspected of madness or indulgence in symbolism."[7] Again, the ghostly space of cinema is tied (albeit here by the way of a disclaimer) with mental states. This section will provide a new angle on the backstory of the film/mind/ghost triad through examining a similar dynamic in Edward Bulwer-Lytton's 1859 novella "The Haunted and the Haunters; or, The House and the Brain."

Today probably most famous for having penned the immortal line, "It was a dark and stormy night,"[8] Bulwer-Lytton (later the 1st Baron Lytton) was not only a well-known writer in his time, but also an early participant in the Victorian "occult revival." This fact manifests clearly in certain of his works of fiction. While fiction, "The Haunted and the Haunters" reflects some contemporaneous theorizations of the supernatural, and its narrator often serves as a mouthpiece for Bulwer-Lytton's ideas. In fact, such was Bulwer-Lytton's credibility in occultist circles that Madame Blavatsky herself reportedly claimed that no author ever wrote about supernatural beings so truthfully.[9] The story's narrator takes it upon himself to investigate an infamous London haunted house where no visitor lasts more than a few hours without fleeing in terror—though no two people relate the same experience. The story is considered an influential example of the Victorian "scientification" of the supernatural, in which hauntings are justified with references to electromagnetism, mesmerism, telegraphy, etc. Alison Milbank refers to it as "the apogee of the naturalized supernatural in the Victorian age."[10] In contrast to such familiar Victorian haunting narratives as Henry James's "The Turn of the Screw" or Charlotte Perkins Gillman's "The Yellow Wallpaper," there is no theme of madness here—quite the opposite, in fact, as the narrator is defined as utterly rational and sane. Nor is there

---

[7] Maxim Gorky "A review of the Lumière programme at the Nizhni-Novgorod Fair, as printed in the *Nizhegorodski listok*, newspaper, July 4, 1986, and signed 'I.M. Pacatus,'" Appendix to Jay Leyda, *A History of the Russian and Soviet Film* (London: Unwin House, 1960), 407.
[8] So began his 1830 novel *Paul Clifford*.
[9] Betsy van Schlun, *Science and Imagination: Mesmerism, Media and the Mind in Nineteenth-Century English and American Literature* (Berlin: Galda + Wilch Verlag, 2007), 136.
[10] Alison Milbank, "The Victorian Gothic in English Novels and Stories, 1830–1880," in *The Cambridge Companion to Gothic Fiction*, ed. Jerrold E. Hogle (Cambridge: Cambridge University Press, 2002), 163. I explore the connections between Bulwer-Lytton's story and Richard Matheson's novel *Hell House* (1971) and its adaptation *The Legend of Hell House* (1973) in Murray Leeder, "Victorian Science and Spiritualism in *The Legend of Hell House*," *Horror Studies* 5.3 (2014), esp. 33–4.

much of what Tzvetan Todorov would call "fantastic hesitation,"[11] where we might wonder if its phenomena are real or imaginary: in "The Haunted and the Haunters," ghostly phenomena do indeed originate in the human mind, but not in the sense that a hallucination might.

The ghosts that the narrator observes in the haunted space have a distinctly proto-cinematic (or "Phantasmagorical" or "lanternic") character. These specters are shadowy approximations of the human form that seem to re-enact a recorded scene, and the narrator appears to both share and not share space with them simultaneously:

> Suddenly [...] there grew a shape,—a woman's shape. It was distinct as a shape of life,—ghastly as a shape of death [...] As if from the door, though it did not open, there grew out another shape, equally distinct, equally ghastly,—a man's shape, a young man's. It was in the dress of the last century, or rather in a likeness of such dress (for both the male shape and the female, though defined, were evidently unsubstantial, impalpable,—simulacra, phantasms) [...] Just as the male shape approached the female, the dark Shadow started from the wall, all three for a moment wrapped in darkness. When the pale light returned, the two phantoms were as if in the grasp of the Shadow that towered between them; and there was a blood-stain on the breast of the female; and the phantom male was leaning on its phantom sword, and blood seemed trickling fast from the ruffles, from the lace; and the darkness of the intermediate Shadow swallowed them up,—they were gone.[12]

Though his servant flees in panic and his dog dies of fright, our intrepid narrator manages to stay steady by telling himself, "my reason rejects this thing; it is an illusion,—I do not fear."[13] And indeed, the ghosts prove unable to affect him.

The use of "Shadow" here is of interest. Not only did Gorky famously characterize cinema as "the kingdom of shadows" and "not life but its shadow" in 1896,[14] but "photographic shadows," "shadow-images," and just "shadows" were privileged descriptors in late nineteenth- and early

---

[11]Tzvetan Todorov, *The Fantastic: A Structural Approach to a Literary Genre* (Ithaca: Cornel University Press, 1975).
[12]Edward Bulwer-Lytton, *The Haunted and the Haunters* (London: Simpkin, Marshall, Hamilton, Kent & Co., 1925), 46–7.
[13]Ibid., 44.
[14]Gorky, 407.

twentieth-century periodical for both photochemical film and X-ray images.[15] The title of the 2011 documentary about the American Film Registry, *These Amazing Shadows*, attests to this rhetoric's persistence. In Bulwer-Lytton's tale, the shadow play seems to be imprinted onto the environment of the haunted house, as if playing and replaying through some quasi-mechanical means. And the explanation is technological, albeit an occult technology: a mysterious device, described as a compass floating in a clear liquid on top of a thin tablet, with astrological symbols in place of cardinal directions. With this object destroyed, the haunting ceases, the house becoming inhabitable. Nonetheless, the narrator theorizes that a living human agency was behind these hauntings, and that ghosts are less motivated, intelligent, ensouled spirits of the dead than residual thoughts and memories willed into a semblance of being by mysterious forces. The narrator reflects on the fact that no two persons told the same tale of their experiences in the haunted house:

> If this were an ordinary imposture, the machinery would be arranged for results that would but little vary; if it were a supernatural agency permitted by the Almighty, it would surely be for some definite end. These phenomena belong to neither class; my persuasion is, that they originate in some brain now far distant; that that brain had no distinct volition in anything that occurred; that what does occur reflects but its devious, motley, ever-shifting, half-formed thoughts; in short, that it has been the dreams of such a brain put into action and invested with a semi-substance. That this brain is of immense power, that it can set matter into movement, that it is malignant and destructive...[16]

Alongside the device, our narrator discovers a miniature portrait dated from 1765, featuring a man described as resembling "some mighty serpent transformed into a man, preserving in the human lineaments the old serpent type."[17] He is identified as a notorious man who fled London on the suspicion of a double murder. This man is presumably the architect of the haunted space, but no more information is provided.

---

[15]Amy E. Borden, "Corporeal Permeability and Shadow Pictures: Reconsidering *Uncle Josh at the Moving Picture Show* (1902)," in *Beyond the Screen: Institutions, Networks and Publics of Early Cinema*, eds. Maria Braun, Charlie Keil, Rob King, Paul Moore, and Louis Pelletier (New Barnett: John Libbey, 2012), 168.
[16]Bulwer-Lytton, 58.
[17]Ibid., 68.

However, in the longer, original version of the story,[18] the responsible party is revealed to be an evil, immortal mesmerist named Mr. Richards. Mr. Richards is heavily associated with empire: the owner of the house encountered him under another name in India, where he was a corrupt advisor to a Rajah, and he now presents himself as an Orientalist residing in Damascus. Mr. Richards is a man of great will, who has willed himself not to die. The narrator tracks him to a London gentleman's club and boldly questions him: "To what extent human will in certain temperaments can extend?" Mr. Richards's answer again invokes empire: "To what extent can thought extend? Think, and before you draw breath you are in China!" The narrator replies, "True. But my thought has no power in China," and Mr. Richards replies, "Give it expression, and it may have: you may write down a thought which, sooner or later, may alter the whole condition of China. What is a law but a thought? Therefore thought is infinite—therefore thought has power..."[19]

Though this discussion of the projectability of thought may not seem supernatural, per se, the conclusions the narrator draws from it are:

> Yes; what you say confirms my own theory. Through invisible currents one human brain may transmit its ideas to other human brains with the same rapidity as a thought promulgated by visible means. And as thought is imperishable—as it leaves its stamp behind it in the natural world even when the thinker has passed out of this world—so the thought of the living may have power to rouse up and revive of the thoughts which the dead—such as those thoughts *were in life*—though the thought of the living cannot reach the thoughts which the dead *now* may entertain.[20]

For several pages, the narrator spells out his (and, by implication, Bulwer-Lytton's) theories of the supernatural and the mind, eventually confronting Mr. Richards for his evils and declaring "execrable Image of Death and Death in Life, I warn you back from the cities and homes of healthful men; back to the ruins of departed empires; back to the deserts of nature unredeemed!"[21]

Reflecting the paradoxical impressions of travel and immobility, motion and stillness, emerging from cinema and other modern media, Mr. Richards

---

[18]For information on the two versions, see Bruce Wyse, "Mesmeric Machinery, Textual Production and Simulacra in Bulwer-Lytton's 'The Haunted and the Haunters; or, The House and the Brain,'" *Victorian Review* 30.2 (2004), esp. 33–4, 55–7.
[19]Bulwer-Lytton, 75.
[20]Ibid., 75–6.
[21]Ibid., 81.

responds to this attempt at banishment by wresting his and the narrator's spirits into another place: "As he spoke I felt as if I rose out of myself upon eagle wings. All the weight seemed gone from the air—roofless the room, roofless the dome of space. I was not in the body—where I knew not—but aloft over time, over earth."[22] The subsequent sequence plays out almost entirely in dialogue, as the narrator witnesses an allegorical (one assumes) depiction of Mr. Richards's ultimate grim fate, the lone survivor of a ship in the frozen north, pursued by foes under an iron sky. Mr. Richards then impels the narrator to sleep, and commands him not to tell any of this story to anyone, while he presumably flees the country and changes his identity.

"The Haunted and the Haunters" is a fascinating muddle, especially in the longer version, but one central recurring theme is projection: the projection of Mr. Richards's will that causes the ghosts to haunt the house, the projection of his and the narrator's consciousness out of their bodies and into an allegorical space, and of course, the shadowy, ineffable phantoms that the narrator confronts in the haunted house. That sequence anticipates many hallmarks of accounts of early cinema spectatorship: uncanny figures that resemble human beings but are shadowy phantasms divested of life force, the traceless appearance from and disappearance into nothingness, the uncertain line between presence and absence, and the demarcation between the naïve, overwhelmed spectator who succumbs to panic and the sophisticated one capable of saying some version of "it is an illusion—I do not fear."[23] These parallels are more than anecdotal, and demonstrate the extent to which these themes were not necessarily unique to cinema, but rather illustrate consistencies between early cinema and the broader history of projected media, especially its entanglement with the supernatural.

The Lesson of Sympsychography

From Bulwer-Lytton's occult projections of 1859, we move to two examples of the mystical projection of thought from 1896, the immediate aftermath of the unveiling of two new and sensational extensions of photography:

---

[22] Ibid., 81–2.
[23] For the separation between naïve and trained spectators, see Stephen Bottomore, "The Panicking Audience? Early Cinema and the 'Train Effect,'" *Historical Journal of Film, Radio and Television* 19.2 (1999), 177–216; Martin Loiperdinger, "Lumière's *Arrival of a Train*: Cinema's Founding Myth," *The Moving Image* 4.1 (Spring 2004), 89–118; Murray Leeder, "M. Robert-Houdin Goes to Algeria: Spectatorship and Panic in Illusion and Early Cinema," *Early Popular Visual Culture* 8.2 (2010), 187–203.

cinema and the X-ray. It is easy to forget that it was Röntgen's discovery that initially inspired greater excitement. The relationship between the X-ray and the supernatural was immediate and reciprocal. Supernatural metaphors helped characterize its ability to penetrate solid surfaces; an early X-ray scientist named Silvanus Thompson prophesized that "we shall now be able to realize Dickens's fancy when he made Scrooge perceive through Marley's body the two brass buttons on the back of his coat."[24] Conversely, occultist and spiritualists welcomed the X-ray as a sensational modern scientific discovery that lent credence to some of their claims: that there was an invisible world and the specially equipped can reveal it. The notion that thought itself would soon be photographed now seemed plausible even beyond occultist circles.

In September 1896, *Popular Science Monthly* carried an article by scientist David Starr Jordan entitled "The Sympsychograph: A Lesson in Impressionist Physics." Jordan was one of the most respected scientists in the United States at the time and the president of Stanford University. The article concerned a curious image, rather resembling a later surrealist photograph: a blurry collage of a series of images of cats (Figure 2.1). The picture, the text tells us, was produced by the seven members of the

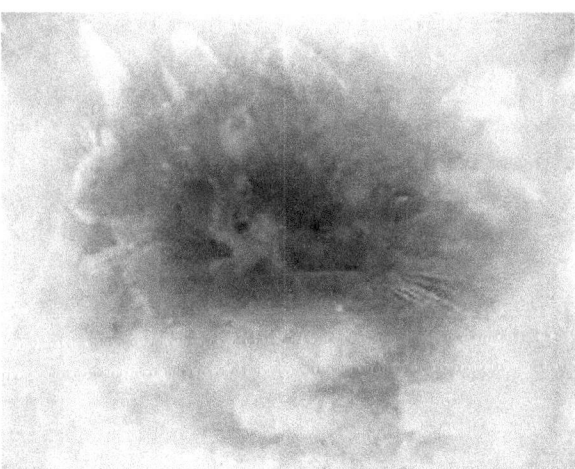

FIGURE 2.1 *From David Starr Jordan's "The Sympsychography: A Study in Impressionist Physics,"* Popular Science Monthly 49 *(September 1896), 601.*

---

[24]Sylvia Pamboukan, "'Looking Radiant': Science, Photography and the X-Ray Craze of 1897," *Victorian Review* 27.2 (2001), 58.

"Astral Camera Club of Alcalde," inspired by Röntgen's experiments. With a specially designed camera, the Club devised a way to capture on a sensitive plate, "as the rays of light are gathered in ordinary photography," those "electric and odic impulses [that] could be transferred from the brain or retina through the eye of each different observer."[25]

The sympsychograph itself claims to record mental impressions of the concept "cat" from each member of the Club:

> They were not to think of any particular cat, but of a cat as represented by the innate idea of the mind or ego itself.... One man's thought of a cat would be individual, ephemeral, a recollection of some cat which he had some time seen, and which by the mind's eye would be seen again ....The personal equation would be measurably eliminated in sympsychography, while the cat of the human innate idea, the astral cat, the cat which "never was on land or sea," but in accordance with which all cats have been brought into incarnation, would be more or less perfectly disclosed.[26]

Again, mystical discourse (buoyed by the sympsychograph's aesthetic resemblance to a spirit photograph), mental spaces, and the image smoothly coexist. The fact that the article tells us that the Astral Camera Club's experiment was conducted on April 1 ought to have been a giveaway (or failing that, the claim that "The next experiment will be by similar means to photograph the cat's idea of man"[27]), and the following issue confirmed that it was a hoax. By then, however, the idea had taken root with some credulous readers. Jordan would recall in his autobiography that "One clergyman even went so far as to announce a series of six discourses on 'The Lesson of Sympsychography,' while many others said they welcomed the discovery as verifying what they had long believed."[28] Though a hoax, sympsychography stands near the beginning of a tradition of attempted or purposed thought photography or "thoughtography," famously manifesting in

---

[25]David Starr Jordan, "The Sympsychograph: A Study in Impressionist Physics," *Popular Science Monthly* 49 (September 1896), 600.
[26]Ibid., 600–1.
[27]Ibid., 601.
[28]Qtd. in Kathryn Ann Lindskoog, *Fakes, Frauds and Other Malarkey* (Grand Rapids: Zondervan Publishing House, 1992), 173.

the *nensha* experiments of Tomokichi Fukurai in Tokyo[29] and, later, the work of the controversial American photographer Ted Serios.[30]

In sympsychography, the purported act of mental projection onto undeveloped film is justified with references to the recent discovery of X-rays; the article argues that "the invisible rays of Röntgen are not light in the common sense, but akin rather to brain emanations, or odic forces, which pass from mind to mind without the intervention of forms of gross matter as a medium."[31] The reference here is to a discredited concept: the odic or odylic force (also sometimes called the von Reichenbach force after its purported discoverer, Baron Carl von Reichenbach), a hypothetic life force used to justify mesmeric *rapport*. What Jordan suggests facetiously, other writers proposed in earnest: an article entitled "Röntgen's Vindication of Reichenbach" appeared in an 1897 issue of the spiritualist/occultist journal *Borderland*, arguing that X-rays were none other than the odic force.[32]

The idea that thought itself can be conceived as a kind of emanations that can stretch beyond the body into the world around us, and even imprint itself as a kind of photography, is born of both science's recent unveiling of new unseen worlds and of the "ghostification" of mental space. And those haunting thoughts so stubbornly failed to remain confined to one's head.

"The Kinetiscope of the Mind"

Tropes of projection and the externalizability of thought also operated in the nascent field of psychical research. Frederick W.H. Myers, cofounder of the Society for Psychical Research and the coiner of the word "telepathy,"[33]

---

[29] These experiments inspired Kōji Suzuki's 1991 novel *Ring* and its various adaptations (*Ring/Ringu* (1998), *The Ring Virus* (1999), *The Ring* (2002)). See Rolf H. Krauss, *Beyond Light and Shadow: The Role of Photography in Certain Paranormal Phenomena: A Historical Survey* (Portland: Nazraeli Press, 1995), 57–8; Anthony Enns, "The Horror of Media: Technology and Spirituality in the Ringu Films," in *The Scary Screen: Media Anxiety in The Ring*, ed. Kristen Lacefield (Farnham: Ashgate, 2010), 32–8.

[30] See Stephen Raude, "The Thoughtographs of Ted Serios," in *The Perfect Medium: Photography and the Occult*, eds. Clément Chéroux, Andreas Fischer, Pierre Apraxine, Denis Canguilhem and Sophie Schmit (New Haven: Yale University Press, 2004), 155–7; María del Pilar Blanco, "The Haunting of the Everyday in the Thoughtographs of Ted Serios," in *Popular Ghosts: The Haunted Spaces of Everyday Culture*, eds. María del Pilar Blanco and Esther Peeren (New York: Continuum, 2010), 253–67.

[31] Ibid., 598.

[32] [Anon], "Röntgen's Vindication of Reichenbach," *Borderland* 4.1 (January 1897), 35–6.

[33] See Roger Luckhurst, *The Invention of Telepathy* (Oxford: Oxford University Press, 2002).

offered a redefinition of the ghost less as a motivated, intelligent being than as a lingering psychic phenomenon (estranging many spiritualists in the process). As Shane McCorristine notes, Myers's conception of "the ghost as an automatic phenomenon implied a radically phantasmagorical and haunted world, a site of previous events, memories and dreams that never disappear from the visual world, but can be relayed through hallucinatory vision."[34]

A similar sensibility, tied explicitly to cinema and other media technologies, is on display in an article in *Borderland* in October 1896, entitled "Suggestions from Science for Psychic Students. Useful Analogies from Recent Discoveries and Inventions." It was authored by the journal's founder, W.T. Stead. Regarded as the founder of the "New Journalism," the forerunner of both tabloid journalism and investigative journalism, Stead would die in 1912 on the *RMS Titanic*. He was also an enthusiastic spiritualist and employed medium Ada Goodrich Freer as *Borderland*'s coeditor.[35] Running from 1893 to 1897, *Borderland* published widely on new developments in psychical research, spiritualism, theosophy and eastern religions, palmistry, precognition, astrology, haunted houses, psychic photography, and even psychic messages received from Mars.

Stead's article begins:

The discovery of the Röntgen rays has compelled many a hardened sceptic to admit, when discussing Borderland, that "there may be something in it after all." In like manner many of the latest inventions and scientific discoveries make psychic phenomena thinkable, even by those who have no personal experience of their own to compel conviction. I string together a few of these helpful analogies, claiming only that they at least supply stepping stones that may lead to a rational understanding of much that is now incomprehensible.[36]

Stead's "new discoveries" include electricity, the phonograph, the telephone, the photograph, the X-ray, the (far from new) camera obscura, and, critically for

---

[34]McCorristine, 179.
[35]See Roger Luckhurst, "W.T. Stead's Occult Economies," in *Culture and Science in the Nineteenth-Century Media*, eds. Louise Henson, Geoffrey Cantor, Goean Dawson, Richard Noakes, Sally Shuttleworth and Johnathan R. Topham (Aldershot: Ashgate, 2004), 125–35; Justin Sausman, "The Democratisation of the Spook: W.T. Stead and the Invention of Public Occultism," in *W.T. Stead: Newspaper Revolutionary*, eds. Laurel Brake, Ed King, Roger Luckhurst and James Mussell (London: The British Library, 2012), 149–65.
[36]W.T. Stead, "Suggestions from Science for Psychic Students: Useful Analogies from Recent Discoveries and Inventions," *Borderland* 3.4 (October 1896), 400.

"VISUALIZING THE PHANTOMS OF THE IMAGINATION"

our purposes here, the kinetoscope.[37] Stead consistently misspells Edison's invention as "kinetiscope"—he may be thinking of the earlier kinetiscope designed by Austrian inventor Franz von Uchatius, which projected moving drawings. Stead divides his section on the kinetoscope into the "Kinetiscope of Nature" (based around the idea of nature to spontaneously record traumatic events and replay them when appropriately sensitive spectators are near) and the "Kinetiscope of the Mind," which deals with the projectability or externalizability of inner images and states. He introduces the latter thus: "The possibility of visualizing the phantoms of the imagination is possessed by some persons in such a high degree that they can compel clairvoyants and sensitives to see as if they were real persons the purely imaginary heroes and heroines of an unwritten romance."[38] Here, Stead assembles a set of shorter anecdotes. The first, entitled "Living Pictures at Will," describes a Frenchman who purchased a sixteenth-century chateau and furnished it in Renaissance style. The decor included a portrait of a nobleman of the House of Valois pictured alongside some "charming girls," and the owner found that by focusing his mental energies on the portrait, it was possible to will its originals to manifest "in a visible and tangible form." A dull vapor would fill the room and become:

> the originals of the portraits sitting there clothed in costumes of the olden times, seated in the armchairs. They were alive, or at least they so appeared, so entire was the illusion (if illusion it was). Their faces were those of persons talking, their eyes moving, their lips opening as if they were conversing together, but the magician could not distinguish an articulate word, the most being a light murmur of voices. The marvellous scene lasted half an hour, then melted into a mist.[39]

Lynda Nead has surveyed such image of paintings and other inanimate works coming to life as a key fantasy of the nineteenth century, one that culminates in cinema:

> The haunted gallery is a powerful metaphor for the uncanny magic of early film. Every still is haunted by the photographic likenesses of those who are no longer there; each time the project is set in motion the figures step out of their frames and come to life. There is, however, an

---

[37] There is also a section on experiments in photographing thought conducted by the French occultist Hippolyte Baraduc, as clarified by the British theosophist Annie Besant.
[38] Stead, 403.
[39] Ibid.

instant of hesitation and doubt—does the image move, can it live?—but the moment cannot be held for long.[40]

In Stead's anecdote, a parallel moment of hesitation is implied in the parenthetic "if illusion it was." Are these actually the ghosts of the portrait models, or merely apparitions that look like them, willed to that shape by the gentleman's mind?

Stead then reproduces a letter from Madame Marie de Manasseine, who claims that she has always possessed "the faculty of representing to myself vividly and objectively all that I desired... on reading the history of a disease, I could at will see the patient and all the pathological phenomena of his disease. On reading the description of a journey, I not only saw mentally, but, as it were, objectively, the scenery described, &c."[41] She honed the skill to conjure and manipulate hypnagogic hallucinations (phenomena of the indeterminate mental state between sleep and waking life), but also notes that

> during my entire conscious life I have, from time to time, a visual phantom or apparition which remains completely independent of my will, and which appears sometimes several times a day, and sometimes more rarely, after longer or shorter periods. This visual phantom consists in a very brilliant star, having the apparent size of the planet Venus. It appears to me ordinarily at a certain distance, suspended in the middle of the room: but sometimes it approaches me and begins to shine over my shoulder, sometimes over my breast.

This phantom often shines above her daughter's head. It interestingly blurs the line between those images born of the human mind (the talent Madame de Manassiene professes to possess in great degree) and the supernatural (she regards the hallucinogenic star as portending "some success or pleasure").[42]

Lastly, Stead reproduces some comments by theosophist C.W. Leadbeater that concern "the projection of a desired spot of a thought-form—that is to say, an artificial elemental moulded in the shape of the projector and ensouled by his thought. Thus form would receive whatever

---

[40]Lynda Nead, *The Haunted Gallery: Painting, Photography, Film c. 1900* (New Haven: Yale University Press, 2007), 104.
[41]Ibid.
[42]Ibid.

impressions there were to be received, and would transmit them to his maker, not along an astral telegraph-wire, but by sympathetic vibration." Leadbeater goes on to address the question of whether an astral body can be solidified into material forms; he says that yes, it can, and it is even possible to produce perfect illusions of the human form, but that "No one connected with any school of white magic"[43] would deign to do such a thing. The astonishing idea of creating a double of oneself and send it out into the world, relaying its sensory impressions back to one's body, is an extreme incarnation of modern technology's ability to create lifelike but lifeless doubles of the human form, wedded to the occult speculations triggered by telegraphy and its descendants.[44]

Stead's article displays how "cinematic" metaphors became available almost immediately to supernatural discourses. Here, the medium is mined for analogic value, both in terms of the recording and replaying of reality of the projectability of phantasmic images through the mind's eye into observable reality. Stead does not contend that they are themselves supernatural, but rather places them within the stock of media metaphors that had served spiritualists for a half century. It is also noteworthy that it was also in 1895–1896 that Sigmund Freud began to formulate his version of "projection."[45] In 1901's *The Psychopathology of Everyday Life*, Freud asserted that

> I believe that a large part of the mythological view of the world, which extends a long way into the most modern religions, is nothing but psychology projected into the external world. The obscure recognition... of psychical factors and relations in the unconscious is mirrored... in the construction of a supernatural reality, which is destined to be changed back once more by science into the psychology of the unconscious.[46]

Again, "projection," in all of its many senses, hangs stubbornly around both the supernatural and the mind, here again understood as being, on some

---

[43]Ibid.
[44]See Jeffrey Sconce, *Haunted Media: Electronic Presence from Telegraphy to Television* (Durham: Duke University Press, 2000); Simone Natale, "A Cosmology of Invisible Fluids: Wireless, X-Rays, and Psychical Research around 1900," *Canadian Journal of Communication* 36 (2011), 263–75.
[45]J. Laplanche and J.B. Pontalis, *The Language of Psychoanalysis* (New York: Norton, 1973), 351. Laplache and Pontalis identify a sense of projection "comparable to the cinematic one: The subject sends out into the external world an image of something that exists in him in an unconscious way" (354).
[46]Sigmund Freud, *The Psychopathology of Everyday Life* (New York: Norton, 1965), 258–9.

level, interchangeable.[47] Of course, to return to Castle, this retreat of the supernatural into the unconscious serves to supernaturalize thought.

One also thinks of that key strand of early film theory that connects cinematic conventions to mental processes. The key example is Hugo Münsterberg:

> [Film] can act as our imagination acts. It has the mobility of our ideas which are not controlled by the physical necessity of outer events but by the psychological laws for the association of ideas. In our mind past and future become intertwined with the present. [Film] obeys the laws of the mind rather than those of the outer world.[48]

Münsterberg was an anti-spiritualist[49] and would likely not have welcomed the comparison, but his theories of cinema materializing the workings of the inner mind work in parallel to contemporaneous supernatural theorizations. In his theories, film becomes just that projected externalization of thought, no less so than Mr. Richards's shadow-phantoms, the sympsychograph's mind cats, or Stead's anecdotes of the living pictures at will, Madame de Manassiene's brilliant star and the ensouled, projected doubles of theosophist fantasies.

"Just Like an Old-Time Movie"

Writes Castle, "By the end of the nineteenth century, ghosts had disappeared from everyday life, but as the poets intimated, human experience had become more ghost-ridden than ever. Through a strange process of rhetorical displacement, thought itself had become phantasmagorical."[50] The entanglement of the projected image with thought and the supernatural

---

[47]For psychoanalysis's relationship to the supernatural, see Roger Luckhurst, "'Something Tremendous, Something Elemental': On the Ghostly Origins on Psychoanalysis," in *Ghosts: Psychoanalysis, Deconsruction, History*, eds. Andrew Buse and Andrew Stott (New Barnett: Macmillan, 1999), 50–71; Pamela Thurschwell, *Literature, Technology and Magical Thinking, 1880–1920* (Cambridge: Cambridge University Press, 2001), 115–150; Carolyn Burdett, "Modernity, the Occult, and Psychoanalysis," in *A Concise Companion to Psychoanalysis, Literature, and Culture*, eds. Laura Marcus and Ankhi Mukherjee (Chichester: John Wiley & Sons, 2014), 49–65.
[48]Hugo Münsterberg, *The Film: A Psychological Study* (Minneola: Dover, 1970), 41. For more on Münsterberg's theories of "psychotechnology," see Giuliano Bruno, "Film, Aesthetics, Science: Hugo Münsterberg's Laboratory of Moving Images," *Grey Room* 36 (2009), 88–113.
[49]See Simone Natale, "Spiritualism Exposed: Scepticism, Credulity and Spectatorship in End-of-the-Century America," *European Journal of American Culture* 29.2 (2010), 133–44.
[50]Castle, 144.

illustrated here is intimately linked to that process, and is clearly not limited to the nineteenth century. In one case from 1976, experimental psychologist Alvin G. Goldstein published an account of his own visual hallucinations, described as "[i]n every respect resembled a Hollywood version of the ghost."[51] While acknowledging that they originated in his mind, Goldstein also makes it clear that media conventions for depicting ghosts gave them shape.

I will conclude with an example I have explored before, from *Stir of Echoes* (1999).[52] As a party trick, Tom Witzky (Kevin Bacon) agrees to be hypnotized by his sister-in-law Lisa (Illeanna Douglas). She says, "Close your eyes," and we see a wipe effect approximate the closing of his eyes. What follows is a rare dream/hallucination sequence to play out entirely in point-of-view, the way dreams generally do. The audience explicitly shares Tom's perspective, but not his vision per se, since his eyes are closed; it is more the case that we are invited to share the gaze of his mind's eye. For a time, the screen is black. We hear Lisa's sonorous voice: "Now, just listen for a moment. Listen to the sounds of the room around you." Her voice dictates what appears in Tom's imagination *and* the film's imagetrack. She instructs him, "Now, I want you to pretend you're in a theatre." The lights come up on a bare proscenium, seen from the audience with eight or nine other spectators present. She clarifies, "A movie theatre," and a huge screen momentously rolls down in front of the stage. "You're the only one there," she says, and the rest of the audience fades away. She says, "It's one of those great old movie palaces," and the bare white screen is replaced by opulent red curtains. "You look around," Lisa says. "It's a huge empty theatre." The camera tracks rapidly backwards in mid air—a movement that is impossible for the human body, but possible for the camera's eye, for a dreamer unpinned from a physical body, or for a ghost. Lisa says that the walls and chairs are covered in black, and blackness crawls down them, wiping out the redness.

"In the whole, pitch black theatre," she says as the camera's gaze again points to the screen, "there's only one thing you can see, and that's the white screen." The light appears, flickering and roiling, and she notes the presence of letters on the screen, black and indistinct. "You begin to drift closer to them in your chair," she says, and the camera does so, until it

---

[51]Alvin G. Goldstein, "Hallucinatory Experience: A Personal Account," *Journal of Abnormal Psychology* 85.4 (1976), 425.
[52]Murray Leeder, "Ghost-Seeing and Detection in *Stir of Echoes*," *Clues: A Journal of Detection* 30.2 (2012), 81–2.

seems like it must be hovering in the middle of the theater (an image we later see visualized in one of Tom's flashbacks). The letters remain hazy until (Tom's) screen fills (our) screen, and Lisa commands them into focus: "The letters spell 'SLEEP.'" She repeats, "Sleep..." and the screen returns to blackness. What follows are two quick, nightmarish flashes, not from his memory, but that of Samantha (Jennifer Morrison), the murdered girl whose spirit occupies his house. Later in the film Tom receives a vision of her death; both images are finally revealed as point-of-view shots from Samantha's perspective.

Throughout the rest of the film, Samantha invisibly haunts not only Tom's house but his mind, as a consequence of this hypnotic trip into the movie theater—the Phantasmagoria—of imagination. This is represented later in the film when Lisa re-hypnotizes Tom and he sees Samantha as a faceless figure sitting in this supposed vacant movie palace of the mind, an ideal visualization of the haunted space of the modern mind. She is there, inexorably, despite Lisa's insistence that he is alone in his mindspace. Despite gender-swapping the hypnotizing in-law, this sequence plays much as it does in Richard Matheson's source novel *A Stir of Echoes* (1958), except that there, the hypnotic space *is* a proscenium theater. The film effectively restages the sequence reflexively, in a cinema within cinema, and evokes a whole set of powerful associations in the process.

I earlier suggested that early cinema's supernatural affinities are attributable to continuities with older media as much as to its novelty. These continuities stretch forward to this day. The discourse around "oldness" (Lightfoot's "old-time movie," *Stir of Echoes*'s picture palace) localizes cinema's ghostliness in older forms and styles. Perhaps old movies, old movie theaters, and even older media forms help inspire more reflection on the triadic relationship between the mind, the supernatural, and projected light. This makes sense if it is truly the case that, as Alice Rayner writes, "[t]echnology has provided the means to make ghosts an ordinary part of consumer culture but in doing so has familiarized and inured the culture against the absences and losses that the medium projects ..."[53] But just as the supernatural affinities of early cinema cannot be explained only through its novelty value, so does the ghost's purported domestication fail to explain its enduring appeal and uncanny power. So long as our minds

---

[53] Alice Rayner, *Ghosts: Death's Double and the Phenomena of Theatre* (Minneapolis: University of Minnesota Press, 2006), 157.

remain haunted, one ventures to say, we will continue projecting our ghosts, onto our screens or otherwise.

Acknowledgments

Thanks to Drs. Colin Williamson (American Academy of Arts and Sciences) and Drew Beard (Portland State University) for their comments on this chapter.

3

Specters of the Mind: Ghosts, Illusion, and Exposure in Paul Leni's *The Cat and the Canary*

Simone Natale

One of the main characteristics of ghosts is that they are able to invite a great variety of interpretations, meanings, and uses. In Shakespeare's dramas and in ancient religious rituals, in gothic novels and in spiritualist séances, in horror movies and in the New Age spiritual movement, specters have been responsible for popular amusements, irrational fears, experimental inquiries, and acts of devotion. This multiform character also shaped the way ghosts have been represented throughout film history on the cinematic screen. Cinematic specters have appropriated different narrative, symbolic, and metaphorical roles—so many that it is perhaps more precise to describe ghost movies as a plurality of genres with a common theme, rather than as an individual genre.

This essay addresses a particular class of ghost movies: those where the existence of the true "protagonist" of these movies, the ghost, is ultimately refused and relegated to the realm of human imagination and trickery. The defining characteristics of these movies are that they tell a ghost story without believing in ghosts; or, to put it in other words, that they propose to the audience an interpretation of the story that denies the status of reality to the world of ghosts and specters. Most haunted house comedies from the 1930s to the 1960s—such as *The Old Dark House* (1932), *The Ghost Breakers* (1940), or *Scared Stiff* (1953)—follow this basic structure; but these types of films also include movies that play more ambiguously with the borders between hallucination and reality, such as Jack Clayton's *The Innocents* (1961), while finally providing a substantial refusal of the ghostly agency.[1] In this chapter, I will focus on the case of Paul Leni's (1927) *The Cat and the Canary*, showing how this film remediated a long tradition of spectacular entertainments based on the rejection of supernaturalism, and how such rejection has important consequences in the narrative frame and in the nature of the gratification invited in their audience.

After providing a brief summary of the plot and the production history of *The Cat and the Canary*, the essay addresses this movie by referring to aspects from the cultural history of ghosts. Particular emphasis is given to how the film can be framed within the tradition of spiritualist exposés, to the characterization of ghosts as creations of our mind, to the use of superimposition effects, and to the question of sound, which paradoxically plays a quite relevant role despite it being a silent movie. Finally, in the conclusion, I interrogate how works of fiction such as *The Cat and the Canary*, by relying on the allure of the supernatural but at the same time refusing to accept its claims, point to the apparently contradictory power of our fascination for the occult.

Dissecting the ghost of *The Cat and the Canary*

Directed by German expatriate Paul Leni in 1927, *The Cat and the Canary* was produced by Universal Pictures in the United States. The film adapted a stage melodrama by American playwright John Willard in 1921 and had premiered in New York in the following year. The plot focuses on the heritance of millionaire Cyrus West, whose relatives aim at his fortune with greed, like cats around a canary. Before dying, West demands that his will be read only twenty years after his death. As twenty years have passed and the day arrives, all the potential heirs meet in West's old mansion, which has acquired the reputation of being haunted by the ghost of its deceased owner. The will nominates the niece Annabelle West (Laura La Plante) as heiress, but with a condition: at the end of the night, she needs to be judged mentally sane by a psychiatrist. If she fails, the heritance will pass to the second person nominated in the will. During the night her mental sanity is strained by seemingly supernatural events, such as a mysterious hand coming out from the mansion's walls and

---

[1] Following Tzvetan Todorov's categorization of the fantastic, the uncanny, and the marvelous, these movies would pertain to the genre of the uncanny, i.e. to those works of fiction where the hesitation between a natural and a supernatural explanation is finally resolved in a decision for the former. See Tzvetan Todorov, *The Fantastic: A Structural Approach to a Literary Genre* (Ithaca: Cornell University Press, 1975).

the sudden disappearance of the lawyer who read the will—just before he could mention the name of the second person nominated in it. The "ghost," however, is finally revealed to be none other than one of West's nephews, Charles Wilder (Forrest Stanley), the second heir nominated in the will. His plans are finally exposed, and the ghostly apparitions debunked as the result of trickery, of the gloomy atmosphere of the old mansion, and of the overexcited imagination of Annabelle and the other relatives.

The film proved to be a critical and popular success, justifying the employment of Paul Leni, who had accepted Carl Laemmle's invitation to move from Germany to Hollywood and become a director at Universal Studios.[2] Leni used some stylistic devices typical of German Expressionism, adapting them to a plot that had already stood the test of the popular theatrical circuit. Particularly noteworthy was his insertion of the Expressionist-style chiaroscuro lightning in an American film, an aspect that would characterize several Universal horror and film noir productions throughout the 1930s and 1940s.[3] Rebecca Gordon notes that while Expressionist lighting is typically used to imply character motivations and to bestow upon people and objects a certain ineffable character, Leni uses light and shadow effects to create both dramatic and comic effects.[4] The film, in fact, is considered one of the first examples, if not the first, of a film genre that functions through the ambiguity between emotional thrilling and humor: the thriller-chiller comedy.

While Leni's *The Cat and the Canary* certainly helped secure the ghost as a relevant trope of cinematic fiction, it is only by looking beyond the temporal and contextual boundaries of film history per se that one might comprehend how the theme and the figures of the ghost acquire and convey meaning on the cinematic screen. Film history and criticism demand what Lynda Nead calls "an integrated approach to visual media," a perspective that focuses on the connections and spaces *across* different media and practices.[5] Tackled from a similar perspective, movies that challenge the existence of ghosts—such as *The Cat and the Canary*—relate to a larger tradition that goes beyond the boundaries of film history to embrace literary and theatrical works, but

---

[2]Kevin Brownlow, "Annus Mirabilis: The Film in 1927," *Film History: An International Journal* 17.2 (2005), 168–78.
[3]Jan-Christopher Horak, "Sauerkraut & Sausages with a Little Goulash: Germans in Hollywood, 1927," *Film History: An International Journal* 17.2 (2005), 241–60.
[4]Rebecca M. Gordon, "Between Thought and Feeling: Affect, Audience, and Critical Film History" (Ph.D. diss, Indiana University, 2007).
[5]Lynda Nead, *The Haunted Gallery: Painting, Photography, Film C. 1900* (New Haven: Yale University Press, 2007), 2.

also popular scientific lectures and magic shows that attempted to expose the deceitfulness of ghostly apparitions.

From spiritualist exposés to cinematic ghosts

In an essay on the intermedial character of early cinema, André Gaudreault suggests that film historians should adopt "a retrospective, rather than a progressive, point of view," addressing cinema in reference to earlier media and practices, rather than to its later evolutions.[6] A similar approach is fruitful not only for the study of early cinema, but in the analysis of other aspects of film history as well. In the specific case of *The Cat and the Canary*, it is by looking at the cultural history of spiritualism and beliefs in ghosts throughout the nineteenth and early twentieth centuries that one may gain insights for the interpretation of the film.

Emerging as a popular belief and a religious movement in the middle nineteenth century, spiritualism was based on the belief that certain persons, called mediums, could establish a channel of communication with the spirits of the dead. This communication was usually performed in meetings or events called séances, where one or two mediums were joined by other sitters in contacting the spirits.[7] The rise of beliefs in spiritualism was counteracted by the emergence of rationalizing attempts that aimed at exposing spiritualist séances as the result of trickery, hallucination, or sensory deception.[8] These were called *spiritualist exposés* and took the form of pamphlet and popular scientific lectures denouncing the falsehood of spirit phenomena (Figure 3.1). Scientists of the caliber

---

[6]André Gaudreault, "The Diversity of Cinematographic Connections in the Intermedial Context of the Turn of the 20th Century," in *Visual Delights: Essays on the Popular and Projected Image in the 19th Century*, eds. Simon Popple and Vanessa Toulmin (Trowbridge: Flicks Books, 2000), 10.
[7]On the emergence of spiritualism in the nineteenth century see, among others, John Warne Monroe, *Laboratories of Faith: Mesmerism, Spiritism, and Occultism in Modern France* (Ithaca: Cornell University Press, 2008); Robert S. Cox, *Body and Soul: A Sympathetic History of American Spiritualism* (Charlottesville: University of Virginia Press, 2003); Ann Braude, *Radical Spirits: Spiritualism and Women's Rights in Nineteenth-Century America* (Boston: Beacon Press, 1989); Janet Oppenheim, *The Other World: Spiritualism and Psychical Research in England, 1850–1914* (Cambridge: Cambridge University Press, 1985).
[8]David Walker, "The Humbug in American Religion: Ritual Theories of Nineteenth-Century Spiritualism," *Religion and American Culture: A Journal of Interpretation* 23.1 (2013), 30–74; Erhard Schüttpelz, "Mediumismus Und Moderne Medien. Die Prüfung Des Europäischen Medienbegriffs," *Deutsche Vierteljahrsschrift fur Literaturwissenschaft und Geistesgeschichte* 86.1 (2012), 121–44; Simone Natale, "Spiritualism Exposed: Scepticism, Credulity and Spectatorship in End-of-the-Century America," *European Journal of American Culture* 29.2 (2010), 133–44.

of Dmitri Mendeleev, William Benjamin Carpenter, Michael Faraday, and Hugo Münsterberg participated in the tradition of spiritualist exposé, challenging the reliability of spiritualist claims through the appeal to fields such as physics and psychology.[9]

The debate on spiritualism, however, went far beyond the realm of experimental science to include a broader range of practices, by which this rationalizing discourse was converted into an established form of live entertainment. Throughout the nineteenth century, popular scientific lecturers discussed the claims of spiritualism and supernatural phenomena, often carrying out their scientific endeavors with a popular and spectacular

FIGURE 3.1 *An illustration portraying the exposure of the celebrated spiritualist medium Eusapia Palladino, performed during a séance organized in New York in 1910 by Dickinson S. Miller, a professor at Columbia University in New York. Note the person under the table who is reaching for Palladino's feet, to prove that she is using them for the moving of the séance table and producing other "spirit" phenomena. From: Joseph Jastrow, "The Unmasking of Palladino: An Actual Observation of the Complete Machinery of the Famous Italian Medium," Collier's Weekly 45.8 (1910), 21–2.*

---

[9]Sofie Lachapelle, *Investigating the Supernatural: From Spiritism and Occultism to Psychical Research and Metapsychics in France, 1853–1931* (Baltimore: Johns Hopkins University Press, 2011); Michael Pettit, *The Science of Deception: Psychology and Commerce in America* (Chicago, London: University of Chicago Press, 2013).

approach.[10] Starting in institutions devoted to the popularization of science such as the London Polytechnic,[11] this tradition of spiritualist exposés began to involve a growing number of stage magicians in Europe and North America. Some of the most famous magicians of the nineteenth and early twentieth centuries, including the American Harry Houdini, delivered magic shows that aimed to expose the tricks practiced by spiritualist mediums during their séances.[12] The audience expected to find in these shows phenomena similar to those observed at a spiritualist séance, but within a different interpretative framework: in contrast to mediums, in fact, magicians openly admitted that their feats were the result of illusion and trickery, rather than of supernatural phenomena.[13] The anti-spiritualist shows of stage magicians, or spiritualist exposés, became one of the most successful forms of stage conjuring, and help to account for the success of magic spectacles as popular entertainment in the nineteenth century.[14] This genre became more and more important as stage magic reached its zenith, between the 1870s and the 1900s.[15]

Spiritualist exposés have been sometimes linked to early and silent cinema. Matthew Solomon describes film as "an anti-spiritualist medium," observing that the tradition of exposés of the trickery of spiritualism was "one of stage magic's earliest and most important contributions to the history of cinema."[16] Indeed, several among the magicians involved in the pioneering of early cinema had carried out in their careers some forms of anti-spiritualist shows.[17] For instance, David Devant, who bought the first Robert W. Paul's projector and entered into film production, previously performed spiritualist

---

[10]Aileen Fyfe and Bernard V. Lightman, eds., *Science in the Marketplace: Nineteenth-Century Sites and Experiences* (Chicago: University of Chicago Press, 2007); Bernard V. Lightman, *Victorian Popularizers of Science: Designing Nature for New Audiences* (Chicago: University of Chicago Press, 2007); Iwan Rhys Morus, "Worlds of Wonder: Sensation and the Victorian Scientific Performance," *Isis* 101.4 (2010), 806–16.
[11]Jeremy Brooker, "The Polytechnic Ghost: Pepper's Ghost, Metempsychosis and the Magic Lantern at the Royal Polytechnic Institution," *Early Popular Visual Culture* 5.2 (2007), 189–206.
[12]Matthew Solomon, *Disappearing Tricks: Silent Film, Houdini, and the New Magic of the Twentieth Century* (Urbana: University of Illinois Press, 2010).
[13]Peter Lamont, "Magician as Conjuror: A Frame Analysis of Victorian Mediums," *Early Popular Visual Culture* 4.1 (2006), 21–33.
[14]Simon During, *Modern Enchantments: The Cultural Power of Secular Magic* (Cambridge: Harvard University Press, 2002).
[15]Lionel A. Weatherly, *The Supernatural?* (Bristol: Arrowsmith, 1891); John Nevil Maskelyne, *Modern Spiritualism: A Short Account of Its Rise and Progress, with Some Exposures of So-Called Spirit Media* (London: F. Warne, 1876).
[16]Solomon, 27.
[17]Eric Barnouw, *The Magician and the Cinema* (Oxford: Oxford University Press, 1981).

exposés in London at the Egyptian Hall.[18] Likewise, Nevil Maskelyne, son of the magician and author of anti-spiritualist pamphlets John Nevil Maskelyne, and a stage magician himself, patented a film projector, the Mutagraph, featuring continuous instead of intermittent motion.[19] At least two of the filmmakers who made the history of the trick film genre, Georges Méliès and George Albert Smith, were inspired by the tradition of spiritualist exposés, to which they hinted in their cinematic production.[20]

Yet, the contribution of spiritualist exposés to the new cinematic technology also concerns the characterization of the figure and the theme of the ghost as represented on the screen. Performing spiritualist exposés, end-of-the-century magicians such as John Nevil Maskelyne, Harry Kellar, and Harry Houdini understood better than anyone else the spectacular and theatrical potential of spiritualism and of beliefs in the supernatural.[21] The tradition they contributed to build provided a significant precedent in which the exposure of the inauthenticity of ghosts was turned into a spectacular practice that—like cinema itself—implicitly hinted at the deceitful and hallucinatory nature of spectatorship.[22] It is within this tradition that, retrospectively, one might include films that represent the ghost as the fruit of hallucination and delusion. In fact, by equating ghostly apparitions to perceptual delusion and depicting the haunted house as a space of deception and trickery, these films take up several elements from the rationalizing discourse of spiritualist exposé.

In *The Cat and the Canary*, beliefs in the supernatural are evoked constantly since the beginning of the film, as the caretaker of the old mansion, Mammy Pleasant (Martha Mattox), states she does not feel lonely in the empty house

---

[18] Edwin A. Dawes, "The Magic Scene in Britain in 1905: An Illustrated Overview," *Early Popular Visual Culture* 5.2 (2007), 109–26.
[19] Dan North, "Magic and Illusion in Early Cinema," *Studies in French Cinema* 1.2 (2001), 70–9.
[20] See Simone Natale, "A Short History of Superimposition: From Spirit Photography to Early Cinema," *Early Popular Visual Culture* 10.2 (2012), 139–42. Méliès possibly attended John Nevil Maskelyne's spiritual exposés at the Egyptian Hall in 1884, when he traveled to London for deepening his knowledge in the magician's secrets. Elizabeth Ezra, *Georges Méliès: The Birth of the Auteur* (Manchester: Manchester University Press, 2000), 8. The long-standing tradition of spiritualist exposés reverberates in some of his movies, such as *L'armoire des frères Davenport* (The Cabinet Trick of the Davenport Brothers, 1902) and *Le portrait spirite* (A Spiritualist Photographer, 1903).
[21] As I showed elsewhere, spiritualist séances often had a spectacular character, being performed by mediums on a theatrical stage and offered to a paying audience as a form of entertainment. Simone Natale, "The Medium on the Stage: Trance and Performance in Nineteenth-Century Spiritualism," *Early Popular Visual Culture* 9.3 (2011), 239–55.
[22] On how cinema invited spectators to reflect on the deceptive nature of their perception, see Simone Natale, "The Cinema of Exposure: Spiritualist Exposés, Technology, and the Dispositif of Early Cinema," *Recherches sémiotiques/Semiotic Inquiry* 31:1 (2014), 101–17.

since she does not need "the living ones." At the same time, however, the film challenges them as "old superstition" or as the fruit of madness and delusion. Like in the case of spiritualist exposé practiced on the stage by professional magicians, the rationalizing discourse of anti-spiritualism is converted into an entertaining and spectacular element. The ghost plays thereby a double role: on the narrative level, it provides the film with a supernatural and occult aura that has the potential to fascinate the audience;[23] on the metaphorical level, it embodies broader cultural concerns regarding the deceitful nature of sensory perception and, more broadly, of the human mind.

The spectralization of the mind

In *The Female Thermometer* (1995), literary scholar Terry Castle explores how during the nineteenth century the word "phantasmagoria" changed its meaning from referring to something external and public, a spectacle conjured through optical tricks and a magic lantern, to describing something internal and subjective: human imagination. She links the emergence of gothic literature in the late eighteenth and early nineteenth centuries with a new consideration of the mind as a space inhabited by "ghosts," for example, by fantasies and imaginations. Castle called this process "spectralization of the mind," a dynamic by which the specters were re-framed in the realm of human mind, as hallucinations and illusions, rather than as supernatural phenomena. This process, Castle argues, continued to shape throughout the twentieth century up to the present day the representation of the ghost with its metaphoric connections to mental states. As Castle notes, in fact, we are used to the metaphor of the haunted consciousness: we speak of being haunted by memories and pursued by images inside our heads.[24]

By treating ghostly apparition as products of all-too-human fears, expectations, and delusions, *The Cat and the Canary* plays a legitimate part in the "spectralization of the mind" described by Castle. The rationalizing discourse that dismisses beliefs in ghosts as pure superstition mitigates the fear that ghosts arouse in the public, creating the condition for the movie's combination of hilarious and mysterious themes. The comical effect relies ultimately on the identification of the character's and the spectator's

---

[23]As Simon During notes, after all, also stage magicians who performed spiritualist exposés had profited from their audience's fascination with the world of the occult (During, 71).
[24]Terry Castle, *The Female Thermometer: Eighteenth-Century Culture and the Invention of the Uncanny* (New York: Oxford University Press, 1995).

position: as the guests in West's old mansion, we feel chilled and tense despite the rationalist assurance that ghosts exist only in our imagination. The characters in the movie refuse the existence of the supernatural, and yet, like us, become anyway the victims of the fear and the fascination that the supernatural evoke. The paradox becomes particularly evident with the arrival of the psychiatrist, a Caligari-like figure who needs to assess if Annabelle is mad: his mesmerist gaze is fixed on Annabelle but a at the same time on the audience, and his inquiry becomes an investigation of the specters not just in the heroine's, but in everybody's mind. "What makes you so nervous tonight?" asks the psychiatrist, to which Annabelle responds only after a long pause—just the time for us to reflect if we would be able to provide an answer, too.

The meaning of superimposition

Among the different kinds of spiritualist exposés performed on the stage or illustrated in popular publications by stage magicians, the exposure of spirit photography—a spiritualist practice based on the belief that it is possible to capture the image of a ghost on the photographic plate—plays a particularly significant role.[25] As skeptics have often underlined, these images can be explained as the product of photographic tricks, such as multiple exposure and other superimposition techniques, which were of common use in photographic practice well before spirit photography emerged. Struggling to demonstrate the inauthenticity of spiritualism, and eager to find all possible visual and spectacular means to do so, stage magicians like Jacoby in Germany (Figure 3.2) and Maskelyne in Great Britain (Figure 3.3) produced images similar to spirit photographs, but openly acknowledged as photographic tricks. In so doing, they contributed to establish superimposition as a visual technique that wavered between fictional and religious contexts, allowing for its association to the worlds of belief and entertainment at the same time.

In *The Cat and the Canary*, superimposition is one of the most effective visual effects employed. This technique is used relatively sparingly, but with meaningful results throughout the film. In early and silent cinema, superimposition effects were used for three main aims: to visually represent ghosts and other supernatural apparitions, to represent hallucinations and thoughts produced by a character's mind, and to depict the events

---

[25]Natale, "A Short History of Superimposition: From Spirit Photography to Early Cinema."

Jacoby im Reiche seiner Geister.
(Sogenannte Geister-Photographien.)

FIGURE 3.2 *"Jacoby im Reiche seiner Geister: Sogenannte Geister-Photographier" ("Jacoby in the Realm of his Spirits: So-Called Spirit Photography"). From: Carl Willmann,* Moderne Wunder: Natürliche Erklärung der älteren wie neueren Geheimnisse der Spiritisten und Antispiritisten, Geisterritierer, Hellseher, Gedankenleser, Heilmedien, Mnemotechniker und Rechenkünstler *(Leipzig: Otto Spamer, 1886), 212.*

FIGURE 3.3 *"A Spirit Photograph: The Wraith of Mr. Maskelyne Appearing to Dr. Weatherly."* From: Weatherly, Lionel A. The Supernatural? *(Bristol: Arrowsmith, 1891) (frontispiece).*

and atmospheres of dreams.[26] In *The Cat and the Canary*, the use of superimposition also displays a range of characterizations and meanings. Yet throughout the movie ghosts are never visually represented as superimposed images. Ghosts are in fact not represented visually at all, but rather embedded in visual or aural events that can be explained rationally or exchanged for supernatural phenomena. The film, in other words, creates the possibility for the choice whether to believe in ghosts or not: the spectators, as well as the film's fictional characters, choose whether to "see" or "hear" a ghost, or to give another interpretation to what they see, hear, and feel.

Rather than representing ghosts as something external, *The Cat and the Canary* posits ghosts as a matter of interpretation, a choice that is taken at the level of our mind. It thus follows the trajectory of the spectralization of the mind. While superimposition is not used to represent "real" ghosts, it is employed to represent the specters of the mind. At the beginning of the movie, for instance, superimposed images of cats hint at Cyrus West's obsessions: the vision symbolizes the greed of his relatives, among which Cyrus feels like a defenseless canary circled by cats.[27] The character's thoughts are depicted as faint, transparent images—a well-established iconography to represent ghosts in media and popular entertainments such as photography, drawing, phantasmagorias, and stage magic shows.[28] To be haunted by specters, in this sense, also becomes in visual terms "to find oneself obsessed by spectral images," as Castle puts it.[29]

Ghosts and the problem of noise

Interestingly, the silent movie *The Cat and the Canary* employs superimposition not only to render mental thoughts, but also sounds and aural events. Superimposition effects are employed to depict visually the noise of the knocking at the door and, in another scene, the stroke of a clock.[30]

---

[26] André Bazin, "The Life and Death of Superimposition (1946)," *Film-Philosophy* 6.1 (2002), 22–30.
[27] The use of superimposition in this scene functions at the same time as an allegorical summary of the plot and as a visualization of Cyrus West's thoughts—with the latter interpretation reinforced by the fact that the image of the cats is superimposed on that of the old man, hinting to the existence of a mental, subjective reality.
[28] See Brooker; Tom Gunning, "To Scan a Ghost: The Ontology of Mediated Vision," *Grey Room*, 189–206.26 (2007), 94–126.
[29] Castle, 123.
[30] A similar strategy was employed in other films of the time, including Sergei Eisenstein's *Strike* (1925). Sergei Eisenstein, *The Film Sense* (New York: Harcourt Brace Jovanovich, 1975), 80.

The trick helps to visualize in a striking manner those sounds that were to provoke the chills of the impressionable characters (and spectators). But the necessity to substitute sound with visual effects in a silent film does not explain alone why the movie employed superimposition, an aesthetic that, as mentioned above, is inextricably linked with the iconographic tradition of representations of ghosts in Western culture. My contention is that this use of superimposition to represent sounds has to do with the status the film gives to the ghost as irrational interpretations of sensorial events.

In 1927, Leni's film came near the end of the era of the silent film. Yet, despite being a silent movie, sound played a peculiarly relevant role in this movie. As Robert Spadoni points out, "this film, had it been a sound film (...) would had been a feast of noise implemented, like the host of visual techniques Leni deployed, to make viewers jumpy."[31] The richness of sensorial chills that also somehow have an (in)audible nature is underlined by the reactions of the film's characters to aural events, and Spadoni reports that the *Motion Picture News* predicted that the film would "score best when presented mostly with mechanical sound effects rather than customary musical accompaniment."[32]

Immaterial by definition, invisible in many cases, ghosts have always entertained a particular relationship with the realm of sound. The first manifestations of spirit agency in spiritualism were rappings, and spiritualist phenomena frequently consisted of noises and sounds. The darkness or semi-darkness of séance rooms forced spirits and mediums to rely on nonvisual experiences. As Steven Connor points out, "the members of the séance would see much less than they would touch, taste, smell and, most importantly, *hear*."[33] In the frame of a spiritualist séance, each sensation and event could be explained and understood as a spirit message. Spirit communications supposedly delivered from the beyond were often barely understandable phenomena, relying on the interpretation of spiritual mediums to become of some meaning to the sitters. Phenomena as different as movements of objects, a sudden current of air, a barely inaudible rap, or the feeling of being touched were interpreted as spirit messages.

---

[31] Robert Spadoni, *Uncanny Bodies: The Coming of Sound Film and the Origins of the Horror Genre* (Berkeley: University of California Press, 2007), 55.
[32] Ibid.
[33] Steven Connor, "The Machine in the Ghost: Spiritualism, Technology and the 'Direct Voice'," in *Ghosts: Deconstruction, Psychoanalysis, History*, eds. Peter Buse and Andrew Stott (New York: St. Martin's Press, 1999), 208. Emphasis in original. See, also, on spiritualism and sound technologies, Anthony Enns, "Voices of the Dead: Transmission/Translation/Transgression," *Culture, Theory and Critique* 46.1 (2005), 11–27.

The status of sensorial perception in this context can be aptly described by referring to the concept of noise in communication theory. According to Claude Shannon's mathematical model of communication, the fundamental aim of communication is to reproduce exactly or approximately a selected message at another point. In order to do so, one needs to distinguish meaningful information from the distortions, labeled *noise*, which may intervene in the process.[34] With Shannon's communication theory in mind, the history of the spiritualist movement in the nineteenth century can be regarded as an effort to transform the noise in information or, in other words, to understand every sensorial event as significant information. In spiritualism the idea of noise was almost completely banned, and every event could be regarded as a spirit message, rather than as interference or distortion. The conventionality of this interpretation was acknowledged even by committed spiritualists. As one recognized, for instance, for the case of table rappings, "the interpretation of sound—its investment with sense—is purely conventional. We may build up a system of laws to enable us to give a proper and uniform expression to it, but we make sound to signify just what is most convenient for us."[35] In 1853, among audible spirit phenomena a spiritualist listed knockings, rappings, jarrings, creakings, and tickings. These "peculiar noises, indicative of more or less intelligence" could be very loud, distinct, and forcible, or less distinct and more gentle, but were all "audible realities."[36] What counted was not the nature of the sound, but the interpretation, which was given to them as evidence of ghostly agency.

If spiritualists conceived aural phenomena within a context banning noise as nonrelevant information, critics of spiritualism had a very different approach to the problem: they considered the knockings and rappings heard by spiritualists at séances as noise, rather than as meaningful information (i.e., the spirit message). Critics hinted at the problem of sensorial perception, whereas noises of ordinary origins could be exchanged for a sign of the presence of ghosts.[37] They stressed that the hearing of anomalous

---

[34]Claude Elwood Shannon, "The Mathematical Theory of Communication," in *The Mathematical Theory of Communication*, eds. Claude Elwood Shannon and Warren Weaver (Urbana: University of Illinois Press, 1949). See also Juan A. Suarez, "Structural Film: Noise," in *Stillmoving: Between Cinema and Photography*, eds. Karen Beckman and Jean Ma (Durham: Duke University Press, 2008).

[35]Napoleon Bonaparte Wolfe, *Startling Facts in Modern Spiritualism* (Chicago: Religio-Philosophical Publishing House, 1875), 24.

[36]Adin Ballou, *An Exposition of Views Respecting the Principal Facts, Causes and Peculiarities Involved in Spirit Manifestations* (Boston: Bela Marsh, 1853), 1.

[37]Joseph Jastrow, "The Psychology of Deception," *Popular Science* 34.10 (1888), 328; George M. Beard, "The Psychology of Spiritism," *The North American Review* 129.272 (1879), 65–80.

sounds implies the possibility of madness or hallucination—that is to say, the existence of the "specters" of the mind.

In *The Cat and the Canary*, the dialectic between ghosts and rationalizing discourses is resolved in the film's dismissal of the possibility that ghosts do exist, in its refusal of the interpretation of noises as signs of spirit presence. The film evokes such spectralization of sound by inserting noises as moments of shock that underline the characters' propensity to believe in the supernatural, being scared and excited by sensorial events. The arrival of Paul Jones (Creighton Hale) in the house just before the reading of the testament, for instance, is introduced by a hectic scene in which he reports hearing a loud noise, possibly a shot—an event that left him shaken and scared. His inability to understand the origin of noises signals the characterization of Jones throughout the entire film: easily impressionable from the atmosphere of the house and the strange event that happen during the night, he more than any other character embodies the film's comical representation of people's sensitivity to supernatural claims and sensorial delusions. Those who believe in ghosts, the film implies, are the ones who are most receptive to the chilling effect of noises.

Superimposition, in this regard, functions within a context where not only visual hallucinations but also aural chills are activated as specters of the mind. As David Toop notes, "the interpretation of sound as an unstable or provisional event, ambiguously situated somewhere between psychological delusion, verifiable scientific phenomenon, and a visitation of spectral forces, is a frequent trope of supernatural fiction."[38] Spiritualism's interpretation of sounds as ghostly events is regarded as a sign of madness and deception; the specter, also in this case, is located in our imagination, rather than in the external world.

Conclusion: The fascination for the spirit

As Vivian Sobchack suggests, special effects "point behind and beyond the film's story to the grounding technology that allows these special imaged instances to exist at all."[39] Superimposition effects, however, recall not only

---

[38] David Toop, "Chair Creaks, Though No One Sits There," in *The Spectralities Reader: Ghosts and Hauntings in Contemporary Cultural Theory*, eds. María del Pilar Blanco and Esther Peeren (London: Bloomsbury, 2013), 291.
[39] Vivian Sobchack, "Science Fiction Film and the Technological Imagination," in *Technological Visions: The Hopes and Fears That Shape New Technologies*, eds. Marita Sturken, Douglas Thomas, and Sandra Ball-Rokeach (Philadelphia: Temple University Press, 2004), 146.

a single technology but rather a set of practices, technologies, and icons that evoke—in contexts as different as spiritualism, magic lantern, stage magic, and photographic amusements—the intervention of the supernatural. In the application of this technique in *The Cat and the Canary*, we find a strategy that characterizes the film's wider appeal to its spectator. Like in the spiritualist exposés performed by stage magicians, the refusal of ghosts comes together with a self-aware usage of the fascination that supernatural claims inspire in the public. The ghost is denied, domesticated, but also employed as a powerful means to attract the audience toward the show. It is used as a chilling, uncanny element, and at the same time as a comic expedient to amuse the viewer, who is encouraged to laugh at the ingenuity of the characters. In such apparently contradictory use of the supernatural trope, Leni's film reminds us that ghosts are often produced by our own mind, but at the same time implies that the occult is enough scary and entertaining to make it a feasible subject for a successful movie. Like other fictional works and spectacular shows that represent ghosts only to deny them, it points to the contradictory power of our relationship with the occult: we are irresistibly attracted by the supernatural, even if we refuse to believe in it. Also, the enlightening and rationalizing endeavors of debunking ghosts, in this sense, are an inherent part of such inescapable fascination for the occult. It is due to this fascination that spiritualist exposés appealed to large masses of people throughout the nineteenth and twentieth centuries. It is due to this persisting fascination, too, that ghost movies denying the existence of ghosts, such as *The Cat and the Canary*, count among successful instances of supernatural fiction in the history of film.

By adopting a retrospective approach and by employing elements that are external to the cinematic screen, this chapter has addressed Paul Leni's *The Cat and the Canary* as pertaining to a wider tradition of spectacular shows that focus on ghosts and yet openly refuse them, relegating the specter to the realm of human imagination. This approach is consistent with media archaeological studies that address cinema and other media as elements of a broad media culture, rather than in isolation from each other.[40] Moreover, by referring to elements from the history of beliefs in ghosts, the chapter aims to call for the necessity to integrate contexts that are usually separated from each other, such as the history of film and the history of religious belief.

---

[40] William Uricchio, "Film, Cinema, Television... Media?," *New Review of Film and Television Studies*, ahead-of-print 12.3 (2014), 266–79; Siegfried Zielinski, *Deep Time of the Media: Toward an Archaeology of Hearing and Seeing by Technical Means* (Cambridge, MA: MIT Press, 2006); Thomas Elsaesser, "The New Film History as Media Archaeology," *Cinémas* 14.2–3 (2004), 75–117.

Literature addressing the cultural history of ghosts is often divided into two separate traditions, which address respectively fictional and "real" (at least, considered to be so) ghosts. While many attempts have been made to question how beliefs in spirits have influenced the work of writers, filmmakers, and TV producers,[41] less attention has been given to the possibility of comparing the experience of those who believe in spirits with those who consume a product of fiction on ghosts. Film scholars often do not take into account how not only ghost movies and horror films but also ghost beliefs and spiritualist practices depend on the fascination—felt by those who believe in ghosts as well as by those who firmly deny their existence—for the occult and the supernatural. The popularity of ghost movies such as *The Cat and the Canary* is built upon this fascination for the occult, upon the emotions evoked by the conception of ghosts—whether we believe in them or not.

Acknowledgments

A first draft of this paper was presented at a screening of *The Cat and the Canary* organized for the presentation of the exhibition "Diversamente vivi: Zombie, fantasmi, mummie, vampiri," National Museum of Cinema, Turin, Italy, in October 2010. I would like to thank Sarah Pesenti Campagnoni and the Mario Gromo Library of the National Museum of Cinema for contributing to the organization of this event, as well as the curators of the exhibition, Giulia Carluccio and Peppino Ortoleva.

---

[41]See, for instance, Pamela Thurschwell, *Literature, Technology and Magical Thinking, 1880–1920* (Cambridge: Cambridge University Press, 2001); Carrol L. Fry, *Cinema of the Occult: New Age, Satanism, Wicca, and Spiritualism in Film* (Bethlehem: Lehigh University Press, 2008); Emily D. Edwards, *Metaphysical Media: The Occult Experience in Popular Culture* (Carbondale: Southern Illinois University Press, 2005).

4

Supernatural Speech: Silent Cinema's Stake in Representing the Impossible

Robert Alford

The most arresting sequence in Paul Wegener and Albert Steinrück's *Der Golem, wie er in die Welt kam* (1920) comes midway through, in the form of a séance of sorts. The film follows the narrative of a community of Jews that finds itself threated by the ruling emperor. In this time of crisis, Rabbi Löw functions not only as the community's spiritual leader, but also as its protector against the emperor's forces. To provide greater support for the Jews, Löw summons the spirit of Astaroth to utter a word that has the power to animate *in*animate objects. The ultimate goal of this arcane ritual is to bring to life the film's namesake golem so that it might serve as a guardian for the threatened population. When Löw summons Astaroth, the spirit's disembodied head appears and the magical word issues spectacularly from his mouth in a stream of mist (Figure 4.1). This visual sequence is thereafter followed by an intertitle that reads, "The word, the terrible life-giving word, I have snatched it from the dark powers. Now I shall call the golem to life." The film's fascination with the word continues as the golem is brought to life through a star shaped medallion that bears the word. The film continues to follow the trajectory of the golem, who at first aids the Jews but then later turns against them in favor of the will of Astaroth, a troubling reminder of both the limits of human power over the divine as well as the enduring, catastrophic potential of "the terrible life-giving word."

FIGURE 4.1 Der Golem, wie er in die Welt kam *(1920, Paul Wegener and Carl Boese, Projektions-AG Union).*

Three years later, Cecil B. DeMille's *The Ten Commandments* (1923) staged a similar text-based spectacle to thematize the power of supernatural speech. The film is divided into two sections: the first recounts the drama of the Old Testament and the second (more extensive) half details the dramas of the McTavish family, a working-class San Francisco clan, as they reconcile the legacy of the Old Testament to the more modern values of forgiveness and tolerance that populate the New Testament. Both sections visualize supernatural speech in spectacular ways. In the film's Old Testament half, Moses receives the Ten Commandments from God atop Mount Sinai, and they barrel forth individually from the clouds styled like lightning. They are one of the film's most extravagant displays of special effects, and the words sparkle and flicker, reading as flame, glitter, and erratic charges of electricity (Figure 4.2). In the film's second half, the commandments haunt the contemporary actions of the McTavish family, especially Danny, a son in the family who has forsaken Christian values for wealth, material pleasure, and sins of the flesh. The commandments appear in a more subdued fashion in the New Testament sequences, but they nonetheless provide a pleasurable visual effect by fading in and out and occupying temporal and visual space within the film's narrative segments. For example, to thematize

FIGURE 4.2 The Ten Commandments *(1923, Cecil B. DeMille, Paramount)*.

Danny's fall after his many transgressions, an intertitle states, "Fighting with his back against the wall—Dan begins to realize, that if you break the Ten Commandments—they will break you." The film then cuts to Danny in the midst of what appears to be a mental breakdown before he confronts and murders his mistress. He soon encounters a painting of his mother (whose death he accidentally caused) when digging through his liquor cabinet, and the words "Thou shalt not kill" hover over the image and propel Danny into a further frenzied state (Figure 4.3). In these later segments, however, the origins of the words are more ambiguous; they might come from God as they did in the film's first half, or they might express Danny's internal thoughts and speech as he begins to comprehend the penalties for his many transgressions and his corresponding fall from grace. Regardless of the source of the words *The Ten Commandments* is much like *The Golem* in that both films provoke spectatorial fascination not only with the utterance of speech that supersedes human comprehension and ability, but also with the enduring legacy of these words as they are repeated by humans who either respect or disavow their linguistic power.

I focus on these films because they both seize upon the expression of supernatural speech as an opportunity to demonstrate the modern powers of the cinema. Although *Der Golem* and *The Ten Commandments* come

FIGURE 4.3 The Ten Commandments *(1923, Cecil B. DeMille, Paramount)*.

from different geographical contexts and are remarkably different objects (the former a popular, but artistic film, and the latter a super-production intent on box-office domination), both of these films reify the capacities of modern technologies by visualizing ancient forms of power. In the process, these films suggest that the cinema might share a metonymic relationship with the powers it pictures and narrativizes in a fashion impossible in other media. *Der Golem* is an early exemplar of the German Expressionist movement in film. As it has been framed extensively using a range of motion pictures—among them *The Cabinet of Dr. Caligari* (1920), *Nosferatu* (1922), and *Metropolis* (1927)—the German Expressionist period responded to the tensions of modern life: the trauma of World War I; the experience of urban modernity; and new developments in science and technology.[1] In its thematization of war and automation, in addition to its angular and fractured mise-en-scène, it is clear how *Der Golem* may have spoken to contemporary experiences of urban life and post-traumatic stress carried

---

[1] See Anton Kaes, "Silent Cinema," *Monatshefte* 82.3 (Fall 1990), 246–56; Anton Kaes, "The Cold Gaze: Notes on Mobilization and Modernity," *New German Critique* 59 (1993), 105–17; Tom Gunning, "Modernity and Cinema: A Culture of Shocks and Flows," in *Cinema and Modernity*, ed. Murray Pomerance (New Brunswick: Rutgers University Press, 2006), 297–315; and Patrice Petro, *Joyless Streets* (Princeton: Princeton University Press, 1989).

from the recent war. It is important to remember, however, that despite the artistic sophistication of these films, they were nonetheless tremendously popular with audiences in Germany, precisely because they gave expression to shared trauma or experiences of modern life.[2] Although American culture at the time was markedly different from that of Weimar Germany, certain films nonetheless engaged in a parallel project that related the popular cinema to modern life. The way films such as *The Ten Commandments* did this, however, was by demonstrating the power of cinema as an innovative modern art form that superseded previous means of expression, and in so doing providing an unprecedented form of entertainment that was meant to appeal to a global audience.

Ironically, the parallel endeavors of German Expressionism and American popular cinema often resorted to anachronistic, ancient subjects to thematize the capacities of the cinema as a modern medium. Even the hypermodernity of *Metropolis* draws from the Biblical legend of the tower of Babel to thematize the tension between the educated elite that rules and the practically enslaved workers that enable the city to function. To contextualize *The Golem*, Astaroth's origin is ambiguous, but it is safe to say that he is related to figures in several ancient systems of belief, including Assyrian and Egyptian. Astaroth remained a prominent figure in Western occult and demonological texts (and as such is also a possible model for the figure of Mephistopheles in Goethe's *Faust*), and he is regularly categorized in the third tier of demons after Lucifer and Belial, and along with Satan, Beelzebub, and Pluto.[3] Appropriately, Astaroth is summoned by recourse to the dark arts and black magic. In contradistinction, *The Ten Commandments* refers to more familiar tenets of Christian belief, and "the finger of God" writes the film's spectacular words in the Old Testament segment. While Astaroth (or at least his disembodied head) actually does appear, God remains invisible, establishing presence in an ethereal sense with the visual and temporal manifestation of his speech the marker of his presence. The choice of both *The Golem* and *The Ten Commandments* to render supernatural speech through visual spectacle (achieved in each case via double exposure) not only sets apart the power of such speech from that which is uttered by mere mortals in intertitles, but it also dramatizes the act of speaking in a way that was unique in silent cinema, in which the only potential avenue for the expression of speech was visual rather than aural.

---

[2] See Joseph Garncarz, "Art and Industry: German Cinema of the 1920," in *The Silent Cinema Reader*, eds. Lee Grieveson and Peter Krämer (London: Routledge, 2004), 389–400.
[3] Julius Goebel, "The Etymology of Mephistopheles," *Transactions and Proceedings of the American Philological Association* 1.151 (1904), 148–56.

I contend that in their efforts to demonstrate the modern power of the cinema, both *The Golem* and *The Ten Commandments* rely not only on anachronistic subject matter, but also on the representation of an act of speaking that was literally impossible to represent. This impossibility stems as much from the nature of what these films represented (supernatural speech) as the inability of the silent cinema to replicate the voice, human or not. Indeed, it is precisely because the voice cannot be heard in these films that it can evoke spectatorial fascination and (counter-intuitively) establish the cinema as a uniquely powerful medium. For example, were *The Ten Commandments* actually to present the voice of God (for which viewers were primed via an intertitle that quotes Exodus 24:17 to say that "the sight of the glory of the Lord—was like devouring fire") audience members would be rightly terrified and would likely flee the cinema were such a spectacle presented through audition rather than vision. The cinema, of course, could not present the voice of God audibly. This impossibility was due both to the technological inability of the cinema to play recorded speech generally, or to channel supernatural voices specifically. To compensate for this lack, the silent cinema developed representational strategies that render supernatural speech visually, and grant it power over the human figures with which it shares narrative and visual space. Rather than frame the conditions of the silent cinema negatively, I wish to consider them positively as a space of fullness and potential that allowed the narration of supernatural speech to yield spectatorial fascination, awe, and pleasure. To demonstrate the limitations of sound cinema to give both visual and aural expression to supernatural speech, I compare *Der Golem* and *The Ten Commandments* to *Bedknobs and Broomsticks* (1971) and DeMille's later *The Ten Commandments* (1956), respectively. Although *Bedknobs and Broomsticks* is a family film, it nonetheless narrativizes (in drastically altered form) the word of Astaroth, and adapts the Golem myth. In these later films, the narration and representation of the power of supernatural speech become a problem to be overcome or temper, rather than a source of potential, precisely because they must aurally register a voice and speech that can never be as phenomenally, narratively, or representationally powerful as the film purports them to be.

Silent cinema, modern life, and the visual representation of supernatural speech

While written speech was not uncommon to the silent cinema, the presentation and narrativization of the words of Astaroth and God in *Der Golem* and *The Ten Commandments*, respectively, is unusual. Unlike intertitles—which convey dialogue spoken between characters that populate the diegetic world, or provide narrative contextualization for the film's events and the actions of the characters—these acts of speaking are thoroughly integrated into the temporal and visual space of the narrative segments of these films. Accordingly, although intertitles convey information that informs the visual world of the film, they nonetheless occupy an interstitial temporal space that runs parallel to the narrative. Intertitles interject in the narrative to duplicated information that the viewer has already seen uttered by the characters on screen if not heard, or they provide context so that the visual world makes more sense. Stated differently, intertitles are secondary to the visual, narrative world of the film, even though this world is indebted to the information that intertitles convey. In both *Der Golem* and *The Ten Commandments*, however, the point of the narrative *is* this specific act of supernatural speech. In turn, the words of God and Astaroth are the action *and also* the intertitle, and these spectacular lexical, figural and narrative displays have more rhetorical power than the other bodies that also occupy visual narrative space. In a sense, the speech of Astaroth and God is formally distinguished from human figures precisely because it can speak for itself without recourse to an intertitle. These words are also privileged narratively, because their enunciation shapes the actions of other figures that also occupy visual space: in the case of *Der Golem*, the titular golem who is brought to life by Astaroth's words; in *The Ten Commandments*, the words of God compel the destruction of Babylon, and later Danny's precipitous downfall.

To be clear, such text-based effects in which words invade narrative space were not unprecedented by the 1920s, even if they were remarkably rare. Another striking example from the 1920s is in *The Cabinet of Dr. Caligari*: a character sees "Du musst Caligari werden," or "You must become Caligari," and the message appears letter by letter, as though being written by a typewriter. Unlike *Der Golem* and *The Ten Commandments*, this speech appears hallucinatory (best allied with the potentially internal speech of Danny in *The Ten Commandments*) rather than supernatural. However, even though it does not have an explicit spiritual association, it does retain a power to transform and refers to modern life as per the bent of German Expressionism, perhaps making a comment about the relationship between the ubiquity of mechanized forms of writing or transcription and their relation to concepts of the self. In a similar sense, the appearance of "Happiness must be earned" in the sky toward the end of *The Thief of Bagdad* (1924) offers a transcendent moral to viewers and comments on the film's narrative, and gestures to both general "life lessons" and the film itself. As explored by Tom Gunning in "Heard over the Phone:

The Lonely Villa and the de Lorde Tradition of the Terrors of Technology," however, the text appeared in the narrative to describe the act of speaking as early as 1907. Edwin Porter's *College Chums* pictured two matted figures talking on the phone over the image of a city, with the content of their telecommunication appearing as animated letters between them.[4] The comparison of *College Chums* to *Der Golem* and *The Ten Commandments* must be qualified because it belongs to cinema's transitional period, the period stretching roughly from 1907 to 1913 (its borders are perpetually debated) in which films moved from a general model of brief, disjointed, and technologically innovative and spectacular films to the model of film that is still common today: longer and narratively coherent.[5] Even though *College Chums* precedes the standardization of intertitles and their informational function, the speech it pictures nonetheless informs the narrative rather than compels it, as is the case with the supernatural speech of *Der Golem* and *The Ten Commandments*.

When *Der Golem* and *The Ten Commandments* were released in the 1920s, a range of discourses in both Europe and the United States had already related technologies of vision and audition to the supernatural, and would have primed audiences for the narrative spectacles of supernatural speech that both films depict. The beliefs of modern spiritualism had associated modern technologies with the inhuman on both continents since the mid-nineteenth century. "Rather than viewing Spiritualism as an escapist desire for disembodiment," argues Dana Luciano, "we might more usefully frame it as an *intensification* of the body: a radical expansion of its terrain, its nature, and its times."[6] In Luciano's reading, spiritualism nullifies physical and temporal bodily boundaries, creating a dynamic conduit between life and death, the present and the past, the phenomenal world and the supernatural. However, it is only through the intervention of technology—such as the camera, the cinema, the telegraph, the telephone, or even electricity alone—that this expansion of the body's temporalities and capabilities can be recorded or validated. The technologized roots of the movement are often traced to the "rappings" that were heard by the Fox sisters in Hydeville, New York, in 1848 after a telegraph was installed in

---

[4] Tom Gunning, "Heard over the Phone: *The Lonely Villa* and the de Lorde Tradition of the Terrors of Technology," *Screen* 32.2 (Summer 1991), 187–8.
[5] In a related sense, the 1916 serial *The Iron Claw* animated the speech of a parrot within narrative temporal space. Here, however, it connotes otherness from the human characters rather than a transcendence of human abilities.
[6] Dana Luciano, "Rejoicing in the Time to Come: Spiritualism's Spectral Erotics" (paper presented at the Queer Bonds Conference, University of California, Berkeley, February 19–21, 2008).

their home, which led the way to later associations between phonographs, telephones, radios, televisions, and spiritualism.[7]

It is, however, a more specific link between spiritualism and modern technologies of audition that informs *Der Golem* and *The Ten Commandments*. In "The Machine in the Ghost: Spiritualism, Technology, and the 'Direct Voice,'" Steven Connor historicizes and theorizes the potentials of electronic technologies of audition to transmit supernatural speech within spiritualist thought. In the context of the séance, the "direct voice" originates from an ethereal being and "speaks independently of the medium's vocal organs."[8] This effectively places the medium as a figure equivalent to a telephonist, or one who operates such machinery.[9] Spiritualists co-opted a wide range of modern technologies to express the direct voice, among them the telephone and the phonograph, and this practice extended well into the 20s in both America and Europe.[10] According to Connor, "the primary purpose of the séance was not to evoke beings from another world," but rather to effect a differently material body in the human phenomenal world that was reorganized for other senses such as taste, touch, and hearing rather than vision.[11] The direct voice was widely understood as the ultimate expression of the supernatural. *Der Golem* and *The Ten Commandments* capitalize on the synaesthetic foundations of the direct voice and offer a parallel conflation of senses: the substitution of vocal audition for vision. While markedly different from the mechanics of spiritualist practice, these films nonetheless use the legacy of spiritualist fixations on the direct voice to render spectacular visual effects, and in so doing provide a visual corollary for mediations of supernatural speech that would be impossible within the confines of the séance where vision was often downplayed. To be clear, I contend not that hearing generally was neglected by these films (indeed, the review of *The Ten Commandments* in the *New York Times* emphasizes that it was with the accompaniment of the orchestration that the sequence atop Mt. Sinai was especially impressive), only that the direct voice was a cultural phenomenon for which audiences were primed, and furthermore that these films sought to sate the public appetite for the direct voice via vision rather than hearing.[12]

---

[7] Jeffrey Sconce, *Haunted Media: Electronic Presence from Telegraphy to Television* (Durham, London: Duke University Press, 2000), 22–8.
[8] Steven Connor, "The Machine in the Ghost: Spiritualism, Technology, and the 'Direct Voice,'" in *Ghosts: Deconstruction, Psychoanalysis, History*, eds. Peter Buse and Andrew Stott (New York: St. Martin's Press, 1999), 212.
[9] Ibid., 215.
[10] Ibid., 213.
[11] Ibid., 208–9.
[12] "Remarkable Spectacle," *New York Times* (December 22, 1923), 8.

In addition to the general context of modern spiritualism, *Der Golem* should be understood within the specific cultural context of Weimar Germany where a range of views on the modern capacities of the cinema would have shaped how audiences perceived the film's depiction of supernatural speech. While not always referring to traditions of religious or pseudo-scientific belief, several German accounts of the cinema in the 1920s characterize the medium as a technology that transcended or enhanced human capacities of perception. For example, in 1920, the same year as the release of *The Golem*, German critic Carlo Mierendorff in his piece "If I Only Had the Movies!!" asserted:

> Film explodes all norms of corporeality... that is the uprooting power of the movies. When the [live] music stops, things become frightening, ghostly, eerie. Then we are no longer in the here and now. Melody, however, gives body to the imagination, makes things intimate. And we live on redeemed and smiling about the whole affair.[13]

I have highlighted this quotation from Mierendorff because it describes not only the ethereal qualities of the cinema, but also asserts that these might be mitigated by the accompaniment of sound. Although Mierendorff speaks here about the live musical accompaniment of a film, his statement nonetheless looks forward to the synchronization of the cinema with electronic speech and sound as a means to ward off the cinema's ghostly effects. Even without looking forward to a sonorized era of cinema, however, Mierendorff nonetheless insists that the visual components of the cinema should be understood through sound, which is especially relevant to *Der Golem* and its visualization of the word of Astaroth.

The following year in the *Prager Presse*, Robert Müller linked the cinema to the expression of the spiritual in his article "The Future of Film":

> Could the spiritual not be photographed? Could not thoughts be rendered in an image? Film has its own sort of monologue; that is *things speak for themselves*. We understand this without difficulty when we see a grimace or a facial expression... Rather than making films about spiritualism, one could make outright spiritualist films.[14]

---

[13]Carlo Mierendorff, *Hätte ich das Kino!!* trans. ed. Jeffrey Timon (Berlin: Erich Reiss Verlag, 1920), 7–34.
[14]Robert Müller, "The Future of Film," *Prager Presse*, trans. Michael Cowan. No. 198 (1921), 7.

While it is not clear in what sense Müller means spiritualism in the preceding quotation (he likely refers to both the spiritualist movement as well as more generally to the human spirit unbounded by the corporeal), he nonetheless characterizes the silent cinema as a technology that is uniquely suited to expose what might elude the human eye.[15] Indeed, Müller positions the cinema as revelatory of the true ontology of a person or object, and here it is only through the lens of the cinematic apparatus (rather than the human eye) that a subject might find its ultimate expression. What is also striking about Müller's statement, however, is that he equates aural and visual expression with his statement that "things speak for themselves." While he clearly does not mean this literally (that one can actually hear through vision in the cinema), he does mean it figuratively, which also indicates that he and others would be predisposed to read synaesthetic aural meaning into the visual world of the cinema. This is especially relevant for *Der Golem*, in which speech, as a narrative figure, is able to speak for itself and also control the actions of humans. What is important about Mierendorff and Müller's quotes more generally as they relate to *Der Golem*, however, is that they both characterize the cinema as somehow providing access to something beyond human perception, and that they associate modern technology with an altered phenomenal experience in which the boundaries of bodies are different from those in day-to-day life.

While *The Ten Commandments* emerged from an American rather a German context, I argue that it nonetheless draws from a similar sense of awe at cinema's capacity to move beyond the limits of the body. Indeed, the equivalence between the divine body of God and the speech that he utters demonstrates the loosened boundaries between body and spirit that were legible to both American and international audiences. Both American and international audiences might have understood the lexical special effects of *The Ten Commandments* through the concept of logos. Typically translated as "the Word" in English Bibles, though translated by Goethe in *Faust* as "die Tat," or "the deed," logos describes the ability of the word of God itself to beget matter. At times, it confers upon God's words the same power or presence as a supernatural being. Logos conflates speech, action, and

---

[15]Malcolm Turvey has historicized such a belief in the capacities of the cinema to transcend human sensory capacities as "revelationism," although he focuses on the work of writer/filmmakers such as Balazs, Vertov, and Epstein. It is worth noting that the beginnings of "revelationism" are contemporaneous with this German popular discourse. See Malcolm Turvey, *Doubting Vision* (New York: Oxford University Press, 2008).

matter, because in the biblical account God *creates* the universe through speech, as in passages from Genesis such as John 1:1-3: "And God said, 'Let there be light,' and there was light." Returning to the text in *The Golem* and *The Ten Commandments*, the cinematic apparatus mimics supernatural presence not only visually (and implicitly aurally) through the presentation of speech, but also because—when viewed through the concept of logos—this particular speech is constitutive of matter and actions later in these films. In *The Ten Commandments*, the word of God stands in for a depiction of the deity, and brings about the demise of both Babylon in the Old Testament story and Danny in the New Testament portion. In *The Golem*, the word of Astaroth not only has life itself, but also brings life to (and later controls) the film's titular clay Golem. Furthermore, even though *The Golem* narrativizes occult myth, it represents the word of Astaroth through Christian conventions for the depiction of logos: the film draws on conventions for representing the Annunciation, or the scene in which the angel Gabriel informs the Virgin Mary that she will bear Jesus Christ. For example, in Simone Martini's *Annunciation*, the Immaculate Conception is given visual expression by the word of God, which flows across the altarpiece's pictorial space from the mouth of Gabriel on the left to impregnate Mary on the right.

The Biblical, lexical display of *The Ten Commandments*, however, was often cited as evidence of the unprecedented capabilities of the cinema as a modern medium, rather than more simply as an illustration of Christian belief. *Photoplay* lavished extravagant praise on the film, and not only called it "the best photoplay ever made," but also noted (after raving about the depiction of the parting of the Red Sea) that "[t]he screen has never approached this beauty or power, yet within a few minutes this too is surpassed in the episode on the mountain top where the voice of God comes thundering and flashing through the darkening skies, bearing the commandments to Moses."[16] While the *Photoplay* review devotes significant energy to describing the Biblical dimensions of the film, the *New York Times* review (titled "Remarkable Spectacle") is more direct in its delineation of the film as a modern marvel. Of the sequence in which Moses receives the commandments, the review notes:

> Coupled with the orchestration there has been nothing on the film so utterly impressive as the thundering and belching forth of one commandment after another, and the titling and photography of this particular effect was remarkable...The sky clouds, and then seems to

---

[16] James R. Quirk, "The Ten Commandments," *Photoplay*, February 1924, 62.

burst, and from the ball of smoke appears golden lettering with one or another of the commandments, stress being laid upon those that are considered the most important, if one may say such a thing.[17]

Of a film that is in its entirety a "remarkable spectacle," the *Times* reviewer highlighted the text-based display of the commandments as being the film's most notable segment, and furthermore devoted a considerable amount of space to a description of this sequence's remarkable visual effects.

To draw an anachronistic comparison, the spectacular lexical effects of *The Golem* and *The Ten Commandments* can be understood as proto "Vital Figures," or technological effects that appear more powerful and full of life (as well as more deadly) than the human actors with whom they share the screen. As described by Kristen Whissel in *Spectacular Digital Effects*—which argues generally that such effects are not excessive, but instead give spectacular visual expression to a film's narrative themes as well as its historical context—the name "Vital Figures" refers to multiple meanings for vital, including "consisting in, constituted by, that immaterial force or principle which is present in living beings or organisms and by which they are animated and their functions maintained"; "maintaining, supporting, or sustaining life"; and also "fatal or destructive to life."[18] To be clear, Whissel makes this argument about digitally rendered characters that are meant to appear somehow more alive than human actors in contemporary, special effects–driven films such as the *Harry Potter* and *Lord of the Rings* series, even as she gestures to historic precedents for vital figures such as the clay golem in Wegener's film, which she even cites.[19] While the golem itself can be understood as a vital figure, I argue instead that the word of Astaroth is more appropriately vital than that which it animates. Indeed, it is the words (and those of God in *The Ten Commandments*) that require spectacular visual effects for their rendering (as opposed to the Golem costume worn by Wegener himself), and it is furthermore the words themselves that confer life onto the golem and also lead him astray later in the film. Similarly, in *The Ten Commandments*, the words hang over and condemn the character of Danny in the New Testament portion and the revelers of Babylon in the film's first segment. Perhaps more importantly in *The Ten Commandments*, the status of the words themselves as the body of God allows them to be understood under the aegis of the vital figure, especially when compared to the "mute"

---

[17] "Remarkable Spectacle," *New York Times* (December 22, 1923), 8.
[18] Kristen Whissel, *Spectacular Visual Effects* (Durham: Duke University Press, 2014), 93.
[19] Ibid., 92.

bodies of the actors that populate the visual space of the film, and which are also guided by the dictates of the commandments.

What is ultimately ironic about the ability of the linguistic spectacles in *Der Golem* and *The Ten Commandments* to command spectatorial awe and demonstrate the modern powers of the cinema is that this possibility relies precisely on the *in*ability of the cinema to render recorded speech or the direct voice. In other words, the fundamental lack of the silent cinema is also its greatest asset in regard to the representation of supernatural speech. The sonorized voice forecloses (or at the very least complicates) the unique potential of the silent cinema to represent the power and effects of supernatural voices. Figures that would trouble spectatorial absorption in the sound cinema (such as the supernatural figures of God or Astaroth, whose inhumanity would be difficult to render through aural means) have the potential to provoke wonder and awe in the silent cinema, where the act of speaking and conveying information within narrative space is extraordinary in itself. Stated differently, the silent cinema is uniquely suited to represent voices as powerful supernatural bodies precisely because *they cannot be heard*, and in turn have to be represented as visual, lexical bodies that are more powerful than the human characters that occupy an equivalent space. Within this context, words themselves are allowed to intervene and reorder both the visible frame, and also the diegesis of the film. In turn, this representational imperative eliminates the threat that the spectator will recognize the human or mechanical origins of the voice, or the way a supposedly supernatural voice has been artificially manipulated to impart the impression of an inhuman being. Indeed, were audiences of *The Ten Commandments* to hear the voice of God it would not be "like devouring fire" as the intertitle states, simply because such an effect would be impossible to produce (or unconvincing and disappointing) through cinematic technologies. Rather than incomplete or lacking, the silent cinema should be understood as a site of narrative potential, in which speech itself might take on superhuman qualities due to the representational limits of the medium. Were the supernatural speech of *Der Golem* and *The Ten Commandments* actually heard, these films would require substantively different approaches to both narrative and representation in order to preserve the apparent power of the cinema.

Sound and the representational burden of supernatural speech

Films that present similar narratives as *The Golem* and *The Ten Commandments* after the conversion to sound face a representational dilemma: they must both thematize the power of supernatural speech and also give this speech aural expression using available technologies. When faced with the reality that a voice with human or mechanical origins will never possess extraterrestrial qualities, sound films that tackle supernatural speech have to develop strategies to compensate for the lack that audible speech would introduce to the spectator. To be clear, when making this claim I refer primarily to films before the advent of digital CGI technologies—indeed, the period before that which Whissel addresses regarding vital figures. I nonetheless insist, however, that there is a certain representational limit for what any sort of technology might effect in order to convey the animating or awe-inspiring power of supernatural speech: for example, the word of Astaroth would never be able to give life to inanimate objects were it heard in the space of the cinema. Several films made after the conversion to sound nonetheless attempt to represent the supernatural speech of both Astaroth and God by recourse to a range of strategies.

DeMille's 1956 *The Ten Commandments* tackles it head on in a way that is only marginally successful. In the later version (which dwells on the drama of the Old Testament and forgoes the earlier film's contemporary family drama), the viewer is actually able to hear a voice speaking as God, though it is clearly human if also mechanically altered. The film visualizes God's presence through an animated pillar of flame that periodically splinters off to transcribe the commandments on stone. In his autobiography, DeMille recounts the difficulty he encountered in representing God's voice:

> The greatest single problem in *The Ten Commandments* was the Voice of God. To reproduce the Divine Voice is of course an obvious and literal impossibility... But what human actor could essay that role? Marvelous as the techniques of sound engineering are, what mechanical device could be equal to that impossible assignment? We tried everything suggested by anyone. Individual actors with fine voices recorded the lines. It seemed most fitting to try a chorus of individuals of all races and creeds, speaking in perfect unison. Was there some way to use a musical instrument, a great organ, and through the magic of the sound department shape its majestic tones into words? We recorded voices under water. We amplified them in deep canyons and from one mountain peak to another and re-recorded their reverberations. We tried everything; and everything was wrong.[20]

---

[20] Cecil B. DeMille, *The Autiobiography of Cecil B. DeMille*, ed. Donald Hayne (Englewood Cliffs: Prentice-Hall, 1959), 431.

DeMille eventually settled on the voice of a man he refuses to identify (though it has been rumored that it is either his own voice or that of Charlton Heston) that was mechanically filtered to render it more powerful. Regardless of the eventual outcome, however, DeMille acknowledges that this sequence was "the greatest single problem" in the making of the film precisely because the constraints of the sound cinema could never adequately render supernatural speech. Accordingly, he later notes that "our solution of that whole problem was imperfect, of course," but also that "any solution of it would be."[21] Although he does not compare this sequence to the equivalent one in the 1923 version of the film, it is nonetheless ironic that the manifold technological advancements manifest in the later film (among them full Technicolor, VistaVision, and a host of sound technologies) only made the representation of that which surpasses human capacity more difficult due to their illusionistic plenitude instead of productive lack.

As a later counterpart to *Der Golem*, *Bedknobs and Broomsticks* reconfigures the narrative of Astaroth's word dramatically to vivify musical, animated sequences and appeal to family audiences (the film was produced and distributed by Disney). The plot concerns the search of self-taught sorceress Eglantine Price, an older woman who lives alone in a small village on England's Dorset Coast during World War II, for the fabled word of Astaroth. Her mission leads her to the animated Isle of Naboombu where she and her orphan wards steal the necklace of the king (a lion who plays soccer), a star medallion inscribed with the magical incantation. While somewhat serious sequences appear in the film (for example, the word of Astaroth is later used to fight against advancing Nazi forces), *Bedknobs and Broomsticks* foregrounds humor and delight before terror or awe in an effort to appeal to children and families. Furthermore, the incantatory abilities of Miss Price are somewhat lacking; the film presents her as a hapless amateur, and a far cry from the foreboding figure of Rabbi Löw. The animating potentials of Astaroth's word are here tamed and displaced to actual animation and musical sequences in order to provide a straightforward sense of pleasure. Although *Bedknobs and Broomsticks* adapts the Golem myth to bring delight to children and families and was not meant to instill fear in the audience, it is nonetheless striking that the film uses a range of narrative and representational displacements (animation, music, humor,

---

[21] Ibid., 432.

and casual misogyny) to tame the vital power of supernatural speech and compensate for the inability of sound cinema to convey such power.[22]

The Ten Commandments (1956) and *Bedknobs and Broomsticks* demonstrate that the sound cinema, as opposed to the silent cinema, is comparatively poorly equipped to thematize the power of supernatural speech. This limitation is as much a result of the representational difficulties of the sound cinema in registering such speech as it is a historical context that is remarkably different from the twenties (i.e., modern spiritualism fell out of favor in the late 1920s and 1930s, and the fascination with the cinema as an expression of modern life has waned). Compared to *Der Golem* or *The Ten Commandments* (1923), the sound films profiled here fall short at communicating the otherworldly nature of God or Astaroth, precisely because they make apparent the ultimately human or mechanical origins of the ostensibly more powerful beings they represent. In these later films, supernatural speech ceases to be an object that (in its structural absence) might give expression to cultural beliefs, and instead becomes a representational narrative burden or an opportunity for amusement. In turn, the "partial" nature of the silent cinema should be understood more properly as a space of potential in which the lack of sound translates to the thickened presence of the ghostly or supernatural, of that which sound might otherwise betray. While it may not be possible to replicate the supernatural power of speech itself in the current technological regime, to confer onto words otherworldly powers because they need to be seen rather than heard, this does not mean that similar effects would not be possible. It is instead important to consider what potential (through lack) the cinema might continue to have, whether spatial, sonorous, or visual, that would surpass the conventions of representation, or appeal to contemporary systems of belief and approaches to the world, and leave open a space that might elicit spectatorial awe, wonder, and even terror at the powers of the supernatural.

---

[22]The use of humor to displace the urgency and power of God's voice has been a similar tactic in later sound films as well, among them the comedies *Oh, God!* (1977) and *Dogma* (1999). In the former, comic George Burns plays God. *Dogma* presents a more complex relationship with the voice of God, but also resorts to stunt casting. Alternative rock singer Alanis Morissette plays God, and upon her appearance she quickly kills several people simply by speaking because they are unable to tolerate her voice. The scene is played for humor, however, as she promptly changes into a tutu and behaves whimsically for the remainder of the scene without speaking.

PART TWO

Cinematic Ghosts from the 1940s through the 1980s

5

Bad Sync: Spectral Sound and Retro-Effects in *Portrait of Jennie*

René Thoreau Bruckner

> *There is the world in the frame where we can identify things…Then there is the other world, that of sound, which is not named or identified…One world is more ghostly than the other, and it's the world of sound.*[1]

> *What a near-perfectly lip-synchronized soundtrack hopes we will forget is that sound film itself is based in an ontological non-identity. First of all, it is a mixed medium.*[2]

> *"Time made an error"*

Walking in the park, starving artist Eben Adams (Joseph Cotten) meets a precocious little girl, Jennie Appleton (Jennifer Jones), playing alone in the snow. After having an odd conversation on a park bench, the two stroll across a covered bridge, and Jennie sings Eben a song:

---

[1] Michel Chion, *Audio-Vision: Sound on Screen* [1990], trans. Claudia Gorbman (New York: Columbia University Press, 1994), 125.
[2] Nataša Ďurovičová, "Local Ghosts: Dubbing Bodies in Early Sound Cinema," *Electronikus Periodika Archívum Datbázis* (The Hungarian Electronic Library), http://epa.oszk.hu/00300/00375/00001/durovicova.htm (accessed April 5, 2014).

> Where I come from, nobody knows
> And where I am going, everything goes
> The wind blows, the sea flows, nobody knows
> And where I am going, nobody knows

There is an intentionally unearthly quality to Jennie's song, both in its lyrics and in Jones's slow, somber vocal performance. But there is something else, something subtly irksome, about this early scene in David O. Selznick's Hollywood swansong *Portrait of Jennie* (1948). A single, long take shows Jennie voicing the song as the two actors cross the bridge. Though her face is mostly obscured by shade, it becomes plainly apparent that the sound of Jennie's voice and the movement of her lips are grossly out of sync with each other. Sound and image momentarily come apart.

Later, it will become clear that Jennie is some kind of ghost, a woman who lived in another time, before Eben's time, and has already died. She has somehow traversed the "distance" between past and present to meet her would-be lover, as if fate were correcting itself. "We were lonely, unloved," she will say in one of their later encounters. "Time made an error." Over the course of the movie, the pair meets a number of times and strolls through the city, haunting New York's public spaces, enjoying a few snatches of impossible romance.

For a number of reasons, *Portrait* stands as an extraordinary example of spectrality in American cinema.[3] As any ghost does, Jennie signifies a troubled time, a problem with presence, a compromise in the integrity of chronological time. Even before her eerie vocal performance, Jennie immediately comes off as anachronistic: Eben mentions her old-fashioned clothes; she speaks of vanished New York architecture and the Kaiser of Germany as if they were current. The film's ghost narrative lends itself to fantastic film technique, and the film showcases a number of *intentionally* ghostly effects. One such example is the exquisite visual effect of a canvas texture which the filmed image occasionally assumes in moments just before Eben and Jennie meet; an example from the register of sound is

---

[3] A more thorough consideration of *Portrait*'s spectral qualities would have to take into account complexities such as (a) the somewhat anachronistic presentation of the concept of the work of art and the masterpiece, given the traditional, less than modern style of the protagonist's painting; (b) relatedly, the commentary on old media/new media that emerges from the fact that this is a film about painting, with an implicit comparison of the two mediums' respective temporalities; and (c) the film's status as a literary adaptation, haunted by its source material, Robert Nathan's 1939 novel—especially important since the time between the book's publication and the film's production—contains the traumatic historical event of World War II.

the score's use of the Theremin, which Jeffrey Sconce calls "Hollywood's signature instrument of the 'otherworldly.'"[4]

However, a less overt sort of ghostliness arises from the fact that the film's production was especially troubled, leading to radical postproduction revision. This essay contends that the finished film's most uncanny qualities emerge primarily incidentally, as *retro-effects*: conspicuous signs of retroactive tampering, like Jennie's out-of-sync singing performance.[5] Such moments add an odd hauntedness to *Portrait*, which also helps reveal the inherent hauntedness of sound film in general. Because retro-effects, like ghosts, emerge in "post," they mark the film in a way that can undermine the linear, chronological time upon which classical Hollywood narrative is built. Hollywood producers like Selznick hope spectators will ignore (or repress) these audible and visible marks. The many cracks in the surface of this film, and of classical films in general, give a glimpse into a certain secret about cinematic time in the sound era, despite all attempts to mask it. Retro-effects help make it possible to hear and see how, as a ghost once helped Hamlet to see, "the time is out of joint."[6]

When lip-sync fails, the inherent duality of sound film becomes perceptible. The most prevalent examples come in the common practice of dubbing a film's dialogue for a foreign language market, in which "good sync" is largely abandoned. "When I go to see a film 'dubbed' in French, I do not merely notice the discrepancy between word and image, I suddenly have the impression that something else is being said over there," explains Maurice Merleau-Ponty. And further,

> When a breakdown of sound all at once cuts off the voice from a character who nevertheless goes on gesticulating on the screen, not only does

---

[4] Jeffrey Sconce, *Haunted Media: Electronic Presence from Telegraphy to Television* (Durham: Duke University Press, 2000), 120.
[5] I have written elsewhere on the "retro-effect" (though only in the visual register) as a component of cinematic temporality. On a retro-effect in *Random Harvest* (Mervyn LeRoy, 1942), see René Thoreau Bruckner, "Lost Time: Blunt Head Trauma and Accident-Driven Cinema," *Discourse* 30.3 (Fall 2008), 373–400. For a consideration of one of *Portrait*'s visual retro-effects, see René Thoreau Bruckner, "'Why Did You Have to Turn on the Machine?' The Spirals of Time-Travel Romance," *Cinema Journal* 54.2 (Winter 2015), 1–23.
[6] Shakespeare's comment on time becomes clearer in the complete line uttered by Hamlet: "The time is out of joint, O cursed spite/That ever I was born to set it right!" Not just time as such, but *the* time, the historical now, is the source of Hamlet's haunting. In his lecture, "Spectres of Marx," Jacques Derrida shows how the subject of the haunting, in *Hamlet* and elsewhere, is always history—a matter of conflict between different times, or between different concepts/uses of time. See Jacques Derrida, *Specters of Marx: The State of the Debt, the Work of Mourning & the New International* (New York: Routledge, 1994), 20–7, 34, 96–8.

the meaning of his speech suddenly escape me: the spectacle itself is changed. The face which was so recently alive thickens and freezes, and looks nonplussed, while the interruption of the sound invades the screen as a quasi-stupor.[7]

Words and gestures—that is, sound and image—are not perceived entirely distinctly from one another; rather, claims Merleau-Ponty, they "intercommunicate through the medium of my body."[8] When voice and image fail to match each other, the visible body acts like a spiritual medium, channeling some other world, or more precisely, some other time.

Referencing Merleau-Ponty's musings on dubbed films, Michel Chion builds his concept of the *acousmêtre* upon the assertion that "a ghost is a perception made by only one sense." In sound cinema, Chion claims, "the world of sound" is "more ghostly" than that of image.[9] The *acousmêtre* is an exemplar of "phantom audio-vision" and acousmatic sound: sound whose source is not visualized at the same time that the sound is audible, thus challenging a viewer's habitual recourse to "causal listening." An *acousmêtre* amounts to a kind of phantom whose voice is not (yet) accompanied by a visible body.

For a fraction of a second, before she has appeared on the screen, the character of Jennie is an *acousmêtre*. In the scene where the couple first meets, Eben finds a parcel on a park bench and, just before he or the audience sees Jennie, a voice from off screen claims, "It belongs to me." The character first arrives as a voice, not an image. However, it would be mistaken to call this a case of disembodied voice. Jennie's voice, like the parcel, belongs to her. She is no more disembodied than she will be a second later, when visible, because bodies in sound film take shape through sound as well as image, not image alone; if the sound film body is embodied at all, Jennie is primarily embodied by her voice, *as sound*—introduced by means of the sonic vibrations given off by Jennifer Jones's body, recorded in a studio at some other time.

Even though this acousmatic status is fleeting—Eben immediately looks up and, in reverse shot, there is a little girl building a snowman—it is significant that Jennie's voice comes first. After about half a second, she can no longer be considered an *acousmêtre* (from here on, she is rarely heard without also

---

[7]Maurice Merleau-Ponty, *Phenomenology of Perception* [1945], trans. Colin Smith (London, Henley: Routledge and Kegan Paul, 1962), 234.
[8]Ibid., 235.
[9]Chion, 125.

being seen), but she can be understood as a related kind of ghost: an audio/visual specter. At times, as in the singing performance described above and some other key moments in the film, her voice and image tend to slip out of sync as if they index separate spaces and times.

"Not of the present nor of the past"

After the young Jennie finishes singing her strange song, Eben is surprised to hear her say, "I wish you would wait for me to grow up so we can always be together." Afterwards, he makes an inspired sketch of her face. When he meets Jennie again, she seems to be growing up inordinately quickly. In subsequent meetings, he comes to understand and accept that Jennie comes from the past; he finds out who she was, when she lived, and how she died. Despite their temporal separation, and despite the periodic nature of their relationship, a romance develops between them. As part of this same process, Eben's artist's block, which he calls a "winter of the mind," begins to thaw. The girl, rapidly becoming a young woman, provides the down and out painter with a link to the past and a spark of inspiration. Eben paints Jennie's portrait, a grasp at immortality—Eben's masterpiece will hang on the wall at the Metropolitan Museum and memorialize both characters.

An art dealer named Matthews (Cecil Kellaway) tells Eben that the portrait represents the ideal woman: "Do you remember my saying that there ought to be something eternal about a woman, not of the present nor of the past? Well, here you've got it." This formulation highlights the rich ambiguity at the heart of this film. It posits an idealized sort of time in which certain things—beauty, woman—do not change. In other words, Matthews's compliment supports a "conservative" time, embracing stasis rather than change. This "something eternal" is "not of the present nor of the past," which can be taken in keeping with the idea that certain things are "timeless" rather than historically contingent. Yet in the very same utterance, the expression can be taken to suggest, perhaps unintentionally, quite the opposite: a heterogeneous mixture, or at the very least a multiplicity, of times that coexist with one another. Not of the present, not of the past, but nonetheless eternal; that is, more than one time at a time, or in one place—on the surface of the canvas—articulating a time in which past and present cannot always be distinguished.

During most of their time together, *Portrait*'s protagonists haunt New York City, and the city is treated as a space in which past and present comingle—

again, it is not so much a "timeless" space as it is a space full of times, plural. They stroll around the city, always in motion—their impossible coupling occurs mainly in passing and in public.

In two of their meetings, however, Eben and Jennie manage to *stop*, and to inhabit Eben's private space, so that Jennie can sit for him as he finishes painting her picture. The second such scene, in which Eben finishes the portrait, is curious. For a moment, Jennie seems to embody a past that envies the present. From her point of view, Eben's present is the future, but is not "her" future, because she won't live to see it. As she poses, she speaks sadly of "things that have never happened," and has a vague knowledge of "things that are going to happen to us." The character seems to perceive that her future with Eben will be, or has been, stolen from her. Having crystallized this insight, or foresight, Jennie stops talking, nods off to sleep, and—in a stunning if heavy-handed visual effect—hardens into a still image that looks more painted than photographed. Looking up from his now-finished painting to see his model this way, Eben panics; he rushes to her as if she looked dead, as if her presence has nearly transformed into the past-ness of a painted picture, still and *silent*.

"The ghost always presents a problem," writes Bliss Cua Lim.[10] Ghost films have the ability to depict "a betrayed past [that] confronts its future (our present), and discovers that it is other than what had been hoped for."[11] As the paradoxical appearance of someone who has died and thus forever disappeared—a presence of the past—the figure of the ghost affects a rupture in the homogeneous and staunchly rational modern construction of time. Thus, the problem of the ghost stems from her ability to prod the audience about its sense of responsibility (toward the past and future, in the present). The specter provokes anxiety because haunting denies the haunted subject's ability to divorce the now from the past. The sudden return of a *repressed* wrong, like an injustice or a lost love, "allows characters (and those spectators who identify with them) to experience *time with the ghost*."[12] In *Portrait*, time with the ghost, which Lim identifies as "nonsynchronism," takes shape in those unplanned eruptions of bad sync. The ghost returns to trouble the present, and the present feels a romantic longing for that very return.

---

[10]Bliss Cua Lim, "Spectral Times: The Ghost Film as Historical Allegory," *Positions: East Asia Cultures Critique* 9.2 (Fall 2001), 287–8.
[11]Bliss Cua Lim, *Translating Time: Cinema, the Fantastic, and Temporal Critique* (Durham: Duke University Press, 2009), 161.
[12]Ibid.

In the film's climax, Eben does lose Jennie. Her death is relived in Cape Cod at Land's End Light, the place where she has already died—or will die, will have died. She has some consciousness of this fact even if she does not remember it (to her, it has not happened yet). When she dies this time, Eben is present to witness it, but powerless to stop it. He sails out to the lighthouse and into the storm that took her years ago. Despite Eben's efforts to save Jennie and undo time's "error," the tidal wave takes her this time, too. He survives, and lives out the fame that his "Portrait of Jennie" has earned him.

The narrative suggests that true love can transcend time. More precisely, however, what is rendered is a picture of love that is "pure," because it can only be glimpsed, with proper faith, in memoriam—love as a mourning for something one *believes* could have or would have been possible, but only in some other time. And as it turns out in this film, this work of mourning makes possible something else: Eben's emergence as an artist of note, a success. Nathan's novel figures his transformation explicitly as a problem of faith: "Sooner or later, God asks His question: are you for me, or against me? And the artist must have some answer, or feel his heart break for what he cannot say."[13] In the film, this direct engagement with religious faith is left implicit, but remains perceptible. (In a memo to the writer of the film's lofty foreword,[14] producer David O. Selznick encapsulates the theme in all capital letters: "NO DEATH WHERE THERE IS LOVE AND FAITH."[15]) In both novel and film, the character of Eben learns that love can transcend death and traverse time, as long as he has faith.

"I wish you would wait for me so we could always be together."

Any film labeled "classical" endeavors to construct a unified world, which entails the presentation of space and time as singular. In the manufacturing of such a world, time comes first, so to speak: for the illusion of spatial integrity to hold up across multiple camera angles, there must exist an orderly (chronological) succession of events in time, linear and homogeneous. For the

---

[13] Robert Nathan, *Portrait of Jennie* (New York: Alfred A. Knopf, 1960), 5.
[14] Selznick commissioned screenwriter Ben Hecht to write a foreword to prepare the audience for the unconventional film they were about to see.
[15] David O. Selznick, *Memo from David O. Selznick*, ed. Rudy Behlmer (New York: Modern Library, 2000), 416.

purpose of the present essay, the imperative to sustain such a homogeneous temporality *defines* classical film style. For this very reason, the classical sound film is definitively anxious and self-conflicted. It bears the difficult task of lashing together multiple times, different modes of presence, as one. This task depends partly on narrative logic, partly on continuity editing, and partly on smooth synchronization between image and sound.

But the marriage of image and sound has always been a rocky one. Though generally locked together, image and sound belong to different temporal registers—different times. A kind of perceptual crisis emerges whenever they fall conspicuously out of sync. Moments of broken continuity and "bad sync" are temporal ruptures, haunted moments, but bad sync is rarely accidental, *per se*; more often it is an inevitable symptom of production and/or distribution conditions—in *Portrait*, it is a product of a conflict between demands of classical narrative style and budgetary strife.[16] Perhaps the most obvious cause of bad sync—dialogue replacement—fulfills a postproduction impulse for which Selznick was well known: the desire to re-write. Usually meant to improve a film, to make up for perceived shortcomings in the script or mistakes on set without incurring the costs of a reshoot, this sort of revision can damage the illusion of unity between image and sound.

Aside from cost-related issues, how to explain why mismatched sound/image moments can sometimes be allowed? It seems that audiences are expected to ignore it, or forgive it, if not miss it altogether. Could it be that the privileging of the visual on the one hand, and of language on the other, excuses occasional lapses in the soundtrack's fidelity? As long as image and sense remain intact, a little fault in synchronization can be written off as insignificant, as if it were only a fault in the sound itself. Sound, apprehended *as* sound rather than linguistic transmitter, takes a back seat to image and sense.

"The situation is clear," writes Christian Metz: "the language used by technicians and studios, without realizing it, conceptualizes sound in a way that makes sense only for the image. We claim that we are talking about sound, but we are actually thinking of the visual images of the sound's source."[17] The privileging of the visual over the aural is at least partly learned—

---

[16]For one account of the production's troubled path, see David Thomson, *Showman: The Life of David O. Selznick* (London: Abacus, 1993), 218–21. For a less damning account, see Joseph Cotten's: "It had all been *terribly* real and extremely uncomfortable [to shoot on location in New York and Connecticut]. David's...decision to return to Hollywood and remake everything he didn't like, was most welcomed by Jennifer and me."Joseph Cotten, *Vanity Will Get You Somewhere* (New York: Knopf, 1987), 81.
[17]Christian Metz, "Aural Objects," *Yale French Studies* 60 (1980), 29.

it has "something cultural" about it, says Metz: "the conception of sound as an attribute, as a non-object, and therefore the tendency to neglect its own characteristics in favour of those of its corresponding 'substance,' which in this case is the visible object."[18] To the contrary, Metz argues, a sound is not merely a characteristic of some physical (and thus visible) object, but constitutes an "aural object" in itself. His key insight—that sound serves to index a film's "objects" just as much as the image does—is crucial for any study of sound film, but his concept of aural objects may suffer from a "blind spot": it places too much value on objecthood. In cinema, neither image nor sound can be understood properly as being made of objects, because granting this status to either one neglects their existence in time. The temporal dimension of cinema—image and sound—conditions its spatial articulations: objecthood exists only in a time that has been "spatialized," to use Henri Bergson's term.[19] Neither image nor sound can be perceived or imagined without duration.

No kind of perception can exist without time, regardless of the sensory organ and/or medium through which it arrives, but more to the point: *time-based* media like phonography and cinematography have an especially strong dependence on the duration in which they operate. The combination of sound and moving pictures can be understood as a binding together of two different temporal registers, two qualitatively different means for capturing, storing, and representing time. The scope of the present essay prevents a fuller discussion of the temporal "inventions" of cinema and sound recording, but suffice it to say that since the end of the nineteenth century, the two technologies have "participated in a ... general cultural imperative, the structuring of time and contingency in capitalist modernity," as Mary Ann Doane writes in *The Emergence of Cinematic Time*.[20]

In a writing that predates her concern with the history of time, Doane analyzes the history of the voice in cinema, arguing that the addition of sound in the late 1920s led to a delicate balancing act. Although sound can make the diegetic world feel fuller and more organically unified, this benefit comes along with a constant risk:

---

[18]Ibid., 30.
[19]Henri Bergson first critiques the habit of spatializing time in his 1896 publication, *Time and Free Will: An Essay on the Immediate Data of Consciousness*, trans. F.L. Pogson (London: George Allen & Unwin, Ltd., 1910), 75–139. See also his later development of the notion in both *Matter and Memory*, trans. N.M. Paul & W.S. Palmer (New York: Zone Books, 1991) and *Creative Evolution*, trans. Arthur Mitchell (New York: Henry Holt & Co., 1911).
[20]Mary Ann Doane, *The Emergence of Cinematic Time: Modernity, Contingency, the Archive* (Cambridge: Harvard University Press, 2002), 3–4.

> The dangers of post-synchronization and looping stem from the fact that the voice is disengaged from its 'proper' space (the space conveyed by the visual image) and the credibility of that voice depends upon the technician's ability to return it to the site of its origin.[21]

That site of origin is not only the space represented in the image, but also the body to which the voice belongs—or more precisely, the *visible* body. Doane characterizes moments of bad sync as "dangers" primarily because, soon after the introduction of sound film, there was a "fear on the part of the audience of being 'cheated'" by the technology.[22]

Classical narrative film technique underwent realignments largely because of the initial discomfort felt by film spectators; film producers felt the awkwardness, too, in trying to integrate sound, which demanded new approaches to rendering both space and time. "It was as if the introduction of sound had caused an immediate 'densening' or 'thickening' of the more permeable spatio-temporal field of the silent film," explains Nancy Wood, "thereby requiring more concrete and exacting definitions of the spatial and temporal dimensions."[23] Stilted and rocky at first, the marriage of the two heterogeneous technologies would take some time to succeed. Techniques of "fidelity" gradually helped audiences repress the inherent "dangers" of sound film. John Belton notes one such trick: "In order to assure an audience that the dialogue and/or sound effects are genuine, the editor must, as soon as possible in a scene, establish synchronization between sound and image, usually through lip-sync."[24] But the early sound film audience's anxiety speaks of something deeper than the mere maintenance of an illusion that feels "genuine." Early sound era adjustments to film form have to do with the fact that, as Doane puts it, "the body reconstituted by the technology and practices of the cinema is a *phantasmatic* body."[25] In any sound film, there remains "the potential risk of exposing the material heterogeneity of the medium."[26] Sound film always produces a doubled audio/visual body that seems to come from two sources, or worlds, at the same time. However, as Doane explains,

---

[21] Mary Ann Doane, "The Voice in the Cinema" [1980], in *Film Theory and Criticism: An Introduction*, 7th edition, eds. Leo Braudy and Marshall Cohen (Oxford: Oxford University Press, 2009), 321.
[22] Ibid., 319.
[23] Nancy Wood, "Towards a Semiotics of the Transition to Sound: Spatial and Temporal Codes," *Screen* 25.3 (May–June 1989), 16.
[24] John Belton, "Technology and Aesthetics of Film Sound," in *Film Theory and Criticism: An Introduction*, 7th edition, eds. Leo Braudy and Marshall Cohen (Oxford: Oxford University Press, 2009), 333.
[25] Doane, 319.
[26] Ibid., 320.

"classical *mise-en-scène* has a stake in perpetuating a unity and identity sustained by this body and in staving off the fear of fragmentation... what must be guarded is a certain 'oneness.'"[27] In short, the perceptual pleasure sought by the classical film (and its ideal spectator) involves the illusion that the body is whole, which requires the broader illusion of a unified space and a singular, homogeneous time in which that body persists.

In fact, however, the experience of sound cinema involves a constant encounter with heterogeneity—difference—which itself may be enough to make certain ghostly moments uncanny or frightening. Taking vision to be the more dominant perceptual register, sound enjoys an essentially irksome quality, bears the potential to reveal things unseen. As such, sound and the technologies of transmitting and reproducing it have long been associated with haunting and matters of the occult.[28] Likewise, it is an understatement to say that spooky stories on film rely heavily on sound for their affect.[29] From "spirit rapping" and creaking floorboards to shrieks, howls, and screams, the soundscape of terror remains central and undeniable. To the point at hand, the horror film (post–silent era) has embraced mismatched sound—specifically, qualitative dissonance between a voice and the body that appears to speak. The intentional mismatching of body and voice has become a commonplace way to indicate that a character has been possessed by an outside force or spirit. For a few examples, see actress Linda Blair's vitriolic scenes of possession in *The Exorcist* (1973), the vocal takeover of Florence Tanner by the haunting spirit of Emeric Belasco in *The Legend of Hell House* (1973),[30] or the finale of *Demon Seed* (1977), in which a half-human, half-robot baby speaks with the ominous digital voice of his father. In cases such as these, an uncanny doubling—that is, the separation between the visible actor and the voice actor—becomes perceptible mainly because the quality of the voice does not appear to match the visible actor's body, but it also has to do with the accompanying tendency for less-than-perfect sync resulting from the dialogue replacement

---

[27]Ibid., 328.
[28]Sconce gives a thorough account of the history of "haunted media" based on the relationship between occult beliefs/practices and audio/visual technologies such as the phonograph, radio, and television. Sconce, 21–91, 124–66.
[29]For a full discussion, see Peter Hutchings, "The Sounds of Horror," in *Horror Film* (New York: Routledge, 2003), 132–47; see also Hutchings, "Music of the Night: Horror's Soundtracks" in *Sound and Music in Film and Visual Media: A Critical Overview*, eds. Graeme Harper, Ruth Doughty and Jochen Eisentraut (New York: Bloomsbury, 2009), 219–30.
[30]For a lucid treatment of the film's voice possession as well as its employment of an electronic soundtrack to index the evil spirit, see Murray Leeder, "Victorian Science and Spiritualism in *The Legend of Hell House*," *Horror Studies* 25.1 (2014), 31–46.

process. In an earlier example of the tactic, Akira Kurosawa's *Rashomon* (1950) has a murdered husband speak through a female spirit medium at his murder trial, and not only does the voice sound like it emanates from some other (and otherworldly) body, it also visibly mismatches the movement of the performer's lips. Here, as in *Portrait*, an uncanny effect results from the actualization of the ever-present potential for the sound–image couple to split up. In and of itself, that constant potential charges every moment of sound cinema with the ability to produce powerfully affective apparitions.

The kind of audio-visual ghost given bodily form in *Portrait* is phantasmatic because, like a time traveler, Jennie comes from the past, back from the dead, and makes the film's space juggle a mixture of different times. Ghosts and apparitions have a way of pluralizing time, as they embody some injustice or unresolved conflict from the past that invades the present and will not leave it alone. When it comes to ghost stories, the classic concept of film spectatorship, as a play between presence and absence, must be adjusted: a cinematic ghost attains *presence-in-pastness*.[31]

Disunity between image and sound allows (at least) two distinct modes of presence-in-pastness to be perceived. A voice from some other realm, inaccessible to the camera's eye, haunts the visible "presence" projected by the image; and simultaneously, the image haunts the disembodied voice, which is "present" in a qualitatively different way. This phenomenon constitutes a two-way form of haunting: sound haunts the visible space-time of the film, and image becomes spectral when separated from sound. Post-synced sound comes from some unseen body in another location (typically indexing an actor's body in a sound booth), and indexes some other time—other than now, but also other than the moment indexed by the image.

In general, voice is assumed to have the ability to induce presence in ways that images simply cannot.[32] There is a difference between sound's commanding mode of presence and the also-powerful presence of moving images; classical sound cinema builds its captivating illusion of presence by mastering both, and mapping sexual difference in the process. "Hollywood's soundtrack is engendered," argues Kaja Silverman, "through a complex system

---

[31]Christian Metz is the primary voice here, and he certainly accounts for the "pastness" implicit in his term "absence," especially given the psychoanalytic framework that structures his theory. In Psychoanalysis, absence and lack are always bound up with the subject's (repressed) past. See *The Imaginary Signifier: Psychoanalysis and the Cinema* (Bloomington: Indiana University Press, 1986).
[32]Kaja Silverman argues that there is a "powerful Western episteme, extending from Plato to Hélène Cixous, which identifies the voice with proximity and the here and now...a metaphysical tradition which defines speech as the very essence of presence." Silverman, *The Acoustic Mirror: The Female Voice in Psychoanalysis and Cinema* (Bloomington: Indiana University Press, 1988), 43.

of displacements which locate the male voice at the point of apparent textual origin, while establishing the diegetic containment of the female voice."[33] It is this very sort of diegetic containment that Jennie, as a badly synced audio/visual phantom, seems to confound.

In *Portrait*, the male voice enjoys a different status than that of Jennie. An unseen man's voice introduces the film's themes even before the camera descends into the diegetic space of New York City; and throughout the film, narrative focalization comes largely through segments of Eben's voice-over narration. Like Jennie, the male protagonist is first introduced by his voice—a temporary *acousmêtre*—but unlike Jennie's voice-off, Eben's voice-over comes from another space and time, the future from which he remembers and narrates this story. It is his story, which is the primary reason he does not come off a ghost, like Jennie (after all, there is no sign given that the couple's meetings happen in present day New York; they could in fact take place in Jennie's time, or in a mixed time zone that is neither Eben's nor Jennie's, where the two meet in the middle). Eben's narrator position allows him to fit comfortably in the classical mold for male figures: as the writer of the story, he attains the status of present, thus encouraging the reading of Jennie as the one doing the haunting.

If the film follows the narrative conventions that Selznick—one of the engineers of classical Hollywood sound film—helped to institutionalize, then it stands to reason that the visual realm should belong to Eben, while Jennie's role should be to "echo" him. "In classical film," explains Amy Lawrence, "sound is conflated with the feminine. Sound itself, as a cinematic register, is 'feminized,' assigned the role of the perpetually supportive 'acoustic mirror' that re-enforces the primacy of the image and of the male gaze."[34] In *Portrait*, sound almost seems to be transmitted through Jennie's body as if she were a receiver, like an antenna or a *medium*—passive mirror of sound. Jennie's defining character quirk is a chattery, flitting quality; from the outset, she does most of the talking. During their first encounter, she volunteers to sing for him—"I know a song. Would you like to hear it?"—and then Jennie gives her eerie, out-of-sync performance on the covered bridge. The early sequence sets the tone for their relationship to come: she performs and he listens. She seems to arrive in order to speak and, through her, Eben and

---

[33] Ibid., 45.
[34] Amy Lawrence, *Echo and Narcissus: Women's Voices in Classical Hollywood Cinema* (Berkeley, Los Angeles, Oxford: University of California Press, 1991), 111. Further discussion of Hollywood's conventions around sound and women, see Alexander Binns, "Women in the Golden Age" in *Sound and Music in Film and Visual Media: A Critical Overview*, eds. Graeme Harper, Ruth Doughty and Jochen Eisentraut (New York: Bloomsbury, 2009), 375–87.

the audience presumably engage in a routine game of narcissistic "visual pleasure" of an audiovisual sort. However, certain forces conspire to allow Jennie's voice to come unhinged, to break from the image, and thus to defy this game's rules.

"Goodbye my darling"

Portrait's most conspicuous, and most ghostly, instances of bad sync come in the film's climactic storm scene, during the reliving of Jennie's death at Land's End Light. Eben rents a boat, succeeds in sailing across time, and tries to take Jennie to safety in the lighthouse, but, content in the knowledge that their love is eternal, she gives in to fate and dies again.

Selznick put a great deal of energy and money into the climax, saying he wanted to end the picture with "tremendous dramatic power and enormous spectacular value, thereby adding a big showmanship element."[35] The image changes from black and white to a green tint; the aspect ratio changes from the Academy standard 1.33:1 to widescreen; the sound changes over to an early version of surround sound—that is, if one was lucky enough to see it in the right theater, such as New York's Rivoli—and the scene's special photographic effects would garner an Oscar for Selznick employee Clarence Slifer.[36] Given that Selznick's company was about to go under, however, the funding of this massive spectacle had limits.[37]

---

[35] David O. Selznick, *Memo from David O. Selznick: The Creation of* Gone with the Wind *and Other Motion Picture Classics, as Revealed in the Producer's Private Letters, Telegrams, Memorandums, and Autobiographical Remarks*, ed. Rudy Behlmer (New York, Toronto: Modern Library/Random House, 2000), 413.

[36] *New York Times* film critic Bosley Crowther, who saw the film at the Rivoli, describes the climax as such: "a green flash of lightning electrifies the screen, which expands to larger proportions and sound vents around the theater roar with the ultimate and savage fury of a green-tinted hurricane." Bosley Crowther, "Portrait of Jennie," *The New York Times*, March 30, 1949 http://www.nytimes.com/movie/review?res=9507E2DB133CE23BBC4850DFB56683 82659EDE (accessed September 21, 2014). John Belton explains that, for the reel containing the storm scene, "a wide angle lens (resembling the Magnascope lens) was used to enlarge the image to 40 by 30-feet," and that "additional speakers were installed in the theater to play back music and sound effects during the final storm sequence." John Belton, "The Rivoli: The First Todd-AO Cinema," In70mm.com. http://in70mm.com/newsletter/1999/59/rivoli/index.htm (accessed September 21, 2014).

[37] Selznick would put much of his studio's properties up for auction within a few months of *Portrait of Jennie*'s release. It would be his last major Hollywood venture. David Thomson writes that making this film "killed a part of David's love for film-making." See Thomson, 218–21.

Comparing one 1947 shooting draft of the script with the final film, it is clear that the storm scene contains Selznick's most obvious re-writes.[38] Without deep pockets for adequate reshoots on a film that had already gone far over budget, he settled for the *dupe*—another name for dubbing, which also carries the sense of infidelity that early sound audiences feared, the potential to be "cheated" by the sound film.

In both the shooting script and the final film, Eben insists that Jennie come with him to the lighthouse before the storm kills them both; Jennie responds, "No, no, Eben. We're just beginning! There is no life, my darling, until you've loved and been loved—and then there is no death."[39] In the script, four more lines of dialogue follow this one before Eben tries again to lead Jennie to safety in the lighthouse; in the film, these four lines are cut out. The script then details a complex sequence following the couple's attempt to reach the lighthouse; but in the film, the sequence is cut down drastically: a bolt of lighting strikes, then Eben and Jennie are shown in long shot, turning to run for the lighthouse in slow motion. They fall sideways against the rocks as waves crash around them.

Despite the noise and danger, Eben speaks in a voice that is strangely quiet: "We must reach the lighthouse." Jennie answers, much less quietly, "But you're fighting nothing, Eben! Nothing!"—a line not found in the script, and quite probably added after the scene had been shot. Although the angle and distance of this shot prohibit us from seeing Jones's mouth, thus releasing the burden of lip-sync, these two lines nonetheless mismatch the image, for two reasons: first, because of the way Eben's voice sounds too soft, too close to the microphone, to be heard in such a violent storm, and secondly, because their voices "move" at normal speed while the image goes in slow motion. In other words, their voices do not sound like they come from the same space we see on the screen; the impulse to re-write has begun to outweigh the imperative to match the sound and image.

But a few moments later comes a more glaring example of bad sync, just in the dramatic pinnacle of this climactic scene. As the two lovers struggle toward safety with waves crashing into them, still in slow motion, they are knocked off of the rocks and out of frame. Cut to a water-filled shot; as the water clears, the camera finds Eben lying on a rock, his outstretched hand holding

---

[38]Paul Osborn, Peter Berneis, Ben Hecht & David O. Selznick, "PORTRAIT OF JENNIE" 1947 SHOOTING DRAFT. http://www.weeklyscript.com/Portrait%20Of%20Jennie%20(1948).txt (accessed July 23, 2014).
[39]Ibid., 116.

Jennie's, which is just visible at the lower left edge of the frame. "Jennie," he says, again sounding too soft to be audible in such a violent storm. Jennie's face is now visible below him. She is dangling over rocks and waves with her lips parted, showing her teeth. We hear her speak a line: "Please Eben, go without me"—again, not from the script, but added in post. For this line, her voice sounds too close and quiet, like Eben's, and her lips make no movement whatsoever. The effect is as if her voice has given up its body and is already communicating from beyond the grave.

In the next shot, a return to the previous angle, the bad sync continues as Eben replies, "No, there's nothing in life, nothing at all without you." And then back to the same high angle on Jennie, who continues to swing from side to side. Her mouth barely moving—and certainly not in sync with the sound—she says, "You must live on, Eben. But with faith!"

As the tidal wave approaches, framed in a closer shot, Jennie says "Goodbye, my darling," now in good sync; Eben can only respond, "Jennie," also in good sync. However, in the subsequent shot—the film's final look at Jennifer Jones—we return to the high angle on her, dangling. To the eye, she appears to speak the line, "Goodbye my darling" once again, but this time there is no sound of her voice at all. One can only lip-read. A rush of water sweeps her away. The wave envelops the lighthouse and even reaches the camera, covering the frame, which fades to black.

The storm sequence serves not only as the film's climax, but also as its wildest display of sound and image out of joint. This is the couple's final encounter. Their two romantically bound bodies, their two times, are about to come apart for good; the film knows it and comes apart, too. These "faults" in the film become effects more ghostly—more radical, untamed, and spectral—than the film's more intentional methods, and thus, they support the film's narrative and thematic goals more effectively. By tampering with Jennie's words, quite probably *as a way to keep her from escaping containment*, Selznick releases an audio/visual ghost. In contrast, the film ends with a full color shot of the "Portrait of Jennie" on the wall at the Metropolitan Museum, accompanied by a the return of Jennie's voice from an earlier scene. She responds to seeing the painting for the first time: "Oh Eben, is it *really* of me? I think someday it will hang in a museum and people will come from all over the world to see it." The voice-over reasserts a measure of control over Jennie's voice, but feels less haunted than it does haughty: a re-inscription of the overt themes of love and faith and that ability of art to achieve an eternal, unchanging time. These final, prescient words, a replayed snippet of sound, hope to make up for the temporal mischief perpetrated by the film's audio/visual foibles.

Post

In certain moments, Jennie almost seems to have undermined the very apparatus of classical film production: when the words spoken on set fail to meet (Selznick's) expectations, writing changes are made, re-recordings are done, and bad sync becomes a part of the picture. This phenomenon is not confined to this film alone, of course; the re-write process characterizes Selznick's approach in general, and is common in classical productions in general. In *Portrait*, the results of that process are more apparent (visible/audible) than Selznick could have meant them to be. If this movie represents a fading classical mode—a mogul's last gasp in Hollywood—which works to contain the woman through sound–image relations, Jennie's out-of-sync voice ironically allows her to escape the imprisonment to which her own voice should sentence her.

Again, Jennie seems to defy the notion of time as *one*. Attempts to bind her time with Eben's succeed for a few ethereal moments, but the marriage falls apart. As her voice comes unhinged from her image, Jennie fractures and shows cinematic time to be disintegrated, plural. Her longing to "always be together" with her impossible loved one, to always be remembered, characterizes the entire dimension of sound (not language, but sound as such) as a cheated past that knows it is to be repressed and resent this. Knowing she has been *duped*, Jennie vexes Selznick's production, invades the present—the image—leading his movie empire to finally give up the ghost.[40]

A survey of recent reviews of *Portrait* suggests that the film is back from the dead, so to speak, markedly better appreciated today than it was in its own time.[41] In a 2001 review, Ed Gonzalez of *Slant* Magazine dubs the

---

[40] It would be a stretch to say that this one film ended Selznick's run in Hollywood, and much more of a stretch to claim that it was the film's bad sync that singlehandedly doomed it box office failure—its budget of over $4,000,000 had no chance of being recouped. The point here is to draw out the inherent tensions between budget (and its accompanying dependence on efficient use of time) and artistic intention. I simply want to suggest that the film's failure to maintain a seamless unity between sound and picture is a symptom of the larger problems faced by studios as the classical era fizzled out. Box office data derived from the Internet Movie Database, http://www.imdb.com/title/tt0040705/business?ref_=tt_dt_bus (accessed July 23, 2014).

[41] Critics' reviews aggregated by RottenTomatoes.com—almost all of which were written since 2001—give *Portrait* a 91 percent fresh rating, and the audience's rating (an aggregate of user ratings) on the site is 85 percent fresh. http://www.rottentomatoes.com/m/portrait-of-jennie/ (accessed August 10, 2014). User ratings on the Internet Movie Database add up to 7.8 points out of 10. http://www.imdb.com/title/tt0040705/?ref_=fn_al_tt_1&licb=0.2228374583646655 (accessed August 10, 2014).

film a "masterpiece."[42] Critic Ken Hanke calls it "a close-to-perfect blend of stylization and unabashed romance."[43] In a capsule on the film's 2004 DVD release, critic Jeffrey M. Anderson notes the sync problems, but praises the film in general: "Strangely, the sound doesn't always match up; Jones's lips sometimes don't match her voice and other sound effects are not quite edited correctly. But it's a wonderful film and well worth the handsome transfer it gets on the new DVD."[44] It can be argued that the unstoppable tidal wave of change in postwar film history foreclosed on the possibility that this movie could be what it seems to aspire to be: a film that gives voice to a ghost and yet functions in the classical Hollywood mold of Selznick's biggest successes. As a relative failure in its time, the film—filled with unwanted retro-effects, cracks in its hermetically sealed audio/visual world—appears now to have been an unconscious suicide leap toward the postclassical cinema to come (note the film's famous influence on both Luis Buñuel and Alfred Hitchcock, for starters[45]). Is it fair to say that *Portrait of Jennie* haunts (post)modern cinema?

---

[42]Ed Gonzalez, *Slant Magazine*, June 27, 2001 http://www.slantmagazine.com/film/review/portrait-of-jennie (accessed March 11, 2014).

[43]Ken Hanke, *Mountain Express*, March 22, 2011 http://mountainx.com/movies/reviews/portrait_of_jennie/ (accessed March 11, 2014).

[44]Jeffrey M. Anderson, "Picture Perfect," *Combustible Celluloid*, http://www.combustiblecelluloid.com/portrait.shtml (accessed March 11, 2014).

[45]Buñuel cites *Portrait* as one of his favorite films, calling it "a mysterious, poetical, and largely misunderstood work." Luis Buñuel, *My Last Sigh*, trans. Abigail Israel (New York: Vintage Books, 1984), 225. As for Hitchcock—a director lured to Hollywood by Selznick—as David Thomson claims, "if *Portrait* had not been attempted, then its onlooker, Alfred Hitchcock, might never have begun to think of *Vertigo*. For *Vertigo* is the eventual realization of *Portrait of Jennie*" (Thomson, 513).

6

"Antique Chiller": Quality, Pretention, and History in the Critical Reception of *The Innocents* and *The Haunting*

Mark Jancovich

In the early 1960s, two ghost films were released that have acquired classic status. The first, *The Innocents* (1961), acquired this status quickly and, as early as 1967, it was identified as a "classic" by Ivan Butler, who has devoted half a chapter to the film in his study of horror and described it being so "superbly" handled that it "is difficult to imagine a better film version of the famous ghost story."[1] The second film, *The Haunting* (1963), developed its reputation more slowly but has eventually come to eclipse the former. Indeed, it has come to be emblematic of a "restrained tradition" of horror that is said to work by suggestion rather than being explicit.[2] For example, in his discussion of horror, Stephen King even takes one sequence from the film to illustrate a key dilemma in horror—whether to leave the door closed and so excite the imagination about what may lie beyond; or to open it, a move that will always achieve an anti climax. If King ultimately argues for the second strategy, despite its inevitable disappointments, he firmly identifies

---

[1] Ivan Butler, *The Horror Film* (London: Zwemmer, 1967), 67. The film was an adaption of a stage play that was itself an adaptation of Henry James's literary classic, *The Turn of the Screw*.
[2] Gregory Waller, "Made-for-Television Horror Films" in *American Horrors: Essays on the Modern American Horror Film*, ed. Gregory Waller (Urbana: University of Illinois Press, 1987), 145–61.

The Haunting as *the* classic example of the former strategy: "it is a door that Wise (the director of *The Haunting*) elects never to open."[3]

If King ultimately saw this strategy as a cop-out, or a failure of nerve, others have repeatedly seen it as a more distinguished route and, if figures such as Prawer ultimately identify Val Lewton as the key proponent of this strategy, *The Haunting* is still seen as one of the foremost examples of this restrained tradition, and Prawer therefore identifies Wise as one of the "masters of cinema" whose horror films were not simply presented as superior to more explicit horror films, but are claimed to demonstrate "how meaningful terror could be projected" rather than (presumably) *meaningless* terror.[4] Nonetheless, while *The Haunting* is more commonly used in this way, *The Innocents* is also discussed in almost exactly the same terms, despite this usage being less common. For example, in her discussion of the gothic, Helen Wheatley uses the film to distinguish between "two opposing poles in Gothic fiction as represented by, on one hand, Jack Clayton's *The Innocents*... and on the other, the prolific output of the Hammer and Amicus studios."[5]

Of course, in this context, it is significant that both of these films are ghost stories rather than, as was the case with most of the output from Hammer and Amicus, "monster movies." In other words, as ghost stories these films were able to eschew explicit monstrous figures and *suggest* the presence of spectral beings through evocation and allusion—a flickering candle, a wafting curtain or an almost imperceptible noise. As such, the ghost film is well suited to the demands of the restrained tradition that resists explicitness and seeks to keep "the door closed." It is also worth remembering that it was a ghost story, *Curse of the Cat People* (1944), that established Lewton's critical reputation as a producer, even if it was one that hinted at a psychological explanation for its uncanny events; and that many examples of the restrained traditions that are cited by Waller, particularly in the case of "made-for-television" horror films, are also ghost stories.

The classic status of *The Innocents* and *The Haunting* has led many critics to see these films as brilliantly original works. Even Carlos Clarens, who is highly critical of *The Innocents* sees it as a rare "attempt to lead the horror genre from the beaten path."[6] The odd thing here is that despite the status of these films today as classic and original, critical responses at the time of their

---

[3] Stephen King, *Danse Macabre* (London: Futura, 1982), 135.
[4] S. S. Prawer, *Caligari's Children: The Film as Tale of Terror* (Oxford: Oxford University Press, 1980), 250.
[5] Helen Wheatley, *Gothic Television* (Manchester University Press, 2006), 28.
[6] Carlos Clarens, *An Illustrated History of the Horror Film* (New York: Putnam, 1967), 146.

initial release were far less positive and actually saw the films as anything but original. On the contrary, the chief complaint about them was precisely that they were hackneyed and predictable; that they were not just formulaic or overly familiar but even old fashioned.

The point here is not to suggest that these original critical responses had access to the "correct" reading of these films, but nor is it to suggest (as is more common) that these responses were simply examples of "failed criticism."[7] Instead, the purpose of this essay will be to explore why reviewers (at the time that these films were released) viewed these films in terms that are different from those that are common today; and in the process, to demonstrate that all readings and responses need to be understood historically as the product of different conditions. In other words, both historical and current readings of these films are historically contingent. Neither has access to the "true" meanings of these films; and the responses of both periods were shaped by historical circumstances.

Nor will this article seek to give a general overview of all critical responses at the time, a task that is not simply daunting but ultimately impossible. Instead it will concentrate on two key sources that have been chosen for strategic reasons. The reviews in *Variety* give a strong sense of how these films were understood and judged by the industry and therefore provide an insight into how films were imagined in terms of their potential audience and their success in achieving their commercial ambitions. Alternatively, in the early 1960s, the *New York Times* was still the publication most associated with legitimate taste, and its foremost critic, Bosley Crowther, was one of the "most influential reviewers" in the United States during the decades that followed World War II.[8]

The first section of the essay will therefore examine the reviews of these two films, and the ways in which they were condemned as old fashioned. In the process, it will also be demonstrated that this judgment was linked to another concern, the ways in which these films were seen as prestige productions that were not sold as low budget horror but as films of quality and distinction. The second section will then move on to explore how these aspirations to quality meant that these films (through their use of literary, theatrical, and other materials, through the personal, both stars and directors, and through stylistic features such as their use of black and white) were linked to earlier classic texts, particularly the quality horror films of the 1940s.

---

[7]Barbara Klinger, *Melodrama and Meaning: History, Culture, and the Films of Douglas Sirk* (Bloomington: Indiana University Press, 1994).
[8]Klinger, *Melodrama and Meaning*, 72.

In other words, it will be argued that while these films have acquired their status as classics through their association with these earlier moments, it was precisely these aspirations to quality that meant that reviewers in the 1960s judged them to be hackneyed and old-fashioned.

The Innocents arrived in the United States with a fanfare of publicity about its London premiere, which was claimed to have succeeded in "breaking records of every major film to play the Carlton Theatre."[9] In a full-page advert in *Variety* that was published on December 6, it was claimed that the film "takes London" with its "strange new experience in shock"; and this advert was clearly designed to generate anticipation for the following week, when the film would have its "Academy Award Opening December 15 in L.A.!" But this anticipation was generated in two carefully balanced ways. The description of the film as a "strange new experience in shock" clearly sought to position the film as a thrilling horror feature that would attract audiences, while the reference to its "Academy Award Opening" simultaneously stressed that this was no low budget horror project but was also a serious quality production from abroad. Consequently, the advert also featured quotes from the London papers that played up both aspects of the film, which was clearly identified as "horror" but also as a "distinguished" and "stylish exercise" in the genre. Reminders of director Jack Clayton's recent success with *Room at the Top* (1959) were also balanced with claims that "as a ghost story" the film was quite simply "the best ever." Indeed, the day immediately following *New York Times* review, *Variety* featured another full page advert that was much more simple and announced that "Deborah Kerr in Jack ('Room at the Top') Clayton's *The Innocents* breaks house record in Los Angeles in Academy Award Opening" and predicted that the film would "possess N.Y." with its "double premiere at Criterion and 72nd St Playhouse."[10]

The *Variety* review also stressed these qualities and described it as a "High-quality spine-chilling drama" that was likely to prove "marquee-bait."[11] Director Jack Clayton was once again associated with *Room at the Top*, and his new film was seen as a "high-quality" feature that would only "enhance the reputation" that he had established with his earlier film. As a result, he is credited with having made "full use of camera angles, sharp cutting, shadows, ghost effects, and a sinister sound track" so that "every trick is employed to keep the patrons' hands clammy with apprehension and anticipation." Of course, this description walks a very thin line between claims to quality and

---

[9] Anon, "Advert for The Innocents," *Variety* (December 6, 1961), 14.
[10] Ibid. (27 December 1961), 14.
[11] Rich. "The Innocents," *Variety* (December 6, 1961), 6.

suggestions of familiarity: "every trick" might not quite be "every trick in the book," but there is a sense that this is a skillful version of material that we know well, even if it is not yet material that has become overly familiar.

Deborah Kerr is also seen as a key "selling point," and she is praised with providing an "excellent performance" while other positive contributions are said to be made by literary luminary Truman Capote and by cameraman Freddie Francis, who would soon develop a career as a director of more low budget horror efforts. In general, then, the film was described as "a powerful and gripping though sombre and disturbing picture" that "catches an eerie, spine-chilling mood right at the start and never lets up on its grim evil theme."

On one level, it was precisely this dual strategy that the *New York Times* condemned. Rather than praise the film as a horror film of quality, Crowther suggested that it was precisely its aspirations to quality that were the problem: the film might prove successful with a highbrow audience that didn't usually frequent horror films, but regular viewers of horror films would find it "bland."[12] Again, Clayton was identified as "the British director who first clicked with 'Room at the Top'" and he was credited with having "done a fine job in infusing this drama with spooky atmosphere and a certain sense of the weird and supernatural." But even here he only succeeded to the extent that he would "clobber the gullible."

Alternatively, in this review, Deborah Kerr was seen as one of the fundamental problems. Her performance as "the supposedly morbid young woman who is the focal figure of the tale" is accused of being too "lucent" so that (while the film should be a "psychological film" study of a "suspiciously frustrated and sexually repressed" woman who "would quickly be labeled psychopathic in this more knowing day") Kerr "neither acts nor looks a repressed or inhibited woman." The problem is that, as the term "lucent" suggests, Kerr is presented as anything but repressed but rather as "alive," healthy and with no suggestion of "mental unwholesomeness."

In other words, the film is claimed to be "inadequately motivated along psychological lines," but this is not just a complaint about its success as a drama, but a more specific complaint about expectations that one might have of it as a horror film. Consequently, it was not simply "the sophisticated viewer" who would complain about this lack of motivation but "certainly one who is used to seeing conventional horror movies." This is a particularly interesting maneuver by Crowther, but one familiar to those who knew his

---

[12] Bosley Crowther, "Screen: 'The Innocents': film From James Tale Is at Two Theatres," *New York Times* (26 December, 1961), 15.

attitude to horror more generally: rather than simply see the "sophisticated viewer" and those "used to seeing conventional horror movies" as separate groups, Crowther implies that the horror connoisseur is actually one of the *most* sophisticated of viewers.

He therefore sees the film as being too "mild and ingenuous" so that only those "who have never seen a movie set in a scary old house, where doors creak, the wind howls around corners, ghosts pace the long, dark halls and hideous spectral faces appear in the windows at night, should find themselves beautifully frightened and even intellectually aroused by Jack Clayton's new picture." Alternatively, "old hands long familiar with the traffic and tricks of horror films will feel a bit bored" or, at best, "let down."

It may have some "interest" and succeed in sending "some formidable chills down the spine" but anyone familiar with horror will find the film predictable, old fashioned, and unconvincing. Furthermore, if the filmmakers fail to "give us a first-rate horror film or psychological film," the two are clearly seen as associated with one another rather than divergent choices. On the contrary, the suggestion is that any psychological motivation was "not sufficiently explained" for horror audience who would not only have been familiar with such explanations but would have had quite sophisticated expectations in relationship to them.

Although it is now the more celebrated of the two films, *The Haunting* received a less positive review than *The Innocents* from *Variety*, who still saw it as a horror film of quality but one where the quality did not elevate it above other horror films but rather compensated for weaknesses in the film by ensuring that it was an effective example of its genre. It was therefore seen as a "slim shocker fortified with cinematic savvy."[13] Again much was made of its director, Robert Wise, whose "artful cinematic strokes" ensure that audiences "will respond to the film's intermittent terror passages" even while "the skill of Wise, his cast and his crew" are "not quite enough to override the major shortcomings" so that audiences "are apt to find the whole unsatisfactory." Similarly the acting is claimed to be "effective all round" while Julie Harris and Claire Bloom are singled out for their effects. It is therefore claimed that Harris "delivers an expertly agitated portrayal, although the character that she plays is a victim of expository fuzziness"; and "lovely Miss Bloom" is praised for the way in which she is supposed to "subtly convey the unnatural forces at play within her character."[14]

---

[13] "The Haunting," *Variety* (21 August, 1963), 6.
[14] The "unnatural forces" here are not the supernatural but the suggestion of lesbianism!

It is also claimed that the film "excels in the purely cinematic departments, principally in the photographic area" so that Wise's "artful surveillance" ensures that his cinematographer "has employed his camera with extraordinary dexterity in fashioning a visual excitement that keeps the picture alive with images of impending shock." In fact, like later critics, the reviewer also credits cinematographer, Davis Boulton, with breathing life into the set so that "the house itself is a monstrous personality, most decidedly the star of the film."

Similarly, sound, music, editing, special effects, and production design are all commended but the film is ultimately condemned for its lack of clarity. If most contemporary critics praise the film as one that works through suggestion and creates disquiet by refusing to be explicit, the *Variety* review complains about precisely this aspect of the film, which is simply read as vagueness, a lack of clarity, and even as a cop-out:

> After elaborately setting the audience up in anticipation of drawing some scientific conclusions about the psychic phenomena field, the film complete dodges the issue in settling for a half-hearted melodramatic climax that is a distinct letdown.

The review even goes one step further and presents the ending as not merely a "letdown" but downright laughable: "the only immediate conclusion that the [surviving characters] can really draw is, 'Let's split, cats, before them crazy poltergeists get fresh ideas.'"

The *New York Times* is equally dismissive but rather than seeing talent as compensating for failures elsewhere, the film is seen as wasting its talent. Consequently the presence of "two such actresses" as Julie Harris and Claire Bloom, who are said to be "very good all the way through" the film, and of "the able Robert Wise," who produced and directed *The Haunting*, are supposed to have made the film's deficiencies both "surprising and disappointing."[15] Certainly, there are supposed to be effective moments of horror, and the film is supposed to be "great" in the sequences where the two female leads "are huddled in a room in that luridly off-kilter mansion, hugging each other in the dark and listening to horrible noises—thuds, screams, gun-fire—outside the door, waiting in paralyzed terror for they know not what." The film also "seems to be getting someplace" when Robert

---

[15]Bosley Crowther, "The Screen: An Old-Fashioned Chiller: Julie Harris and Claire Bloom in 'Haunting,'" *New York Times* (19 September, 1963), 23.

Johnson's scientist confronts Harris on a spiral staircase "when she, poor thing, has given alarming evidence of going understandably mad."

But despite these sequences, the film is ultimately condemned as one that "simply makes more goose pimples than sense." In other words, once again, as in the case of *Variety*, the film's refusal to be explicit, for which so many critics have praised the film in more recent years, was seen as simply incoherence or opaqueness. The film is therefore said to give "clear intimations that Miss Harris is obsessed by the notion that she killed her mother," which "might remotely explain why she has hallucinations, hears noises and all that sort of thing," but it is also claimed that the film never develops these intimations or explains why others also experience these phenomena.[16]

Ultimately, then, for all its sheen of quality, the film is seen as a meaningless affair so that there is "really no point to it" and everything is simply designed "to make your blood run cold. And that's the total purpose of the picture, as nearly as I can see." The point here is NOT that there is anything wrong with a film that is "a shocker, plain and simple";[17] and, back in 1946, the *New York Times* had praised a number of films for dispensing with any pretense or pretension and simply following "the time-tested theory that moviegoers are seldom more satisfied than when a film causes them to experience cold chills." Indeed, these quotes are taken from a 1946 review of another classic horror film featuring a spiral staircase, Robert Siodmak's *The Spiral Staircase* (1945). In other words, while Crowther and his colleagues championed serious films that sought to advance the art of film, they celebrated films that made no claim to anything more than horrific entertainment. Conversely, they were highly critical of "pretentious" films that sought to pass themselves off as something that they were not—either entertainments that pretended to be something grander (often to their detriment as entertainments); or art films that failed to entertain or to advance the medium. Indeed, the review of *The Haunting* makes an interesting jibe about "psychic symbolism" on that grounds that "after watching all those pictures at the Film Festival, I'm looking for symbolism everywhere," a comment that seems to be more critical of the Film Festival offerings than Wise's horror film.[18]

---

[16]For more recent critics, the implication is actually clear. Both Harris and Bloom's characters are psychic and the phenomena that appear to be the result of a haunting are not simply in their minds but are an unconscious psychic projections (although there is some uncertainty about whether it is Harris or Bloom's psychic powers that is causing these manifestations). In other words, the implication is that, like the monster in *Forbidden Planet* (1956), these phenomena are monsters from the id.
[17]T.M.P., "At the Palace," *New York Times* (7 February, 1946), 35.
[18]Crowther, "An Old-Fashioned Chiller," 23.

Consequently, when Crowther refers to the film as an "antique chiller" that features "just about everything in the old-fashioned blood-chilling line," this can be understood in a number of ways. On the one hand, the film is accused, for all its pretensions to quality, of being an overly familiar, and even outmoded, exercise in cinematic horror, on the other, it is precisely its aspirations to quality that make it outmoded through the ways in which the film works to remind one of earlier "classic" horror films, such as The Spiral Staircase.

One of the key problems with understanding 1960s horror is that most accounts place Hammer at the center of the story. Certainly, Hammer was phenomenally successful for a small studio, and was widely imitated, but, as Kevin Heffernan has stressed, companies such as Hammer and AIP were not merely producers of low budget horror in the late 1950s and early 1960s, but were explicitly setting their sights on the middle-bracket picture through their use of classic properties, larger budgets, color photography and star performers.[19] The success of Psycho, in 1960, only encouraged this strategy; and, as Kapsis points out, Psycho was a product of Hitchcock's own contradictory aspirations; he wanted both the security of commercial success and the prestige of artistic recognition.[20] In Psycho, then, Hitchcock planned to capture some of the art-house cache of Les Diaboliques (1955) while working in a genre that had one of the few reliable markets, the teenage horror audience.

Indeed, in the early 1960s, horror was not simply a low-end game, and the period was witnessing a significant boom in major studio horror productions, particularly in the aftermath of Psycho. The prestige horror films of this period were a diverse and complex group and extend well beyond the mid-1960s, although these later developments will not be sketched out here so that we can focus on the key contexts for both The Innocents and The Haunting.

One feature that is particularly relevant to The Innocents is the relationship between the British new wave and horror. While it may seem strange that the director of Room at the Top would turn to horror for their next film, Clayton was by no means the only figure to make such a transition. In 1964, for example, Karel Reisz's first feature after his new wave classic, Saturday Night and Sunday Morning (1960), was another collaboration with Albert Finney, who was cast as a psychotic killer in Night Must Fall (1964). While Tony Richardson would ultimately take a different path and move into another key genre associated with Britishness, the historical drama (Tom Jones

---

[19]Kevin Heffernan, Ghouls, Gimmicks and Gold: Horror Films and the American Movie Business, 1953–1968 (Durham: Duke University Press, 2004).
[20]Robert E. Kapsis, Hitchcock: The Making of a Reputation (Chicago: University of Chicago Press, 1990).

(1963), *The Charge of the Light Brigade* (1968)), his breakthrough new wave film was the 1959 film version of John Osborne's play *Look Back in Anger*, adapted by the master of television horror, the great Nigel Kneale (creator of the *Quatermass* programs). It should also be noted that even Clayton's own new wave film, *Room at the Top*, had starred Simone Signoret, a French actress that had achieved international stardom a few years earlier with her performance in the art-house horror hit *Les Diaboliques*.

Many of the prestige horror films of the 1960s also associated themselves with the female centered horror films of the 1940s, and even resuscitated the careers of many of the female stars of this period. Strangely, Joan Fontaine, who was one of the key stars of the 1940s films, and had starred in *the* pivotal film of the 1940s cycle, *Rebecca* (1940), came late to the 1960s horror film, and only made one significant film, *The Witches* (1966), which was written by Nigel Kneale. However, her sister, Olivia De Havilland, made a series of horror films in the 1960s and 1970s.[21] Bette Davis and Joan Crawford also resurrected their careers in the 1960s after their appearance in *Whatever Happened to Baby Jane?* (1962), a film that spawned a series of imitators and turned the two actresses into major horror stars for the rest of the decade and, in Davis's case, well beyond.[22]

Although the key star of the 1940s female-centered horror films, Ingrid Bergman, avoided this path, she had already starred (in 1959, only two years before the release of Clayton's film) in a television version of same theatrical adaptation of *The Turn of the Screw* as *The Innocents*. Even Barbara Stanwyck appeared in a horror film for William Castle, *The Night Walker* (1964), while Ross Hunter produced a glossy reproduction of the 1940s horror film with Doris Day, *Midnight Lace* (1960)

While there was also a series of films featuring younger and more fragile female stars (Carol Lynley in *Bunny Lake Is Missing* (1965), Audrey Hepburn in *Wait Until Dark* (1967), and Mia Farrow in *Rosemary's Baby* (1968)), Deborah Kerr's casting in *The Innocents* needs to be seen in the context of these 1940s

---

[21]During the 1960s and 1970s, De Havilland appeared in several horror projects including, *Lady in a Cage* (1964), *Hush...Hush, Sweet Charlotte* (1964) and *The Screaming Woman* (1972).

[22]Crawford's horror films include *What Ever Happened to Baby Jane?*, *Straight-Jacket* (1964), *I Saw What You Did* (1965) *Berserk* (1967), *Journey to the Unknown* (for which she was the host, 1969) and *Trog* (1970). She also made an appearance in Rod Serling's horror television series, *Night Gallery* (1969).

Davis's horror films of the period include *What Ever Happened to Baby Jane?*, *Dead Ringer* (1964), *Hush...Hush, Sweet Charlotte* and *The Nanny* (1965), although this career continued well into the 1970s when she appeared in a range of film and television horror vehicles including *Burnt Offerings* (1976), *The Dark Secret of Harvest Home* (1978), *Return from Witch Mountain* (1978), and *Watcher in the Woods* (1980).

stars. After all, Kerr had largely achieved stardom through a 1940s film about isolation, sexual repression, and madness that was directly associated with the 1940s horror cycle, Powell and Pressburger's *Black Narcissus* (1947).[23] Indeed, the complaint about Deborah Kerr can even be understood in this context, given that *Black Narcissus*, like many 1940s horror films, operated around female duality (women who are themselves divided such as Irene's victim-monster in *Cat People* (1942) or are doubles of one another, most explicitly in De Havilland's dual role in *The Dark Mirror* (1946)). In other words, while *Black Narcissus* featured similar themes of mental disintegration as *The Innocents*, Deborah Kerr was cast as a "healthy" and "wholesome" woman, and was placed in opposition to Kathleen Byron's role, which *Variety* described as "the picture's plum...the neurotic half-crazed Sister Ruth."[24]

The casting of Michael Redgrave is also interesting in this context, given that he appeared in two key 1940s horror films, the British classic *Dead of Night* (1945) and *Secret Beyond the Door* (1947), which was produced and directed in Hollywood by Fritz Lang. Even Peter Wygard, who plays the ghost of Quint in Clayton's film would appear the following year in *Night of the Eagle* (1962), an adaptation of a classic 1940s horror novel, Fritz Leiber's *Conjure Wife* (1943), that was filmed as *Weird Woman* (1944) for Universal's Inner Sanctum series, a horror series that featured the studio's principal horror star of the period, Lon Chaney.

Nonetheless, while *Conjure Wife* had, by the 1960s, become a classic of horror literature, it was still very much a classic of popular generic literature. In contrast, *The Innocents* not only aspired to quality through its use of literary and theatrical sources, like many 1940s horror films, but even associated itself with a key figure of the literary canon, Henry James.[25] These literary references also tended to privilege a version of the gothic that either explicitly placed the story in the historical past (a familiar Hollywood strategy for suggesting notions of quality) or in a contemporary setting that removed signs of modernity (as in *The Haunting*, which even concerns modern science plunged back into a gothic past that threats to overwhelm it). Indeed, both

---

[23]Mark Jancovich, "'Psychological Thriller': British Cinema, Horror and the Cultural Contexts of *Dead of Night*," in *Speaking of Monsters: A Teratological Anthology*, eds. Caroline Joan S. Picart and John Edgar Browning (London: Palgrave, 2012), 39–53.
[24]Cane, "Black Narcissus," *Variety* (7 May, 1947), 18.
[25]While many 1940s films drew on literary and theatrical sources that were hardly literary classics at the time, but rather represented the respectable, middlebrow end of the popular market (*Rebecca*; *Dragonwyck* (1946)), others explicitly sought to associate themselves with literary classics (Charlotte Bronte's *Jane Eyre* (*Jane Eyre*, 1944) and Henry James, *The Aspern Papers* (*The Lost Moment*, 1947) and *Washington Square* (*The Heiress*, 1949)).

Experiment Perilous (1944) and *Hangover Square* (1945) shifted the period setting of their source material and transferred their action back to a vaguely imagined "Victorian Past."

Furthermore, as both Peter Hutchings and I have argued, there is a long tradition in which "the Gothic" is privileged over "Horror" and works to draw distinctions between different types of material. Moreover, the gothic is often associated with a legitimate aesthetic traditions, while horror is associated with debased popular entertainments,[26] distinctions that can even be seen as being evoked through the mise-en-scène of these films. In the late 1950s, both Hammer and AIP were, as we have seen, attempting to upscale their projects in order to break into the middle-bracket, and one of the key ways in which they did this was through increased budgets that put more emphasis on an opulent mise-en-scène, a key feature of which was their use of color.[27] In contrast, both *The Innocents* and *The Haunting* used black and white photography, not only because they had less to prove in terms of their market position but also because of the connotations of color at the time. If color was important for Hammer and AIP to break into the middle-bracket, highbrow cinema was still associated with black and white. In the art film, black and white was often associated with realism (as was the case with the British new wave cinema with which Clayton was associated) or with restraint and respectability.

If *The Haunting* differed from *The Innocents* insofar as it did not feature stars that were associated with the 1940s horror films,[28] it was the film's

---

[26]Peter Hutchings, "Tearing Your Soul Apart: Horror's New Monsters," in *Modern Gothic: A Reader*, eds. Victor Sage and Allan Lloyd-Smith (Manchester: Manchester University Press, 1996), 89–103; and Mark Jancovich, "Genre and the Problem of the Reception: Generic Classification and Cultural Distinctions in the Promotion of the *Silence of the Lambs*," in *Hollywood Spectatorship: Changing Perceptions of Cinema Audiences*, eds. Melvyn Stokes and Richard Maltby (London: British Film Institute, 2000), 34–44.

[27]Heffernan, *Ghouls, Gimmicks and Gold*.

[28]Certainly these stars still provided a sense of quality, particularly due to their associations with both Britishness and the theater. For example, Richard Johnson was a distinguished actor with a strong theatrical, and even Shakespearean, background, but he had no association with the 1940s horror film and tended to specialize in upper class, often military, types. Claire Bloom had enjoyed an illustrious career before *The Haunting* and had starred alongside Charlie Chaplin in his acclaimed postwar film *Limelight* (1952), and in Richardson's film adaptation of *Look Back in Anger*.

The two key American actors had no more relation to horror at the time, and certainly not the 1940s horror films. Russ Tamblyn had a small role in Joseph Losey's postwar fantasy *The Boy with Green Hair* (1948) and would end up in David Lynch's *Twin Peaks* (1990–1991). But, in the 1960s, he was better known for musicals such as *Seven Brides for Seven Brothers* (1954) and Wise's *West Side Story*. Certainly, he had appeared in the fantasy *Tom Thumb* (1958) and (along with Claire Bloom) *The Wonderful World of the Brothers Grimm* (1962) but little more. Similarly, Julie Harris had little direct association with horror but was a distinguished star of theater, film, and television

director, Robert Wise, who carried these associations. It is even worth remembering that *The Haunting* was made by Wise in the brief period between his two massive middlebrow color spectacles, *West Side Story* (1961) and *The Sound of Music* (1965); and the choice of *The Haunting*, and the decision to film it in black and white, can be seen as references back to an earlier period in the director's career, references that aimed to emphasize his cultural credentials at a time when these credentials were under potential threat due to his association with cinematic projects that were massively successful in commercial terms but were simultaneously less respectable in critical terms.

Nor was Wise the only big name director who turned his hand to horror during the 1960s. Between *Ben-Hur* (1959) and *Funny Girl* (1968), William Wyler directed *The Collector* (1965), a horror film based on John Fowles's first novel. Also in 1965, Otto Preminger followed a series of massive middlebrow projects (*Exodus* (1960), *Advise and Consent* (1962), *The Cardinal* (1963)) with *Bunny Lake Is Missing*, a psychological horror film that starred Laurence Olivier and Noel Coward, and was written by respected British dramatist Sir John Mortimer. Certainly in a different league, but no less significant, was Terence Young, who directed *Wait Until Dark*, after directing three key Bond films of the early 1960s—*Dr. No* (1962), *From Russia With Love* (1963), and *Thunderball* (1965)— and just before his move into major middlebrow historical drama with *The Mayerling* (1968).

Nonetheless, if it was not uncommon for prestige directors to make horror films in the 1960s, Wise was different from these others in several ways. *The Haunting* has come to acquire a reputation that far outstrips any of these other films and one reason for this is that, unlike these other directors, it was designed to remind one of Wise's relationship to some of the most revered horror films of the 1940s, even some of the most revered films of the 1940s. He had edited *Citizen Kane* (1941) for Welles, a film that is often listed as one of the greatest films ever made; and his association with Welles proved vital to his career. Not only was Welles explicitly associated with horror throughout the 1930s and 1940s,[29] but Wise's association with Welles also led to an association with the figure usually seen as representing the key

---

and had received numerous Tony, Emmy, and Grammy awards. One of her first film appearances was in Elia Kazan's *East of Eden* (1955), Kazan having built a film career directing the realist thrillers that emerged out of the 1940s horror cycle (see Mark Jancovich, "'Terrifyingly Real': Psychology, Realism and Generic Transformation in the Demise of the 1940s Horror Cycle," *European Journal of American Culture* 9 (2012), 25–39), and she had already appeared in a television adaptation of *The Heiress*. But it was only after *The Haunting* that she became strongly associated with horror.
[29]Mark Jancovich, "Shadows and Bogeymen: Horror, Stylization and the Critical Reception of Orson Welles during the 1940s" *Participations*, 6.1 (2009), 1–27.

contribution to horror in the 1940s—producer Val Lewton, a figure who is often cited as the foremost exponent of suggestion and restraint with horror. Furthermore, Wise's first assignment as a director was on Lewton's *Curse of the Cat People*, the film that marked the critical (if not the commercial) turning point in Lewton's reception as a producer and established his films as cinematic classics to the present day.[30] Wise then went on to direct another two films for Lewton, including the horror classic *The Body Snatcher* (1945) before moving on to other projects, the first of which was yet another horror film, *Game of Death* (1945), a remake of the 1932 horror classic *The Most Dangerous Game*.

Conclusion

As we have seen, then, while *The Innocents* and *The Haunting* are often revered as brilliantly original films today, they were seen quite differently at the time of their original release, and it was precisely their aspirations to cinematic quality that was identified as the root of the problem. In other words, these films are now celebrated as classics due to the markers of quality that were used to distinguish these films from supposedly inferior low budget productions, but critics at the time objected to these films on the grounds that these markers of quality often sought to associate these films with earlier and more respectable moments in the horror film. As Barbara Klinger has noted, since the 1960s, it has become common to present "Old Hollywood" as more authentic through an opposition to supposedly crass and commercial contemporary products, and for some contemporary films to assume an aura of respectability through an allusion to this earlier moment and through a repudiation of contemporary mores.[31] This is the strategy that both *The Innocents* and *The Haunting* used early in the 1960s, but it was also one that backfired on them at the time: rather than marking these films as superior to low budget horror films, the association with respectable horror films from the past was condemned by some critics who saw these films as "antique" and "old-fashioned."

---

[30] Mark Jancovich, "Relocating Lewton: Cultural Distinctions and Generic Negotiations in the Critical Reception of the Val Lewton Horror Films," *Journal of Film and Video* 64 (2012), 21–37.
[31] Klinger, *Melodrama and Meaning*.

7

Shadows of Shadows: The Undead in Ingmar Bergman's Cinema

Maurizio Cinquegrani

A young peasant is climbing a ladder from a field in Dalarna, a central region of Sweden, to the sky above his farm and here is given advice about life and love by his dead father and his ancestors.[1] This is one of the most remarkable scenes from Victor Sjöström's *Ingmarssönerna* (*Sons of Ingmar*, 1919), a film where it is not the dead who return but the living who can temporarily travel to the afterlife. More commonly, Swedish films portray the deceased as if they return as ghosts to haunt, warn, help the living, or to find redemption. In the silent era, the pioneering work of Sjöström and Mauritz Stiller had seen a consistent use of ghosts for narrative purposes and their appearances were rendered through a sophisticated use of staging and cinematography. In Stiller's *Herr Arnes pengar* (*Sir Arne's Treasure*, 1919)—an adaptation of Selma Lagerlöf's novel of the same title (1904)—a ghost returns to denounce the perpetrator of a heinous act and the narrative follows the conventional model of gruesome unfinished business between the dead and the living. Elsalill (Mary Johnson) is the only survivor of Sir Arne's family, slaughtered by

---

[1] *Sons of Ingmar* is the first film of a trilogy adapted from Selma Lagerlöf's novel *Jerusalem* (1901–1902), and also including Sjöström's *Karin Ingmarsdotter* (*Karin Daughter of Ingmar*, 1920) and Gustaf Molander's *Ingmarsarvet* (*The Heritage of Ingmar*, 1926).

mercenaries seeking their treasures. Years later, Elsalill and one of the mercenaries meet again; they do not recognize each other and fall in love. Elsalill is then led to a revelation about the true identity of the man by the ghost of her dead sister, Berghild (Wanda Rothgardt). Berghild is a benign ghost protecting her living relative, and her ghostly apparition on screen is the result of Gustaf Boge and Julius Jaenzon's sophisticated use of that process known as multiple exposure and consisting of the superimposition of two exposures to create a single image.[2] Jaenzon was also responsible for the use of this device to show the journey to the afterlife of David Holm (Sjöström) and Georges (Tore Svennberg) in Sjöström's *Körkarlen* (*The Phantom Carriage*, 1921). David, the last person to have died before the clock struck twelve on December 31st, is destined to take over from Georges the role of driver of the phantom carriage and to collect the souls of those who will die in the following year. Their ghostly figures superimposed on the wintry Swedish landscape provide some of the most remarkable sequences from the silent era.

Forty years later, the famous ghostly dance of death observed by Jof (Nils Poppe) at the end of Ingmar Bergman's *Det sjunde inseglet* (*The Seventh Seal*, 1957) portrays the dead in a corporeal manner and yet in a way that echoes the ethereal ghosts of Sjöström and Stiller's films. Reminiscent of earlier haunted screens in Swedish cinema, Bergman's ghosts and his fantasies of spectrality emerge with close ties to a broader series of cultural influences. Bergman's spectral presences, as this chapter aims to demonstrate, are complex presences echoing gothic and pagan traditions, national and international literature. At times mere hallucinations dissolving into thin air, Bergman's ghosts can also be corporeal and animated dead bodies. This characteristic is reminiscent of a pre-gothic narrative tradition provided by Scandinavian and Icelandic sagas, where specters inhabit the barrows in which they were enclosed and that are known as *draugr* or *haugbúi*.[3] They leave their burial sites to prey on men and maintain intellect and a residual personality. This is a character trait that, as we shall see, emerges at a symbolic level in Bergman's ghostly narratives. The present investigation thus aims at an in-depth reassessment of this aspect of Bergman's cinema and his

---

[2]This technique was pioneered as early as in the 1890s by filmmakers like Georges Méliès and Robert W. Paul, and consistently used to give shape to ghostly presences on screen.
[3]N.K. Chadwick, "Norse Ghosts: A Study in the Draugr and the Haugbúi," *Folklore*, 57.2 (June 1946), 50–65. See also Ármann Jakobsson, "Vampires and Watchmen: Categorizing the Medieval Icelandic Undead," *The Journal of English and Germanic Philology*, 110.3 (July 2011), 281–300.

narratives eerily populated by spectral presences caused by disturbances in the acts of dying and grieving.

Ghosts on the wild strawberry patch

Bergman's characters are regularly caught in the process of mourning and their connection with the voices of the past is often an expression of the inability of the present to be self-sufficient and provide atonement. His cinema reflects the differences in strands of hauntology deriving from Jacques Derrida and from Nicolas Abraham and Maria Torok. According to the former, the secrets of the ghosts are unspeakable inasmuch as they cannot be articulated in any comprehensible language; for Derrida, hauntology is the encounter with the otherness of the ghost, the structural openness directed by specters of the past toward the living. According to Abraham and Torok, the secret of the ghost is a riddle, a jigsaw puzzle to be solved; the spectral thus needs to be restored to the order of knowledge with the result of exorcising its effects on the living.[4] As we shall see, Bergman's cinema explores the ambiguity between the desire to divest oneself of the dead and a nostalgic yearning for the past; it displays a tension between attempts to understand the spectral, to restore it to the realm of logic, and, on the other hand, the need to embrace what is uncanny and incomprehensible about the ghost. In *Såsom i en spegel* (*Through a Glass Darkly*, 1961), Karin (Harriet Andersson) and her brother Minus (Lars Passgård) stage for their father (Gunnar Björnstrand) a play called "The Artistic Haunting," the tale of a prince who chooses fame over love. As Frank Gabo suggests, with this play Minus tries to open his father's eyes to the truth about his shortcomings as a parent and as a writer.[5] This message underlies the gothic shell of the play, which shows Karin in the role of the ghost of the princess of Castile, forever inhabiting her own burial site. The princess died at childbirth and cannot rest because her husband forgot her and turned to other women immediately after her death, thus providing a disturbance in the symbolic rite of her burial. She returns to collect an unpaid symbolic debt, a recurring narrative device in Bergman's film and one that echoes Slavoj Žižek's evaluation of the return of

---

[4] See Jacques Derrida, *Specters of Marx: The State of the Debt, the Work of Mourning & the New International* (London and New York: Routledge, 1994); Nicolas Abraham and Maria Torok, *Cryptonymie: Le Verbier d el'homme aux loups* (Paris: Aubier Flammarion, 1976).

[5] Frank Gabo, *The Passion of Ingmar Bergman* (Durham: Duke University Press, 1986), 273.

the dead as the result of a disturbance with their obsequies, often induced by the ambivalence of the act of mourning.[6] Bergman's cinema illustrates this contrasting desire to keep the dead with us and to get rid of them.

Bergman addresses the theme of death, and the representation of different ways of responding to and coming to terms with it, in continuity with earlier films. From Sjöström's work he has borrowed the theme of redemption in the impediment of death, exemplified by Isak Borg's story in *Smultronstället* (*Wild Strawberries*, 1957). The Swedish title can be translated as "the wild strawberry patch"—a place that is associated in Sweden with both the short Scandinavian summer and with the short season of youth in the life of a man or a woman.[7] *Wild Strawberries* is a time journey to this short season and to later events in the life of Isak Borg (Sjöström), who evaluates the choices he made in life during a long car ride from Stockholm to Lund and through a series of nightmares, daydreams, and reveries. Isak revisits earlier stages of his existence and, among others ghosts, Isak's long-dead father and wife, as well as the younger versions of his still-living mother and childhood love, guide him through this journey. In *The Phantom Carriage*, the protagonist David Holm was a violent man who found redemption through the love of a Salvation Army girl, Edit (Astrid Holm). In *Wild Strawberries*, Isak Borg finds peace and accepts his mortality as he daydreams of his young parents waving from the shore of a lake on a bright summer day. Isak's mother is still alive and she appears to be a cold and unloving woman; her ghostly apparition in Isak's reverie thus confirms Baruch Spinoza's claim that the belief in ghosts is to be understood as an answer to "men's desire to recount things not as they are, but as they would like them to be."[8]

In *Wild Strawberries*, the ghosts lead the living away from their present and into the past; they tell unfinished stories and claim their presence in the lives of those who survived them. Bergman's filmic spaces are invaded by the uncanny and by shadowy presences, and often turned into a land of specters; his ghosts take the shape of long-lost loves, deceased parents, lovers and siblings, blurred memories, and unpayable debts. In Bergman's

---

[6]See Slavoj Žižek, *Looking Awry: An Introduction to Jacques Lacan through Popular Culture* (Cambridge, MA: MIT Press, 1992).
[7]See also Peter Cowie, *Ingmar Bergman: A Critical Biography* (London: Martin Secker & Warburg, 1992), 87–90.
[8]Baruch Spinoza, "Une idée des spectres: Correspondance entre Spinoza et Hugo Boxel, 1674," at http://www.vacarme.eu.org/article367.html; translated by Colin Davis in *Haunted Subjects: Deconstruction, Psychoanalysis and the Return of the Dead* (Houndmills, Basingstoke, Hampshire, and New York: Palgrave Macmillan, 2007), 3.

cinema the dead have great power over the living. This is exemplified for instance by the pastor's dead wife in *Nattvardsgästerna* (*Winter Lights*, 1962), whose memory prevents Tomas (Björnstrand) from loving Märta (Thulin); Tomas is thus unable to kill the dead and complete the process of mourning. In this regard, Bergman was influenced by the work of Sjöström and, when summoning the dead, he occasionally adopted a similar visual style.[9] In *Sommerlek* (*Summer Interlude*, 1951), a double exposure is used to introduce Henrik (Birger Malmsten) and his return from death. During a rehearsal, prima ballerina Marie (Maj-Britt Nilsson) unexpectedly receives the diary of her first love, Henrik, a young man with whom she fell in love on a summer vacation thirteen years earlier, and who died at the end of that season as the result of a diving accident. As she opens the diary, the ghostly and smiling image of Henrik introduces a reverie as it literally emerges from the handwritten pages by means of double exposure. This appearance guides the woman to a journey in time and space to the small island where they had conducted their relationship; the central part of the film consists of several long flashbacks taking Marie and the viewer back to that long-gone summer. In one of the final sequences of the film, Marie opens the diary again and this time it is the eerie image of herself as a younger woman that emerges from those pages. Henrik had until then survived in the unconscious of Marie or in what Nicolas Abraham and Maria Torok call *cryptophore*, the repository of a crypt constructed to preserve the dead from being ultimately lost in the afterlife.[10] Bergman implies here that, while the image of young Marie is forever bound to that of Henrik, after this journey in time the woman is finally able to move on and, as she closes the diary, to "bury" her dead lover. Unlike Tomas in *Winter Lights*, Marie has been able to complete the process of mourning.

In Bergman's cinema, the return of the dead is not always aimed at helping the living and, when compared to earlier Swedish films, a more complex and often ambiguous level of interaction between the two is normally presented. The complexity of this theme is a reflection of Bergman's own connection with the undead, as he explained in his autobiography:

> Ghosts, devils and demons, good, evil or just annoying, they have blown in my face, pushed me, pricked me with pins, plucked at my jersey. They have

---

[9]Ingmar Berman, *The Magic Lantern: An Autobiography* (London: Hamish Hamilton, 1988), 179–82; originally published as *Laterna Magica* (Stockholm: Nordstedts Förlag, 1987), translation by Joan Tate.
[10]Abraham and Torok, 254–55.

spoken, hissed or whispered. Clear voices, not particularly comprehensible but impossible to ignore.[11]

These voices and presences, as well as the very act of writing and directing, can be ascribed to what Jacques Derrida called "animated work that becomes that thing, the thing that, like an elusive spectre, engineers a habitation without proper inhabiting, call it a haunting of memory and translation."[12] Ghostly reveries and the creative process are often paired in Bergman's cinema and allow the merging of past and present. In *Efter repetitionen* (*After the Rehearsal*, 1984), Henrik Vogler (Erland Josephson), the filmmaker's alter ego, is directing a new production of August Strindberg's *Ett drömspel* (*A Dream Play*, 1901). After a rehearsal—as in *Summer Interlude*, this is presented as a meaningful moment in the creative process—he engages in a conversation with Anna Egerman (Lena Olin), the daughter of Vogler's former lover and *protégé* Rakel Egerman (Thulin). Anna, who plays Indra in Vogler's production of *A Dream Play*, talks of her hatred for her dead alcoholic mother. Vogler later falls into a reverie and is visited on stage by the ghost of Rakel, while Anna remains seated on a couch at the center of the stage, first as her adult self and then as a 12-year-old girl. Here, Bergman uses a recurring narrative device where a breach in the barriers separating the worlds of the living and the dead allows the two to meet and address the disturbances in the rite of mourning. Rakel's presence is corporeal, not rendered through multiple exposures. In Bergman's cinema the dead often maintain a very physical presence, just like the *draugr* in Norse sagas, and often reiterate the shortcomings of their lives. In *Efter repetitionen*, it is the living who bear a grudge against the dead and the return of a drunken Rakel, whose bitterness is reminiscent of the ghost of Isak's wife in *Wild Strawberries*, does nothing to address the disturbance in the symbolic act of grieving caused by the profound hatred felt by her own daughter. In *Summer Interlude* on the contrary, dead Henrik comes back to teach a lesson to his long-lost love, just like Michael Furry in James Joyce's *The Dead* (1914), and to bring the rite of mourning to an end with Marie's realization that both youth, exemplified by their time at the wild strawberries patch near the lake, and summer are over.

---

[11] Bergman, 204.
[12] Derrida, 180.

The corpse and the return

FIGURE 7.1 Cries and Whispers *(Ingmar Bergman, 1972, Svensk Filmindustri)*.

In Bergman's cinema, returns from death are often difficult to decipher, whether the undead materialize without any aid or are awakened by others. Like Rakel, Andersson's character in *Viskningar och rop* (*Cries and Whispers*, 1972) returns to haunt the living. Agnes is dying of cancer and the film depicts her final days in the family home surrounded by her sisters Maria (Liv Ullmann) and Karin (Thulin), and her maid Anna (Kari Sylwan). After her death she apparently returns to life for a brief moment; her body is already decomposing and yet she returns to collect a debt and asks her sisters for the love and care she was denied in life. Laura Hubner and Peter Harcourt suggest that the sequence is not only dreamlike but, like some of the reveries in *Wild Strawberries*, an actual dream had by Anna after the death of her sister.[13] Bergman claimed that Agnes is not a ghost but someone whose death "has been caught up halfway out into the void," and Agnes herself explains to Anna that she is dead but cannot go to sleep and cannot leave until

---

[13] Laura Hubner, *The Films of Ingmar Bergman: Illusions of Light and Darkness* (Houndmills: Palgrave Macmillan, 2007), 109; Peter Harcourt, "Ingmar Bergman's *Cries and Whispers*: A Discussion," *Queen's Quarterly* 81.2 (Summer 1974), 250.

her business with the living is finished.[14] When Anna enters the bedroom, Agnes's corpse is shedding tears. Anna suggests that it is only a dream and Agnes denies this possibility, or at least the fact that she should be the one having the dream: "perhaps it's a dream for you, but not for me." In *Cries and Whispers*, Agnes's return from death echoes that concept of spectrality discussed by Žižek as the "fundamental fantasy of contemporary mass culture" and exemplified by the idea that the return of the dead is caused by a "disturbance in the symbolic rite" of their burial.[15] This disturbance finds a resolution in the final sequence of the film, when Anna opens the dead woman's diary and, like Henrik in *Summer Interlude*, Agnes returns to life in a long flashback depicting Anna and the three sisters on a bright autumn day before the young woman's health had deteriorated. The diary, as a cinematic device that allows the return of the dead, makes explicit a belief in spectrality suggesting that the present is not as self-sufficient as it claims to be. In the flashback, the three sisters are walking in the garden and then run toward their childhood swing—their own patch of the wild strawberries—and sit there while Anna pushes them gently. Agnes's second return from death achieves what her first return did not; she has recollected a glimpse of the care she had mostly been denied in life:

> I could hear their chatting around me. I could feel the presence of their bodies, the warmth of their hands. I wanted to hold the moment fast and thought: come what may, this is happiness. I cannot wish for anything better. Now, for a few minutes, I can experience perfection. And I feel profoundly grateful to my life, which gives me so much.

This reconciliation is unusual for Bergman's undead. In films such as *Ansiktet* (*The Magician*, lit. tr.: "The Face," 1958) and *Vargtimmen* (*Hour of the Wolf*, 1968), ghostly matters are often left unresolved. In the latter, Bergman bends the boundaries between hallucinations, ghosts, reveries, and nightmares. The title is a reference to the time in the middle of the night when the ghosts are most powerful and when, according to the main character, "most births and deaths happen." Painter Johan (Max von Sydow) is haunted by demons from his past as well as by threats from the present, in the form of ex-lovers, neighbors turning into monsters, and other visions. His wife, Alma (Ullmann), possibly begins to share Johan's hallucinations when an old lady wearing

---

[14]Ingmar Bergman, *Four Stories: The Touch, Cries and Whispers, Hour of the Wolf, A Passion*, translated by Alan Blair (London: Marion Boyards, 1977), 86.
[15]Žižek, 22–3.

a white dress appears in front of her, out of thin air, and claims to be 217 years old. The old lady in white tells Alma to read her husband's diary, where she will discover that Johan is still obsessed by the memory of his former lover. Bergman does not provide answers to logical questions regarding this apparition and the identity of the old lady and the reason for her intervention is not revealed. Purposely ambiguous, the nature of this ghostly character remains unidentified; Bergman avoids restoration to the order of knowledge and, in a Derridean manner, allows the viewer to encounter what is strange and impossible to articulate about the ghost.

FIGURE 7.2 Hour of the Wolf *(Ingmar Bergman, 1968, Svensk Filmindustri).*

In *The Magician*, Granny Vogler (Naima Wifstrand) claims to be a witch and also claims, perhaps lying, that she has been living for over 200 years. She is not a ghostly figure but she appears to be the connection between the supernatural pagan rituals and the trivial tricks of travelling magicians Albert Emanuel and Manda Vogler (Sydow and Thulin). As the Vogler's carriage goes through an eerie forest, Granny says that she has seen ghosts walking, sighing, and wailing in the forest after sunset; when they hear a scream, she claims that it comes not from a fox but from a creature "on two thin legs, bloody and maybe with a head hanging by a sinew, without eyes and with a rotten hole for a mouth." This description fits that of the *draugr* in Scandinavian sagas, a dead corpse inhabited by a spirit. Vogler identifies the source of the scream in a figure lying below a tree; Granny crosses herself and pronounces the protection spell against the leaving dead: "Gash in the eye, blood in the mouth, fingers gone, broken neck. He calls you down; he calls you out, beyond the dead, the living, and the living dead beyond the raised hands." What they find is an alcoholic dying former actor, Johan Spegel (Bengt Ekerot). He dies inside Vogler's carriage and his final words suggest that he was already dead when they found him: "I always longed for a knife. A blade that would free me from substance [...] A sharp blade that purged all impurity. Then the so-called spirit would rise up and out of this meaningless cadaver." On the one hand, Bergman implies that Spegel's condition had deteriorated to the point where he was beyond cure when the Voglers found him. On the other hand, Granny's allusions to the undead provide a more esoteric reading of this character as a corporeal ghost, a reading which is confirmed by later events in the film. Spegel's body has been hidden in a coffin and during a stormy night in the small village he returns to life in order to steal vodka from a dinner table. Like Rakel's in *After the Rehearsal*, his drinking habits persist after death. He ambiguously claims that he did not die and yet he is "better as a ghost than as a person" as he has become convincing, something he never was an actor. He claims he is already in disintegration and goes back to the coffin, like a *draugr*, and apparently dies again. His corpse will be disembodied in one of Vogler's pranks; again like a *draugr*, only the destruction of his corpse will prevent Spegel from coming back.

Sunday's children at the time of the wolf

The physicality of some of Bergman's undead, such as Spegel or Agnes, coexists with a more ethereal ghostly presences, largely influenced by the work of August Strindberg. In Strindberg's *Spöksonaten* (*The Ghost Sonata*, 1907), the Student is said to have been born on a Sunday and, according to the Old Man, this is what has given him the gift to see ghosts and things that are not necessarily occurring in the present moment.[16] Bergman, who staged the play four times between 1941 and 2000, was significantly influenced by *The Ghost Sonata* and in 1992 wrote the script for *Söndagsbarn* (*Sunday's*

---

[16]August Strindberg, *Miss Julie and Other Plays*, translated by Michael Robinson (Oxford and New York: Oxford University Press, 1998), 257.

Children), a film directed by his son, Daniel.[17] An autobiographical story, *Sunday's Children* focuses on Pu, a young boy who is said to possess the gift and whose thoughts linger on the ghost stories told by the servants. With their special connection with the dead, many of the characters created by Bergman in his films, including Vogler in *After the Rehearsal*, Anna in *Cries and Whispers*, or Alma in *Hour of the Wolf*, are "Sunday's children." For Bergman, cinema becomes the ideal medium to explore this connection. In *The Magician*, Spegel looks at Vogler's magic lantern and the projection of a slide representing a skull wearing a wig. He calls it a "shadow of a shadow"; actors are shadows and the magic lantern, as much as cinema, projects their own shadows. This is a claim with a Shakespearean influence and one that will resonate again in the haunted images of Bergman's *Fanny och Alexander* (*Fanny and Alexander*, 1982), the story of another Sunday's child.

FIGURE 7.3 The Magician *(Ingmar Bergman, 1958, Svensk Filmindustri)*.

Like Pu and Bergman himself, Alexander (Bertil Guve) is fascinated by the ghost stories told by his father at bedtime and he is also drawn to his magic lantern and its flickering shadows of shadows. His father, Oscar

---

[17]See Egil Törnqvist, "Bergman's Strindberg," in *The Cambridge Companion to August Strindberg*, ed. Michael Robinson (Cambridge: Cambridge University Press, 2009), 149–63.

(Allan Edwall), suddenly dies from a stroke while rehearsing the role of the ghost of Hamlet's father at the Ekdahl family's theater. Like King Hamlet, Oscar will reappear as a ghost on several occasions, unable to leave his family behind and regularly causing an uncanny fracture in normality which brings Alexander to confront the idea of absence or loss. After his father's funeral—a rite that in Bergman's films often fails to consign the dead to their own domain—Alexander falls asleep while playing with his magic lantern; he is woken by Fanny (Pernilla Allwin) and shown the ghost of his father playing the piano in the living room. Oscar, who is wearing a white suit, looks back at them, apparently unable to speak; he appears a second time when their mother, Emilie (Ewa Fröling), announces she is going to marry Edvard Vergérus (Jan Malmsjö), the local bishop. The children, Emilie, and the bishop are praying in the sitting room when Alexander sees Oscar walking slowly and silently toward them. Again, during Emilie and Edvard's wedding ceremony, Alexander sees his father's ghost standing in the hallway with a worried expression on his face. Oscar appears again to his own mother, Helena (Gunn Wållgren), in what is possibly a dream she has on a rainy afternoon at their summer house. He tells Helena about his worry for the children, now in the hands of the bishop. Like Elsalill's sister in Stiller's *Sir Arne's Treasure*, Oscar feels the need to protect the surviving members of the family and explains this to Alexander in his final apparition. The children are rescued by the Ekdahl family and are smuggled to the house of Isak Jacobi (Josephson), Helena's former lover. Alexander spends the night exploring Isak's curiosity shop, and here his dead father appears for fifth time. He finally speaks to his son and explains that he has lived his life for his wife and children; death does not change anything; he cannot leave them and worries for them. He appears to be powerless and unable to help his living family. And yet, Oscar's message is now delivered and his mission fulfilled as his apparition will ignite the events leading to the mysterious death of the bishop in a fire.

Oscar's ghost epitomizes the difficulty in separating the past from the present that characterizes Bergman's narratives and the ways in which the present, in his films, is always constructed through deferral of the past. After his father's apparition, Alexander is led by Isak's nephew, Aaron (Mats Bergman), to see another, very different kind of undead: a *draugr* in the form of a luminous mummy that inexplicably breathes and turns its head in its own coffin. Alexander and Aaron later discuss ghosts: "Uncle Isak says we are surrounded by realities, one outside the other. There are swarms of ghosts, spirits, phantoms, souls, poltergeists, angels and demons." Alexander has already encountered these realities, including malevolent spirits. While staying at the bishop's palace, Alexander lies to Fanny and one of the maids

(Andersson) about meeting the ghosts of Edvard's former wife and two young daughters who drowned in a river outside the palace while trying to escape the bishop's tyranny. He claims that the bishop was responsible for their death and he is subsequently forced to spend the night in the cold and dark attic. Here, Alexander expects to see his father: "Father. If you are going to visit me, please remember I'm scared of ghosts and that you're actually dead. I don't understand why I have to see dead people when it makes me sick." Alexander's attitude toward his father's ghost reflects the ambivalence of the act of burial: he wants to be rid of him for good and yet he is angry for having been left behind. In this regard, Alexander's ambiguity echoes Žižek's suggestion that the desire of the living to keep the dead among them coexists with their will to stop them from returning and interrupt normality.[18] But in this sequence Oscar does not appear and Alexander is instead visited by the ghosts of the bishop's daughters; they take the side of Edvard and threaten the boy. Another malevolent spirit is introduced in the final sequence of the film. Emilie and the children have now returned to the family house; Alexander, who is no longer seeing Oskar and has thus completed his process of mourning, will soon be taunted by another ghost, that of Edvard. The boy is destined to live like Bergman himself, in the words of Antonius Block (Sydow) in *The Seventh Seal*, "in a world of ghosts, prisoner of his dreams." In one of the final scenes of the film, the bishop's ghost hits Alexander on the head and says, "You cannot escape me." Edvard himself has now returned to collect what Žižek calls an "unpaid debt" and to silently close some unfinished business.[19]

Conclusions

A remarkably intense and equally unusual heat wave affects the city of Stockholm. As the wave eventually subsides, the men, women, and children who have died in the previous two months come back to life. This is the premise of Ajvide Lindqvist's novel *Hanteringen av odöda* (*Handling the Undead*, 2005); with their rotting flesh and dilapidated skin, these returned ones can be placed in the tradition of the *draugr*.[20] The undead in Lindqvist's

---

[18] Slavoj Žižek, *The Puppet and the Dwarf* (Cambridge, MA, and London: MIT Press, 2003), 100.
[19] Žižek, *Looking Awry*, 22.
[20] The undead, in the form of ghosts or vampires, are recurring presences in the work of Lindqvist, with the former also appearing in *Människohamn* (*Harbour*, 2008) and the latter featuring in *Låt den rätte komma in* (*Let the Right One In*, 2007).

work are always tragically lonely: "I'm twelve"—Eli the vampire tells Oskar in the film adaptation of Lindqvist's *Låt den rätte komma in* (*Let the Right One In*, 2008)—"but I've been twelve for a long time." *Let the Right One In* is one of the most successful Swedish films of all times and yet, as a horror film, it has hardly followed a prolific cinematic tradition. Indeed, while horror elements and atmospheres can be traced in several Swedish films, *Let the Right One In* is the first vampire horror film made in Sweden.[21] Ghost films in the traditional sense are entirely absent from the country's film production. The secularity of Swedish society and the nation's limited interest in popular folklore may well be responsible for the lack of significant horror films. The portrayal of the disturbances involved in the concept of spectrality and the interaction between the living and the dead thus emerge in Swedish cinema from films that do not belong to the horror genre. Bergman's cinema arguably offers the most prolific and complex exploration of spectrality in Swedish cinema. The director filled a gap in the national cinema of Sweden and, as this chapter has aimed to demonstrate, reinvented a series of influences deriving from drama, silent cinema, pagan beliefs, and popular stories, and filtered these sources through his search for answers to questions about the afterlife, the silence of God, redemption, and nostalgia.

---

[21] Peter Pontikis's *Vampyrer* (*Not Like Others*) followed *Let the Right One In* in 2010. Both films were anticipated in 2006 by Anders Banke's *Frostbiten* (*Frostbite*), a comedy horror about vampires.

8

Locating the Specter in Dan Curtis's *Burnt Offerings*

Dara Downey

According to Anne Rivers Siddons, "a house askew is one of the most not-right things in the world."[1] Author of *The House Next Door* (1978), a novel about a brand-new house that destroys the lives of everyone who lives in or near it, what Siddons articulates here is the uncanny power that domestic space has to shape the lives of those who inhabit it—a power that, depending on the house, is not necessarily benevolent. Nevertheless, both scholarly interpretations and cinematic adaptations of literary texts featuring houses that are "askew" and therefore dangerous often display a stubborn desire to divert attention away from the capacity of houses to haunt, and toward the actions and mental states of the human beings who occupy these spectral spaces.[2] This tendency, I would argue, is particularly evident in Jack

---

[1] Anne Rivers Siddons, qtd. in Stephen King, *Danse Macabre* (1981) (London: Time Warner, 2002), 305.
[2] This is particularly (though by no means exclusively) the case in relation to Henry James' *The Turn of the Screw* and Shirley Jackson's *The Haunting of Hill House*; see, *The Turn of the Screw*, eds. Deborah Esch and Jonathan Warren (New York and London: Norton, 1999). In relation to Jackson, see Roberta Rubenstein, "House Mothers and Haunted Daughters: Shirley Jackson and Female Gothic," *Tulsa Studies in Women's Literature* 15 (1996), 309–31; Tricia Lootens, "Whose Hand Was I Holding?: Familial and Sexual Politics in Shirley Jackson's *The Haunting of Hill House*," in *Haunting the House of Fiction: Feminist Perspectives on Ghost Stories by American Women*, eds. Lynette Carpenter and Wendy K. Kolmar (Knoxville: Tennessee University Press, 1991); Judie Newman, "The Reproduction of Mothering: *The Haunting of Hill House*," in *American Horror Fiction: From Brockden Brown to Stephen King*, ed. Brian Docherty (Basingstoke: Palgrave MacMillan, 1990), all reprinted in *Shirley Jackson: Essays on the Literary Legacy*, ed. Bernice Murphy (Jefferson: McFarland, 2005); as well as Darryl Hattenhauer, *Shirley Jackson's American Gothic* (New York: State University of New York Press, 2003).

Clayton's *The Innocents* (1961), a film version of Henry James's *The Turn of the Screw* (1898), Robert Wise's *The Haunting* (1963), an adaptation of Shirley Jackson's *The Haunting of Hill House* (1959), and Stanley Kubrick's *The Shining* (1980), based on Stephen King's 1977 novel of the same name—all texts concerned with the relationship between individuals and houses. All three novels are profoundly ambivalent in their presentation of the spectral phenomena around which they revolve, allowing the reader to interpret these phenomena either as "real" or as nothing more than the productions of the protagonists' disordered psyches—but, crucially, never permitting the reader to be certain one way or the other. All three films, by contrast, emphasize the crumbling psychic integrity of their protagonists to the point of obscuring the supernatural agency of the haunted (or rather haunting) house.

A notable exception to this general rule (in which film versions downplay the ambivalence central to their literary source material) is *Burnt Offerings* (1976), directed by Dan Curtis, based on Robert Marasco's 1973 novel of the same name. Curtis's film is unusually explicit about the imprisoning and dangerous qualities of domestic space, the structure of its plot drawing attention to the ways in which the cinematic and critical foregrounding of mentally unhinged individuals actively obfuscates the domineering nature of a house. In *Burnt Offerings*, the specter of female insanity conjured up by *The Innocents* and *The Haunting* and of male violence notoriously dramatized in Alfred Hitchcock's *Psycho* (1960) function as smoke screens within the plot itself, distracting the female protagonist from the more insidious violence wielded by the system of domesticity through the material spaces of the home. In other words, the house in *Burnt Offerings* exploits gendered stereotypes in order to conceal the extent to which it actively enforces certain kinds of gender roles, particularly for women.

Specifically, the heroine, Marian Rolfe, views the house that she insists her family rent for the summer as an opportunity to carve out some independence for herself within a marriage where she feels increasingly trapped by her increasingly sexually aggressive husband, Ben. Turning away from him during their time there, to his frustration, she seizes upon the endless household tasks that the house seems to demand as an excuse to spend more time alone. However, both film and novel imply that doing so is in fact not merely futile but contradictory, binding Marian more tightly within the confines of middle-class domesticity, even as it transforms her into an avatar of monstrous femininity. The house in *Burnt Offerings* is therefore ultimately revealed as a kind of demon lover, not only vying with Ben for Marian's time and affection, but actively seeking to take him out of the picture altogether. In order to do so, it exploits the assumption so common to gothic film and fiction—that all men barely contain their base desires for physical and sexual violence and domination beneath a thin veneer of respectability—so as both to poison Marian's feelings toward Ben, and to conceal its own vampiric nature.

In order to illustrate this, it is necessary to begin by examining how *Burnt Offerings* is situated within the context of twentieth-century films about women's vexed relationship with men and houses. From here, I examine the ways in which Curtis's film (as part of a wider canon of haunted-house films) figures the interaction between the house that dominates the action and visual range, and Marian, played by Karen Black. Finally, I move on to a discussion of housework, in order to suggest some of the ways in which the physical and sociocultural spaces of the home can themselves become haunting, actively hostile presences, particularly for those women enjoined by cultural pressure, not only to spend most of their time in such spaces, but to devote to them their entire energy, concern, and indeed affection. The house in *Burnt Offerings* therefore serves as a powerful symbol for the ways in which domestic ideology effectively tricked women throughout the twentieth century in the United States (and indeed in Europe), enticing them with the promise of privacy, self-determination, and meaningful work. Faced with such appealing possibilities, *Burnt Offerings* suggests, middle-class American women became the dupes, not of individual men, or of their own damaged psychologies, but of a wider system of patriarchal ideology, of which the house was the most insidious and ubiquitous avatar. Under its seductive sway, like Marian, who is ultimately transformed into the living ghost haunting a mansion that she loves better than her husband and son, millions of women threw themselves willingly and enthusiastically into self-forged chains.

Filming the villainous husband

Central to an understanding of the position of *Burnt Offerings* within horror film more generally is its use of a married female protagonist (rather than the virginal young girls who dominated eighteenth- and nineteenth-century gothic novels by Ann Radcliffe, J. Sheridan Le Fanu, and their ilk, and who resurfaced as the Final Girls of the slasher-film craze that emerged in the 1970s). It should consequently be recognized as a direct continuation of what Mark Jancovich terms the gothic or "paranoid" women's films of the 1930s and 1940s, such as *Rebecca* (1940) and *The Secret Behind the Door* (1948). Jancovich makes a strong case for reading such films as horror, not least because doing so acknowledges that the horror genre is capable of accommodating "women's concerns" relating to marriage, childbirth, and childrearing, and especially the home.³ As he admits, the recognition of such films as part of the genre has been severely hampered by the critical assumption that "the horror spectator [is] essentially masculine in character"—that horror films exist purely to gratify the male gaze with objectified images of beautiful women in peril, thereby automatically and universally precluding depictions of feminine subjectivity, let alone female heroism or feminist issues.⁴

With the decline of the gothic-paranoid film in the 1950s, the success of *Psycho* and *Peeping Tom* in 1960 briefly swung the pendulum back in favor of depictions of male violence and female victimhood.⁵ However, as Richard Nowell points out, "Hollywood's horror output during the decade that followed the 1968 release of *Rosemary's Baby* was dominated by supernatural domestic melodrama before giving way to youth-centered horror in the late 1970s."⁶ Films produced by the members of the Motion Picture Association of America were characterized by:

> one of the most distinctive marketing trends of the 1970s: targeting big-budget chillers toward mature women in ways that differed [...] from earlier horror marketing [...]. Largely jettisoned were images of women in jeopardy—partially dressed, cowering, screaming, and vulnerable—and in their place came, for the most past, images of strong, focused female characters.⁷

Nevertheless, film companies were slow to capitalize on the success of the adaptation, and it was several years before American cinema screens would show "similarly lavish supernatural horror films that focused on thirty-something women and parenthood," such as *The Exorcist* (1973) and later *The Omen* (1976) and *Burnt Offerings*.⁸ Moreover, as Nowell argues, just as

---

³Mark Jancovich, "Bluebeard's Wives: Horror, Quality and the Gothic (or Paranoid) Woman's Film in the 1940s," *Irish Journal of Gothic and Horror Studies* 12 (Summer 2013), 20.
⁴Ibid. 22. See also Peter Hutchings, "Masculinity and the Horror Film," in *You Tarzan: Masculinity, Movies and Men*, eds. Pat Kirkham and Janet Thumin (London: Lawrence and Wishart, 1993), 84–94, 84f.
⁵See Andrew Tudor, *Monsters and Mad Scientists: A Cultural History of the Horror Movie* (Oxford, Massachusetts: Basil Blackwell, 1989), 48.
⁶Richard Nowell, "'There's More Than One Way to Lose Your Heart': The American Film Industry, Early Teen Slasher Films, and Female Youth," *Cinema Journal* 51.1 (Fall 2011), 125, referring to Vivian Sobchack, "Bringing It All Back Home: Family Economy and Generic Exchange," in *The Dread of Difference: Gender in the Modern Horror Film*, ed. Barry Keith Grant (Austin: University of Texas Press, 1996), 143–64.
⁷Nowell, 125. See also Jancovich, 27.
⁸Nowell, 125.

this trend reached its peak, the industry realized that profit from such films was by no means assured, and with *Carrie* (1976), moved on to targeting younger women directly as both protagonists and audiences. *Burnt Offerings* is therefore situated in a brief yet significant period in which older, married, domestically positioned women's concerns were seen as central to mass-market, big-budget horror films.

Vitally for my purposes here, in terms of plot, the tradition (both cinematic and literary) from which *Burnt Offerings* emerged barely deviates from conventional gothic gender dynamics, carrying the structural opposition of male villainy and female persecution into the sanctified realms of married life. In the books and films termed "marital Gothic" by Michelle Massé, the narratives commence immediately after marriage, instead of ending at this point, as Radcliffean gothic does.[9] Even more radically, where "straight" gothic plots such as that of Louisa May Alcott's *A Whisper in the Dark* (1889) orchestrate the vanquishing of the male villain so that the heroine can marry a good man and live happily ever after, the marital gothic of Hollywood cinema and mid-twentieth-century novels conflates these two male characters into a single menacing figure—the husband. As the heroine and first-person narrator of Victoria Holt's novel *Bride of Pendorric* (1963) asserts, "I had married a man who had seemed to me all that I wanted in a husband... then suddenly it was as though I were married to a stranger."[10] According to Jancovich, so prevalent in mid-century Hollywood cinema was the figure of a "woman who feels threatened or tortured by a seemingly sadistic male authority figure, who is usually her husband," that contemporary critics began to see gothic or paranoid women's films as archetypal, "identify[ing] them explicitly as retellings of the fairy tale of Bluebeard and his wives."[11]

Many conventional female-gothic texts imply that men are not only potentially responsible for women's imprisonment in the home, safeguarding their own freedom and economic dominance by insisting that women belong at home and only at home, but are also empowered by the privacy surrounding domestic space to behave abusively and even violently. From Edith Wharton's "The Lady's Maid's Bell" (1902), "Kerfol" (1916), and "Mr. Jones" (1928), to *What Lies Beneath* (2000) and *Gothika* (2003), victim-heroines are pitted against men whose controlling and violent behavior is

---

[9]Michelle A. Massé, "Gothic Repetition: Husbands, Horrors, and Things That Go Bump in the Night," *Signs: Journal of Women in Culture and Society* 15.4 (Summer 1990), 679–709.
[10]Quoted in Kyra Kramer, "Raising Veils and Other Bold Acts: The Heroine's Agency in Female Gothic Novels," *Studies in Gothic Fiction* 1.2 (2011), 25.
[11]Jancovich, 21.

both ignored and sanctioned by societal norms. As is made explicit by the iconography (if not necessarily the plots) of twentieth-century women's films, however, a third party necessarily structures and makes possible abusive marital relationships—the house, under the sheltering eves of which patriarchal violence is permitted to flourish. Indeed, many of the films discussed by Jancovich hint that the privacy of the single-family dwelling is all but responsible for the terrible things that occur within it. As Mary Ann Doane notes, "An advertising poster for *Dark Waters* (1944) asks, 'Have you ever really been afraid? … of a man? … of a house? … of yourself?'"[12] A recent blog post both lampoons and celebrates this trope as it features in Charlotte Brontë's *Jane Eyre* (1847) and the cult of handsome, brooding villains that it and other gothic texts have spawned in twenty-first century popular culture (including the *Twilight* books and films), precisely by drawing sharp attention to the role played by domestic space in such productions. Reducing the plot of Brontë's novel to a compact stage or film script, when Jane is sent to work as a governess in the mysterious Thornfield Hall, having previously occupied not one but two gloomy mansions, the post imagines a personified plot as situating the house as a suitor:

> THE PLOT: You know how people really like love triangles?
> JANE EYRE: With HOUSES?
> THORNFIELD HALL: Hiiii. I'm bachelor number three, tall, dark and brooding![13]

This is essentially what Norman Holland and Leona Sherman refer to as "the image of woman-plus-habitation," which, they assert, has survived almost unchanged from the eighteenth right up to the twentieth centuries (and, as I argue below, into the twenty-first).[14] The two most prominent haunted house films from the decade's end, *The Amityville Horror* (1979) and Kubrick's *The Shining*, both feature husbands who are manipulated by evil houses into becoming bearded, axe-wielding maniacs who are a clear threat to their wives and children. Focusing on what Suzanne E. Hatty calls

---

[12]Mary Anne Doane, *The Desire to Desire: The Women's Film of the 1940s* (Bloomington: Indiana University Press, 1987), 136.
[13]Sarah Rees Brennan, "Jane Eyre, Or: The Bride of Edward 'Crazypants' Rochester," *Sarahtales* (22 December 2011) (http://sarahtales.livejournal.com/193457.html, accessed April 14, 2014).
[14]Norman N. Holland and Leona F. Sherman, "Gothic Possibilities," *New Literary History* 8.2 (1977), 279. See also the 2013 *Huffington Post* feature on mid-twentieth-century cover designs for contemporary gothic novels, http://www.huffingtonpost.co.uk/2013/12/17/women-running-from-houses-gothic-horror-book-covers-pictures-_n_4459737.html (accessed July 8, 2014).

"'the problem of men,' the perceived contribution of men to newfound levels of civil disorder" in late twentieth-century American life, both versions of *The Shining* explicitly associate deviant masculinity—masculine behavior at odds with familial and social norms—with monstrosity.[15] King's protagonist, Jack Torrance, is an English teacher with a history of alcohol-fuelled violence, against both his son Danny and a former student. With Danny and his wife Wendy, Jack takes a job as a caretaker in the isolated Colorado mountaintop Overlook Hotel during the winter months, and is gradually possessed by the demonic forces residing there. The narrative traces Jack's descent "from college-educated man to wailing ape in five easy seconds," as he succumbs (at the hotel's bidding) to his inner rage, becoming drunk on ghostly liquor, attempting to murder his family as his predecessor has done before him, and ultimately dying in a conflagration that destroys the entire hotel, leaving homeless the spirit that has rendered it evil and haunted.[16] In Kubrick's less overtly supernatural version, Jack, as played by Jack Nicholson, and upon whose twitching facial features the film dwells at length, appears to be murderously insane from the beginning, rather than under the sway of a malevolent building. At the film's climax, when he gives into violent urges that, it seems, he has always barely suppressed, Jack, chasing his son Danny with an axe, becomes lost in a hedge maze in the hotel's grounds and dies of exposure, still incoherently hollering Danny's name.

As will become clear, King's novel has much in common with Marasco's earlier *Burnt Offerings*; the differences, however, are illuminating. In both the novel and the film, family man Ben (Oliver Reed), also an English professor, nearly drowns his son David in the swimming pool of their lavish holiday home. What begins as relatively innocent "roughhousing," as Ben repeatedly pulls David under the water until the boy can hardly breathe, seems to spin out of control, and the boy is forced to strike his father in the face with a snorkeling mask. It is also by the side of the pool that Ben attempts to pressure Marian into sex, first cajoling her into skinny-dipping, and then pinning her to the ground when she refuses his advances. This is a complex scene, one central to an understanding of the film as a whole. The disturbing spectacle of what nearly becomes marital rape is undercut by Marian's odd reaction to seeing a light come on in the window of the room occupied by

---

[15]Suzanne E. Hatty, *Masculinities, Violence, and Culture* (Thousand Oaks: Sage Publications, 2000), 3, 67.
[16]Stephen King, *The Shining* (London: Hodder, 2007), 119. See Joseph Grixti, *Terrors of Uncertainty: The Cultural Contexts of Horror Fiction* (New York and London: Routledge, 1989), 64, for a discussion of Jack's imperfect repression of his bestial urges.

Mrs. Allardyce (an old woman who they never see but who they must leave food for every day), at the top of the house which looms above them as they struggle. Seemingly made more uncomfortable by the thought that the house and its mysterious occupant might be able to see her interaction with Ben than by his advances themselves, this scene quickly ceases to be about Marian's desire to determine what happens to her own body, alerting us instead to the extent to which the house has begun to control her. Rather than rejecting Ben so as to assert self-determination, she does so because she has given herself to the house instead, in a relationship that prefigures that between Jack Torrance and the Overlook Hotel.

What this scene (somewhat problematically) implies is that the threat apparently posed by husbands to women and children is a red herring, and that the house itself is the "real" source of fear and peril—or rather, that the very structures which produce and regulate the family can function as demonic forces, structures haunted, not by ghosts as such, but by the problematic power and gender relations they encode and enforce.

The malevolent house

What renders this idea so difficult for films like *The Haunting* and *The Shining* to swallow, to the point where they rapidly substitute human madness for systemic evil, is the deep-rooted notion that, in Siddons's words, a house "is an extension of ourselves; it tolls in answer to one of the most basic chords mankind will ever hear. My shelter. My earth. My second skin."[17] This is both the domestic ideal and the assumption that runs behind much gothic scholarship regarding haunted houses—that an absolute homology exists between owner/occupier and house. A significant proportion of critics working on the genre repeatedly assert that horror fiction abandoned the obvious and rather factitious locale of the haunted ancestral castle at some point around the middle of the nineteenth century. Since then, they argue, horror in all its guises is now "correctly" located in the haunted psyche rather than the haunted house, which, many agree, was only ever a metaphor for the haunted psyche anyway.[18] Such assertions have become so commonplace in criticism of gothic fiction and film as to constitute an almost unquestioned

---

[17]Siddons, quoted in King, 305.

[18]See, for example, Richard Davenport-Hines, *Gothic: 400 Hundred Years of Excess, Horror, Evil and Ruin* (London: Fourth Estate, 1998), 303, 325, Tudor, 57f, Clive Bloom, *Gothic Histories: The Taste for Terror, 1764 to the Present* (London and New York: Continuum, 2010), 143.

(and unquestionable) orthodoxy.[19] However, a significant proportion of American gothic fiction and film implies otherwise—that, rather than being mere projections of and haunted by our darker memories and desires, a house harbors thoughts and wishes of its own, that have nothing to do with us as individuals, and that are often inimical to our plans—even our sanity and our very lives.

While we may like to imagine that our homes and their contents body forth and express our innermost selves, as Daniel Miller notes, "quite often we are not the agents that create the material environment that becomes the medium of representation." He adds, "The very durability and physicality of things make them liable to represent attributes which were not those than an individual desired them to convey: for example, that they are actually torn rather than whole, or not quite the same as the object they were supposed to replace."[20] People are therefore often "thwarted by the prior presence of their houses and the orders of their material culture," potentially to the point where they "come to see their lives as formed through the influence of the home itself."[21] In this way, "the objects around us can embody an agency that makes them oppressive and alienating and may in turn be projected in a personified form as the ghost that haunts us. In short, where we cannot possess we are in danger of becoming possessed."[22] Asserting that ghost stories "mythologize this problem by positing the agency as belonging to the house itself and its possessions," Miller argues that "It is, after all, the house and its possessions that are possessed; we merely observe these ghosts and poltergeists to our terror."[23] Even Sloan Wilson's *The Man in the Gray Flannel Suit* (1955), a realist novel ultimately convinced of the value and goodness of monogamous marriage, opens with a direct attack on the family home as psychic space, in a manner which posits the home as a sentient and far from benign entity. The Rath family is described as living in a

---

[19]See Fred Botting, *Gothic* (Abingdon and New York: Routledge, 1996), 19–20 for a discussion of the ubiquity of Freudian interpretative frameworks; and Robert Mighall, *A Geography of Victorian Gothic Fiction: Mapping History's Nightmares* (Oxford: Oxford University Press, 1999), for a good case against such readings. See also Allan Lloyd Smith, "Can Such Things Be?: Ambrose Bierce, the 'Dead Mother' and Other American Traumas," in *Spectral America: Phantoms and the National Imagination*, ed. Jeffrey Andrew Weinstock (Madison: University of Wisconsin Press), 57–77, for an essay that makes some effort to move away from psychosexual interpretations of supernatural texts and towards something more culturally and historically grounded, but that still relies on psychoanalytical theoretical models.
[20]Daniel Miller, "Possessions," in *Home Possessions: Material Culture Behind Closed Doors*, ed. Miller (Oxford and New York: Berg, 2001), 107–21, 120.
[21]Miller, "Behind Closed Doors," 1–19, 10. See also 111.
[22]Miller, "Possessions," 120.
[23]Ibid., 112.

"house that had a kind of evil genius for displaying proof of their weaknesses and wiping out all traces of their strengths," the interior of which is declared to be "vengeful."[24]

However, as *Burnt Offerings* implies, it is upon the stay-at-home middle-class housewife that the full force of the home's malevolence fell in twentieth-century America. The rise of suburbia and the explosion in single-family housing following the Second World War transformed the housewife, arguably even more completely than nineteenth-century ideology had, into little more than an extension of the house itself, put on display by and as a vital component of the disciplinary mechanism that it was her job to maintain. It is this social role, and the social and cultural coercion behind it, that both Marasco's and Curtis's *Burnt Offerings* dramatize in supernatural form. The vampiric Allardyce house, a vast estate, owned by an elderly brother and sister (who seem almost to worship the ramshackle old place) comes with a suspiciously diminutive price tag, and effectively seduces Marian Rolfe, an obsessive cleaner and purchaser of furniture and ornaments, from the moment she spots an advertisement for it in the newspaper. Marian persuades Ben to rent the house for the summer, and they settle in with Ben's elderly aunt (Aunt Elizabeth, played by Bette Davis in the film version) and their young son David (Lee H. Montgomery). Throwing herself into tidying and polishing the opulent but decaying mansion, Marian rapidly begins to believe that it is somehow inherently tied to her, to the point where she is convinced that, as the original book asserts, "The house was absolutely essential, a vital part of herself which she recognized immediately." Luxuriating in the opportunity it offers her both to escape from the dust and heat of their city apartment, and to show off her skill as an expert housekeeper, Marian thinks, "the house was everything she had always wanted; it was [...] a reflection of what she was or could be inside, at her best."[25]

The only "catch," as Ben repeatedly calls it, is that they must leave food three times a day outside the locked door of the siblings' ailing mother, who occasionally eats the meals but who never appears in the flesh, as it were. While her husband sees this routine as a burden, Marian, who becomes ever more impatient with her son David's untidiness and carelessness and begins to loathe Ben's increasingly ardent caresses, can find peace and solitude only in the beautifully decorated sitting room that serves as an ante-chamber to old Mrs. Allardyce's private quarters, a place she guards jealously against the intrusion of the rest of the family. Obsessed by cleanliness and

---

[24] Sloan Wilson, *The Man in the Gray Flannel Suit* (1955) (London: Penguin, 2005), 1.
[25] Robert Marasco, *Burnt Offerings* (London: Coronet, 1974), 75.

neatness in her own home, housework becomes a sort of religion for her during her stay at the Allardyces', and the more that she devotes herself to it, the lovelier the house as a whole becomes. However, Marian pours most of her energies into this forbidden section of the house, which is depicted in the film as heavily draped and cluttered with Mrs. Allardyce's "collection" of what appear to be family photographs. The window of the antechamber, which is an inaccessible haven in Marasco's book, is positioned by Curtis to look straight out on the swimming pool that effectively symbolizes the appeal of a house of this kind to the apartment-dwelling Rolfes, a luxury to which Ben's academic salary could never normally stretch. What Curtis's film makes clear is that this direct connection between Mrs. Allardyce's rooms and the pool is central to Marian's relationship with the house and with her husband and son. It is in this pool that, early on in the film, Ben first finds a pair of glasses with an ominous hole in one lens, and later, as detailed above, it is also where he is apparently overtaken by violent urges towards both David and Marian.

It is here that novel and film diverge most widely. In the third and final pool scene, David tries to impress his father with his newfound swimming skills, primarily because Ben has slipped into a kind of catatonic trance following Aunt Elizabeth's sudden death and his own repeated hallucinations of a leering, demonic hearse driver connected to his own mother's funeral. David splashes helplessly toward the deep end of the pool, with Ben watching from a deck chair but unable to intervene. Curtis's film has Marian glimpse the tableau from the window of Mrs. Allardyce's room, and she rushes to help her son, but is prevented by the doors of the house, which lock themselves against her, and she only rescues David at the last minute. In Marasco's novel, by contrast, Marian is completely helpless against the house's barriers, unable even to catch more than a brief glimpse of her son and husband dying, alerted to their deaths only by the brightening color of the walls around her. Alone and apparently accepting of her fate, and appealing to the old woman's locked door for her lingering affection for Ben and David to be "'*burn[t] out of [her]!*,'" Marasco's Marian, while horrified and numb, is far more explicitly complicit with the now-gleaming house, and never leaves it again.[26]

As this implies, the house renews itself through sacrifice—it demands Marian's work, her love, the lives of her family, and finally, it demands her very self. Curtis's *Burnt Offerings* ends as Ben, who has been woken out of his trance by the sight of Marian rescuing David, bundles the family into the car and prepare to leave. If the audience are fooled into thinking that

---

[26]Marasco, 230, italics in original.

the film will end more happily than the book, however, they are mistaken; predictably, Marian insists on going back to tell old Mrs. Allardyce that they are leaving. When there is no sign of her several minutes later, Ben goes looking for her, and (in a neat gender-reversal of the Bluebeard trope) opens the door to the forbidden chamber, only to find his wife alone in what should be Mrs. Allardyce's room, transformed into a hideous and wizened crone. Staring at her in shock, he is violently propelled out the window and through the car's windscreen below, in the film's only real moment of gore. David is then summarily dispatched by a falling bell tower[27]—presumably the last vestige of the house's old skin that it has now fully shed, sated with the blood of the Rolfe family, and with a new feminine presence ensconced at its heart—until the next hapless family stumble into the Allardyce siblings' trap. Having had even the memory of her family "burnt" out of her, Marian has, it would seem, become a housekeeper so efficient that she need only remain there to keep it vibrant and beautiful—until, that is, it has drained all the life out of her and must find another willing victim.

In this regard, the endings of both film and novel align Marian with Eleanor in *The Haunting* and Jack in Kubrick's *The Shining*. Jackson's *The Haunting of Hill House* opens with a lengthy passage describing the house, which states:

> No live organism can continue for long to exist sanely under conditions of absolute reality; even larks and katydids are supposed, by some, to dream. Hill House, not sane, stood by itself against its hills, holding darkness within; it had stood so for eighty years and might stand for eighty more. Within, walls continued upright, bricks met neatly, floors were firm, and doors were sensibly shut; silence lay steadily against the wood and stone of Hill House, and whatever walked there, walked alone.[28]

This passage is repeatedly almost unchanged at the close of the novel, implying strongly that Eleanor (the emotionally fragile protagonist who takes part in a psychic investigation and who rapidly becomes convinced that the apparently haunted Hill House desires her in some way) has in fact been cheated by the house. As she becomes increasingly obsessed by the house and begins to participate in the poltergeist activity that has made it famous, the other members of the investigation send Eleanor away for her own good, but, convinced that, by killing herself, she will join the ghosts or other entities

---

[27] I saw this film during a horror festival in Dublin, and David's death was met by cheers and applause from the otherwise unimpressed audience.
[28] Shirley Jackson, *The Haunting of Hill House* (1959) (London: Robinson, 1999), 3.

that inhabit it, she deliberately crashes her car in the driveway. We are told that "In the unending, crashing second before the car hurled into the tree she thought clearly, *Why* am I doing this? Why am I doing this? Why don't they stop me?"[29] This, combined with the repeated assertion that whatever "walks" in Hill House continues to do so "alone" following her death, would appear to indicate that her death is futile, engineered by the house's own supernatural malevolence, which first promises and then denies her a ghostly afterlife within its walls. Wise's film, by contrast, depicts Eleanor's voice, hovering spectrally over a shot of the house itself, saying "'and we who walk here, walk alone.'" The cinematic Eleanor is therefore now one of them, whoever or whatever they are: she has been correct about the house and its intentions, and will remain there, undead, forever.

Similarly, in Kubrick's film, Jack's death is followed by a shot of a group photograph (hanging on one of the hallways) of the hotel's guests in evening wear on Independence Day in 1921, who Jack now appears to have joined. His contented face beams out at us from the photograph, and it is reasonable to conclude that, like Eleanor, Jack has finally found somewhere to belong, in a timeless realm of eternal celebration within the hotel from which he will never be released—nor, it would seem, does he wish to be. *The Haunting* and *The Shining* therefore depict their protagonists as living happily ever after in the structures that have oppressed and violated them, while all the time implying that these characters were always already insane, that nothing external has harmed them. Both films initially downplay the supernatural agency of the houses in which their action takes place, only ultimately to interpose an overtly supernatural ending, in which human ghosts occupy these houses, once again obscuring the malevolent animation attributed in the original novels to the houses themselves. Even as the visual register of both films tells one story—that the house looms over everything and is the monster that we should fear—the plots tell another, situating the human subject as all that should hold our attention. To a certain extent, it is possible to attribute this alteration to the demands of cinematic medium itself, which tends to set up a figure-and-ground structure, emphasizing human emotion and action over the environment, which is reduced to mere backdrop, however evocative or detailed. Nonetheless, *Burnt Offerings* does not appear to be constrained by such limitations—indeed, as indicated above, Curtis's film depicts Marian as struggling again the house's malign influence even more than the novel does, leaving little room to doubt that the Allardyce mansion is a haunting presence that exists independently of the protagonists' mental

---

[29]Jackson, 245–6. See Lootens in Murphy for a discussion of this moment.

states. Moreover, it is far more explicit than either *The Haunting* or *The Shining* about what exactly is going on here. Rather than simply becoming a ghost, forever walking the halls of her eternal home, by the sanguinary finale, Marian has become an active and sustaining component of the very entity that recruits women to commit themselves to work at the expense of all else—the home.[30]

Demonic housework

Although, at the end of both film and book, Marian has become the supernatural being that the misty-eyed Allardyces refer to as "'our darling!,'" she is also a victim having had the life, color, and human emotion burnt out of her by a house that lures her in with its beauty and size, but that proves an exacting master. What is important to remember is that Marian's single-minded absorption in housework, which leads her to shout at and shake Davey for breaking a crystal bowl, and to remain in the house to work during Aunt Elizabeth's funeral, was experienced by countless middle-class married women in twentieth-century America. The kind of housework that Marian engages in is essentially what Kathryn Allen Rabuzzi labels "demonic," a form of unpaid labor so compulsive that "every moment of every single day is precisely accounted for." Rabuzzi continues, "Housework is certainly not done by these women because it needs doing—it is done because they feel compelled to do it."[31] As she contends, when housework takes on the characteristics of the demonic, "the performer is so submerged by her ritual tasks that she hardly continues to exist apart from her work," but is almost literally "swallow[ed] up" by it.[32] Nor was this surprising, when paid work outside the home was still largely denied to married women in 1970s' America. Confined to a relatively small canvas, many housewives sacrificed themselves almost maniacally to their work, to the point where improvements in technology actually exacerbated rather than ameliorated the tendency of ordinary housework to cross the line into demonic possession. As Betty Friedan illustrates, one survey conducted for market research during the mid-fifties

---

[30] It is worth noting that, in King's novel, Jack dies and the Overlook is destroyed precisely because he has failed in his professional duties. Charged by the manager to "dump" the pressure on the massive furnace, Jack is so hell bent on killing his family that he forgets his job, and both he and the hotel are consumed in an enormous explosion.
[31] Kathryn Allen Rabuzzi, *The Sacred and the Feminine: Towards a Theology of Housework* (New York: Seabury Press, 1982), 116.
[32] Rabuzzi, 116–17.

revealed that a certain electronic cleaning appliance—long considered one of our great labor savers—actually made "housekeeping more difficult than it need be." From the responses of eighty per cent of those housewives, it seemed that once a woman got this appliance going, she "felt compelled to do cleaning that wasn't really necessary." The electronic appliance actually dictated the extent and type of cleaning to be done.[33]

According to Margaret Horsfield and Ruth Schwartz Cowan, what was especially troubling about this situation was the extent to which middle-class women imposed grueling work routines upon themselves. Horsfield sees technological development as producing "monsters making formerly impossible standards now possible," prompting women to participate "whole-heartedly in [...] buying and using ever more mechanisms to clean our homes, little reckoning the hidden cost and the high irony involved."[34] While Curtis's *Burnt Offerings* is at a disadvantage in relation to Marasco's novel, in that the visual medium denies us direct access to Marian's thought processes, even behind Karen Black's occasionally manic glare, it is evident that the Allardyce house is the greatest opportunity for self-expression that she has been offered in many years. As Mary Douglas puts it, "Dirt offends against order. Eliminating it is not a negative movement, but a positive effort to organize the environment. [...] In chasing dirt, in papering, decorating, tidying we are [...] positively re-ordering our environment, making it conform to an idea."[35] Cleaning can therefore function as a medium of control, permitting women to carve a space for themselves out of the otherwise patriarchal home, in which they had (and often still have) little or no financial or social power. Consequently, for Rabuzzi, "the traditional housewife is not simply a victim; she is also, typically, an idol or priestess."[36] Moreover, she argues that

> The ritual enactment of housekeeping typically links its performer back in time to the company of female ancestors [...]. To do a task precisely as you observed or were taught by your mother or grandmother is to experience a portion of what they each once did [...]. The ritual enactment

---

[33]Betty Friedan, *The Feminine Mystique* (1963) (London: Penguin, 1992), 190.
[34]Margaret Horsfield, *Biting the Dust: The Joys of Housework* (New York: Picador, 1998), 139. See also Ruth Schwartz Cowan, *More Work For Mother: The Ironies of Household Technology from the Open Hearth to the Microwave* (New York: Basic, 1983), 70.
[35]Mary Douglas, *Purity and Danger: An Analysis of the Concepts of Pollution and Taboo* (London: Ark, 1996), 2.
[36]Rabuzzi, 101.

of housework thus helps provide continuity from one generation of women to another. Consequently, although housework as it is generally practiced is a solitary occupation, some sense of community is provided by the *method* of doing, when that method reflects the performance of earlier women.[37]

As both book and film make clear, Marian Rolfe's fate—becoming the "idol or priestess" at the center of the Allardyce house—is by no means unique. We are led to believe that the brother and sister who rent it to the Rolfes have done this countless times before, as testified to by the vast "collection" of photographs—featuring blankly frightened-looking people in costumes ranging from late nineteenth century to contemporary, as well as numerous scenes of the house looking clean and new—that populate the antechamber and the reception rooms. Since it is implied that the house's organizing principle ("'our mother! Our sainted darling!'" as the Allardyces call her, with infinite reverence and awe in their voices) is always female, what we can take from *Burnt Offerings* is that hundreds of housewives have, like Marian, been seduced by the house into being *both* its victim and its agent. Encouraged to take their housewifely zeal to the extreme, to the point of deliberately endangering the very people supposed most to benefit from women's unpaid work (men and children), Curtis's film, by having Marian first save her family and then defenestrate her own husband, graphically dramatizes the unreasonable demands which domestic ideology placed upon the middle-class American housewife.

While the ending may position Marian as the nexus of evil in the film, then, the bulk of the narrative implies that *neither* her apparently heartless absorption in the house *nor* Ben's intimate violence should be interpreted as the specters haunting the frame. Indeed, as the foregoing examination of housework implies, even the Allardyce house itself is not entirely to blame. Beautiful as it may be, its seductive wiles can only succeed because they are undergirded by the system of domestic ideology that not only coerces housewives into devoting all their time and energy to housework, but actively pits house against husband and child in a battle of affection, from which only the house emerges unscathed.

---

[37]Rabuzzi, 102.

9

The Bawdy Body in Two Comedy Ghost Films: *Topper* and *Beetlejuice*

Katherine A. Fowkes

Ghosts usually bring to mind dark and stormy nights, gothic horror, and spooky haunted houses. But in Hollywood cinema, ghosts are just as easily employed as full-fledged characters in dramatic or comedic genres. While there are hundreds of such films, and a great deal of variety among them (everything from the 1947 classic *The Ghost and Mrs. Muir* to more light-hearted fare like Bill Cosby's 1990 *Ghost Dad*), this essay will focus on two notable ghost comedies from different eras. While it is clear that both *Topper* (1937) and *Beetlejuice* (1988) are comedies, this pairing may at first seem strange. In addition to the differences in plot and the films' different historical and cinematic contexts, each film is also inflected by different film genres. *Topper* is considered a classic screwball comedy while Tim Burton's film riffs on the conventions of Gothic horror. Indeed, as a seminal work in Burton's oeuvre as a creative auteur, *Beetlejuice* almost belongs to its own "genre." Despite their many differences, however, several aspects link the two films. Both films employ clever but often simple visual effects related to the ghosts and/or the afterlife (although here again Burton's signature artistic design provides a uniquely stylized mise-en-scène). Both films introduce a married couple as a double-protagonist only to kill them off in car accidents near the beginning of the film. And while not conventionally considered a screwball comedy, *Beetlejuice* also features the physical slapstick humor that characterizes the genre. Perhaps most importantly, both films employ ghost characters in the service of a similar message. In both cases the ghosts bring a refreshing liberation from narrow-mindedness, stuffiness, snobbishness, and a lack of engagement with life. While it may seem ironic for dead characters to be used as a device to provoke a better appreciation of life, this function seems to be one that comedy ghosts are particularly well suited to fulfill, particularly through challenging ideas about the dignity and mastery of the human body.

From antiquity, the idea of ghosts has raised questions about physicality and the human body. In *The Haunted: A Social History of Ghosts*, Owen Davies recounts that over the centuries, alleged real-world ghost sightings in Britain have gone hand in hand with serious theological and philosophical questions about whether or not a person "lives" on in some fashion after death. Conundrums such as whether or not the spirit of a person can persist independently of the body become even more complicated when a spirit is said to conveniently "materialize" fully clothed,[1] a convention of ghost lore exploited by fictional ghosts of all kinds. In comedy ghost films, this convention facilitates stories in which ghosts can operate as full-fledged characters rather than merely spectral wraiths whose main purpose is to serve as a device to induce fear in the living characters.

In *Topper*, the Kerbys rise fully intact and clothed after crashing their car into a tree. As they sit on a nearby log, they eventually notice their dead bodies nearby and realize they've become ghosts, a limbo they blame on their failure to do any good deeds while alive. They decide that livening up their stodgy banker, Cosmo Topper (Roland Young), will qualify as the good deed that will allow them to move on (presumably to heaven). They succeed, but not before causing a great deal of humorous mischief which at first threatens to destroy Topper's marriage, but ultimately saves it. In *Beetlejuice*, the Maitlands also appear to the audience as intact, fully clothed characters that make their way back to their small-town country home after a car crash. They soon discover not only that they are ghosts, but are also unable to leave the house. When the obnoxious and pretentious Deetz family from New York City moves in, the Maitlands' purgatory becomes truly hellish. Particularly offensive to Barbara Maitland (Geena Davis) is the wife and stepmother, Delia Deetz (Catherine O'Hara), who replaces the Maitlands' antiques and old-fashioned country décor with her trendy modern furnishings. In contrast to *Topper*, the ghosts in *Beetlejuice* do not intentionally try to "liven" things up, but by the end of

---

[1] Owen Davies, *The Haunted: A Social History of Ghosts* (Houndmills, Basingstoke: Palgrave Macmillan, 2007), 19, 33–4; see also R.C. Finucane, *Ghosts: Appearances of the Dead & Cultural Transformation* (Amherst: Prometheus Books, 1996), 82, 209.

the film they have inadvertently done so through their attempts to evict the odious family from their home. In the process, they poke fun at the Deetzs' pretentious values, and ultimately create a situation where both families agree to share the house in harmony.

In *Topper*, the Kerbys' mischievous good deed fits nicely within the purview of the screwball genre, which Ed Sikov characterizes as connoting "lunacy, speed, unpredictability, unconventionality, giddiness, drunkenness, flight, and adversarial sport."[2] This perfectly describes our introduction to the Kerbys as George (Cary Grant) and Marion (Constance Bennett) speed drunkenly along in their roadster, George sitting on his seat back so he can steer with his feet. In fact, it is precisely the Kerbys' drinking and reckless disregard for appropriate speed limits that cause the crash that leads to their death. Kathrina Glitre writes that screwball comedy is characterized by "instability and inversion—a world turned upside down..."[3] In *Topper*, the values of mainstream society are inverted. Instead of celebrating respectable manners, hard work, adult responsibility, and sobriety, screwball comedies more often favor flouting the law. They celebrate light-hearted play, flirting, drinking, dancing, and silliness. This is a world where in order to enter a nightclub George and Marion are invited to swoop down a giant slide like little kids in a playground. By the end of the film, Topper has learned to be more playful and learns how to drink, dance, and enjoy life. His controlling and sexually repressed wife (Billie Burke) is initially horrified by Topper's behavior, fearing that their reputation and social status will be ruined by Topper's arrest in a drunken brawl. But the emphasis on being socially acceptable is turned on its head when, much to Mrs. Topper's surprise, her socialite acquaintances find the formerly henpecked Topper to be refreshing and exciting, thus making the Toppers the center of attention. By the end of the film, Mrs. Topper has also been transformed from a prissy snob to a more permissive and flirtatious wife, further ratifying the movie's exhortation to embrace the physical pleasures of life.

As characters in a screwball comedy, the Kerbys hardly need an excuse to act in an eccentric manner. Yet their decision to embroil Topper in their antics is solely the result of their ghostly state, and their ghostly state provides the chaos and confusion so common in screwball comedies. The beauty of film ghosts is that their manifestations and physical capabilities

---

[2]Ed Sikov, *Screwball: Hollywood's Madcap Romantic Comedies* (New York: Crown Publishers, 1989), 19.
[3]Kathrina Glitre, *Hollywood Romantic Comedy: States of the Union, 1934–1965* (Manchester: Manchester University Press, 2006), 25.

can be conveniently adapted to fit the needs of the story. So while in some movies, ghosts have no corporeal presence, in *Topper* the Kerbys are able to manipulate objects just as they had in life. And while some movie ghosts remain invisible to other characters (but often not the movie audience), the Kerbys are able to make themselves invisible or visible at will. Their motivation for becoming invisible (to both characters and audience) is that remaining visible uses up some of their limited amount of "ectoplasm" (the source of their ability to be visible). Becoming invisible also conveniently allows them to follow Topper wherever he goes without revealing their presence to others. In turn, their invisible manipulation of objects and people causes chaos and confusion for the other characters and much humor for the film viewer.

Particularly in comedies, ghosts may serve as malleable devices for creating comedic situations when living characters experience strange but usually benign disruptions to their daily routines. In such films, a character may express fear and confusion at hearing voices or witnessing the effects of an invisible presence moving a solid object. The "joke" is thus carried out at the characters' expense. Film viewers don't share in the frightened characters' reactions but instead experience the situation as humorous since the viewers are almost always in the superior position of knowing that the ghost is both "real" and that its intentions are at best well-intentioned and at worst mischievous. In ghost comedies, characters that experience anomalous phenomena often question their sanity or attribute the experience to inebriation.[4] In *Topper*, alcohol actually plays a large part in the positive transformation of Topper while also playing a part in the invisible ghosts' creation of visual humor.

In one scene, after having drunk too much champagne, the formerly dignified and teetotalling Topper is made to look ridiculous as his limp and comatose body seemingly hauls itself through the lobby of a building. Naturally, the bystanders are completely flummoxed by this odd behavior, and the illusion is quite convincing to the film audience due to Roland Young's skillful pantomime. In another scene, having beaten up an impossibly large number of bystanders with the help of the invisible Kerbys, Topper stands before the judge in a tipsy, disheveled state. Since the Kerbys are invisible, the judge and the audience see only that Topper's jacket, tie, and handkerchief somehow magically straighten themselves. His hair, too, seems to have a life of its own, as it rearranges itself without his intervention. Throughout

---

[4]Katherine A. Fowkes, *Giving Up the Ghost: Spirits, Ghosts, and Angels in Mainstream Comedy Films* (Detroit: Wayne State University Press, 1998), 98–9, 178 n.53.

the film, bystanders witness hats, pens, chairs, and a host of other objects appear to move by themselves.

The humor of these scenes taps into several theories of comedy. Much of the humor stems from the slapstick indignities wreaked upon hapless human bodies that are manipulated, and in some cases, harassed by the invisible ghosts (as are many of the unwitting bystanders throughout the film). As Andrew Stott writes, a character in a slapstick comedy "is continually prone to attack through either a bodily revolt or loss of self-control, or from an external source that aims to dismantle his dignity".[5] Throughout the film, the invisible ghosts create slapstick humor that fulfills the movie's screwball mission to dismantle traditional notions of dignity and acceptability.

Related ideas tendered by the French philosopher Henri Bergson in 1900 seem particularly apt here. One of his central ideas is that the human body becomes comical when it seems to operate mechanically rather than of its own volition.[6] This applies to the first case where Topper is so drunk that he would otherwise be unable to walk, and yet is propelled along as if some kind of crazed automaton. Similar humor can be found in other comedies that employ ghosts who interact with living characters that others can't see.[7] A reversal of this principle applies to the other examples cited above, namely that inanimate objects may appear comical if seeming to move or operate on their own. This explains why it may seem funny when the wind turns an umbrella inside out. W.H. Auden uses this example, explaining, "The operation of physical laws upon inorganic objects [is] associated with a human being in such a way that it is they who appear to be acting from personal volition and their owner who appears to be the passive thing [....]The activating agent, the wind, is invisible, so the cause of the umbrella turning inside out appears to lie in the umbrella itself. It is not particularly funny if a tile falls and makes a hole in the umbrella, because the cause is visibly natural."[8]

Another facet of humor is incongruity stemming from reversals or inversions.[9] In these examples from *Topper*, the inversion is that of a stodgy, respectable banker acting crazily and uncharacteristically being arrested in

---

[5]Andrew Stott, *Comedy: The New Critical Idiom* (New York: Routledge, 2005), 93.
[6]Henri Bergson, *Laughter—An Essay on the Meaning of the Comic* (Lexington, KY: CreateSpace Independent Publishing, 2014), 13.
[7]Fowkes, Ibid., 99.
[8]W.H. Auden, "Notes on the Comic," in *Comedy, Meaning and Form*, ed. Robert Corrigan (San Francisco, CA: Chandler Publishing, 1965), 62.
[9]Bergson, 35.

a drunken brawl. This inversion, again, is just one of many in a movie that celebrates both the process and the outcome of disrupting the life of a stuffy banker and his even more strait-laced wife.

One interesting aspect in the conversion of Topper and his wife concerns their sex life, which the ghosts help rejuvenate by the film's end. As Stott writes, "sex is probably the single most persistent theme in comedy..."[10] The movie must deal with this in a clever way due to the era's Production Code, which dictated what kind of content was appropriate for Hollywood movies. Screwball comedies such as *Topper* essentially exhibit a reaction to censorship that recalls the ghosts' mission to save Topper. That is, they use humor to cleverly promote the idea that Mrs. Topper's so-called "respectable" notions about sex are boring if not risible, and that sex and playful flirtation are thoroughly acceptable and desirable. By employing double entendres and silly slapstick antics, the film delivers what Andrew Sarris has famously described as a "sex comedy without the sex."[11]

Although Marion's invisibility might seem to challenge Hollywood's typical objectification of women, Marion's body still serves as a spectacle, objectified even as a ghost. Isn't it handy that this ghost is magically able to change into different fashionable and sexy evening dresses at whim? Marion "zips" herself into different outfits as she teases Topper and encourages him to admire her legs. In one scene, invisibility is no deterrent to our imagination as Marion's naked presence in the shower is made known only through the special effects showing various shower items moving of their own accord. In the face of the Production Code, the film seems to have profited from the interplay between invisibility and traditional spectacle (an idea reused in the 1940 film *The Invisible Woman*).[12] Does a naked woman become acceptable movie fare if you can't actually see her? Or is the spectacle merely the clever visual effects? The marketing for the film even plays on this confusion with press releases exclaiming "See an invisible beauty take a bath!"[13]

In an earlier scene, Marion makes Topper take her to a lingerie store where she invisibly tries on a pair of panties, much to the shock of the other customers and sales reps who see only a pair of panties hovering in front of a mirror. In an effort to calm things down, Topper grabs the underwear and he and Marion flee the building. Later Mrs. Topper finds the panties and is scandalized, thinking that Topper must be having an affair, but also shocked

---

[10]Stott, 15.
[11]Qtd. in Sikov, 20.
[12]Thanks to Murray Leeder for this observation.
[13]Fowkes, Ibid., 137–8.

by the very sexiness of the panties themselves. Today's viewers may have a hard time believing these are particularly revealing underwear, but a similar pair of panties causes much embarrassment to Katharine Hepburn's character when the back of her gown is torn away in the 1938 *Bringing Up Baby*, another Cary Grant screwball comedy. As with the shower scene, the panties were subject to much scrutiny by the censors.[14] Interestingly, by the end of the film, Mrs. Topper trots out the panties to prove to Topper that she has changed and is willing to wear such risqué items if it means saving their marriage.

Although many have noted that it was *Topper* that put Cary Grant on the screwball map, his role in this film tends to "vanish" a bit as Constance Bennett's character, Marion, becomes the key player in attempting to loosen Topper up by flirting with him. In the scene where Topper drinks too much champagne, Marion jumps down from her perch on a tall bookcase. Although Topper gamely tries to catch her, they end up on the floor with Marion astride Topper. George is not amused, but it is yet another slapstick gambit that permits the inkling of a sexual interaction in the face of censorship. As the film progresses, Marion pursues Topper and George pursues Marion, finding her and Topper at an inn where the two are drinking and dancing together. He expresses his jealousy but Marion insists she is succeeding in their good deed. They make up by the end of the film but the specter of infidelity has at least been raised. By broaching the issue of infidelity and then reconciling both couples, the film treads the line of Production Code respectability, but ultimately suggests that marriage need not be the prison Topper had experienced at the beginning of the movie.

Throughout *Topper*, the body becomes the locus of change for the characters. In death, the "disembodied" Kerbys still manage to function as living bodies as they revive Topper's spirits and marriage, thus redeeming their own hedonistic ways and presumably allowing them to move on to heaven. Throughout the movie, the body is celebrated through drinking, where the spirits of alcohol combine with the Kerbys' ghostly spirits to create a more relaxed and yet more "spirited" Topper. Much is made of Topper allowing himself to dance despite Mrs. Topper's presumed disapproval. Even physical fighting contributes to Topper's blossoming since it coincides with a more feisty and less milk-toast version of manhood. And of course, the movie repeatedly validates Toppers' sexual renaissance by celebrating Marion and Topper's flirtation, Topper's dancing, Marion's invisible shower and the ubiquitous pair of sexy panties. The portrayal of sexuality may be

---

[14] Billy Rose Theater Collection, The New York Public Library at Lincoln Center, New York.

circumscribed by the dictates of the Production Code, but it nevertheless remains key to the ghosts' good deed.

Beetlejuice also features dancing, sexual innuendo, visual humor, and slapstick violence as the Maitlands attempt to expel the Deetz couple and their morose teenage daughter, Lydia (Winona Ryder), from their beloved house. Far from being reckless hedonists who have never done a good deed, the Maitlands are nothing if not wholesome. Adam Maitland (Alec Baldwin) is so sweet and kind that he lovingly preserves the life of a spider at the film's opening (the spider is one of the movie's first clever references to the horror genre when what at first appears to be an enormous spider crawling over a roof is soon revealed to be an ordinary garden spider crawling on a house in the model town being built by the Maitlands). In another attempt to save an animal, this time a dog, the Maitlands swerve and end up plunging their sensible car off a bridge (compare to the Kerbys' souped-up roadster which Topper ends up buying as one of his first acts of marital rebellion). It is thus their goodness that causes the Maitlands' death, and makes even more inexplicable their purgatorial imprisonment as ghosts (more on this later).

Unlike the Kerbys, the Maitlands' flirtatious teasing at the beginning of the movie is less sexual than it is playful, indicative of a happy couple who enjoys life despite their obvious chagrin at being childless. Their wholesomeness is reflected in their attire, particularly Barbara Maitland's old-fashioned looking country dress. And, unlike the Kerbys, the Maitland's never change outfits because it is unnecessary for the story: These outfits already perfectly serve as the visual opposites to the chic, urban attire of the Deetzs and their friends. Barbara's pale, flowery dress also contrasts nicely with Lydia's black goth attire (in some scenes complete with a funereal-looking veil). In addition, the Maitlands' wide-eyed and fresh-faced appearances contrast markedly with the title character, Beetlejuice (Michael Keaton), a decrepit and lewd trickster whom the Maitlands eventually summon to help them "exorcise" the Deetzs from the house. His stringy strands of hair, ghostly (ghastly) white face and the dark circles around his eyes announce his similarity to a corpse while his striped outfit recalls a prison inmate and perhaps the costume of a carnival barker. His suit thus alludes to two aspects of his character—one, to the fact that he had once been a manager-type in the afterlife, before his rogue behavior caused him to be banished (to return only upon being summoned by name three times). He is thus literally imprisoned and ends up being dug up by the Maitlands from their model town cemetery. The carnival allusion recalls his role as a trickster, a type of character who causes humorous mischief and often represents an inversion of values characterized by traditional medieval carnivals, where social roles are temporarily reversed.[15] As I have argued elsewhere, the film as a whole also uses its vision of the afterlife to poke holes in a number of generic conventions, turning upside down a number of cultural stereotypes and conventions of horror movies.[16]

Like the Kerbys, the Maitlands can manipulate objects, but unlike the Kerbys they cannot become invisible or invisible at will. Instead, their dilemma is that no one can see or hear them so that when they attempt to haunt their own house to expel the Deetzs their plan fails miserably. While the Kerbys are not restricted to one location, the Maitlands (despite their ineptitude at haunting) nevertheless fulfill the stereotype of haunted house ghosts. This is ironic because the beginning of the movie shows them staying at home for their vacation to continue with the loving restoration of their house and their ongoing hobby of building the model replica of their town. Alive, they had their chance to be free, but dead they are now prisoners in the house that they once loved. In fact, they are doubly imprisoned because in attempting to avoid the toxic Deetz family, they find themselves hiding in the attic with their model town. Perhaps they were doomed from the start since from the beginning their white country house displays distinctly Gothic features (picture *Psycho*'s (1960) Gothic mansion, but painted a cheery white).

While most of the humor in *Topper* is the result of the Kerbys' success at haunting, a good portion of the humor in *Beetlejuice* is the result of the Maitland's *failure* to successfully haunt. Difficulty in communicating with the living is a common problem for comedic and dramatic ghosts such as found in *Ghost* (1990), *Always* (1986), and *Truly, Madly, Deeply* (1991), to name just a few examples. In these movies a ghost character attempts unsuccessfully to give a message to a loved one to help the loved one move on with life.[17] But in *Beetlejuice*, the desire to "communicate" is not to deliver a message or help a living character but merely to hew to the horrific ghost's mission to be scary. Their ineptitude creates an inversion of horror conventions, reminiscent of an inversion found in *The Wizard of Oz* (1939) when Dorothy meets a supposedly ferocious lion who turns out to be just a pussycat.

---

[15]Mikhail Bakhtin, *The Dialogic Imagination*, Trans. Helen Iswolsky (Bloomington: Indiana University Press, 1984), Katherine A. Fowkes, "Tim Burton and the Creative Trickster: A Case of Study of Three Films," in *The Works of Tim Burton: Margins to Mainstream*, ed. Jeffrey Andrew Weinstock (New York: Palgrave Macmillan, 2013).
[16]Fowkes, Ibid.
[17]Fowkes, 1998, Katherine A. Fowkes, *The Fantasy Film* (Oxford: Wiley-Blackwell, 2009), 81–91.

As in many ghost movies, it is a matter of narrative convenience that the ghosts in *Beetlejuice* are able to manipulate objects (a tool to eject a "skeleton" key from the attic door, a piece of chalk, etc.) and yet fail to do this in front of the Deetzs who would surely be frightened, as in *Topper*, by objects that move by an unseen hand. The Maitlands receive little hope from a book they find entitled, *The Handbook for the Recently Deceased* which claims that the living usually won't see the dead. When Adam asks Barbara, "can't or won't?" she replies that it just says "won't," a clue to the fact that here, as in many ghost films, some characters may possess the ability or the willingness to perceive ghosts and others may not. In *Ghost*, for example, it is the reluctant medium Oda Mae, while in other films it may be a child who is either more sensitive than adults (as in *The Sixth Sense* (1999)) or who is still young enough to be open to unusual phenomenon. Likewise in *Beetlejuice*, it is the child, Lydia, who discovers the ghosts' presence. While outwardly cynical, Lydia possesses enough childlike imagination to be open to the unexpected—in contrast to her father and stepmother who epitomize narrow-mindedness. Nevertheless, Lydia is still disappointed to find that the ghosts fail to meet her expectations, being not at all scary but in fact pleasant and friendly.

After having followed instructions in the handbook to draw a chalk door on the wall to seek assistance in the afterlife, the Maitlands encounter a dingy waiting room inhabited by a host of mutilated characters waiting to see equally grotesque social workers. Bergson describes life as constant change and writes that while change is serious, rigidness conversely invites humor.[18] So perhaps it is unsurprising that in this afterlife the dead bodies "incorporate" their last moments in changeless form. That is, each of the character's bodies in the afterlife exhibits plainly, but humorously, the cause of death.[19] For example, a woman in circus attire is shown literally sawn in half with both halves waiting separately on a couch, and nearby an impossibly charred corpse bides his time by chain smoking. This portrayal of the afterlife riffs on ghost lore and ghost stories where headless ghosts or other wounded spirits haunt perhaps to avenge their murder, to expose the murderer, to make known an injustice or to conclude some other unfinished business after an untimely demise. It is also a joke about the idea that the afterlife might be subject to certain bureaucratic rules, seen in movies such as *Defending Your Life* (1991), *Here Comes Mr. Jordan* (1941), and its remake *Heaven Can Wait* (1977) not to mention the military afterlives portrayed in

---

[18]Bergson, 33–4.
[19]Finucane traces this idea back to antiquity (16).

A Matter of Life and Death (1946) and *A Guy Named Joe* (1943). Furthermore, it is a joke about mindless bureaucracy in general: For an appointment with a case worker, dead people have to take a number as if waiting in line at a bakery but in this case the numbers climb into the billions. In another reflection of mindless bureaucracy, neither the Maitlands nor the audience ever learn why they have been imprisoned in their house for 125 years even though (unlike the Kerbys) they seem likely to have done some good deeds. The movie also never explains why the drowned Kerbys don't stay waterlogged for the rest of the film, but again, this is most likely another example of how malleable film ghosts are in suiting the needs of the narrative or even the logistics of filming—having two actors remain soaked in each scene would be quite annoying for everyone involved! Since part of the point of the film is to violate conventions and mindless adherence to norms, the humorous portrayal of an afterlife that perpetuates blind obedience to rules fits nicely with the movie's overall theme. And the vision of the afterlife as a mindless bureaucracy recalls the type of humor Bergson describes regarding human bodies as automatons (see below) in that it shows the entire universe operating like a giant mindless machine.[20]

Beetlejuice thus relies on a number of the same types of comic maneuvers as *Topper*, namely inversion and the conflation of the body with mechanical movement. Other instances of incongruity stemming from inversion include the fact that the ghosts try to "exorcise" the living rather than the reverse. And not only are the Maitlands seriously inept at being scary, the living in this film are ultimately more ghoulish than the dead. The living are likewise, metaphorically less "alive" than the ghosts. Lydia, while imaginative enough to perceive ghosts, sulks and pouts her way through the first half of the movie, her make-up induced paleness and dark-circled eyes recalling Beetlejuice and corpses (as well as the bereaved). She even expresses her desire to be dead at one point, although the Maitlands disabuse her of suicide as a solution to her supposed boring life. Lydia's stepmother, Delia, is reminiscent of Mrs. Topper in that she is obsessed with status instead of enjoying her life. The hideous sculptures she creates are less a creative outlet than they are a point of vanity in styling herself a talented artist. And although Charles Deetz (Jeffrey Jones) expresses the desire to relax and enjoy the country, several scenes show him incapable of doing so. In one scene, he sits tensely in a chair, his leg twitching nervously as he proclaims stiffly, "Ten minutes! I'm already perfectly at ease! It's perfect!" Instead of

---

[20]Bergson, 38.

relaxing and enjoying the serenity of the countryside, he is soon scheming to buy up the little town to capitalize on its rustic appeal (and later in the film puts together a plan to exploit the Maitlands as a tourist attraction). The film doesn't just invert ideas about the living and the dead; it also breaks down the binary altogether in creating a "spectral spectrum" of the "truly alive" (Lydia at the end of the film), the metaphorical dead (the Deetzs), the ghostly dead (the Maitlands), and Beetlejuice who seems to be more a reanimated corpse than a ghost.[21]

Another type of humor discussed by Bergson concerns incongruity and "jokes" arising from situations in which two interpretations of events are simultaneously possible such as occurs linguistically with puns and double entendres. An example of humor arising from two overlapping interpretations occurs when Delia Deetz and her pretentious interior decorator, Otho (Glenn Shadix), first explore the Maitlands' country home, making a tour of each room. When they open a bedroom closet we see Barbara hanging gruesomely by a noose as she reaches up and pulls her face off. The camera cuts to Delia and Otho's shocked reactions. But a second later, they whisk Barbara easily aside as if she's just a dress on a hanger as Otho complains: "We just have to *pray* that the other closets are bigger than this one!" The joke relies on two frames of reference, the first being the viewer's knowledge that Barbara is expecting shock and fear, and the second being Delia and Otho's investigation of what to them is a house that needs to be thoroughly remodelled. For one moment these two scenarios overlap when the viewer may at first believe their shock and horror is due to encountering a corpse, only to learn that they have looked right past Barbara to the inadequacy of the closet. The doubled interpretation also applies to the "hanging" corpse which doubles as something mundane "hanging" in a closet.

Having failed to make their presence known, the Maitlands consult their caseworker, Juno, who exhorts them to avoid Beetlejuice at all costs and instead to try harder to improve their haunting techniques. At this point, the ghosts realize they must conform to the expectations that people have about ghosts, a point Davies makes in discussing how ghost hoaxes in the real world have often operated: Recreate the stereotypical aspects that people are expecting or the hoax may fail.[22] One of these stereotypes concerns white sheets, which probably derives from an old ritual of wrapping dead bodies in white. Occasionally at night, people wearing white might even be mistaken for ghosts.[23] However, as a widespread believe in this convention

---

[21] Fowkes, 2013, 235–44.
[22] Davies, 165–74.
[23] Ibid., 20.

faded over time, it eventually became just a cliché of Halloween costumes. As Davies observes, these days no one could hope to create a successful ghost hoax this way. Indeed, Davies traces the demise of the horrific white-sheeted ghost to silent slapstick films, several of which used the device for comic purposes. While he cites Harold Lloyd as well as Laurel and Hardy movies (including a sight gag in which a character's hair stands on end, as in *Topper*), he gives much credit to Hal Roach's studio that (surprise!) went on to produce *Topper* in the sound era.[24] (Interestingly enough, it was in part the new cinematic techniques needed to create synchronous sound that permitted some of the effects used in *Topper*, just as the synchronous sound encouraged screwball comedy's snappy dialogue.)[25] When the Maitlands disguise themselves in Delia's designer sheets, complete with holes for eyes, it's not surprising that Lydia thinks the ghosts are living people dressed up as ghosts. It is not until she takes several pictures of them that she notices that they have no feet in the photos, evoking another ghost-stereotype that ghosts slowly and effortlessly glide instead of walk.[26] And in another joke that relies on two competing frames of reference, Lydia at first only hears the Maitlands' poorly executed ghost-moaning from another room and mistakenly believes it to be her father and stepmother having sex.

As in *Topper*, a preoccupation with money and status is repeatedly mocked, eventually to be replaced by an appreciation of life, epitomized by the joyful music and dancing at the end of the film, accompanied by a final inversion when the "haunted" house becomes the home for the unusual family configuration of the living *and* the dead. But this turn of events hinges in part upon overcoming the havoc wreaked by Beetlejuice when the Maitlands desperately call on him for help. Where in *Topper*, flirtatious sexuality is celebrated, here it is shifted to Beetlejuice and sublimated in the Maitlands who can't seem to have children, as well as with the Deetzs when Delia is shown sleeping alone with "Prince Valium," as Lydia puts it.

Beetlejuice's decrepit body and his lewd and frequently gross behavior (eating flies, grabbing his crotch) recall a meeting point between horror and comedy but one that allows a further distinction between the different attitudes displayed by the two. As described by Julia Kristeva, bodily fluids, such as blood and pus, excrement, etc., are seen as disgusting and "other" from the rest of the body. They are experienced as something to be rejected,

---

[24]Ibid., 214.
[25]Fowkes, 1998, 137, John Brosnan, *The Story of Special Effects in Cinema* (New York: New American Library, 1974), 44.
[26]Davies, 18.

what Kristeva, Barbara Creed, and others call the "abject."[27] While horror films capitalize on the abject as horrific and disgusting (corpses, blood, etc.), many ghost comedies simply avoid it precisely by creating disembodied specters who, like the ghosts in *Topper*, bear no marks of the violence that killed them: "...the abject qualities associated with the bodily corpse are glossed over and replaced by an idealized version of the body, one physically resembling the living body representing the non-material 'spirit' of the individual."[28] But the abject can also invite humor in the right context for the precise reason that the physical body can serve as an antidote to the pretensions of superiority. Drawing on Bakhtin's analysis of carnival, Stott writes:

> By foregrounding the functions of what Bakhtin calls the "lower bodily stratum," the genitals, the anus, urine, excrement, and excrescences, and invoking the abject body as a risible concept to be laughed at rather than feared, its power of horror may be lifted and our fear of decay and degeneration alleviated. But the comedy of abjection is also a confirmation of the frail foundations of civility...[29]

Thus, the biggest difference in the treatment of the body between *Topper* and *Beetlejuice* is that the former celebrates the "life" that animates and gives joy to the body (and here we might note a play on Bergson's use of the French term "esprit" meaning "wit" and "esprit" meaning "spirit"), and *Beetlejuice*'s acknowledgment of the baseness of the body and the tenuousness of the superficial niceties designed to ignore this fact.

Beetlejuice is in a state of perpetual hyperactivity, and much of his humorous banter consists of his manic parodies of popular culture, including bad T.V. ads and carnival barkers. He also physically sprouts carnival-themed appendages near the end of the film. At one point he parodies a pretentious professional who becomes increasingly outraged when challenged to explain his credentials as an exorcist: "Well...I attended Julliard...I'm a graduate of the Harvard Business School. I travel extensively. I lived through the Black Plague and had a pretty good time during that. I've seen *The Exorcist* about a hundred and sixty-seven times, and it keeps getting funnier every single time I see it!" That Beetlejuice finds *The Exorcist* (1973) funny is meant to be another humorous inversion in the movie, and yet it alludes

---

[27] Julia Kristeva, *The Kristeva Reader*, ed. Toril Moi (New York: Columbia University Press, 1986), Barbara Creed, "Horror and The Monstrous Feminine: An Imaginary Abjection," *Screen* 27 (1986), 44–70.
[28] Fowkes, 1998, 58–9.
[29] Stott, 87.

once more to the sometimes very fine line between horror and comedy described so well by William Paul in his book *Laughing Screaming*. Paul extensively examines both "gross-out" comedies and "gross-out" horror films, noting that while the animal nature of the human body can lead to horrific scenes of graphic gore, it can also be used for humor—reminding us again that despite our pretensions, we are simply animals and not immune to the unsavory aspects of our bodily functions. Paul writes of a Western hierarchy that privileges the spiritual over the physical, a tendency that certain comedies capitalize on through their gross-out humor (what he calls "Animal Humour").[30] But Paul also discusses *The Exorcist* in detail, examining the graphic scenes where the possessed child, Regan, vomits, urinates on the floor, and violently thrusts a crucifix into her crotch. Most viewers found these scenes to be horrifying (in part because of the religious frame of the story), and yet a certain percentage of the audience found them to be laughable, either due to a defensive disavowal of the graphic images or perhaps because the scenes were so over the top that they became a squeamishly laughable spectacle. We may thus enjoy the "bawdy" body in a comedy *but* we may also enjoy the spectacle of the "bestial" body even *as* it horrifies (otherwise why would people go to horror movies for entertainment?). In reference to Regan's failure to control her bodily fluids, Paul writes, "There is a kind of defiant pleasure in regression, in wallowing in dirt as a way of rejecting social constraints. We take a fierce pride in our body's ability to produce disgusting emissions, finding pleasure in them precisely because they are disgusting."[31] This seems to describe both Beetlejuice as a character, as well as our enjoyment of his repeated transgressions of social niceties, even at the expense of the Maitlands. And the dichotomies of both comedy/horror and the spiritual/physical are nicely captured in movies where ghost characters have the capacity to conflate these categories, something Tim Burton movies excel at as they celebrate ghosts and skeletons and other traditionally macabre elements in the context of comedy.

Shortly after referring to *The Exorcist* as a comedy, Beetlejuice's head suddenly and repeatedly spins around three hundred and sixty degrees, recalling an infamous scene in that film where Regan's head turns fully around. But whereas in *The Exorcist* the movement is slow, uncanny, and accompanied by scary growls and sound effects, here the movement is sped

---

[30]William Paul, *Laughing Screaming: Modern Hollywood Horror and Comedy* (New York: Columbia University Press, 1994), 292–4.
[31]Ibid., 314.

up to resemble something mechanical or motorized. Here again, we see how Bergson's theory of the mechanical "encrusted" in the body creates humor. The Maitlands appear horrified but Beetlejuice simply quips, "Don't you hate it when that happens?" The line is funny because it takes what is normally impossible and horrific and makes it seem both commonplace and trivial, likening the event to some slightly embarrassing mishap to be ruefully laughed at later—as if having one's head spin clear around was equivalent to having spinach in one's teeth. His lecherous advances toward Barbara are humorous in part because they're relatively benign (his later intentions toward Lydia notwithstanding). They're also outlandish, striking a contrast with Barbara's calm wholesomeness. At one point he grabs her roughly and plants a big smacker on her lips, reminiscent of Bugs Bunny planting a wet one on Elmer Fudd. He "gooses" her in more ways than one, but his behavior is more like a third grader than an adult and so we can laugh at the Maitlands' outrage. At one point he "cheekily" attempts to get a look under Barbara's dress by lifting the hem with a stick when her back is turned. But it is precisely his outlandish behavior that causes the Maitlands to put Beetlejuice back in the model town (by saying his name again three times) and strive to do a better job at haunting.

The Maitlands thus take a cue from Beetlejuice's arsenal of tricks and finally succeed in making the Deetzs acknowledge their presence by harnessing their powers over the bodies and voices of the Deetzs and their snotty dinner guests. As we watch both Delia and Charles attempt to impress their guests and deflect attention from Lydia's embarrassing remarks about ghosts, the group suddenly finds themselves lip-synching and dancing to the strains of Harry Belafonte. By this time, the Maitlands have made friends with Lydia who is thus spared the indignity. Not only does this scene show the Maitlands to be successful in using their ghostly powers, it is also the first time in the movie that Lydia laughs, making the moment a major turning point in the film. Once again, there is humor to be found as bodies seem to move mechanically against their will. An incongruous inversion also occurs as the sophisticated, wine-sipping group are deprived of their dignified masquerade and are made to wag their rear ends at each other. At the end of their dance, what looks like shrimp on the table turns into giant hands that unceremoniously grab their faces, sucking them down into their dinner plates. The scene is an interesting contrast to the dancing in *Topper*, which is evidence of Topper's learning to enjoy life. Here, while the dancing represents the same thing—shaking the stuffiness out of the Deetzs and their guests—it is also done at their expense. As Bergson explains, human freedom and mastery are the stuff of serious drama. "What, then, is requisite to transform all this into a comedy? Merely to fancy that our seeming freedom conceals the strings of a dancing-Jack, and that we are, as the poet says...humble marionettes..."[32] By the end of the film, however, Lydia has been effectively adopted by the Maitlands and as a reward for earning an "A" on an exam, requests that the Maitlands cause her to dance in just such a way. Thus by the end of the movie, Lydia has embraced the mechanical-in-the-body humor while combining it with the idea of physical movement and music as a celebration of life.

In conclusion, both *Beetlejuice* and *Topper* use the device of ghostly bodies to celebrate and promote an appreciation of physical, earthly joy. While in *Topper*, the sexual body is central to the plot, in *Beetlejuice*, the title character's bawdy humor is still a celebration of the body despite the Maitlands' repulsion precisely because it provides humor for the viewer. It is funny for the same reason that it is funny in *Topper* when the ghosts use their powers to "goose" the other characters (which George Kerby literally does to an unsuspecting woman near the end of the film). That is, an emphasis on the human body—even in its ghostly state—can potentially provoke either horror or humor, but in these films our animal nature is a reminder that we are alive...if only we can remember to enjoy it.

---

[32]Bergson, 30.

PART THREE

Millennial Ghosts

10

"I See Dead People": Visualizing Ghosts in the American Horror Film before the Arrival of CGI

Steffen Hantke

Introduction: Seeing is believing

One of the lasting contributions of M. Night Shyamalan's *The Sixth Sense* (1999) to the American horror film is its popular catchphrase "I see dead people." (Figure 10.1). As cinematic genres go, the horror film has produced the occasional catchphrase, especially in its rare yet memorable incarnations as a blockbuster—one might think of William Friedkin's *The Exorcist* (1973) with its rich trove of demonic bon mots. But the device of the catchphrase belongs to the big, loud, spectacular action films that have become the bread and butter of the U.S. film industry and that dominate the global summer box office regardless of local and national cinematic traditions and commercial practices. The smaller, nastier, bleaker films that make up the hard core of horror usually get by without a catchphrase. This is especially true for one subgenre of horror, the ghost film, which tends to gravitate toward the quieter, less exuberant, and less emphatically self-referential side of the horror film genre. Exception to this rule may be horror comedies like *Ghostbusters* (1984) or *The Frighteners* (1996), but then they tend to owe their cinematic life more to the blockbuster and the action film than the horror genre. If the catchphrase in *The Sixth Sense* merits critical attention, it is because the film, remarkably enough, is both a creepy, quiet, intimate little horror film *and* a smashing blockbuster success. How special effects in *The Sixth Sense* contributed to the film's odd intermediary position will be one of the points of the discussion to come.

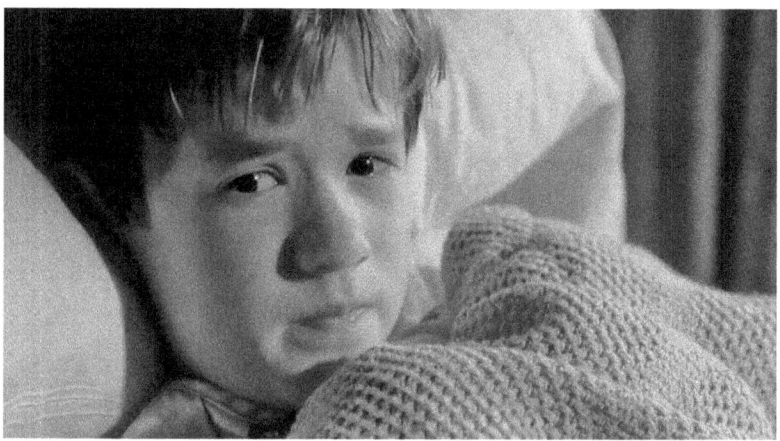

FIGURE 10.1 The Sixth Sense *(1999, M. Night Shyamalan, Hollywood Pictures)*.

More important than Shyamalan's commercial success, however, is the catchphrase's articulation of a key issue of the horror genre at large—the varying degrees to which the monster becomes visible in the course of a film. This specific film, as we all know, plays ingenious games with this issue, letting us see "dead people" early on and all the time, and yet reserving the recognition of this diegetic fact to the very end as its spectacular final plot twist. While the issue of "seeing dead people"—that is, the visual staging of monstrosity in all its shapes and forms—in virtually all horror films is tied to matters of production and technology (i.e., the relative sophistication of prosthetic and makeup effects) and aesthetic preference and generic typology (i.e., the privileging of films that "leave something to the imagination" over films that "show everything"), it is one of the accomplishments of *The Sixth Sense* that it finds a new and surprising way of linking the issue of visibility to the cognitive dimension inherent in all ghost films: how do we know whether we have actually seen a ghost? Critical discussions of the film have interrogated this dynamic as to its thematic and affective dimension. Aviva Briefel, for example, recognizes *The Sixth Sense* as a prime example of a cluster of films about "spectral incognizance." The catchphrase, according to Briefel, provides the key to an interpretive process which "force(s) us to reconsider our role as spectators at the moment in which (the film links) the protagonist's cognition to his or her death."[1] While the moment of cognitive breakthrough in *The Sixth Sense* happens to be constructed so as to "reassur(e) viewers of their safety,"[2] the link between cognitive certainty and visibility is less interesting (after all, everybody knows that "seeing is believing") than the one between the cinematic apparatus and the text it produces on the one hand, and the spectral presence of the ghost as a potent signifier of death on the other.

This link between the cinematic apparatus and death goes back to cinema's constitutive technology, photography. In his musings on photography, Roland Barthes has drawn attention to the fact that, on the one hand, the "photograph is literally an emanation of the referent. From a real body, which was there, proceed radiations which ultimately touch me, who am here";[3] it captures "the *necessarily* real thing which has been placed before the lens, without which there would be no photograph."[4] On the other hand, Barthes links this materiality of the photographic image to death; from the immobilization of the subject in the frame to its visual imprint after the subject's demise, death permeates the technology ("that rather terrible thing which is there in every photograph: the return of the dead").[5] Critics discussing especially cinema during the silent era have made that connection as well. In her discussion of F.W. Murnau's *Nosferatu* (1922), Stacey Abbott extends Barthes's ideas into the realm of the cinematic, noting that, not by coincidence, cinema evolved simultaneously with late nineteenth-century and post–World War I spiritualism, and out of technologies like magic lantern shows and various forms of the phantasmagoria, all of which explored the uncanny possibilities of the emergent medium in regard to spectral presences constructed exactly around the nexus of visibility, death, and the cinematic (or pre-cinematic) apparatus.[6] Given the fact that this thematic nexus plays a significant role in all horror films, but that it is thematically constituent in horror films about ghosts, the question whether we actually "*see* dead people" or not

---

[1] Aviva Briefel, "What Some Ghosts Don't Know: Spectral Incognizance and the Horror Film," *Narrative* 17.1 (January 2009), 98.
[2] Ibid., 95.
[3] Roland Barthes, *Camera Lucida: Reflections on Photography*, Trans. Richard Howard (New York: Farrar, Straus & Giroux, 1981), 80.
[4] Ibid., 76.
[5] Ibid., 9.
[6] Stacey Abbott, "Spectral Vampires: *Nosferatu* in the Light of New Technologies," in *Horror Film: Creating and Marketing Fear*, ed. Steffen Hantke (Jackson: University Press of Mississippi, 2004), 3–20.

suggests a link between ghosts as aesthetically framed and technologically produced cinematic phenomena that is worth exploring.[7]

The scopophilic demand in horror films for the audience to see the monster, addressed extensively in critical discussion, is thus the demand in the ghost film to see the ghost's unique feature, spectrality—the ghost's impossible ontological liminality—visually arrested, fixed, and represented in a stable cinematic image. This image may come with connotations of "otherworldliness," but as a cinematic signifier it is very much present.[8] The following discussion of ghosts in the horror film will examine this image—the ghost's visual presence in the cinematic text—first in its classic manifestations, throughout the 1940s and 1950s, and then in light of the transition of Hollywood filmmaking from the classic to the post-classic period, especially in regard to so-called neo-horror emerging in the late 1960s and early 1970s. It will finally move to the 1990s and early 2000s, which marked the most crucial technological transition within this entire historical time span—that from the analog photographic to the digital manipulation of the cinematic image, or, in other words, the arrival of computer-generated imagery (closing with a brief outlook to the prodigious output that continues to the present day).

Rather than opening the door to an examination of the prodigious and creatively diverse outpouring of cinematic production initiated by computer-generated imagery (CGI) after the start of the new millennium the final section of this discussion will focus on the ten-year period starting in the mid-1990s and thus on the historical arrival of digitalization and the impact it had on the ghost film as it faced the challenge of continuing, modifying, or challenging stylistic conventions (particularly in regard to computer-generated effects like morphing) it had inherited from its immediate predecessors. The historical arc drawn in the discussion, which begins with a fully developed technical and stylistic inventory of techniques for representing ghosts in classic Hollywood filmmaking, terminates with the first uses of CGI as a genuinely new technical device introduced, for better or worse, into a relatively steady

---

[7] The emphasis in this discussion on the visual as the privileged sensual path to cognition is not to omit the importance of sound in the representation of the ghost. From the ominous knocking sounds produced in the middle of the nineteenth century by Leah, Margaret, and Kate Fox in evidence of ghostly manifestations in their residence, to the elaborate sound effects accompanying the appearance of the ghost in horror films, the issue deserves critical attention far beyond the scope of this essay.

[8] The term "otherworldliness," used by Christopher Frayling in his commentary on Jack Clayton's *The Innocents*, serves as an umbrella term for various manifestation of mixed, dual, or ambiguous ontologies that define the ghost. See Christopher Frayling, Commentary Track, *The Innocents*, Fox Searchlight (DVD 2005).

VISUALIZING GHOSTS IN THE AMERICAN HORROR FILM BEFORE CGI

and familiar stylistic framework. The guiding questions throughout are: how do American films make us "see dead people," and how do the cultural and technological tools that create the cinematic ghost determine what this ghost will look like?

Spectral presences in negative spaces: Classic Hollywood ghosts

In a key scene in Alfred Hitchcock's *Rebecca* (1940), Maxim de Winter (Laurence Olivier) describes to his nameless second wife (Joan Fontaine) the circumstances surrounding the death of his first wife, the eponymous Rebecca. The conversation takes place in a boathouse, which provides the scene of a crime that ends with Rebecca's accidental death (presumably), a death that has provided the narrative and atmospheric foundation of the continued spectral presence of Rebecca on the Manderley estate and in the lives of those who knew her. The scene in question serves as a flashback, albeit a flashback without some of the stylistic markers that conventionally announce a transition from the diegetic present to the past (such as haze or wave effects or musical cues). As Maxim's voice describes the fight between himself and Rebecca—a diegetic narration coming from outside the frame—Hitchcock's camera travels to the details and locations mentioned in what serves as a voice-over. Prompted by the line, "She was lying on the divan...," a brief cut to Fontaine's face precedes a cut to that exact piece of furniture, complete with a full ashtray and an indentation suggestive of a body in repose. As the narration continues, the camera follows Rebecca's imaginary rise from the divan by panning up. While Maxim recounts their conversation, the camera slowly pans to the left, finally bringing him back into the frame as his story has reached the point where he recalls Rebecca standing face to face with him. Sometime during the sequence, the camera's point of view has dissociated itself from Fontaine's perspective as a listener, just as it has not yet re-attached itself back to Olivier as a narrator. Though the spaces it has traversed are empty, the scene conjures up Rebecca, presumed to be dead, as a spectral presence in the room interposed between the two characters.

Hitchcock's strategy of marking the presence of the ghost—or the character endowed with sufficient ontological ambiguity to function at least temporarily as a ghost—by emphasizing the empty space it occupies reverberates through other films, some from the period, others far beyond its reach. Otto Preminger's *Laura* (1944), another film about a woman presumed to be dead

(Gene Tierney), features scenes that show the detective investigating her disappearance and presumed murder, Mark McPherson (Dana Andrews), in the woman's apartment. As his gaze attempts to reconstruct the assumed murder and its victim, Preminger's camera travels around the space emphasizing its emptiness, as if to trace the imprint the absent body has left on the objective world left in its wake.

The lasting impact of Hitchcock's device can be felt in horror films long after the classic Hollywood period. In a brief montage sequence at the very end of *Halloween* (1978), John Carpenter revisits several of locations in which key scenes of the film have just taken place. With a nod to Yasujirō Ozu's signature montages, these locations are now shown to be empty, depopulated, and innocuous; they barely show traces of the horrific events inscribed upon them. Though the emphasis on embodied physical violence moves this particular film far out of the reach of the ghost film, it is exactly this sequence that endows the character of Michael Myers, the film's central monster, with qualities associated with the ghost. The suggestion of a spectral presence—not hidden, as he would have been in his bodily incarnation as Michael Myers, but spectrally present in his incarnation as "The Shape" (the name under which the character appears in the film's closing credits)—is achieved by emphasis on a narratively inscribed empty space fully visible within the frame.[9]

Visualizing the spectral presence of the ghost by registering its negative imprint on the space surrounding it is, of course, the strategy that explains why so many horror films about ghosts are really films about the space they haunt. In fact, combing through the history of ghosts in horror films, one might find more films about haunted houses—from *The Haunting* (1963) and *The Legend of Hell House* (1973) to *The Shining* (1980) and the two adaptations of Susan Hill's *The Woman in Black* (1989/2012)—than about ghosts themselves. Hitchcock's *Rebecca* is at least as much, if not more, the story of Manderley than of Rebecca. It has been commonplace to refer to the house in these films as a character in its own rights, and yet as a tool in the service of visualizing the spectral presence of the ghost, the haunted house serves as a precisely circumscribed, idiosyncratically inscribed negative space akin to the one Hitchcock's

---

[9]In an extended discussion of the "Michael (Myers)-as-ghost subtext" of *Halloween*, Murray Leeder not only comments on the final sequence of tableau shots (in which Michael "is nowhere to be seen, but his presence in felt in all things"), but also points to various other moments in the film when Carpenter's camera construes Michael's presence in Haddonfield in reference to empty or negative spaces (from the displaced tombstone to the blackness in shadows from which his figure is expected to emerge). See Murray Leeder, *Halloween* (Leighton Buzzard: Auteur, 2014), 53.

camera is outlining inside the (albeit less personal and randomly chosen) secondary space of the boathouse in *Rebecca*.

Robert Wise's *The Haunting* constructs Hill House through a variety of devices as an overdetermined space: extreme high and low angle shots, discontinuous editing, extreme wide angle lenses creating visual distortion, and cluttered deep focus shots in which characters are either dwarfed by the surrounding space or stand out against it in uncomfortable proximity to the camera. Each elaborate mise-en-scène in the film allows for the enactment of agency without a visible agent: the source of the booming sound that wakes up the members of the temporary household remains concealed behind a closed door; objects that move or appear to move enter the frame without a cut or reframing move by the camera bringing their causing agent into visibility. Effect without cause is suggested by keeping the agent outside of the frame. As the invisibility of that agent suggests the absence of agency altogether, the house itself appears uncannily animated as it registers the imprint of unseen forces (Figure 10.2).

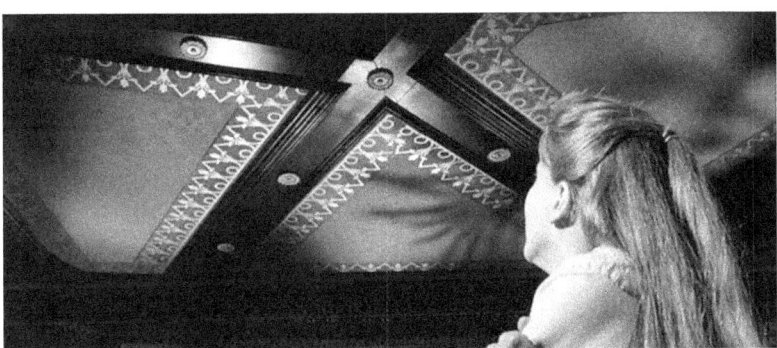

FIGURE 10.2 The Haunting *(1963, Robert Wise, Argyle Enterprises)*.

Again, as in the case of the montage sequence at the end of Carpenter's *Halloween*, post-classical Hollywood will take its cue from these conventional visual strategies. In a famous scene in *The Shining*, Kubrick has his camera in an elevated position above and in front of Danny Torrance (Danny Lloyd), who is playing on the floor of a long hallway in the haunted Overlook Hotel. The camera moves out in a backward tracking shot, opening up the frame to include a wider field of vision, when a ball rolls vertically into the frame and comes to rest right in front of Danny. With a hard cut, Kubrick then moves the camera behind Danny, placing him in the center of the shot as the camera looks down that same hallway in a deep focus shot, revealing that it is completely empty. As Danny gets up and starts moving in the direction from which the ball came, the film cuts back to a reverse angle shot twice and then begins a backward tracking shot with Danny in the center of the frame. The sequence ends with a forward tracking shot from Danny's point of view scanning the hallway in its spectacular emptiness before turning right toward the open door to the infamous Room 237 (more about what happens in that room later).

Whenever the classic ghost film does not have the camera look at an empty space or visualize agency without a visible agent to suggest spectral presence, it tends to project the ghost into an empty space constructed by way of editing. Jack Clayton's *The Innocents* (1961), for example, pursues this space as a matter of ontological uncertainty as the narrative wavers between the point of view of its central character, Miss Giddens (Deborah Kerr), and a more objective perspective. In one scene, Giddens spots the ghost of Quint at the top of a tower during her walk through the surrounding gardens. As she squints into the sun, a haze effect is carried over from the point-of-view shot to the reverse-angle shot that shows her shielding her eyes. When Clayton cuts back to her point of view—this only after some time has passed while she has walked up to the building—the figure is gone, vanished in the interval between the two structurally aligned, yet temporally separated point of view shots. "Usually, when the apparitions appear," John Tibbetts concludes about Clayton's visual strategies, "they are presented either from her foreground point of view in a deep-focus two-shot or via the simple means of eyeline cutting. Either way, the viewer participates in her point of view. When the camera shifts to a more omniscient angle, however, the phantoms vanish."[10] In order to sustain the cognitive destabilization of the viewer, however, Clayton introduces "significant variations in this schema," at times suggesting the objective presence of the ghosts (as, for example, in a scene in which "Quint appears at the window *behind* Giddens") against the dominant strategies insinuating that Giddens, emotionally overwrought, is an unreliable observer.

The fact that an individual film does not have to limit itself to a single representational method is also borne out by Lewis Allen's *The Uninvited* (1944), a film that deploys the visual strategy perhaps associated the most with ghost films from the classic Hollywood period—the double exposure.

---

[10] John C. Tibbetts, "The Old Dark House: The Architecture of Ambiguity in *The Turn of the Screw* and *The Innocents*," in *British Horror Cinema*, eds. Steve Chibnall and Julian Petley (London: Routledge, 2002), 112.

In the course of the story about a cliff-side mansion haunted by two female ghosts, Allen largely follows Hitchcock's lead, having his camera roam the inside of the mansion attached to a particular character in search of the origins of mysterious sounds or unexplained physical phenomena. A large upstairs studio room is of special significance in bearing the imprint of the spectral presences, and yet it is not in that room but on the staircase leading up to it where the film, in the final dramatic climax, has the spectral presences manifest themselves in a double exposure. The image announces itself with a cloudy, flowing movement of a shawl blown around by a wind that is clearly not part of the diegetic space. From this flowing movement the ghostly figure of one of the two dead women haunting the house emerges. The image itself is held in a medium long shot so as to accommodate both the figure and the surrounding space; given the lack of ambient movement, it is possible that the moving figure is even superimposed upon a still image of the staircase. Unlike similar scenes in *The Innocents*, however, the empirical veracity of the apparition is not in question. Two objective observers are included in the scene, just as the film's narrative logic insists that the visual manifestation of the ghost is a logical culmination of a process that escalates from inexplicable sounds to minor physical effects. Seeing the dead woman's body is the final logical step in a process from which incredulity, at this late point in the story, has already been eliminated.

The unifying aesthetic concept that emerges from all these examples of films from the classic Hollywood period also happens to correspond loosely to Kristeva's concept of the abject—that is, that it "disturbs identity, system, order"; that it "does not respect borders, positions, rules"; that it favors "the in-between, the ambiguous, the composite";[11] and that, in fact, this categorical unruliness is far more significant than the "dichotomous categories of Pure and Impure, Prohibition and Sin, Morality and Immorality" associated with abjection.[12] Following Kristeva's definition, ghosts are visually constructed as occupying a space that exists in the gaps between the increments, fragments, or partial components of the cinematic text—gaps which, owing to cinema's illusion of the moving image in a field of visual plenitude, are rarely acknowledged by the medium's audience. One might think of these abject gaps and ruptures in the seemingly smooth cinematic text as, in their more radical manifestations, a negative or a non-space, or, in

---

[11] Julia Kristeva, *Powers of Horror: An Essay on Abjection*, Trans. Leon S. Roudiez (New York: Columbia University Press, 1982), 4.
[12] Ibid., 16.

its more moderate manifestations, as a liminal space.[13] In some instances, the cinematic ghost exists in the interval of the cut between two takes; it exists in the interval between two structurally aligned yet temporally separated point-of-view shots; it exists in the interval between the space recorded in the present and the events projected upon it in the past (by voice-over or narrative extrapolation); it exists in the space between the two recorded images of the double exposure (either temporally, as one image is projected onto an already existent one, suggesting a temporal order; or spatially, as two images occupy the same position within the frame, rendering both sufficiently transparent to register the simultaneous presence of one and the other).

While some cinematic ghosts during the classical Hollywood period show signs of bodily decay, and thus manifest abjection specifically as a visual marker of the corpse—and thus meet Kristeva's more directly applicable conditions of abject materiality—the pale face, the shadowy rings under the eyes, the spidery hair, and all the other subtle and not-so-subtle signs that ghosts are "dead people" are not the primary markers of where spectral abjection resides. While horror film monsters predicated conceptually on physical materiality would manifest the abject primarily as something performed in front of the camera's lens and captured by the photographic image, the spectral presence of the ghost relocates this site of abjection from something existing prior to, or separate from, the cinematic apparatus to the site of the cinematic apparatus itself. While the zombie and, to a slightly lesser extent, the grossly physical vampires of recent years haunt the world in front of the camera, the world recorded by the machinery of cinema, the ghost in classic Hollywood filmmaking haunts the camera, that very machine, itself.

Nonetheless it is important to remember that all "(c)inematic representation depends on our acceptance of absence"; that is to say, the "play of presence and absence is central to the movies" in the sense that "presence and absence in the realm of representation" regulate the audience's completion of the fragmentary information provided by the cinematic image.[14] While conventions of narrative continuity, especially

---

[13] "It is curious that Lacanian film theory should have supposed that we 'misrecognize' the image as a plenitude when the film image since Griffith has been something we are to accept as a fragment (...) Presence is not an illusion in the movies, nor absence a fact: presence and absence are conventions of cinematic representation." See Gilberto Perez, *The Material Ghost: Films and their Medium* (Baltimore: Johns Hopkins University Press, 2000), 25–6.

[14] Perez, 25. Expanding his discussion of photography to the moving image, Barthes comes to the same conclusion: "cinema, whose raw material is photographic," produces an incomplete text in the sense that "the photograph, taken in flux, is impelled, ceaselessly drawn toward other views ..." See Barthes, 89.

within the classic Hollywood style, rely on the suppression of the awareness that the photographic image is by its very nature incomplete, fragmentary, and in need of supplementation before it is able properly to signify—that is, that it would have to undergo technological manipulation in order to become a cinematic image (the best example of that would be the dominance of continuity editing obscuring the editing process rather than drawing attention to it)—the visual conventions of the ghost film tend to desublimate this repression of spectatorial self-awareness by emphasizing exactly those gaps in the cinematic text that the classic Hollywood style is working so hard to conceal.[15]

Two qualifying remarks are necessary at this point. While the stylistic conventions of classic ghost films relegate the ghost to the negative spaces within the cinematic text, and while this spatial and conceptual assignment works to render the cinematic apparatus itself abject, this process of signification does express unease with the technology of cinema but is qualitatively different from films that posit the ghostly hauntings of media technology as an explicit theme. As affectively impressive as films like *Poltergeist* (1982) or *Ghostwatch* (1992) may be in depicting the medium of television as haunted or uncanny (Manning's film actually is a made-for TV movie, masquerading as a news program, while Hooper indicts the rival medium from the lofty heights of cinema), the question whether their visual style corroborates this explicit thematic agenda is an entirely different one. In some films, theme and style may work in unison, but as these cases differ from one specific case to the next, it would be an overgeneralization to assume that every film about spectral media makes its point visually by projecting abjection onto the cinematic apparatus itself.

It is also important to note here that the liminal space occupied by the ghost may overlap with the horror film's traditional reluctance to reveal the monster in its full abject glory, and its tendency—as a matter of dramaturgy or one of non-narrative spectacle—to delay, obstruct, and impede this visual revelation as long as possible. Clearly, the fact that *The Uninvited*, having run through a variety of visual strategies only to resort to double-exposure in its final dramatic scene, is saving the best for last in what the audience is likely to experience as a visual, and thus dramatic, escalation. Nonetheless, the ghost that becomes visible in that final double-exposure scene is not revealed in a grand climax of abjection to be in a state of repulsive decomposition; its

---

[15]The reference to the classic Hollywood style depends on the standard definition of characteristic features formulated by David Bordwell, Janet Staiger, and Kristin Thompson, *The Classic Hollywood Cinema: Film Style & Mode of Production to 1960* (London: Routledge, 1985).

abjection resides elsewhere. While narrative conventions in a film like *The Uninvited* still work toward preserving the smooth surface of the cinematic text, the stylistic conventions employed for the visual manifestation of the ghost work against these efforts. The final outcome of these two counterforces may not be a spectator fully conscious of the ruptures in the cinematic text and thus able to articulate the experience and integrate it into the overall aesthetic experience of the film. More likely, the play of two opposing forces produces an experience in which the spectator, compelled by narrative conventions, would experience the visual manifestation of the ghost as something intrinsically cinematic.

Full frontal: From neo-horror to CGI

Before computer-generated effects made their impact broadly felt during the 1990s, post-classical horror films underwent a period of stylistic experimentation encouraged by the loosening of visual restraints on the horror film. As so-called neo-horror upped the ante on graphic abjection, it is hardly surprising that films about ghosts were never a significant part of this new wave. To find a neo-horror ghost film, one must turn to a director removed from canonical neo-horror auteurs. Though it is difficult to reduce the creative diversity of neo-horror to a few stylistic devices, an auteurist filmmaker like Stanley Kubrick, who took on the ghost story with *The Shining*, would work deliberately against the stylistic conventions of the classic Hollywood period—precisely because of their historical obsolescence, their gradual hardening into clichés without the power to surprise, delight, and terrify a savvy horror audience. Kubrick retrieves the ghosts haunting the Overlook Hotel in *The Shining* from the negative spaces assigned to them by the conventional stylistic devices of classic Hollywood filmmaking, and places them squarely in front of the camera. Though point-of-view shots still align the appearance of the Grady twins with Danny's subjective perception, or that of the dead woman in the bath tub of Room 237 to that of Jack Torrance, Kubrick's reverse angle shot tends to linger on the monstrous figure with calm detachment. Coupled with camera positions that vary between medium close-ups and medium long shots, the gaze remains steady as the Grady twins simply walk out of the game room rather than vanish into the dead space between two successive shots or between the two simultaneous shots of a double exposure. Similarly, the dead woman in Room 237 remains steadily framed dead center, no matter how often Kubrick cuts back and forth between her and Jack Torrance's reaction shot. Like the Torrances, who may or may not be imagining these ghostly apparitions, the ghosts within the Overlook Hotel occupy positive cinematic space, fully visible and endowed with emphatic materiality.

As either an exacerbating factor or as an inevitable conceptual side effect of Kubrick's departure from the classic visual conventions, *The Shining* not only moves its ghosts from negative into positive cinematic space; it also imagines their spectral bodies—now visually accessible to unprecedented degrees—as bearing the marks of corporeal abjection. Wendy Torrance is greeted by a man in a tuxedo sporting a gruesome open head wound (Figure 10.3). The woman in Room 237 is gradually revealed to be in a state of advanced decomposition when Jack Torrance embraces her, evoking the dread of close proximity to the abject body Kristeva associates with the corpse. In a hallucinatory moment following their first encounter in the film, Danny Torrance sees the Grady twins as dismembered corpses surrounded by pools of blood. Again, their visual presence, though interrupted by reverse-angle reaction shots of Danny's horrified face, is very much located in each shot of the sequence rather than shifted into the interstitial spaces opened up by the montage.

FIGURE 10.3 The Shining *(1980, Stanley Kubrick, Warner Bros)*.

Though Kubrick's auteurist excursion into the horror film, and, specifically, into the ghost story, is hardly representative of the transformation of the genre at large, it aligns itself with the move by neo-horror away from more spiritual conceptions of horror and toward body horror. When directors like David

Cronenberg, George Romero, and Wes Craven—aided by an increasingly visible cadre of special effects experts like Tom Savini, Stan Winston, or Chris Walas, each of whom, in turn, being elevated to start status within his own rights—moved the horror film toward body horror, the ghost became a marginal figure. None of the landmark horror films of 1970s and 1980s neo-horror deal with ghosts, and among the few notable exceptions, a film like *The Shining* follows the general trend by breaking with classic conventions in favor of corporeal abjection as well.[16]

When ghosts do finally return to the horror film—with a cycle of films that, having been initiated by the massive box office success of *The Sixth Sense*, includes *Stir of Echoes* (1999), *What Lies Beneath* (2000), and *The Others* (2001)—the technical sophistication, the broadly creative and specifically visual possibilities, and the increasingly affordable availability of computer-generated effects seem to have been one of the engines driving the return of the ghost as a viable horror film trope. While many of the first reviewers responding to the films in this cycle comment on what they perceive to be their old-fashioned quality, a stately pace and quaintness deriving perhaps from the absence of graphic gore typical of much horror film in the previous decade, it is worthwhile examining some of their visual strategies, aided by CGI as a technology unavailable to previous decades of filmmaking.[17]

In a key scene in Zemeckis's *What Lies Beneath*, which is particularly revealing as to the use of CGI, the character of Claire Spencer (Michelle Pfeiffer) awaits her husband Norman (Harrison Ford) at home. What he does not (yet) know, and the audience is led to suspect, is that Claire's body has been taken over by the ghost of a young woman, Madison Elizabeth Frank (Amber Valetta), murdered by Norman Spencer. As Claire sits astride

---

[16] A similar movement also occurs during the 1980s when, inspired in part by the cyperpunk movement in science fiction, and in part by domestic and imported splatter films, the splatterpunk movement within horror fiction shifts horror away from its more spiritual dimensions and settles is squarely within the realm of the abject body. Even the 1970s and 1980s cycle of vampire films, following the spectacular success of Anne Rice's *Interview with the Vampire* (1976), redefines the vampire no longer primarily as a spiritual menace and more as a figure of embodied sexuality.

[17] In his review of *What Lies Beneath*, Elvis Mitchell praises Robert Zemeckis as being "accomplished at good old-fashioned unclean fun" (*New York Times*, July 21, 2000), citing the film's stately pace as a characteristic feature. A.O. Scott, reviewing *The Others*, sounds the same note: "There is something refreshing about seeing a young filmmaker (Mr. Amenabar is 29) embrace old-fashioned conceits with such sincerity and care" (*New York Times*, August 10, 2001). See Elvis Mitchell, Review of *What Lies Beneath*. *New York Times*, July 21, 2000, http://www.nytimes.com/movie/review?res=9506E1DE163AF932A15754C0A9669C8B63 (accessed on February 17, 2015), A.O. Scott, Review of *The Others*. *New York Times*, August 10, 2001, http://www.nytimes.com/movie/review?res=9C0DE7DF153FF933A2575BC0A9679C8B63 (accessed on February 17, 2015).

Norman in a sexually suggestive pose, the camera frames Pfeiffer's upper body and head in a low-angle shot, lit with a soft key light from the left, in an approximation of an over-the shoulder shot from Norman's perspective. At the cue of the scene's punch line "I think she is beginning to suspect something," spoken by Pfeiffer, prompting Ford to ask, "Who?" Pfeiffer leans down to reply, "Your wife." The downward movement is accompanied by a digital morph of Pfeiffer's face into that of actress Amber Valetta. While the forward movement brings the face of first Pfeiffer, then Valetta closer to the camera, and thus into full visibility, it accompanies but also distracts from the sequential progress of the morphing. Pfeiffer's sharply outlined, somewhat bony face begins to elongate, especially around the chin; her thin lips begin to round out, and her eyes move out. The transformation takes place in a single take of around two or three seconds, before Zemeckis cuts to Ford's face for a reaction shot, and then breaks off the scene with a number of fast cuts in the course of which Norman throws off Claire who, landing on the floor next to him, is now played unambiguously by Pfeiffer again as she turns toward the camera.[18]

Though the abrupt ending of the morphing sequence still follows the classic convention, at least to the degree that it conceals the reverse transformation in which Amber Valetta/Madison Frank turns back into Michelle Pfeiffer/Claire Spencer, the moment that announces the film's originality and stylistic novelty is still the single continuous take that shows the initial facial transformation in close-up. The fact that the scene became iconic after being used as the final punch line in the film's trailer (not to mention being parodied by one of the films in the *Scary Movie* franchise) with exactly that morphing shot as the trailer's final image suggests its central importance to the film's overall visual aesthetic (and, by extension, perhaps to the horror film in its first significant responses to CGI).

The shot combines two stylistic elements, each of which deserves a closer look. First, the shot plants the facial transformation squarely into the positive cinematic space, insisting on Barthes's dictum about the "thereness" of the photographic subject. Though its duration is rather limited, the display of the digital transformation of one face into another is deliberate and conspicuous, and thus construed to be spectacular. Second, the rapid editing that marks the end of the morphing sequence *signals*, but

---

[18]The use of CGI for morphing sequences came into circulation with the 1991 music video for Michael Jackson's "Black or White." The video features a sequence, much admired at the time, in which one face in full-frontal close-up morphs into another, again and again. The same year also saw the release of James Cameron's *Terminator 2*, a landmark in the application of the technology to feature film.

does not actually *perform*, a return to the older visual style and its attempt to relocate the visual manifestation of the ghost into negative cinematic space. The frenzy of the physical action of Norman throwing Claire off translated into a similarly frenzied, though brief, succession of shots, acts, upon casual viewing, as a signal that something more visually arresting might be happening outside the frame, in between cuts, or in the inaccessible space within the frame created by Pfeiffer's face being turned away from the camera. Within the narrative progression of the scene, however, this impression is misleading. Though Madison turns back into Claire, the transformation would merely be a reverse version of the earlier morph, and thus, in its repetitiveness, redundant (both as a narrative element, and as visual spectacle). The second time around, we would neither need to see it to believe it, nor would it be as exciting as the first time. The frenzied conclusion of the morphing scene thus evokes negative space but does not actually assign the ghost to it. As a visual gesture, its function is to connect the technological novelty of the morphing scene to the tradition of visual representation of spectral presence. Reviewers who experienced the film as old-fashioned and traditional may have picked up on exactly those gestures that run throughout the film. Stylistically speaking, *What Lies Beneath* is oddly in tune with classic Hollywood, and oddly out of tune with its immediate predecessor, neo-horror.

If a horror film from around the turn of the millennium is consciously placing itself in the history of visual style marked by classic Hollywood conventions, it is likely that it is also conscious of post-classic but pre-CGI neo-horror films. If this is the case, then the one element conspicuously absent from the morphing sequence is that of the abject body. Unlike the dead lady in the bath tub of Room 237 in *The Shining*, the ghost of dead Madison Frank is not only ravishingly beautiful but, more importantly, physically intact. If corporeal abjection is conspicuously absent from this representation of the ghost, *What Lies Beneath* ends with a scene that provides it as the film's spectacular climax. This is an action sequence in which Claire fights off her husband Norman as both struggle inside a car that has gone over the railings of a bridge and is sinking into a lake. As the ghost of Madison Frank intervenes in the struggle, helping Claire to escape and trapping Norman, her murderer, inside the submerged vehicle, she is visualized entirely as a computer-generated entity, complete with skeletal fingers and arms, tattered bluish flesh dissolving in strips from all over her frame, and wispy hair waving in the current. As she floats away from the camera, her mission accomplished, Zemeckis uses CGI to have her morph back into a digital simulacra of Amber Valetta, the abject body replaced by an intact, albeit fully digital, one. While this morphing sequence is more conspicuously artificial than the earlier one—and thus occurs in exactly the reverse direction than the earlier sequence, that is, as the body moves away from the camera, from a medium close-up to a medium long shot—it does begin with the digital representation of corporeal abjection in alarming proximity to the spectator's point of view.

While the morphing sequences in films like *What Lies Beneath* improve upon older techniques used to achieve similar visual effects—from time-lapse photography to well-timed series of overlapping dissolves—they create the impression of a smooth cinematic surface, without the fissures of earlier technologies that draw attention to the negative spaces that "lie beneath" this surface (or above, besides, and around the cinematic frame). To the degree that the digital morphing is convincing—that is, the degree to which it creates a smooth textual surface and seamless continuity the audience is willing to accept—the spectral really does move out of the negative and into the positive cinematic space. Textual elements that suggest, mimic, or signal toward the older conventions may serve as reminders of a long visual tradition, but they hardly perform the cultural labor of classic Hollywood films. As CGI enters the picture, the function of these stylistic markers has changed as they become dissociated from the abject. In the best case scenario, they signal historical continuity as a homage to earlier forms of filmmaking; they become, in short, meta-textual signifiers. In the worst case scenario, their function is purely ornamental; stripped of an essential signifying function, they are reduced to a stylistic affectation, a mere mannerism or stylistic atavism as the genre is driven by new technologies toward new forms of expression. If the reviewers of these films who found them oddly "old-fashioned" had focused on their meta-textual dimension, they may have appreciated them more for adding an awareness of the subgenre's historical development to the ghost film that had not been part of its thematic inventory. Which is not to say that, barring this meta-textual dimension, the reviewers are off target with their critique that, on a level more directly and affectively accessible to the audience, the films fail to create images that are as genuinely new as the digital technology they have at their disposal.

The digital ghost: Some thoughts on coming attractions

In a film like *What Lies Beneath*, the addition of graphic displays of corporeal abjection (achieved either with the help of traditional means like makeup and prosthetics, or, yet again, CGI) further emphasizes this attempt at relocating the ghost from the cinematic machinery itself to the empirical world surrounding this machinery. It is hardly a stretch to read the next cycle of horror films in which ghosts inhabit contemporary technology—from the haunted television sets, cell phones, and Internet sites that cropped up all over the so-called J-horror cycle in which the American horror film appropriated tropes of Japanese cinema by way of "Americanized" remakes (e.g., *The Ring* (2002), *Pulse* (2006), and *One Missed Call* (2008))—as attempts to the same end.[19] Many of these films readily acknowledge contemporary technologies as abject and thus deny them the corporate and heavily commodified technophilic promise of bodily transcendence. But as they indict the digital for being implicated in a regime of mortality, the cinematic apparatus generating these images—which is, of course, increasingly enthralled by the digital—seems oddly exempt from this take on technology. In an odd act of disavowal, cinema in the age of the digital either considers itself a technology so outdated and irrelevant that it is hardly worth the critical effort; or, more likely, it fails to recognize the distinction between analog and digital because the interpenetration of both categories is so pervasive that the boundary is, for all practical intents and purposes, already largely irrelevant. In their failure to interrogate the cinematic apparatus, most J-horror films are more like Tobe Hooper's *Poltergeist*, ranting against television from the vantage point of cinema—that is, construing their own media delivery system as superior to the one they are criticizing—than Lesley Manning's *Ghostwatch*, which implicates itself as a made-for-TV movie masquerading as a news report in the critique of the medium it delivers.[20]

Where this argument is difficult to sustain, however, is in its assumption that, starting around 2000 and increasing gradually toward the present moment, computer-generated effects and the digital in general do in fact succeed in creating a smooth textual surface. But does CGI really come without the

---

[19]While J-horror may provide a general example of how Hollywood appropriates other national cinematic traditions, the cycle's ability to reveal how divergent styles—especially in regard to the visualization of cinematic ghosts—enter American filmmaking is limited by the fact that digital media made themselves felt globally at about the same time. A brief cycle of American horror films during the first half of the 1990s (including Rachel Talalay's *Ghost in the Machine* (1993) Brett Leonard's *Virtuosity* (1995), and John Flynn's *Brainscan* (1996) prefigure the arrival of the digital ghost in J-horror. For a full discussion, see Steffen Hantke, "Network Anxiety: Prefiguring Digital Anxieties in the American Horror Film," in *Digital Nightmares: Wired Ghosts, CCTV Horror and the Found Footage Phenomenon*, eds. Linnie Blake and Xavier Aldana Reyes (to be completed, London: I.B. Tauris 2014).

[20]For further reading on *Ghostwatch*, see Murray Leeder, "*Ghostwatch* and the Haunting of Media," *Horror Studies* 4.2 (2013), 173–86.

interstitial spaces in which cinematic ghosts perform the cultural labor of producing abjection? How smooth is that textual surface really? As much as CGI may have changed the relationship between the cinematic apparatus and the ghost as a marker of abjection, one might speculate whether films like *Paranormal Activity* (2007) and the cycle of digital found-footage horror films that came after strive toward the recognition that even CGI ultimately fails at closing the rifts and fissures in the surface of the cinematic text. Its failure is marked, most obviously, by the fundamental fact that CGI, like all techniques available to classic Hollywood films, "requires much of the labour and cost of making popular live-action films to be dedicated to postproduction rather than production, with principal shooting often constituting only a small percentage of a project's time and budget."[21] As smooth as the textual surface produced by CGI may appear, and as compelling as its predisposition toward positive space may thus appear, it still implies the negative space between production and post-production, between the photographic image and its subsequent manipulation (regardless whether this manipulation happens to be analog or digital).

The most recent cycle of horror films, all of which announce explicitly, even emphatically, that they are shot not with the usual analog but with digital equipment finally seem to make the thematic transition at which J-horror failed, suggesting that their own digital technology may, in fact, provide a space for abjection. In contrast to the analog technology of celluloid emblematic of cinema, these films are shot with web cams, surveillance cameras, and cellphone cameras, each producing images of, at best, mediocre quality. Superficially, these imperfect images ask audiences to read them as markers of documentary veracity, immediacy, and authenticity. At the same time, though, the digital medium also produces a text rife with the rifts, fissures, and ruptures that open the way to negative space. Though close readings of films as varied as *The Last Exorcism* (2010) or *V/H/S* (2012) might discover a broad range of specific techniques, the visual tradition of classic Hollywood filmmaking, which used to locate the ghost in negative cinematic space, appears to perpetuate itself with these films, more so than in the preceding cycle. While there is no question that, after neo-horror had largely abandoned the ghost, CGI helped to revitalize it as a viable monster for the horror film, it may have taken at least one cinematic cycle for the genre to adapt the new technology to its long-standing association with abjection. While "old-fashioned" films like *What Lies Beneath* and *The Others* are still

---

[21] Kristen Whissel, *Spectacular Digital Effects: CGI and Contemporary Cinema* (Durham, NC: Duke University Press, 2014), 3.

being produced (e.g., *The Awakening* (2011) and *The Woman in Black* (2012)), and while the J-horror model seems to have lost most of its momentum but continues to produce the occasional late manifestation, it is the found-footage film with its total digitalization of the image that promises to return the ghost as a marker of abjection to the space where it all began, deep in the heart of the cinematic apparatus.

11

Spectral Remainders and Transcultural Hauntings: (Re)iterations of the *Onryō* in Japanese Horror Cinema

Jay McRoy

Introduction

Over the last two decades, a specter has been haunting the production of horror cinema around the globe. That specter is the figure of the *onryō*, or the avenging spirit of Japanese folklore. A paranormal, primarily female, entity most frequently depicted through distinct visual markers like funereal white attire, long black hair, and pallid, staring visages, the *onryō* has been a recognizable figure since their codification during Kabuki performances of the Edo period. The *onryō* is far from the only *Yūrei*, or ghostly creature, to occupy many of Japanese cinema's darker works; it is, however, one of the most prevalent. At once mimetic and ambiguous, the *onryō* is a hybrid being that emerges in the interstitial space between the world of the living and the "realm of the dead." It has also undergone a host of subtle and flagrant transformations within the Japanese popular imaginary over the last sixty years, a period of intense cultural and sociopolitical reconfiguration. This chapter explores the visual representation and narratological alteration of these ethereal figures as indicative of a nexus of hauntings that has transformed, and continues to transform, the horror genre in Japanese cinema. Specifically, this essay moves from a careful consideration of the *onryō* in classic films like

Kenji Mizoguchi's Kaidan, *Ugetsu* (1953) and Kineto Shindo's *Kuroneko* (1968), works that variably merge the *onryō* with a myriad of spectral manifestations (like the *oni* [demon] and *bakeneko* [ghost-cat]), to an extended exploration of the radically reimagined *onryō* that most contemporary film viewers have come to associate with works like Hideo Nakata's *Ringu* films (1998–2005) and Takashi Shimizu's *Ju-on* cycle (2000–2006).

"The art of ghosts": The Kaidan, the *onryō*, and Japanese cinema

In Ken McMullen's 1983 film *Ghost Dance*, Jacques Derrida, the legendary literary and cultural theorist, states that "cinema is the art of ghosts, a battle of phantoms." Since its advent in the last decade of the nineteenth century, motion picture art has emerged as the most conspicuous aesthetic medium through which the past continues to cast its shadows in the flickering light of now. Across an increasingly vast array of screens, spectacles staged for the camera's lens play out again and again for new eyes. The absent remains present, and the spirit (*Zeitgeist*) of times gone by communicates its ineffable meanings to viewers who in turn project their own unique perspectives on the projections transpiring before them. The film casts its hallucinatory spell through the optical illusion known as "persistence of vision,"[1] the process by which our brains allow us to perceive series of still images as uninterrupted actions unfolding in time.

In Japan, cinema has been working its uncanny "magic" on audiences for over a century, but supernatural narratives in the forms of folktales and dramas have possessed audience's imaginations for far longer. Informed by Shinto beliefs that the spirits of the dead imbue all of nature with benevolent and malicious energies, as well as Buddhist conceptions of an afterlife in which agitated souls seeking peace wander between the realm of the living and the world of the dead, narratives about angry ghosts and haunted environments have been fixtures of Japanese popular culture since at least the Heian era (794–1185), but reached their most extensive popularity during the Edo Period (1603–1886) in the form of Kaidan (supernatural tales). Comprised of an amalgam of religious beliefs and antiquated superstitions, Kaidan were integrated into Nōh, Bunraku, and *Kabuki* theatrical traditions. Passed

---

[1] Frank Eugene Beaver, *Dictionary of Film Terms: An Aesthetic Companion to Film Art* (New York: Peter Lang, 2007), 189.

down from generation to generation, Kaidan proved extremely popular as entertainments and—with the Meiji Restoration, a political shift that marked the return of imperial rule to Japan in 1868—as a cultural export that inevitably nourished Orientalist imaginings of east Asian cultures throughout the United States and Europe.

Given the popularity of Kaidan in the form of folktales, theatrical productions, and celebrated collections of short stories, it may come as no surprise that filmmakers soon embraced these oft-told tales as raw material for contemporary cinematic works designed to chill audiences and, more often than not, convey ideas that may have been more difficult to articulate through less overtly fantastical genres. As this chapter illustrates, ghosts both operate within, and exceed, the boundaries imposed by conventional narrative diegesis. They are literary and cinematic conceits that, as metaphorical constructions, function as "social figure[s]."[2] In this sense, the process of haunting is more than merely a plot device. The spectral entities that trouble the living in works of Japanese horror cinema are often rife with profound psychological, philosophical, and political implications. As Avery Gordon note, "[t]o study social life, one must confront the ghostly aspects of it."[3] One must, in other words, acknowledge the variably abstracted historical revenants that, like repressed collective memory, perpetually return to trouble the living. The ghosts in these films provide more than a means to unsettle audiences or frighten them out of their comfort zones. They offer an avenue through which spectators may confront larger cultural and historical traumas that, by virtue of their "representational (im)possibilities," inform contemporary ideologies.

Arguably the most popular and frightening supernatural figure in Japanese popular culture is the *onryō*, or "avenging spirit." These "wronged," primarily female, entities that return to exact their wrath upon those living beings that have harmed them, *onryō* can be traced back to at least the eighth century. Almost exclusively the result of distressing/"unnatural" circumstances, their deaths, either by their own hands or at the hands of patriarchal violence, typically follow a prolonged period of abuse or neglect. These traumatic fates frequently bind the *onryō* to the physical location where their lives came to an end, and although the majority of narratives featuring these paranormal figures depict them directing their attacks (be they physical or psychological) against those most immediately responsible for their rage, *onryō* have

---

[2]Avery F. Gordon, *Ghostly Matters: Haunting and the Sociological Imagination* (Minneapolis: University of Minnesota Press, 1997), 7.
[3]Ibid., 7.

also been represented as capable of summoning extreme environmental phenomena, from lightning strikes to earthquakes. "Drawn from the Kaidan...but melded with both the demonic woman of Nōh theatrical tradition (such as *kyojo-mono* and *shuven-mono*) and the kabuki theatre," the *onryō* is, as Linnie Blake notes, both "abject" and "hybrid."[4] Many tales containing *onryō* thus posit these entities as simultaneously sympathetic, in that their physical suffering and untimely deaths evoke our pity, and frightening, in that their ghostly forms (most frequently draped in funereal white and sporting long black hair), coupled with an unyielding desire for retaliation, mark them as distinctly uncanny entities whose behaviors belie culturally coded notions of "appropriate" sex and gender roles. Indeed, it is this dialectical relationship between commiseration and fear that make the *onryō* so compelling, resulting in their standing as one of the most enduring figures in Japanese literature and film.

Even the ghosts are haunted: Kenji Mizoguchi's *Ugetsu Monogatari*

Ugetsu Monogatari is one of Kenji Mizoguchi's later works and, as such, reveals the sensibilities of a master filmmaker operating at the height of his creative powers. Mizoguchi bases his Kaidan on three short fictions. The first two are "The House in the Thicket" and "The Serpent's Lust," translations/retellings of Chinese tales of the macabre by the popular Japanese author, Akinari Ueda. The third source is "How He Got the Legion of Honor," penned by the French prose master Guy de Maupassant. A critical and commercial success upon its release, *Ugetsu* is set within a painstakingly detailed recreation of Japan's feudal past, and throughout the narrative, Mizoguchi explores the ethical and human cost of militarism, avarice, and hubris. These concerns, far from encased within the sarcophagus of historical specificity, resonated powerfully with Japanese and international audiences recovering from the dehumanizing brutality of the Second World War. In Japan, the losses incurred during the war had a particularly devastating impact upon the "national psyche," and this trauma was foremost in Mizoguchi's mind as he crafted *Ugetsu*.

---

[4] Linnie Blake, "'Everyone Will Suffer': National Identity and the Spirit of Subaltern Vengeance in Nakata Hideo's *Ringu* and Gore Verbinski's *The Ringm*," in *Monstrous Adaptations: Generic and Thematic Mutations in Horror Film*, eds. Richard J. Hand and Jay McRoy (Manchester: Manchester University Press, 2007), 214.

The struggle to endure the chaos of a nation at war underlies *Ugetsu*'s plot, which follows the exploits of two poor but ambitious artisans—Genjurô, a humble potter with a desire for wealth, and Tôbei, Genjurô's somewhat bumbling assistant who dreams of becoming a samurai—and their wives, Miyagi and Ohama. Attempting to salve the sting of unfulfilled aspirations, and haunted by their illusions as to what constitutes an idealized masculinity, Genjurô and Tôbei rupture the cohesion of their respective families. While selling their wares at a crowed local market, Genjurô and Tôbei abandon their spouses for the opportunity to enhance their individual (and, by extension, their families') social status. Tôbei spies samurai in splendid armor walking through the market and, inspired by the power and virility that these highly skilled warriors represent to him, purchases the best armor he can afford. He then sets out on a series of misadventures that serendipitously culminate in his steady, if somewhat comical, ascension in the ranks and esteem of his fellow soldiers. It is only after he discovers that his wife has been reduced to working in a brothel that he realizes the folly of his ways and abandons his militaristic pretensions.

Genjurô's quest, however, assumes a more complex, and considerably darker, trajectory when the beautiful and noble Lady Wakasa, accompanied by one of her servants, purchases a piece of pottery that she wishes delivered to Kutsuki mansion. Sensing an opportunity for upward mobility and enchanted by the image of idealized femininity that Lady Wakasa represents for him, Genjurô quickly becomes enamored with the seductive and quietly ethereal woman who, unlike the classic *onryō* of Japanese folklore and kabuki theater, does not seek vengeance upon those who wronged her while she was alive. In fact, Lady Wakasa does not appear to pose any immediate threat to Genjurô. He remains by her side when he learns of the massacre that decimated the inhabitants of Lady Wakasa's crumbling manor, and even after he discovers that Lady Wakasa's deceased father haunts the decaying residence, Genjurô is so entranced by her nobility and gentle bearing that he agrees to marry her. Only after a Buddhist priest adamantly warns Genjurô that Lady Wakasa is in fact a *yurei* (restless spirit) does he decide to perform the exorcism necessary to break her spell over him.

Borrowing conceits from Nōh theater, like the make up that pales Lady Wakasa's face and the dance she performs for her spellbound guest, the supernatural and almost dream-like sequences at Kutsuki Mansion contrast with the film's more overtly realistic moments. This vacillation between the portrayal of a lyrical, highly stylized fantasy realm and a more overtly representational depiction of sixteenth-century Japan is perhaps one of *Ugetsu*'s most remarkable elements. Not only do these transitions function as a means of further differentiating Genjurô and Tôbei's parallel quests to improve their statuses within the operant class and gender hierarchies, but they also illustrate Mizoguchi's extraordinary range as a filmmaker. This is especially evident when one considers the ease with which Mizoguchi moves between these divergent visual styles without disrupting—or otherwise calling undue attention to—the film's tonal modulations. In other words, Mizoguchi successfully maneuvers the viewer through stylistically disparate narrative threads without jeopardizing the work's integrity as a Kaidan, or as a single, integrated piece of humanist cinema.

This visual distinction between the world of the living and the liminal spaces occupied by the ghostly Lady Wakasa is perhaps best illustrated by Mizoguchi's brilliant juxtaposition of two extended sequence shots. In the first of these, Genjurô and Lady Wakasa, framed in an extreme long shot, enjoy each other's company in an idyllic landscape that could easily pass as a cinematographic reproduction of an *ukiyo-e* (floating world) woodblock print, a genre of graphic art defined by its portrayal of the natural world as temporary, inconstant, and fleeting. The implication of transience that such an image calls forth is appropriate given the theme of impermanence woven throughout *Ugetsu*. Additionally, there is an intentional air of artificiality to the sequence, as if we are not seeing the world as it really is, but rather the world as Genjurô wishes it to be. Stylized (and perhaps subjectivized) to the point of allegory, this ideal, bucolic moment immediately precedes one of the film's most disturbing events. In an intricate tracking shot, the camera follows Miyagi (Genjurô's seemingly forgotten wife) as she tries to make her way down a dirt path in a forest near her hometown. Suddenly besieged by marauding soldiers, Miyagi struggles to save herself and the life of her son, who remains strapped to her back throughout the entirety of the assault. In a long shot that keeps us at a precarious remove from the action, she is stabbed and left to die on the side of the road. Her suffering is protracted and palpable. Her fingers claw futilely at the earth as the soldiers depart; her heart-rending screams of agony and despair mingle with the cries of the child on her back. This juxtaposition of powerful sequence shots is indicative of *Ugetsu*'s vacillation between intervals of heightened formalism and stretches of social realism/humanism. Furthermore, such visual and tonal collisions reinforce the recurring motif of abandoned women left to fend for themselves in brutal, masculinist cultures, as well as Mizoguchi's concerns surrounding the ruinous impact of war on those least involved in the political skirmishes.

Perhaps *Ugetsu*'s most memorable sequence, however, occurs relatively early in the film. In a series of beautifully executed shots designed to evoke a sense of unease and telegraph the film's impending supernatural components,

Genjurô and Tôbei's families cross a body of fog-enshrouded water so that they can sell their pottery at market. As they move over the lake, they encounter a second, apparently un-piloted vessel. Upon closer examination, they discover that the ship's lone occupant is a frail, mortally wounded man who uses his last breaths to warn of murderous pirates. If one were to classify *Ugetsu* exclusively as a Kaidan, such an exchange could be interpreted as foreshadowing the dangers that await our protagonists—a reading that, in this case, would not be precipitous. Each of the boat's passengers eventually meets with misfortunes that forever alter the trajectory of their lives and the lives of their loved ones, and this occurs despite Genjurô's attempt to ensure his wife and child's safety by forcing them ashore. However, if we further expand our analysis of this mist-laden crossing, understanding it not simply as a genre convention pregnant with ill portent, but rather as an event that literalizes the film's theme of the transience of all things, a wider and more rewarding understanding of Mizoguchi's Kaidan emerges. Enveloped by a dense, obscuring mist, the boats and the murky water upon which they float function as an interstitial space that effectively severs the remainder of the film from the coherent period locales in which Mizoguchi sets the narrative's initial action, and to which he returns, albeit in an uncanny fashion, in the film's final scenes.

This mist likewise requires the audience to peer intently at the screen in order to gain a modicum of spatio-temporal orientation. It is also arguably *Ugetsu*'s richest and most durable metaphor, providing insights into humanity's struggle to find satisfaction and value in an evanescent world in which cultures too often impose impossible demands based on gender and class inequality. *Ugetsu*, then, is a profound, and profoundly moving, examination of the illusions to which we adhere in the face of oppression and impermanence. In this sense, *Ugetsu* is about the power of illusion. While very much a foundational component of the culture Genjurô and Tôbei inhabit, the gender codes that these men see as compulsory are ultimately social constructions that help perpetuate a larger, ever more pervasive ideology surrounding the performance of masculinity and femininity. These illusions haunt the characters, and it is perhaps within these illusions that *Ugetsu*'s true horrors reside, for it is Genjurô and Tôbei's surrender to these illusions that ultimately tears their families asunder. Like the spectral Lady Wakasa who, even in death, is haunted by the spirit of her warrior father, the characters that populate Kenji Mizoguchi's *Ugetsu* wander through a transitional realm, performing the only identities they know how to perform and struggling to remain adaptable in a society that all too often erects seemingly intractable social edifices in the face of inevitable and unavoidable transformations.

In A Cat's Eye: Kineto Shindō's *Kuroneko*

Like Kenji Mizoguchi's *Ugetsu*, Kineto Shindō's Kaidan, *Kuroneko* challenges simple genre classifications and anticipates the reimagining of the *onryō* that many film viewers have come to associate with works like Hideo Nakata's *Ringu* films (1998) and Takashi Shimizu's *Ju-on* cycle (2000–2006). Helmed by a visionary director who created his own production company rather than compromise his aesthetic vision, *Kuroneko* follows the corporeal and spectral travails of two brutally violated women whose posthumous compulsion for exacting bloody retribution functions as a cultural barometer for considerations of national, sexual, gendered, and class identities based on inequities that are every bit as pertinent today as they were in the 1968, or, for that matter, the Sengoku Period (mid-fifteenth to early seventeenth century), during which the film's action is set.

Based loosely on the Japanese folktale, "The Cat's Revenge," *Kuroneko* tells the story of Yone (Nobuko Otowa) and her daughter-in-law, Shige (Kiwako Taichi), who are raped and murdered, only to return as ethereal hybrid entities that recall classic representations of the *onryō*. Adorned in funereal white flowing kimonos, their meticulously powdered and made up faces framed by dark black hair, the spirits of Yone and Shige vacillate between enacting stylized performances of an idealized, quasi-aristocratic femininity, and assuming the shape of grotesquely anthropomorphic felines that tear open the throats of lone Samurai with a feral abandon. In this sense, *Kuroneko*'s avenging spirits represent a significant departure from *Ugetsu*'s mournful, restless ghost. As Yone and Shige's attacks escalate in number and frequency, Gintoki, a young and resourceful peasant-turned-samurai, is assigned the task of confronting the pernicious *onryō*. The ensuing verbal and tactical exchanges between Gintoki, Shige, and Yone result in a series of bleak, often heartbreaking misrecognitions and discoveries that renders *Kuroneko* every bit as poignant as it is frightening.

Although Yone and Shiga's vengeance marks them as *onryō*, the phantasmatic fusion of the (post)human with the animal/feline suggests motifs most frequently associated with the *bakeneko-mono* (ghost-cat story), a Japanese horror convention evidenced in films such as *Black Cat Mansion* (1958) and *The Ghost of Otama Pond* (1960). One can even argue for *Kuroneko* as an early example of a rape-revenge film. Yet even here one must be cautious, for unlike works such as Ingmar Bergman's *The Virgin Spring* (1960), Meir Zarchi's *I Spit on Your Grave* (1978), and Takashi Ishii's *Freeze Me* (2000), the displaced aggression visited upon random travelling Samurai more closely anticipates the most expansive iterations of the rape-revenge formula, like Abel Ferrara's *Ms. 45* (1981) and Coralie Virginie Despentes' *Baise-moi* (2000).

It is in the sequences during which the ghostly apparitions commune directly with the living, however, that Kineto Shindō most explicitly veers *Kuroneko* toward an impressionistic theatricality that evokes Kabuki and Nōh traditions without ever breaking away from a visual logic grounded firmly within the art of cinema. Double exposures and inventive, virtually seamless split screens allow for the depiction of a world literally unmoored from the spatial and temporal "laws" that demarcate the mortal sphere from the realm of the dead. Characters move about one another like dancers gracefully pirouetting and weaving on a stage, but Shindō's direction and deliberate framing disallows the optical promiscuity afforded spectators at a play. Shindō's expressionistic spot lighting illuminates precise portions of the frame while casting the remainder into inky shadow. In some scenes, backgrounds appear to float behind foregrounded action, a mechanical distortion resulting in the portrayal of a world at odds with itself. Accentuated by Hikaru Hayashi's percussive score, these hybrid moments, with their virtuosic convergence of styles and tropes, recall the *onryō*'s radical alterity—an otherness that combines the Kaidan with the "demonic woman" conceit of "Nōh...and Kabuki...[theatrical] tradition."[5]

Shindō's synthesis of theatrical trappings with conventional Japanese horror tropes invests natural landscapes with a distinctly poetic quality. This undermining of mimesis in favor of cinematic abstraction likewise allows for a remarkably expansive social critique. As Colette Balmain posits, by refusing to "contain" Yone's and Shige's wrath "to those who have committed the offense against them," their rage confronts the nexus of gender biases and power imbalances inherent within "Japanese paternalism as a whole."[6] Without the protection of Yone's son (Shige's husband), and geographically isolated on a patch of land surrounded by a wild expanse of thick bamboo, the women are in a precarious position. Though they struggle against the warriors' libidinous assaults, they are easily overpowered. Additionally, unlike the marauding soldiers who seem conspicuously at odds with their immediate environment (the warriors clumsily hack their way through the vegetation and throw themselves onto the edge of a small stream in a

---

[5]Ibid., 214.
[6]Colette Balmain, *Introduction to Japanese Horror Film* (Edinburgh: Edinburgh University Press, 2008), 75.

desperate attempt to quench their thirst), Yone and Shige, in both their living and undead manifestations, are far more acclimated to the natural world. This association is made all the more salient via the correlation of their ghostly incarnations with the predatory skills and graceful movements of the black cat, a mischievous trickster figure in Japanese folklore and the only living creature we see being the least bit attentive to the women's violated and partially incinerated corpses. As humans, Yone and Shige glean enough food during a time of famine to feed themselves; as spirits, they move effortlessly in the utter darkness of the bamboo forest at night, acrobatically leaping as if carried by the wind as they guide the traveling samurai upon which they prey through a dense arboreal labyrinth.

Though it may be a bit of an overstatement to label Shindō a feminist filmmaker or to describe *Kuroneko* as a film predominantly concerned with the plight of women in a phallocentric culture, Yone and Shige are nevertheless sympathetic characters victimized by an aggressive masculinity that objectifies them and ultimately deems them disposable. The prejudices that sustain social hierarchies and their ideological underpinnings, however, are rarely singular or easily reducible, and *Kuroneko* foregrounds injustices that are systemic and trans-historical. By perpetually compromising verisimilitude, Shindō's hyper-stylized flourishes position *Kuroneko* as a narrative that exceeds any pretenses toward historical specificity, allowing Japanese and international filmgoers of the late 1960's to recognize aspects of the Sengoku period's cultural turbulences within their own immediate political climates. In this sense, *Kuroneko* has as much, if not more, to say about the (inter) national climate of 1968 as it is about 1468. Likewise, if the enthusiasm with which cinephiles continue to embrace the film is any indicator, the unrest and frustration that accompanied the social upheavals of the late 1960s still resonates in the early twenty-first century, where economic divisions in most nations are more extreme than ever.

Indeed, class difference and the structures of domination and exploitation that accompany such divisions deeply inform *Kuroneko*'s *onryō*. Like the bamboo forest through which their restless spirits hunt for wayward samurai, peasants like Yone and Shige are at once omnipresent and, for all intents and purposes, invisible—especially to those whose financial acumen and social power allow them to overlook the suffering of others. They are emblematic of the voiceless masses that have little choice but to capitulate to the whims of the ruling elite. Even the eponymous black cat, whose lithe movements and haunting eyes contribute to some of the film's most powerful and enduring images, carries an allegorical weight that extends beyond its immediate cultural connection with roguish attitudes: "I like the idea of using the cat," Shindō states, "because I could thus express the very low position in society which certain people occupy."[7] In a society stratified along sex and class divisions, and in which an affluent few wield great power while an overwhelming majority scramble to divvy up the scant remainders, it should come as no surprise when human beings are forced to scavenge like beasts.

The *onryō* and contemporary horror cinema

Japanese horror cinema's "return" to international prominence in the mid-1990s was one of the most exciting events in world cinema during the waning years of the twentieth century. Helmed by some of the most daring, visually inventive, and genre-troubling directors working in film, television, and the direct-to-video markets, Japanese horror films soon appeared everywhere from the programs of prestigious international film festivals to the shelves of commercial video rental stores. In the process, directors as diverse as Shin'ya Tsukamoto (*Tetsuo, the Iron Man* [1989], *Tokyo Fist* [1995]), Kiyoshi Kurosawa (*Cure* [1997], *Pulse* [2001]), Takashi Miike (*Audition* [1999], *Ichi the Killer* [2001]), Hideo Nakata (*Ringu* [1998], *Dark Water* [2002]), Takashi Shimizu (*Tomie: Re-Birth* [2001], *Ju-on: The Grudge* [2002]), and Shion Sono (*Suicide Club* [2001], *Noriko's Dinner Table* [2005]) quickly rose in prominence to become some of the premier names in international horror film. For cinephiles and fans of motion pictures steeped in the grotesque, the gory, and the macabre, contemporary Japanese horror cinema's vivid reworking of the motifs and themes that made films like Mizoguchi's *Ugetsu* and Shindō's *Kuroneko* so striking proved a welcome contribution to a genre perceived as increasingly uninspired. This was especially true for audiences tired of the annual parade of unimpressive sequels to franchises that had seemingly long ago run their course. Even self-referential horror-comedy hybrids, like Wes Craven's *Scream* (1996), which at least in their initial iterations were widely viewed as clever revisions of the troubled horror film scene, soon proved tepid and redundant as producers, eager to capitalize upon the success of these parodic features, returned "to the well" again and again with diminishing returns.

In a genre rife with femicidal butchers, bio-mechanical monstrosities, sinister serial killers, and homicidal teens, the figure of the *onryō* proved its resilience within the Japanese cultural imagination by becoming arguably the

---

[7]Joan Mellen, "'My Mind Was Always on the Commoners': Shindō on *Kuroneko* in His Body of Work," *Currents*, The Criterion Collection (Official Web Page), October 28, 2011, http://www.criterion.com/current/posts/2026-my-mind-was-always-on-the-commoners-shindo-on-kuroneko-in-his-body-of-work (accessed on February 17, 2015).

most conspicuous signifier in the resurgence, both nationally and globally, of Japanese horror cinema. Few horror aficionados today will fail to recognize the image of the tragic yet vengeful Sadako from Hideo Nakata's wildly popular *Ringu* (1998). Standing in her loose white gown, her nailless hands hanging limp at her sides, a single eye staring out through long raven tresses—Sadako soon rose to the status of international horror film icon, ascending to a pop culture pantheon comprised of such immediately recognizable entities as F.W. Murnau's Nosferatu, James Whale's Frankenstein's Monster, Wes Craven's Freddy Kreuger, and Clive Barker's Pinhead. In short, during the late 1990s, Sadako became, for a burgeoning generation of audiences, virtually emblematic of the *onryō*; at once strikingly contemporary and evocative to Japan's rich literary and theatrical traditions, Sadako became the very face of Japanese horror cinema.

However, although the success of Nakata's *Ringu* cemented Sadako's status as one of the most internationally recognizable figures in contemporary horror film, the early 1990s saw *onryō* proliferating across screens throughout Japan in video (aka v-cinema) and made-for-television features and anthologies aimed primarily at teen audiences. Often set in high schools and similar locales with which the works' intended audiences could immediately relate, these Kaidan blended conventions from traditional *onryō* narratives with references to popular urban legends and allusions to social problems, like bullying and teen suicide. This amalgamation of signifiers lent these eerie tales an immediacy that resonated with an emerging generation of spectators that, like many young people around the globe, found themselves suddenly confronting an array of radical physiological and social transitions/transformations. It is at least partially because of these texts that Koji Suzuki's 1991 horror novel, *Ringu*, and its now legendary cinematic adaptation by Hideo Nakata, met with such enormous critical and commercial success. Setting box office records in Japan as the highest grossing horror film to date, *Ringu* garnered rave reviews from a plethora of film critics and quickly spawned numerous motion picture adaptations (*The Ring Virus* [Park Eun-Suh, 1998], *The Ring* [Gore Verbinski, 2002]), sequels (*Spiral* [Jōji Iida, 1998] and *Ringu 2* [Hideo Nakata, 1999]), and even a prequel (*Ringu 0: Bāsudei* [Norio Tsuruta, 2000]).

Deviating significantly from Suzuki's novel, Nakata's film involves an urban legend about a cursed video tape that soon proves all too horrifyingly real for an investigative reporter named Rieko Asakawa, her potentially psychic son, Yoichi, and her scientist ex-husband, Ryūji Takayama. Compelled to investigate a potential connection between this allegedly haunted tape and mysterious deaths of several teenagers found with expressions of abject horror contorting their youthful faces, Asakawa retraces a deceased teen's final weeks until she discovers the cursed video cassette at a resort on the Izu Peninsula. She watches the tape and immediately afterwards answers a ringing telephone that to hear a voice that, she believes, indicates that she has only seven days left to live. Working together, Asakawa and her ex-husband, Takayama, study the images on the tape, eventually tracing its origins back to a psychic woman, Shizuko, whose ability to predict future events resulted in a confrontation with reporters. During a heated press conference, a particularly aggressive journalist threatens Shizuko. Shizuko's daughter, Sadako, fearful for her mother's safety, reacts by killing the reporter with a single thought. In the wake of these events, tragedy befalls both mother and daughter as Shizuko kills herself and Sadako dies at the hand of her scientist father, who has been studying her and her mother's uncanny supernatural abilities. The Scientist pushes Sadako down a well, leaving her to rot. Hoping to quell Sadako's vengeance, Asakawa and Takayama recover her remains, but they soon discover that Sadako's rage endures when, several days later, her ghost emerges from a television screen and, in one of the most memorable scenes in horror cinema, frightens Takayama to death. Realizing that her ex-husband had viewed a copy of the cursed tape, and discovering that while she was momentarily distracted, her son, Yuichi, also viewed a copy of the cursed tape, Asakawa deduces that the only way to escape Sadako's wrath is for her to create a yet another copy of the tape for someone else to view. The film ends with Asakawa telephoning her father and informing him that she has a videotape that she would like him to watch.

Like Mizoguchi's *Ugetsu Monogatari* and Shindō's *Kuroneko*, Nakata's film deploys the conceit of the *onryō* as a means of exploring a nexus of cultural anxieties. In *Ringu*, these concerns span from trepidation over the impact of emerging technologies (particularly media technologies) to apprehension stemming from transformations in gender codes and their impacts upon the structure and function of families in contemporary Japan. Viewed through this lens, the cursed videocassette, through which Sadako enacts her vengeance, represents not only the potentially alienating and culturally corrosive impact of modern information technologies, but also the forms of media(tion) through which, as Colette Balmain suggests, "the repressed past reasserts itself,"[8] ultimately demanding that we acknowledge our complicity in our individual and collective disavowals of personal or historical traumas. That this demand for realization—that is, the refusal to be consigned to silence by censuring social and/or patriarchal power structures and their attendant ideologies—comes from an *onryō* coded as explicitly feminine is crucial. It is,

---

[8] Balmain, 170.

importantly, a room full of *male* journalists that "vehemently reject Shizuko's uncanny psychic abilities and apocalyptic predictions" and react virulently not only to the extent to which "Shizuko's...knowledge exceeds that of the patriarchal scientific community," but also to her voicing of this knowledge, her desire to "insert herself into the realm of public discourse."[9] What's more, it is this patriarchal "fear and anger over Shizuko's skills that evokes Sadako's demonstration of her even more threatening mental acumen: her ability to kill with a thought."[10] Thus, it is significant that Asakawa's scientist ex-husband is incapable of breaking the curse that provides a posthumous outlet for Sadako's rage, just as it is vital that it is Asakawa who uncovers the final deadly secret behind Sadako's "technologically inscribed vengeance— the cursed videocassettes representing a mode of mass communication that [Shizuko's and Sadako's] male persecutors...would have found too terrifying to even imagine."[11] Indeed, by selecting her own father as the next victim in the viral chain of individuals destined to confront Sadako's fury, Asakawa actively continues/enables Sadako's vengeance, if only through a process of eternal deferment.

The impact of disrupted gender codes upon traditional family dynamics likewise informs much of *Ringu*'s narratological and thematic content through the juxtaposition the unconventional/scandalous family comprised of the suicidal Shizuko, her powerful yet troubled daughter, Sadako, and the murderous scientist father, with the cordial-yet-"broken" family constituted by Asakawa, her son, Yuichi, and the ineffectual scientist father, Takayama. Though the fatal triad that culminates in the creation of *Ringu*'s memorable *onryō* is clearly the far more explicitly monstrous and dysfunctional grouping, Asakawa's autonomy, as evidenced by her commitment to her career as an investigative journalist, indirectly contributes not only to her encounter with cursed videotape, but also to her ex-husband's subsequent demise and her son's exposure to the accursed tape's deadly contents. In this sense, by combining Sadako's unquenchable rage with a fairly reactionary scenario that posits Asakawa's independence as potentially harmful to those closest to her (i.e., her family), Nakata's *Ringu* ultimately mollifies any progressive potential inherent in its critique of a phallocentric power structure that, in its refusal of feminine agency, leads to the *onryō*'s very emergence.

Shifting gender roles and their impact upon the domestic and larger cultural sphere similarly inform the content of Takashi Shimizu's *Ju-on: The*

---

[9] Jay McRoy, *Nightmare Japan: Contemporary Japanese Horror Cinema* (Amsterdam, New York: Rodopi, 2008), 87.
[10] Ibid., 87
[11] Ibid.

Grudge. Produced primarily for a youth market, *Ju-on: The Grudge* was part of an immensely popular franchise in Japan, eventually spawning a series of Hollywood remakes, two of which featured the popular U.S. television and film star Sarah Michelle Gellar, whose celebrity largely resided in her appeal to teenage audiences. A self-proclaimed "eighties splatter movie kid" (Macias, para 18),[12] Shimizu combines a subtle variation on popular cinematic representations of the *onryō* with visual and narrative tropes culled from late 1970s and early 1980s Hollywood stalker/slasher films like *Halloween* (1978), *Friday the 13th* (1980), and *A Nightmare on Elm Street* (1984). This tantalizing collision of "an American and Japanese style"[13] resulted in a tantalizing cinematic hybrid that doubtlessly contributed to the film's continued transcultural appeal.

The abstract montage that opens *Ju-on: The Grudge* is especially striking and effectively locates the home as the sociocultural epicenter of the *onryō*'s vengeful rage. Beginning with establishing shots of a seemingly anonymous residential street, followed by low angle shots of a vine-clad house, Shimizu then cuts to a rapid montage of unsettling images: a mouth gnawing bloody fingertips, the blade of a Stanley knife clicking slowly out of its plastic casing, a woman's lifeless eyes framed by streaks of blood, a young boy drawing pictures of a long-haired woman on a sheet of paper before scampering away to hide in a closet, a black cat screeching as it is grabbed roughly by the back of its neck. Intentionally disorienting and confusing, these shots nevertheless allow audiences a glimpse into the violent act that has most likely resulted in the eponymous "grudge," a "curse" that, in keeping with the *onryō* archetype, originates when one "dies in the grip of a powerful rage." Like Sadako's wrath, the "grudge" in Shimizu's film spreads virally, killing all those with whom the spirits come into contact and, in the process, birthing new curses.

As the episodic plot of *Ju-on: The Grudge* unfolds, the audience slowly discovers that the film's eponymous curse originated with the murderous assault by Takeo, a husband and father whose violent actions resulted from suspicions over his wife's (Kayako's) fidelity. While the film's narrative makes it clear that Kayako died by her husband's hands, exactly how their son, Toshio, met his fate is left vague. Toshio is described only as having "disappeared," but from the film's initial vignette, it is clear that both the mother and the son haunt the site of the carnage presented in the film's opening sequence, eventually taking the lives of those who move into, or even temporarily visit, the home.

---

[12] P. Macias, "The Scariest Horror Ever? Juon, Director Takashi Shimizu Interview," *Japanattack*, March 9, 2006, http://japattack.com (accessed on February 17, 2015).
[13] Ibid.

If, as Susan Napier argues, Japanese men "[c]onfronted with more powerful and independent women ... have suffered their own form of identity crises,"[14] then the core of Shimizu's film is the ultimate nightmare for a phallocentric culture: the patriarchal paradigm assaulted at its very foundations. The film's fragmented, impressionistic opening montage, then, can be understood not only as illustrative of a profound social disorientation, but also as emblematic of a residual, reactionary compulsion to re-establish/maintain a regime of masculine dominance.

Of course, similar "gender trouble" has long informed North American and European horror cinema, and so Shimizu's appropriation of visual tropes from U.S. slasher films of the late 1970s and early 1980s seems fitting, particularly given the often neoconservative agendas of such texts and how these political subject positions, as critics like Barbara Creed and Carol Clover have illustrated, inform the shifting alignments of the spectator's gaze. This is not to suggest that apparently ideologically recuperative productions lack the potential, in spite of themselves, to advance progressive political perspectives. By displaying "the significant dreams and nightmares of a culture and the ways that a culture is attempting to channel them to maintain its present relations of power and domination," even the most overtly conservative horror films inevitably expose the "hopes and fears that contest dominant hegemonic power relations."[15] In other words, even if the films Shimizu cites as inspirational—like *A Nightmare on Elm Street* and *Friday the 13th*—seemingly promote reactionary political and ideological agendas by "punishing" certain behaviors (e.g., sexual promiscuity, drug use) while "rewarding" others (e.g., chastity, self-reliance within gender constraints, the willingness to resort to violence when necessary), it remains possible also to view these texts as engaging in "an unprecedented assault on all that Bourgeois culture is supposed to cherish—like ideological apparatuses of the family and the school."[16]

Like Nakata's *Ringu*, *Ju-on: The Grudge* is at once ideologically recuperative and socially progressive. Consider, for instance, a sequence early in the film during which an ill-prepared social worker encounters a neglected elderly woman sitting passively near her own feces-soiled bedding. Although the anticipation of a potential encounter with the film's *onryō* permeates the

---

[14]Susan Napier, *Anime: From Akira to Princess Mononoke* (New York: Palgrave, 2000), 80.
[15]Douglas Kellner, *Media Culture: Cultural Studies, Identity, and the Politics between the Modern and the Postmodern* (London, New York: Routledge, 1995), 111.
[16]Tanya Modleski, "The Terror of Pleasure: The Contemporary Horror Film and Postmodern Theory," in *Studies in Entertainment: Critical Approaches to Mass Culture*, ed. Tania Modleski (Bloomington, Indianapolis: Indiana University Press, 1989), 158.

scene a forbidding tone, the carefully composed *mise-en-scène*, lensed from a height reminiscent of Yasujirō Ozu's famed *tatami* shots, provides a somber, disquieting meditation on generational differences and what cultural theorists like Hayao Kiwai would describe as the collapse of the traditional "Japanese-style extended family."[17] While such a scene conveys a nostalgic yearning for waning social and familial order very much steeped in patriarchal conventions, Kayako and Toshio—the film's *onryō*—enact their uncontainable wrath as a result of violence over a *perceived* infidelity, the murderous husband's/father's violence a monstrous symbol of an abusive and antiquated "official culture."

Unlike traditional *onryō*, however, Kayako and Toshio are hybrid entities that navigate an interstitial space between the spectral and the biological; clearly constituted as paranormal/other-worldly, this matriarchal pairing merges a dangerous corporeality (they can physically attack and manipulate their victims' bodies) with an eerie, ghostly quality without adhering absolutely to one convention or the other. Like many *onryō*, they can seemingly appear and disappear; their hair and appendages do not adhere to the physical laws of material reality. At the same time, they are not bound to the spaces in which they died; they can physically attack and manipulate their victims' bodies. This uncanny mother and son become even more disturbing, as well as less exclusively linked to Japanese horror cinema conventions, when one factors in the masterful camera work of Shimizu's cinematographer, Tokushô Kikumura. In keeping with "classic" and contemporary works of Japanese cinema, Shimizu allows tension to build deliberately throughout each of *Ju-on: the Grudge*'s numerous nonlinear episodes. Many of the expected, culturally specific trappings of filmic terror are present: the long black hair framing wide staring eyes, ominous tatami shots of sliding closet doors, shadowy apparitions that render their human victims virtually paralyzed with fear. However, true to his "eighties splatter movie kid" roots, Shimizu also incorporates a distinctly U.S. slasher/stalker film aesthetic, most obviously by aligning the viewer's gaze not only with the central characters' perspectives, but with that of Kakayo and Toshio as well. Such compositions and camera movements allow us, by turns, to "stalk" and "be stalked."

Like a skilled composer, Takashi Shimizu modulates our exposure to the monstrous and the horrific in *Ju-on: the Grudge*, finally building to a crescendo at the culmination of each movement/episode. By frequently relegating

---

[17]Hayao Kiwai, "Violence in the Home: Conflict between Two Principles: Maternal and Paternal," in *Japanese Culture and Behavior*, eds. T.S. Lebra and W.P. Lebra (Honolulu: University of Hawaii Press, 1986), 303.

motion to the extreme edges of the frame, the audience glimpses certain actions peripherally, creating the impression that we may have just witnessed a flash of something—as if from the corner of our collective eye. During other moments, most particularly the climactic sequences that inevitably bring each of the film's episodes to a sudden close, Shimizu culminates our rising dread by propelling us face-to-face with Kakayo and/or Toshio in all their monstrous alterity. Finally, *Ju-on: The Grudge* is a film that disallows its characters, and, by extension, its audience access to those conventional "safe spaces" to which people commonly retreat when fear escalates or the tension becomes too much to take. Peering through fingers does not distance the imperiled characters from that which frightens them; rather, it forces immediate confrontation with the horrific. Likewise, pulling the covers up over one's head does not provide a buffer zone but, instead, reveals that the monster you most fear has been in bed with you the whole time.

Conclusion

As with any literary, dramatic, or cinematic genre, the Kaidan has transformed throughout the years. So has its most compelling figure, the *onryō*. While certain key features and motivations have endured, others have changed in keeping with our rapidly changing media and cultural landscapes. As a result, these alterations have informed, and will undoubtedly continue to inform, not only the stories we tell, but also how we tell those stories and, ultimately, what the stories we tell reveal about us. It is for this reason that out of all the tales we tell ourselves about ourselves, ghost stories remain at once among the most alluring and the most unnerving. For ghosts haunt our lives in the most intimate of ways. Our imaginations, dreams, and memories exist only and always as chimeras, hallucinations, and phantoms; the very foundations of the way we think and feel are, in the end, merely shadows of the "real." They are specters, and a specter, as Jacques Derrida reminds us, "is always a revenant. One cannot control its comings and goings because it begins by coming back."[18] If there has been one common thread in the Kaidan explored in this chapter—or, indeed, in practically all of the ghost stories we tell ourselves—it is that the harder one tries to repress, oppress, or simply push away those parts of our experience we least wish to recognize,

---

[18] Jacques Derrida, *Specters of Marx: The State of the Debt, The Work of Mourning & the New International* (New York: Routledge, 1994), 11.

the powerfully they will return. Thus, rather than hiding in fear from these "ghosts" and the "vengeance" they portend, we should exorcise them by allowing them to speak. We should exorcise them, in other words, "not in order to chase [them] away...but...to grant them the right to...a hospitable memory...out of a concern for justice."[19]

---

[19]Ibid., 220.

12

Painted Skin: Romance with the Ghostly Femme Fatale in Contemporary Chinese Cinema

Li Zeng

The epic 2008 film *Hua pi/Painted Skin*, a Hong Kong/mainland China/Singapore coproduction, cowritten and directed by renowned Hong Kong director Gordon Chan (with Andy Chin and Danny Ko as codirectors), has provoked critical discussions among Chinese scholars and critics about film adaptation and Chinese ghost films.[1] *Painted Skin* is based on a short ghost story of the same title in *Liaozhai zhi yi/Strange Tales from Liaozhai* (*Liaozhai* in short), a collection of supernatural tales written by Pu Songling (1640–1715).[2] Pu's classic story tells about the seduction of a married man by a malicious ghost disguised as a beautiful woman and the man's subsequent violent death. Its relatively complete narrative (compared to other, sketchier stories) and graphic description of the man's violent death makes "Painted Skin" one of the best known horror tales in this collection. The story has been adapted into a number of films and television dramas in Hong Kong, which has a long tradition of horror cinema (Stephen Teo has

---

[1] For example, see Zheng Fei, "On the Film Adaption of 'Painted Skin'" (lun dianying huapi dui xiaoshuo huapi de gaibian), *Movie Review/ Dianying pingjie* 4 (2009), 30–1; Ling Peng, "Love Elements in the 2008 Film *Painted Skin* and Its Realistic Significance," (2008 dianying huapi de aiqing yuansu ji xianshi yiyi) *Film Literature/ Dianying Wenxue* 4 (2010), 88–9. These are mainland Chinese journals.
[2] Songling Pu, *Strange Tales from Liaozhai* (Liaozhai Zhi Yi) V1. Trans. Sidney L. Sondergard (Fremont: Jain Publishing Company, 2008).

said that the ghost story "defines Hong Kong's horror genre"[3]). In contrast, mainland Chinese cinema has shied away from this ghost tale due to censorship directed at superstitious and horror materials. It is in this context that the release of *Painted Skin* in China and its success as the third-highest grossing film of the year drew substantial attention from media scholars and film critics.

Painted Skin drew a lot of people to the theater out of curiosity. Most of the comments posted on fan websites suggest viewers' familiarity with Pu's story and indicate their interest in seeing a modern adaption of a classic horror tale.[4] Those who were expecting a horror film might have been disappointed, as Chan's big-budget all-star blockbuster adaptation is an erotic melodrama mixed with martial arts elements, CGI effects, and some horror scenes. It presents a triangular love relationship between a man and two women (his wife and a fox-spirit—the mythological Chinese character of a fox that transforms into a woman), and depicts an enchanting supernatural woman who is devoted to the man and is willing to sacrifice everything for love. Critics attributed the success of this film to the mix of elements that had "proved successful at the mainland box office at the time."[5] While recognizing that martial arts elements and CGI spectacle are important factors, I call attention to the film's powerful rendering of the malicious ghost in Pu's story. Chan's *Painted Skin* creates a powerful anti-heroine—the ghostly femme fatale, who, I argue, represents the most compelling force that drives the film narrative and has evoked a cultural resonance in Chinese audiences.

To demonstrate the cultural significance of the ghostly femme fatale, this paper first does a close analysis of the anti-heroine in *Painted Skin* and compares her with ghosts/fox-spirits in mainland Chinese films of the 1980s and the early 1990s. The ghostly femme fatale differs from her precedent counterparts in her strong agency and subversion of the male-dominated system. Nevertheless, I will argue that it is not a feminist film because the phallocentric discourse of the control of the "monstrous-feminine," to use Barbara Creed's term, still shapes this modern adaptation.[6] The paper then

---

[3]Stephen Teo, *Hong Kong Cinema: The Extra Dimensions* (London: British Film Institute, 1997), 221.
[4]For instance, there are more than three thousand comments on and reviews of Chan's *Painted Skin* on mtime.com, one of the largest Chinese movie fan websites, http://movie.mtime.com/59588/reviews/short/new.html (accessed on July 30, 2014).
[5]Andy Willis, "*Painted Skin*: Negotiating Mainland China's Fear of the Supernatural," *Asian Cinema* 22.1 (2011), 26.
[6]Barbara Creed, *The Monstrous-Feminine: Film, Feminism, Psychoanalysis* (New York: Routledge, 1993).

discusses the reception of *Painted Skin* in relation to contemporary Chinese films dealing with triangular love relations. In particular, Teng Huao-Tao's *Xingzhong yougui/Matrimony* (2007; the literal translation of the Chinese title is *Ghost in Heart*), a ghost horror film, will be analyzed as a comparison. It argues that *Painted Skin* is resonant with other Chinese films in its expression of anxiety about women's sexual autonomy and moral degeneration, but it also significantly differs from them in its ambivalence toward the ghostly femme fatale on the other hand, refusing a simplistic reading.

As this paper is a study of a contemporary film adaption of a classic horror story, it is helpful to give a more detailed account of Pu Songling's story and Chan's film before moving to a close analysis. In Pu's "Painted Skin," a scholar named Wang encounters a beautiful woman, a ghost in disguise, and starts a lascivious relationship. One day Wang accidently sees the ghost, in the shape of a horrific demon, painting a human skin and then putting it on. Terrified, he seeks help from a Taoist exorcist, who gives him a fly swatter to hang outside his bedroom to keep the ghost away. Feeling betrayed and resentful, the ghost breaks into the bedroom, rips open Wang's chest, takes out his heart and devours it. The story ends with the ghost's elimination by a Taoist monk and Wang's resuscitation.

Chan's film takes place early in the Han dynasty, during which there were frequent wars between the empire and neighboring tribes. During a battle, General Wang (Chen Kun) from the Han army "rescues" Xiao Wei (Zhou Xun), a fox-spirit who feasts on human hearts to keep her youthful human appearance. Xiao Wei falls in love with the general and tries to replace his wife Peirong (Zhao Wei). To turn Wang against Peirong, Xiao Wei uses her power to change Peirong into a demon. In the climax, Wang tells Xiao Wei that he has fallen in love with her, but he cannot break his bond with his wife. Wang kills himself to exchange his life for Peirong's. Heartbroken, Xiao Wei gives up her "essence" to revive the couple, and her body dissolves in the air.[7] Parallel to the main romantic triangle, there are other love relations, including former general Pang Yong's (Donnie Yen) unrequited love for Peirong, and a charlatan spirit's unreturned love for Xiao Wei.

Deborah Cartmell and Imelda Whelehan propose a constructive theory to study an adaptation:

> At its best an adaptation on screen can re-envision a well-worn narrative for a new audience inhabiting a very different cultural environment,

---

[7] In Chinese folklore, "essence" determines a supernatural entity's existence and power. A supernatural entity may spend hundred of years to produce the "essence."

and their relationship to the "origin" may itself change enormously. An adaptation may be an act of criticism and reparation simultaneously; a text may well have outlived its usefulness or become too tired for contemporary tastes.[8]

This paper studies *Painted Skin* as a modern adaptation shaped by intertextual references and cultural contexts. *Painted Skin* is a product targeted at a market that restricts explicit horror films, and is an updated text that is built on contemporary cultural relevance.

The ghostly femme fatale

Commenting on China's notorious censorship, Laikwan Pang notes that an anti-superstition film policy is almost "idiosyncratically Chinese" in terms of "its breadth, variation and relevance."[9] Thus, it is not really a surprise that Gordon Chan changed the ghost character into a fox-spirit and diluted the horror element by emphasizing a love triangle. In Pu's stories, fox-spirits and ghosts are often interchangeable characters, as they both can take on human appearance and represent men's erotic fantasies. Nevertheless, there are some differences. For example, eating human hearts to maintain a youthful human appearance is associated with ghosts rather than fox-sprits. Thus, the heart-eating character in Chan's film is familiar to Chinese audiences as a ghost, even though she is presented as a fox-spirit. At one point the film makes an explicit comment on the fox-spirit as a ghost. In that scene, an exorcist claims that Xiao Wei is a demon. The other characters respond, "Only *ghosts* would believe your words." The camera moves to Xiao Wei. It is not difficult for the audience to understand this self-reflexive humor and figure out that the identity switch is a masquerade to avoid trouble with Chinese censorship regarding superstitious materials.[10]

---

[8] Deborah Cartmell and Imelda Whelehan, *Screen Adaptation: Impure Cinema* (London: Palgrave Macmillan, 2010), 23.
[9] Laikwan Pang, "The State against Ghosts: A Genealogy of China's Film Censorship Policy," *Screen* 52.4 (Winter 2011), 461.
[10] Chinese audiences are familiar with strategies that Chinese filmmakers use to avoid censorship. For example, there were a number of semi-horror films made in China at the turn of the twenty-first century. These films, if ghosts are involved, usually end with a rational or scientific explanation. Chinese audiences are used to such patterns. See my article on Chinese contemporary horror, Li Zeng, "Horror Returns to Chinese Cinema: An Aesthetic of Restraint and the Space of Horror," *Jump Cut: A Review of Contemporary Media* 51 (2009), n.p.

Chan's *Painted Skin* creates a more developed, complicated, and ambiguous female character than the ghost in Pu's story. Instead of being pure evil, Xiao Wei is a combination of a malicious ghost and an amorous ghost. She is both a fetishized object of the male gaze and a woman with strong agency who dominates every scene in which she appears.

This duality is efficiently presented in the pre-credit sequence, which foregrounds Xiao Wei's dangerous sexuality and demonic power. Xiao Wei is introduced with a high angle shot showing her lying seductively on a fur blanket in a military tent, surrounded by male soldiers who look at her lustfully. A panning shot moves slowly and sensuously from her ankle, along her almost-naked body, to her face. The military chief carries her to a bed. He tells her that he will give her anything she wants, even his heart. Xiao Wei looks at him with a seductive smile and says gently, "Really? ... Oh, I've got it." From the terror in the man's eyes, we know that she has taken out his heart. Xiao Wei's beauty is immediately revealed to be a disguise for monstrosity. The previous voyeuristic pleasure of looking at her eroticized body turns into the horror of witnessing a "castration." This scene provides a powerful rendering of the fascinating and fearful femme fatale, a dream and a nightmare for men.

Xiao Wei's transformation into an amorous ghost starts in the same scene. After she kills the chief, Wang, the general from the opposing army, fights his way into the tent. A close-up shot shows Xiao Wei looking at him with amazement and desire. Mistaking her for the victim of a rapist, Wang says to her, "Come, I will get you out." At that moment, Xiao Wei decides to become his woman—as happens to all the Cinderellas who fall in love with the heroes who come to their rescue. Except in this case, the woman in love is more powerful than the hero. As the viewer has just witnessed Xiao Wei's chilling supernatural power, Wang's act of "heroism" seems ironic.

From the outset the film highlights gender and sexuality as a central theme. The pre-credit sequence immediately troubles conventional concepts of femininity and masculinity. Seeing Xiao Wei lying next to the murdered military chief, covered in blood, Wang assumes Xiao Wei is a victim, rather than the other way around. His assumption reflects his own culturally influenced ideas about femininity and masculinity, with the former associated with victimization and vulnerability, and the latter with power and heroism. As the story unfolds, Wang's masculine ideal of heroism continues to prevent him from recognizing Xiao Wei's monstrosity beneath her human skin, when all evidence points toward her as a heart-eating demon. Xiao Wei understands the function of gender roles in the patriarchal world, and plays a gender game to win Wang's favor and his soldiers' admiration. She hides her monstrous-feminine nature to perform the role of a traditional woman: she claims that she was a poor maid to gain Wang's sympathy and protection; she stays at home, waiting to please him; and she kneels before Peirong and Wang and asks them to accept her as Wang's concubine. This masquerade of conventional femininity fools the men in the military town where the film is set. Xiao Wei's "performative femininity" challenges fixed gender roles, resists the conventional definitions of masculinity and femininity, and thus is "subversive."[11]

Those who buy into the conventional gender roles are the prey of Xiao Wei. In one of the film's few horrific scenes, Xiao Wei takes off her human skin and reveals her true identity to Peirong, who is the opposite of Xiao Wei and represents the virtues of a traditional wife. In front of Peirong, she kills a soldier, one of her many admirers, by ripping out his heart. The moment is shocking because the killing happens so quickly and she executes the horrific act so easily. The soldier, skilled at fighting, does not anticipate Xiao Wei's power, hidden beneath a human skin, a masquerade of feminine subjection.

Xiao Wei occupies the dominant position both in the narrative of *Painted Skin* and in the film frame. She may be a fetishized object for the viewer's gaze, but she is the desiring subject in the film. When she and Wang appear in the same scene, Xiao Wei looks at him without hiding her desire. When Wang looks at her, she always returns the look, and Wang looks away. She pursues Wang in her aggressive way while Wang tries to keep his distance. But Xiao Wei's sexuality overpowers his rationality. Wang's desire for her body is captured in two sensuous dream scenes: in the first, Wang watches Xiao Wei with a red scarf around her naked body, walking in a desert; in the second, Xiao Wei swims naked toward him and then they make passionate love.

Xiao Wei plays the game dauntlessly within the male-dominated world. Even Pang Yong, a martial arts master, fails to destroy her. In the end she chooses self-destruction out of her genuine love for Wang. This ending is more powerful than that of Pu's story, in which Taoist exorcists eliminate the ghost and bring the male victim back to life. In the film her uncompromising power makes Xiao Wei a woman of strong agency and subjectivity with few counterparts in either Chinese or Hong Kong ghost films.

Nevertheless, Chan's *Painted Skin* is not the feminist film some critics have seen it as.[12] The film continues the narrative of the containment of

---

[11] Judith Butler, *Gender Trouble* (New York: Routledge, 1990).
[12] For example, see Ling Peng, 2010; Li Junhui, "*Painted Skin*: The Predicament of Women's Love and the Deconstruction of Male Power" (Dianying huapi: nuxing qing'ai de kunjing yu nanxing quanli de xiaojie), *Film Literature/Dianying Wenxue* 1 (2009), 60–1.

the monstrous-feminine and the affirmation of women's traditional virtues, which structure both Pu's story and other Hong Kong film adaptations. Pu's story reflects an ideology similar to that underlying the Western Medusa myth—men who saw Medusa, with her tortured visage and hair consisting of writhing serpents, were immediately turned to stone. The Medusa myth "is mediated by a narrative about the *difference* of female sexuality as a difference which is grounded in monstrousness and which invokes castration anxiety in the male spectator."[13] In "Painted Skin," the "fear of castration" is reflected in the ghost's violent punishment of Wang (taking out his heart is a symbolic castration), after he has seen her monstrous body. The ghost, with her excessive sexuality and superpower, is the "Medusa," the "monstrous-feminine."

In his extensive study of the ghostly women in Chinese supernatural folklore and literature, Wan Xianchu argues that female ghosts represented men's discontent with feudal ethics, which repressed sexual desire and individual freedom.[14] Not belonging to the human world, and thus not confined by its stringent social rules and ethics, the ghost was a figure through which men could release their repressed desires and fulfill their erotic fantasies. Therefore, there were many ghost-mortal man romance stories. However, the male fantasy was also mixed with anxiety about female sexual power. The seductress-demon in Pu's "Painted Skin" embodies this contradiction: she is desirable but destructive.

In Chan's *Painted Skin*, Xiao Wei is both amorous and monstrous in her desire for Wang. By desiring, she transgresses the social hierarchy of male domination and female submission. She looks, desires, and takes; thus she is to be punished.[15] Janey Place states that the monstrous-feminine is constructed within/by a patriarchal ideology. The "ideological operation of the myth (the absolute necessity of controlling the strong, sexual woman) is thus achieved by first demonstrating her dangerous power and its frightening results, then destroying it."[16] It is not difficult to see the mechanism of the same myth underlying Chan's *Painted Skin*. Xiao Wei, who is a threat to the phallocentric system, is removed.

Xiao Wei evokes the femme fatale from American noir films of the 1940s and 1950s: "frustrated and deviant, half predator, half prey, detached yet

---

[13]Creed, 2.
[14]Xianchu Wan, *Chinese Female Ghosts* (zhongguo nügui) (Guilin: Lijiang chubanshe, 1991), 185.
[15]Laura Mulvey, "Visual Pleasure and Narrative Cinema," *Screen* 16.3 (1975), 6–18.
[16]Janey Place, "Women in Film Noir," in *Women in Film Noir*, ed. E. Ann Kaplan (London: BFI, 1980), 45.

ensnared, she falls victim to her own traps."[17] Nevertheless, Xiao Wei differs from the femme fatale in the nature of these "traps." In American noir, the femme fatale's goal is not the man, not the "home" where women are expected by society and culture to perform their traditional gender roles. What she does and desires obviates traditional femininity and threatens the patriarchal order, for which she is punished. Xiao Wei's trap, which she herself sets up, is to be accepted into the domestic space. She transforms from being fatal for men to being "fatal for herself."[18] In a sense, Xiao Wei is defeated by her desire to fit into the traditional feminine role. She starts to lose her power from the moment when Wang offers to "rescue" her. Her deadly power, so chillingly represented in the pre-credit sequence, is subsumed by her desire to become a traditional wife serving the patriarch of the family. By choosing self-sacrifice, she adopts the traditional feminine virtue represented by Peirong. In self-sacrifice/self-destruction, Xiao Wei submits to the traditional world, and completes her transformation from the monstrous-feminine to the traditional-feminine. The tear-jerking melodramatic ending reflects the same ideology: the elimination of the excessive "Other"—the powerful ghostly femme fatale—is necessary for the return of order.

The amorous ghost in Chinese cinema

Though Chinese cinema avoids materials about vengeful ghosts like the one in Pu's "Painted Skin" story, the character Xiao Wei is not completely new to mainland Chinese audiences. She has a close kinship with the amorous ghosts that populated the Chinese screen in the 1980s and 1990s. In the first decades of the P.R.C., ghost literature and plays were condemned as superstition and remnants of feudal society. After the Cultural Revolution (1966–1976), some formerly taboo subjects, including ghost tales, could be addressed in print. In addition to repackaged collections of classical supernatural tales, some writers began to experiment with new forms of ghost stories.[19] Popular media also reflected great interest in the tales about ghosts and fox-spirits in the *Liaozhai* collection of stories. Film adaptations included *Jing bian*/*A Spirit* (1983), *Gui mei*/*Ghost Sisters* (1985), *Hu yuan*/*Romance with a Fox* (1986),

---

[17]Raymond Borde and Etienne Chaumeton, "Towards a Definition of Film Noir," in *Film Noir Reader*, eds. Alain Silver and James Ursini (Pompton Plains: Limelight Editions, 2006), 22.
[18]Ibid., 22.
[19]See Wang, 2004; Chen, 2009.

and *Gu mu huang zhai/Inside an Old Grave* (1991), to name a few. *Liaozhai* was even adapted into a 74-episode television serial in 1986 (although *Painted Skin* was excluded).

The female specters in these films and TV shows were usually humanized—beautiful, kind, and loving—and were seldom portrayed in ways to frighten or disgust the viewer. The exclusive focus on the amorous ghosts and the narrative form of melodrama differentiated Chinese ghost films from the Hong Kong ghost cinema. The increase in Chinese ghost films in the 1980s and the early 1990s reflected the mainland industry's shift away from propaganda-oriented productions to entertainment. The popularity of those films also was attributed to a new consumer culture as well as to a new politics of the body that emerged during that period. The ghost films constructed and presented the female ghost in ways intended to entertain an audience, offering the sorts of narrative and visual pleasures that were denied in the socialist revolutionary cinema prior to the 1980s, including the pleasure of consuming the spectacle of the female body. The propaganda-loaded socialist films of the Maoist era, as Shuqing Cui argues, masculinized women, negated sexual difference, and subjected women's bodies to the nationalist discourse.[20] The amorous ghost provided convenient material to address the new body politics and to legitimate the male gaze at pleasurable female bodies.

Xie Tieli's *Gu mu huang zhai/Inside an Old Grave* (1991), which interweaves four *Liaozhai* stories ("Lian Suo," "Jiao Na," "Painted Skin"/ "Hua pi," and "Nie Xiaoqian"), serves as a good example to illustrate the gendered narrative of this period.[21] A scholar named Yang Yuwei falls in love with Lian Suo, a virgin ghost, and helps to revive her body. But Lian Suo's snobbish parents will not allow the young couple to marry unless Yang succeeds in the imperial exam, through which he can acquire an official position. On his way to the exam, Yang is helped by Jiao Na, a fox-spirit who is proficient in medicine, and by Nie Xiaoqian, a laurel tree-spirit (a ghost in the original story) whom he indirectly frees from a demon's control. He also encounters a ghost who disguises itself as a beautiful woman who seduces men and then kills them. At the end of these erotic adventures comes Yang's success at the imperial exam and his marriage to Lian Suo.

---

[20]See Shuqin Cui, *Women through the Lens: Gender and Nation in a Century of Chinese Cinema* (Honolulu: University of Hawaii Press, 2003), 55; Yue Meng and Jinhua Dai, *Emerging from the Horizon of History* (Fuchu lishi dibiao) (Beijing: Zhongguo renmin chubanshe, 2004), 31.

[21]"Painted Skin" is a less than 10-minute scene. It is mainly used to link the other ghost stories, and does not emphasize the horror element. The male protagonist has no encounter with the ghost.

Inside an Old Grave is a kind of erotic Chinese *Odyssey*. The supremely beautiful and seductive female specters, which previously could only be imagined by readers, were for the first time presented in images for the viewer's voyeuristic pleasure. The scene in which Jiao Na performs a medical treatment on Yang highlights her body rather than her intelligence. Wearing a transparent dress through which her body contour is discernible, she leans toward the male patient who is lying in bed and gently feels his pulse. We see the sexy young doctor through the male patient's eyes. If the mise-en-scène invites erotic imaginings and evokes desire for Jiao Na, this desire is satisfied in the following, almost soft-core pornographic, scene. Yang is ill because of having had sex with Lian Suo (a traditional belief held that sexual infatuation with a ghost could damage a man's health). To be fully cured, Yang must have sexual intercourse with a virgin, and in fulfillment of the patient's (and the viewer's) desire, the virgin is Jiao Na. Medically treating a ghost or a human through sexual intercourse is another male fantasy common in supernatural tales. The original story "Jiao Na" does not have this sex-treatment plot. This film added more erotic elements to satisfy the male viewer's desire to see the female body.

Lian Suo's story is also excessively eroticized. Lian Suo, the original object of the scholar Yang's desire, is a talented virgin ghost who writes beautiful poems. However, as the story develops she becomes merely a sexually desirable object. Yang wants to have sex with her on the first night they meet, but she refuses, fearing that her "*yin*" substance will harm him. When her "*yang*" substance becomes stronger, she invites Wang to have sex with her and tells him she can become a human through receiving his semen. A phallocentric ideology underlies the "*yin/yang*" dichotomy between the female ghost and the male human: "While *Yin* is generally viewed as referring to cold, negative, weak, destructive, passive, and feminine qualities, *Yang* is often associated with hot, positive, strong, creative, dynamic, and masculine attributes."[22] The "semen" invokes the "lack" in the ghost and the phallic power in the man. The sex scene is only subtly implied, but there is a sensuous scene in which Yang offers his blood to Lian Suo to complete the process of her becoming human. While they are both lying in bed, Yang cuts his arm with a knife, letting the blood drip into Lian Suo's naval. The camera lingers, voyeuristically, on the dripping blood and Lian Suo's naked belly.

---

[22] Jianguo Chen, *The Aesthetics of the "Beyond": Phantasm, Nostalgia, and the Literary Practice in Contemporary China* (Newark: University of Delaware Press, 2009), 50.

Just as with the representation of Xiao Wei in *Painted Skin*, the camera highlights the eroticized body of the female specter in early 1990s Chinese ghost films as the fetishized object of male desire. However, Xiao Wei differs from the amorous ghosts in that she is the one that drives the narrative. Although her appearance always causes a pause in the narrative, it is not the classic Hollywood narrative of women freezing "the flow of action in moments of erotic contemplation."[23] It is rather Xiao Wei's fascinating and powerful presence that disrupts the narrative flow and demands attention.

Another difference between the early ghost films and Chan's *Painted Skin* lies in the power structure between the female ghost and the male protagonist. In the former, femininity is defined by the desirability of the woman's body, whereas masculinity is defined primarily by action. *Inside an Old Grave* follows the typical phallocentric narrative: the female ghosts "freeze the flow of action in moments of erotic contemplation"; the male character forwards the story and makes things happen. Yang is the adventurer, moving from one ghost to the next, linking the four narrative segments. In spite of their supernatural abilities, the female ghosts and fox spirits usually rely on the mortal man to save them. Yang offers Lian Suo his semen and blood so that she can become human; he helps Jiao Na and her family escape a deadly thunder attack; he indirectly frees Nie Xiaoqian from the oppression of a demon. Similarly, in the 1985 film *Ghost Sisters*, the scholar helps two ghosts, first to get justice and then to be reborn (in the original story, the scholar is put in jail by his enemy and is later saved by the ghosts.)

In these narratives the female ghost's sexual power is balanced by her vulnerability; her dependence on the man alleviates her potential threat to the patriarchal system. In contrast, Xiao Wei's transformation from the monstrous to the feminine is not through men. Her "rescuer" Wang is not her savior. Overpowered by Xiao Wei's sexuality, Wang loses his ability to see things objectively and rationally, which are important qualities for a military leader. His misjudgment is partially responsible for many people's deaths, including his soldiers'. Wang fails to protect his wife and his soldiers, and thus is far from being a hero. In reversing the power structure, *Painted Skin* becomes a more powerful film than the previous Chinese ghost-scholar romances, and the ghostly femme fatale carries more agency and stronger subjectivity than her amorous ghost sisters.

---

[23]Mulvey; Ibid.

Allegorical reading in the contemporary context

Painted Skin has been read as a metaphor for marriage and family crisis in contemporary China.²⁴ Wang Shen's struggle, having to choose between his wife and another woman he desires passionately, would not be an issue in the *Liaozhai* world, where polygamy was legal and ethically acceptable. Wang's dilemma, however, can be felt acutely by contemporary Chinese viewers, who have been experiencing tremendous changes in the social, cultural, and domestic domains since the early 1990s. Along with China's rapid economic transition and commercialization have come the deterioration of traditional values and a rising divorce rate. An increasing number of television dramas (such as *Lailai wangwang* (1998) and *Qian shou* (1999)) and films (such as Feng Xiao Gang's *Shouji/Cellphone* (2003) and *Yisheng tanxi/A Sigh* (2000)) deal with the subject of marriage crisis. They revolve around the confrontation between a seductress and a homemaker and usually end with the victory of the latter. The male protagonist is usually the victim of the women's war.

I will compare a mainland-produced ghost film, Teng Huao-Tao's *Xingzhong yougui/Matrimony*, released two years before *Painted Skin*, to illustrate the recurrent narrative of female confrontation and marriage crisis. *Matrimony* is set in 1930s Shanghai. A radio hostess Xu Manli (Fan Bingbing) dies at the beginning of the film in a car accident. Her fiancé Shen Junchu (Leon Lai) is distraught by her death and lives in mourning. Later, he accepts his mother's arrangement and marries Sansan (Rene Liu), but he is emotionally remote to his wife. Gradually, Sansan wins Junchu's love with her patience, obedience, and devotion to the marriage and the family. Manli's ghost becomes jealous and threats Sansan's life. At the climax, when Manli is going to take over Sansan's body and kill her, Junchu intervenes. Only then does the ghost lover retreat. The film ends with the revelation that what we have just seen does not really happen and that it is a story that Manli is reading on the radio (it is a typical ending of a Chinese horror film to avoid censorship of superstition and ghost materials).²⁵

The similarity between *Painted Skin* and *Matrimony* is substantial. The confrontation between the two female characters forms the core of the film narrative and they represent opposite feminine attributes: the monstrous-feminine and the traditional feminine. Manli is almost another version of Xiao Wei. She is a strong independent woman with a career as a radio

---

²⁴See Peng, 2010; Fei, 2009.
²⁵For a study of contemporary Chinese horror films, see Zeng; Ibid.

host; she wears red clothes, which symbolize her passion and desire; she is manipulative and knows how to take advantage of Sansan's innocence and love for Junchu to get what she wants. In contrast, Sansan is another version of Peirong. She is an obedient housewife who endures her husband's neglect and patiently performs her role as a loving companion, bringing him food and tea, and as a dutiful daughter-in-law. Her dream is to have a family where "after dinner, the husband reads while the wife does housework," according to Sansan's voice-over. Her purity is indicated by the white dresses she wears.

In both films the mortal man remains relatively passive and victimized. Same as Wang in *Painted Skin*, Junchu is torn by his feeling for both women, and is not aware of the ghost's danger until she threatens his wife's life. Facing the choice between the aggressive ghost and the virtuous homemaker, both men choose the latter. At the end of *Matrimony*, Manli asks her audience the following question: "If you were Junchu, how would you choose?" This question can also be seen as addressing the male audience in the theater watching this film. *Matrimony* and *Painted Skin* seem to convey a regressive and conservative message: the sexually liberated and desiring woman is the source of moral degeneration, and the traditional feminine is the ideal male companion and the family guardian.

As I have argued elsewhere, these films and TV dramas reflect "anxieties around women's sexual autonomy" in contemporary China.[26] They reinforce a phallocentric ideology about femininity and masculinity. *Painted Skin*, with a similar narrative, is thus seen by many Chinese audiences as a modern adaptation of an antiquated story to address a current social issue: Xiao Wei is the temptress that threatens the stability of the family, while Peirong is the virtuous homemaker that keeps the family intact. However, I would argue that *Painted Skin* is more ambiguous than *Matrimony* and other above-mentioned films in gender representation.

Painted Skin shares the recurrent narrative of the female confrontation. To emphasize the conflict between the ghostly femme fatale and the traditional feminine, *Painted Skin* casts two Chinese superstars in the lead female roles—Zhou Xun, star of *Suzhou he/Suzhou River* (2000) and *Ye yan/The Banquet* (2006), and Zhao Wei, star of *Shaolin Soccer* (2001) and *Ye Shanghai/The Longest Night in Shanghai* (2007). Chan added several scenes between Xiao Wei and Peirong. The crucial scene in Pu's story, in which the ghost reveals her monstrous body under Wang's gaze, is

---

[26]Li Zeng, "The Road to the Past: Socialist Nostalgia in Postsocialist China," *Visual Anthropology* 22 (March–June 2009), 108–22.

changed in this film to Xiao Wei's purposefully revealing herself to Peirong to demonstrate her destructive power.

However, in their confrontation, Xiao Wei is the one that occupies the center of the screen and captures attention from spectators in the diegetic world as well as from the audiences watching the film. Her dominance in a gender relation makes her a more compelling character than Peirong. When Peirong fails to find support from her husband, she seeks help from her former lover, Pang Yong. The film includes three grand fighting scenes to demonstrate Donnie Yen's martial arts skills. Xiao Wei does not flinch before him. His masculinity becomes a spectacle for momentary entertainment. Instead of the traditional feminine character, it is the powerful monster that provides female audiences pleasure of empowerment.[27] Although she chooses self-destruction and Wang and Peirong live happily ever after, the film ends with the image of a fox—Xiao Wei. The femme fatale initiates the narrative and completes it.

The ambivalence toward the ghostly femme fatale makes *Painted Skin* a more powerful film than *Matrimony* and the other above-mentioned films that deal with themes of seduction and marriage crisis. This ambivalence refuses a simplistic reading of the film as one that reinforces patriarchal ideology and denigrates female subjectivity and women's sexual autonomy.

Conclusion

Through a close analysis of the ghostly femme fatale in *Painted Skin* in relation to the amorous ghost in Chinese cinema, this paper has demonstrated that *Painted Skin* creates a stronger female character with agency and subjectivity. Although being fetishized as an object of the male gaze, she provides the female audience with the pleasure of empowerment with her uncompromising power over the male-dominated world. Nevertheless, this paper points out that the ghost/fox-spirit's female agency is weakened by the patriarchal narrative of the control of the "monstrous-feminine." The femme fatale, with her excessive sexuality and transgressive power, poses danger to the patriarchy-dominated family structure, and as a consequence, her elimination through self-destruction is the solution for the return of order and the status quo.

---

[27] Isabel Cristina Pinedo, *Recreational Terror: Women and the Pleasures of Horror Film Viewing* (New York: State University of New York Press, 1997).

The ambivalence about the power of the ghost/fox-spirit and her danger evoked a resonance in the mainland audience. Many people read *Painted Skin* as an allegory about moral degeneration and marriage crisis in contemporary China. However, while sharing similar themes and the narrative structure of female confrontation with other contemporary Chinese films, *Painted Skin* cannot be read simply as a film that denigrates women's sexual autonomy as a source of moral degeneration. The ghostly femme fatale remains a more compelling and powerful character than the traditional homemaker.

The female body and its sexuality is often the site where social and cultural conflicts are addressed and negotiated. This dynamic continues in the sequel to *Painted Skin, Painted Skin: The Resurrection* (2012), a mainland production, in which the male protagonist is seduced by the sexual fox-spirit and in the end blinds himself to resist potential temptation. In a more dramatic and sensational way, the sequel continues to warn against the danger of women's excessive sexuality. These supernatural films reflect a cultural anxiety and ambivalence toward women's sexual autonomy and the deterioration of traditional values in an increasingly commercialized society. The patriarchal ideology, the control of the "monstrous-feminine," still dominates the narrative of these supernatural tales. Nevertheless, it is important to recognize that it is the sexually aggressive and physically invincible phantoms that demand screen time, inspire sequels and remakes, and keep drawing audiences to the theater (*Painted Skin: The Resurrection* was the highest grossing film of the year in China). Those ghostly figures will continue to be rewritten and redefined, fascinating a changing modern audience and challenging viewers to question the phallocentric ideology that creates them.

13

"It's Not the House That's Haunted": Demons, Debt, and the Family in Peril Formula in Recent Horror Cinema

Bernice M. Murphy

Haunted house movies were in short supply at the American box office during the first decade of the new millennium. The nation's most commercially successful horror films in the years immediately following the September 11th terrorist attacks generally bypassed the supernatural in favor of horrors of a human nature which either dramatized the moral and ideological quandaries raised by the so-called War on Terror that followed or obliquely re-enacted the scenes of mass death conjured up by the catastrophe.[1]

This is no longer the case. Since the 2007 release of Oren Peli's *Paranormal Activity*, the supernatural horror film has once again become immensely popular at the American box office. In the chapter that follows, I will therefore discuss *Paranormal Activity* and three high-profile haunted house movies that followed in its wake: *Insidious* (2010), *Sinister* (2012), and *The Conjuring* (2013). As we shall see, these films on one level represent a commercially

---

[1] For more on post-9/11 horror cinema, see: Aviva Briefel and Sam J., Miller, eds. *Horror After 9/11: World of Fear, Cinema of Terror* (Austin: University of Texas Press, 2011); Kevin J. Wetmore, *Post 9/11 Horror in American Cinema* (London: Continuum, 2012).

savvy return to the kind of "Old School" scares found in the most prominent haunted house movies of the 1970s and early 1980s. However, as well as shamelessly setting out to evoke the plot lines and decidedly nonironic atmosphere of established genre classics they also tap in to the rich seam of economic and class anxiety currently afflicting the American middle classes, a tendency which arguably has much to do with their commercial success.

Like Peli's debut, the films discussed here originated with Blumhouse Productions, which was established by former Miramax executive Jason Blum in 2000. The success of *Paranormal Activity* helped turn Blum into "Hollywood's first micro budget mogul."[2] The industry consensus is that Blumhouse has achieved a remarkable degree of success in a relatively short space of time because the company has embraced a nontraditional production model that depends upon "… a very simple and alluring logic: make movies fast and for a price—$5 million or less—and then spend the $20 million or $30 million needed to release them in theatres only if they have a shot at selling at least $25 million worth of tickets."[3] The "Blum Formula" also "relies on stars willing to work for cheap on a hefty backend."[4] The centrality of the horror film to the company's profile is made clear in the "About Blumhouse" section of the company website, which cites all of the films discussed here (except for *The Conjuring*) alongside dystopian home invasion hit *The Purge* (2013) and its sequel, *The Purge: Anarchy* (2014).[5]

The company's films share many of the same on-screen and off-screen personnel. *Saw* director/co-writer James Wan helmed *Insidious, Insidious: Chapter 2* (2013), and *The Conjuring*. He is also lined up to direct *The Conjuring 2*, which is due to be released in 2015. John R. Leonetti served as Director of Photography on *Insidious* and *The Conjuring*, and directed the latter's spin-off *Annabelle* (2014). Leonetti also worked with Wan on his post-*Saw* efforts *Death Sentence* (2007) and *Dead Silence* (2007). As well as portraying the "lipstick-faced demon" in *Insidious*, Joseph Bishara composed the scores for both *Insidious* and *Insidious: Chapter 2* and *The Conjuring*, as well as *Annabelle* and Blumhouse's 2013 release *Dark Skies*. Kristen M. Burke

---

[2]Marisa Guthrie and Tatiana Siegel, "How Horror Took Over Hollywood," *Hollywood Reporter*, October 18, 2013, http://www.hollywoodreporter.com/news/american-horror-story-walking-dead-645007?page=show (accessed April 10, 2014).

[3]For information on the alleged downsides to the Blumhouse "micro budget" model, see: Kim Masters, "Jason Blum's Crowded Movie Morgue," *The Hollywood Reporter*, March 7, 2014, http://www.hollywoodreporter.com/news/jason-blums-crowded-movie-morgue-683212 (accessed April 11, 2014).

[4]Guthrie and Siegel, "How Horror Took Over Hollywood."

[5]http://blumhouse.com/ (accessed June 17, 2014).

was costume designer on both *Insidious* installments as well as *The Conjuring* and *Paranormal Activity 2*, while Kirk M. Morri edited *The Conjuring* and both *Insidious* films. To a lesser extent, there is also some recycling of onscreen personnel: Ethan Hawke stars in *Sinister* and *The Purge*, while Patrick Wilson features in the first two installments of the *Insidious* series as well as *The Conjuring*.

This "high-quality assembly line" depends upon "stories that have either a universal theme or a very sellable concept."[6] The "universal theme" most frequently exploited by Blumhouse is that of the family being terrorized in its own home by supernatural forces. Even the storylines of nonsupernatural horror Blumhouse efforts such *The Purge* (2013) and *Dark Skies* (2013) revolve around the same basic template, except that in the former, demons have been replaced by murderous thugs, and in the latter, extraterrestrials (both also feature a suburban setting). I'll begin therefore by briefly discussing the striking level of thematic conformity and plot repetition found in *Paranormal Activity*, *Insidious*, *Sinister*, and *The Conjuring*, before examining their depiction of middle-class economic anxieties in more detail.

The first major plot device that unites these films is the ever familiar "child in peril" trope. Children serve as conduits to the supernatural in all of these films. *Paranormal Activity* at first appears to be an exception, but as the story progresses, troubled protagonist Katie's disclosure of her troubled childhood underlines the fact that the demonic entity causing the haunting came in to her life when she was very young. Children and/or teenagers also feature as prominent elements in all subsequent installments of the franchise.

Insidious essentially replicates the plot of *Poltergeist* (1982).[7] Both films involve a young family with three children trying to recover a "lost" child who has been spirited away to a parallel realm somehow existing within the family home (a similar plot device features in *Sinister*, as we shall see). In each instance, the aid of a no-nonsense female psychic and male assistants is enlisted (although *Poltergeist* also has a motherly female scientist). Children are also targeted in *The Conjuring*. The youngest child in the Perron family, April (Kyla Deaver), finds a creepy music box in the trunk of a tree; her older sister Christine (Joey King) is menaced in her sleep; their sister Cindy (Mackenzie Foy) is, like Katie in *Paranormal Activity*, Dalton in *Insidious*, and Trevor in *Sinister*, a sleepwalker (disordered slumber features in all of these films). It eventually transpires that the Perron's new home was cursed in the

---

[6]Ibid.
[7]Which itself resembles Richard Matheson's 1962 *Twilight Zone* episode "Little Girl Lost."

1860s by a woman named Bathsheba, the descendant of a Salem witch, who killed her own infant so that she could make a pact with Satan. Having been transformed into a demonic entity, she now tries to make mothers who inhabit the house replicate her bloody actions.

The child-centric nature of the hauntings in all of these films reaches its apotheosis in *Sinister*, in which it is ultimately revealed that a demonic entity known as "Baghuul the Child Eater" can use images as a gateway to our reality. The missing children whose mysterious fate is investigated by protagonist Ellison Oswalt (Ethan Hawke) were lured away to the demon's "netherworld" so that their souls could be devoured. Though it initially seems as if Ellison's son will be targeted, in fact, it is his young daughter, Ashley (Clare Foley), who is "taken over" by Baghuul. In the film's grim climax, she hacks the rest of the family to death before joining Baghuul and the other "missing" children in his realm.

One thing that distinguishes later Blumhouse haunted house narratives from *Paranormal Activity* is that unlike Peli's film none of them are straightforward found-footage narratives (perhaps because this would impinge upon the uniqueness of the *PA* series). *Insidious*, *Sinister*, and *The Conjuring* are all presented to us as glossy Hollywood productions whose inherent artificiality is never in doubt (although *The Conjuring* is presented a retelling of a "true" story—just like *The Amityville Horror* (1979)).[8] However, *Sinister* and *The Conjuring* do include important sequences which are shot as though being recorded on authentically grainy 8mm or, in the case of the latter, 16mm film.[9] *Sinister* foregrounds the importance of its intermittent found-footage component by opening with a grainy 8mm recording of a family strung up with rope like prisoners at the scaffold before being murdered by an unknown assailant (later revealed to be their demon-possessed youngest child). Many of the film's most atmospheric moments subsequently involve the scenes in which the Ellison psychs himself up to watch the increasingly disturbing 8mm style footage of further family massacres that he has found in the attic of his new home. The film's re-creation of the distinctive look of older film stock highlights the fact that these murders have been going on for decades. In addition, in an age where

---

[8] Kimberly Jackson notes of *The Blair Witch Project* and *Paranormal Activity* that they use many of the same devices to try and make the viewer believe that the events onscreen are "real": the actors and the characters have the same names, the characters film themselves, and there is "black screen verbiage like that used in documentaries to explain what happened before or after the events chronicled." *Technology, Monstrosity and Reproduction in Twenty-First Century Horror* (Basingstoke: Palgrave Macmillan, 2013), 63.

[9] A technique also used in the recent Hammer film *The Quiet Ones* (2014).

digital video has achieved commercial dominance over film, the simulation of the film style serves multiple purposes. It signifies an attempt to evoke both jolting "realism" as well as the second hand "spookiness." *Sinister*'s target audience of 18–34-year-olds may vaguely recollect from childhood viewings of 1970s and 1980s genre classics.

This is also the case with the relatively brief use of simulated 16mm footage in *The Conjuring*. We are told early on that demonologists Ed and Lorraine Warren (Patrick Wilson and Vera Farmiga) always record supernatural events in order to provide evidence should further clerical intervention be required. Some disturbing footage of an exorcism-gone-bad is shown at one of their speaking engagements, both as a means of illustrating the terrible toll this event took on Lorraine, but also as way of setting up the impromptu exorcism that occurs during the climax of the film. A key sequence during which the investigators try to contact the demonic entity that is terrifying the Perron family is also presented to us in this distinctive style, which is again probably intended to make the audience briefly experience the kind of "this is happening in real time" unease found in the *Paranormal Activity* films.

The remarkably consistent thematic similarity between the films also extends to the way in which each of them uses technology. As is usually the case in haunted house narratives more generally, technology—be it recording equipment or otherwise—is always associated with male characters. Micah in *Paranormal Activity* insists upon documenting the strange events plaguing his girlfriend despite her increasingly anxious pleas that he stop. "Specs" (Leigh Whannell) and "Tucker" (Angus Sampson), the assistants who accompany psychic Elise Rainier (Lin Shaye) to the Lambert house in *Insidious*, arrive, like their counterparts in *Poltergeist*, laden down with all manner of audio-visual and ghost detecting equipment. In *The Conjuring*, the Warrens employ a college student named Drew (Shannon Kook) who is in charge of their AV gear and specialized monitoring devices. Ellison in *Sinister* spends much of the film obsessively viewing footage on his 8mm projector.

What the presence of technology wielded by male characters also does here is affirm the impossibility of trying to record, control, or expel malevolent supernatural forces in any strictly "rational" manner (one could reasonably object to this problematic suggestion that rationality is a specifically masculine trait, but it should also be pointed out that in all of these films, the urge to "document" or engage with the supernatural also backfires upon the men concerned). In yet another indication of the extremely formulaic nature of these films, it's a paradigm that recurs throughout the haunted house sub-genre—one need only think of Shirley Jackson's Dr. Montague's ultimately disastrous attempts to scientifically prove the existence of ghosts in *The*

Haunting of Hill House (1959) or of Dr. Lionel Barrett, who tries to conquer the "Mount Everest of Haunted Houses" with a machine known as "the reversor" in Richard Matheson's *Hell House* (1971).[10] As in the likes of *Poltergeist, The Others* (2001), and *The Orphanage* (2007), in *Insidious* and *The Conjuring*, the ability to psychically connect with "the other side" is also an ability found mainly in female characters (Dr. Fredrich's in *Paranormal Activity* is a rare exception, although Micah in particular has doubts about his authenticity).

Another plot device that unites all four Blumhouse films is that they posit the existence of sinister parallel worlds existing alongside our own. The camera that keeps rolling throughout *Paranormal Activity* impassively records supernatural incursions in a manner that emphasizes the suggestion that below the cosy facade of everyday life there are malevolent entities looking for a chance to "break through." Adding to our unease is the fact that many of these uncanny eruptions happen while Micah and Katie are asleep (or, in Katie's case, unaware of her actions). *Insidious* emphasizes a similar sense of disquiet by depicting the netherworld known as "The Further" as it is accessed by protagonist Josh Lambert (Patrick Wilson) during his bid to rescue his son Dalton. "The Further" is populated by lost souls with a fondness for sporting painted faces and eerie recordings of "Tiptoe Through the Tulips." They use Josh's breach of the walls between their world and ours (through astral projection) as a chance to "cross over." The same theme resurfaces in *Sinister's* focus on Baghuul's Pied-Piper like ability to lure children to the "other side." The film ends as Baghuul himself suddenly pops into frame both to provide one final scare, but also to reinforce the idea of evil "breaking through" the cinematic fourth wall (as in the film's close relation *Ring* (1998)). Lorraine's psychic visions in *The Conjuring*—only she (and the audience) can see the shadowy entity that has literally attached itself to the backs of the terrorized Perron family– also emphasizes this by now very familiar sense of other worlds existing alongside our own.

As we shall see, this recurrent depiction of the family home as an inherently insecure milieu ripe for invasion by sinister forces also taps in to the kind of powerful uncertainty which increasingly characterizes middle-class life in the United States. This feeling of instability is further emphasized by the fact that the demonic entities in each film considered here are ultimately successful in their attempts to break through. What's more, the story in each instance also climaxes with the demonic possession of one of the protagonists, who then murders (or attempts to murder) his/her fellow

---

[10]Richard Matheson, *Hell House* (New York: Tor, 1971; 1999), 15.

family members. By using this particular plot point so frequently, the films further emphasize that the assumed stability of the American family unit is always under threat, and that loved ones can be "taken over" by forces that want nothing other than to cause pain and despair. This strain of insecurity within the nuclear family is also one that can be linked to the resonant undercurrent of economic anxiety contained in the films.

Another important similarity shared by all four films is the fact that the ghostly has been completely displaced by the demonic. It is a tendency that owes much to the demonic entities that tormented the Lutz clan in *The Amityville Horror*, which, along with *Poltergeist*, serves as these films most significant cinematic antecedent. The way in which the various demonic entities are depicted is remarkably consistent, and as we shall see, again highlights the way in which the Blumhouse production model taps in to current middle-class anxieties. The films all have as a major plot point the belief that moving house in order to escape a demon is futile, because it will follow you. It's a notion first dramatized in *Paranormal Activity*. Dr. Fredrichs blanches upon hearing the couple's story, and tells them that demons are a type of entity related to "something that is not human" which attaches itself to a victim and proves very difficult to remove. As Katie later cries, in what will become a familiar refrain in the films that follow, "It's not the house, it's me. Wherever I go, it goes."

Exactly the same plot point recurs in *Insidious* (and even furnishes the movie's tagline).[11] When Elise arrives to aid Josh and Renai, whose seemingly comatose son Dalton is still the focus of disturbing activity despite a house move, she declares, "Your son isn't in a coma. Falling off a ladder had nothing to do with this. His physical body's here, but his spiritual body is not. And the reason ... is because ... it's not the house that's haunted. It's your son." Dalton's ability to astral project has left him vulnerable to the attentions of a demon seeking a human body so it can walk in our world, and his soul is now trapped in "The Further." In *Sinister*, Ellison moves his family back to their beloved old home in the final moments of the film in a bid to protect them, but in fact, this decision actually ensures their collective demise. Yet again, the demon has followed them, and in fact, the process of moving house was vital to ensuring that events played out according to Baaghul's nefarious plan.[12]

---

[11] The tag line reads: "It's not the house that's haunted."
[12] The reason why Baghuul needs his victims to move house is never adequately explained: all we are told is that each murdered family had recently moved into a house that was the site of a previous family massacre carried out at the demon's behest.

The preeminence of the demonic rather than the ghostly threat in these films is further highlighted by the fact that professional demonologists come to the forefront in *The Conjuring*, which purports to tell the "true" story of one of the most dangerous cases ever tackled by Ed and Lorraine Warren, self-described "Demonologists, ghost hunters, paranormal researchers." The Warrens stress the fundamental inhumanity of the entities causing all of the trouble in by what are by now wearily familiar terms to any regular horror moviegoer. "Annabelle," the evil doll featured in the opening scene, has been used as a conduit by "something that's never walked the earth in human form. The force possessing Annabelle is "something demonic" striving to take possession of its victims in order to enter the human world. The same is true of Bathsheba, who appears to somehow be both simultaneously a demon and a kind of ghost (she was, after all, a real person at one time, but is also clearly allied with the demonic). Lorraine tells the terrified Perron's that "It doesn't matter where you go. This dark entity has latched itself to your family, and it's feeding off you." Ed elaborates, "Sometimes, when you get haunted, it's like stepping on gum—you take it with you." Like a bad credit history, the demons in these films can never be shaken off by a mere change of address.

For all of their similarities, however, it should be acknowledged that *The Conjuring* is the only film discussed here in which conventional religiosity is overtly referenced. The Warrens are devout Catholics who work closely with the church. They also make use of religious artifacts during their investigations (Lorraine even holds a rosary in her hand in many scenes). Yet the view of the demonic espoused in *The Conjuring* is still essentially the same as that encountered in the earlier Blumhouse films, all of which espoused a much more secular, or at least, nondenominational view of matters (as was the case in *Poltergeist*, in which Christianity is only referenced once, in passing. There is never any suggestion, unlike as in *The Amityville Horror* (1979) or *The Exorcist* (1973), of clergymen belonging to any denomination being called in). This important difference between *The Conjuring* and earlier Blumhouse haunted house films may be due to the fact that it alone is explicitly "based on a true story" and, as such, has to at least play lip service to the well-known religiosity of the *real* Ed and Lorraine Warren. For instance, during her meeting with Danny Lutz in the 2012 documentary *My Amityville Horror*, Lorraine brandishes both a piece of what she believes to be "the one true cross" in addition to a picture of the Italian mystic Padre Pio. This also helps explain why it is that *The Conjuring* is the only film considered here that has a happy ending in which the demonic threat is conclusively dealt with (even if it is just a skirmish that forms part of a much larger battle between good and evil).

For all of their obvious replication of themes and plot devices, however, what is most striking about the films considered here is the manner in which they implicitly and explicitly reference the financial crisis has adversely affected the lives of millions of ordinary American families. The significance of middle-class economic anxiety in the films being produced by Blumhouse is first of all emphasized by the fact that they have helped re-establish the idea of the suburban-set haunting for a new generation of cinemagoers. (*The Conjuring*, which is set in a rural farmhouse and features a blue-collar family under threat, is again the sole exception here. It does however feature many of the same plot devices and anxieties seen in the suburban-set films).

Writing in 2008 on the topic of suburban set haunted house narratives, I noted that "one is much more likely to encounter a serial killer or psychotic mass murderer in suburban set horror films of the 1980s and 1990s than a house that is haunted in the traditional sense," in part because "Americans these days are more afraid of the people next door than of the dead that lie beneath their feet."[13] The recent re-emergence of the suburbia-set haunted house story in the form of *Insidious*, *Sinister*, and *Paranormal Activity* highlights the fact that the kinds of economic and class anxieties that helped inform the likes of *The House Next Door* (1978), *Poltergeist*, and *The Amityville Horror* have recently re-emerged with a vengeance. This can partially be attributed to the fact that economic crash has deepened the preexisting suspicion that the suburban way of life is one that cannot (and indeed, *should* not) be maintained.[14]

As Leigh Gallagher noted in 2013, "The housing crisis, in which the binging on residential mortgages led to the overbuilding of millions of homes, hit the suburbs especially hard: builders erected more single-family houses than at almost any time in history and covered record amounts of farmland with new subdivisions. Many of those houses now sit empty." Yet, she continues, the housing crisis "only concealed something deeper and more profound happening to what we have come to know as American suburbia. Simply speaking, more and more Americans don't want to live there anymore."[15]

---

[13]Bernice Murphy, *The Suburban Gothic in American Popular Culture* (Basingstoke: Palgrave Macmillan, 2009), 135.
[14]See, for instance, James Howard Kuntsler, *The Geography of Nowhere: The Rise and Decline of America's Man-Made Landscape* (New York: Touchstone, 1994); J.R. Short, B.F. Hanlon and T.J. Vicino "The Decline of Inner Suburbs: The New Suburban Gothic in the United States." *Geography Compass* 1.3 (2007), 641–56.
[15]Leigh Gallagher, *The End of the Suburbs: Where the American Dream Is Moving* (New York: Penguin, 2013), 5.

Of course, locating this kind of connection between the haunted house story and contemporaneous economic unease is by no means a new critical approach. As Andrew Smith usefully outlines, there is a long tradition of connecting the eighteenth- and nineteenth-century gothic in particular to middle-class anxieties about financial insecurity and precarious social status. As he rightly notes, while it would be reductive to "reduce the gothic to a solely class bound analysis," "such ideas help us to critically read specific issues about power which are relevant to a discussion of ghosts and money."[16] It has also been the case then that the haunted house in late twentieth-century American cinema has previously been subject to this line of critical inquiry. In his influential discussion of *The Amityville Horror* in *Danse Macabre* (1981), Stephen King described it as a prime example of the horror film as "economic nightmare," a reading that Dale Bailey expanded, rightly noting that "Jay Anson wasn't the first writer to employ the haunted house as a symbol of the sometimes grim realities of American life."[17] Given the rather obvious (and oft noted) potential for drawing parallels between the specter of supernatural incursion and the specter of looming bankruptcy, it is hardly surprising then that at a time when the American middle classes have been through severe economic uncertainty last seen in the early 1970s, the haunted house movie has made such a major comeback.

As my earlier discussions of the most prominent characteristics of the Blumhouse "assembly line" have indicated, it is therefore my belief that their haunted house films dramatize the ever-deepening sense of insecurity and crisis besetting the nation's middle classes in particular. Underpinning many recent discussions of the lot of the middle-class family in modern American society is a sense of profound pessimism and concern about its rapidly waning prospects. Bestsellers such as Timothy Noah's *The Great Divergence: America's Growing Inequality Crisis and What We Can Do About It* (2012) and George Packer's *The Unwinding: Thirty Years of American Decline* (2013) have argued that the past forty years have seen a steadily accelerating downturn in income and quality of life for the American middle class that shows no sign of slowing (in fact, the opposite is the case). Both Noah and Packard highlight the fact that the prolonged "Golden Age" which lasted from the end of World War II until around 1973 will likely never be recaptured, as the income gap between those at the higher end of the scale and those in the middle

---

[16]Andrew Smith, *The Ghost Story 1840–1920* (Manchester: Manchester University Press, 2010), 12.

[17]See: Stephen King, *Danse Macabre* (London: Warner, 1981), 163–170, Dale Bailey, *American Nightmares: The Haunted House Formula in American Popular Fiction* (Bowling Green, OH: Bowling Green State University Press, 1999), 67.

ceaselessly widens. As Noah puts it, "The American Dream is less attainable than it once was. And it was never as attainable as many people wanted to believe."[18] This sense of decline has been solidified by recent studies which have found that the although the United States is still the world's richest large country, the American middle class is no longer the world's wealthiest, in large part because of the increasing income inequality identified above.[19]

It is relevant for our purposes too that the ceaseless desire for home ownership—which helped fuel the disastrous trend for overextended mortgage debt—was a major factor in the economic crash. As Robert J. Shiller notes, "US homeownership rates rose over the period 1997–2005 for all regions, all age groups, and all income groups."[20] During the same period, the U.S. census showed an 11.5 percent increase in the number of owner-occupied homes.[21] The purchase of many of these homes had been facilitated by the emergence of so-called subprime mortgages, which were "provided to borrowers who would not normally be regarded as trustworthy. Many of them were so-called NINJA loans, extended to people with no incomes, no jobs, and no assets."[22] When the housing bubble that had to a considerable extent be financed by subprime mortgages began to implode in 2007, the effects were devastating: "by autumn 2009, over 40% of all US mortgages were either delinquent or in foreclosure," and the global financial markets began to enter a prolonged free fall whose effects are still being felt today.[23] As has already been noted, the effects of this free fall had a hugely detrimental effect upon the suburbs in particular—very many of the homes being foreclosed were, after all, in such neighborhoods.

It should be noted however that suburbia functions in these films mainly as backdrop rather than as an overt focus of the narrative, unlike in some older suburban house stories (for instance, *Poltergeist* very explicitly critiques the perceived complacency, greed, and disrespect for the past that popular culture often associates with such developments). The use of the suburban setting in three of these films does, however, reinforce the bourgeois credentials and complacency of our protagonists. For instance, although they are still in

---

[18] Timothy Noah, *The Great Divergence: America's Growing Inequality Crisis and What We Can Do about It* (New York: Bloomsbury, 2012), 27.
[19] David Leonhardht and Kevin Quealy, "The American Middle Class Is No Longer the World's Richest," *The New York Times*, April 22, 2014, http://www.nytimes.com/2014/04/23/upshot/the-american-middle-class-is-no-longer-the-worlds-richest.html (accessed June 18, 2014).
[20] Robert J. Shiller, *The Subprime Solution: How Today's Global Financial Crisis Happened, and What to Do About It* (Princeton: Princeton University Press, 2009), 1.
[21] Ibid.
[22] Howard Davies, *The Financial Crisis: Who Is to Blame?* (London: Polity, 2010), 133.
[23] Ibid., 2007.

their mid–late twenties, Micah (Micah Sloate) and Katie in *Paranormal Activity* inhabit a spacious home in the suburbs of San Diego (a detail which perhaps helps emphasize the film's status as a relic of the "pre-crash" era). The film makes it clear that Micah is the one with the financial muscle: we soon infer that the technological toys showcased in the film have been purchased by him. Katie, a college student, is far less impressed by all of this equipment, anxiously asking, "Seriously, what did you throw down for that?" to which Micah glibly replies, "About half as much as I made today"—an answer which sets up a recurring pattern in the film, whereby he glibly dismisses her concerns. Relationship problems surrounding money surface even more explicitly in *Sinister:* washed-up true crime writer Ellison's motive for moving his family into the "murder house" lies in his desire to write a book that will salvage his ebbing reputation and secure his family's financial security (although ego plays a role as well).

The connection between home ownership, financial anxiety, and supernatural terror in all four films is further highlighted by the fact that in *Insidious, Sinister,* and *The Conjuring,* the protagonists have just moved in. As Barry Curtis notes, this is a recurrent trope in haunted house movies as far back as the 1944 film *The Uninvited*:

> As in many other haunted house films, there is a scene of packing and unpacking. This very characteristic moment is a promise of new beginnings, but also prefigures tensions between old possessions and new contexts. The room, filled with cardboard boxes or draped with dust sheets, is poised at a vulnerable point of transit and porosity, when the narratives of the new inhabitants are weakened and receptive and the narratives of the new home are at their most influential.[24]

The upheaval of moving also inevitably delays the family's realization that something is very wrong with their new abode. Renai (Rose Byrne) and Josh Lambert (Patrick Wilson) in *Insidious* initially attribute their Dalton's complaint that he doesn't like his new room to unfamiliarity with his new environment. Renai's comment that "I just want things to be different in this house" suggests that despite the couple's seemingly happy marriage, preexisting discontent percolates just below the surface. The purchase of a new home also represents one of the biggest and most anxiety-spawning financial transactions any of us will ever make. It is perhaps hardly surprising, therefore, that as in *The Amityville Horror,* the protagonists of *Sinister* and *The*

---

[24]Barry Curtis, *Dark Places: The Haunted House in Film* (London: Reaktion Books, 2008), 171.

Conjuring seem to have at the back of their minds the niggling worry that they have severely overextended themselves this time. In fact, economic disquiet directly informs these moves from the outset. As noted already, Ellison has moved his family far from their actual home (a spacious mansion which he can no longer afford) to a dreary looking tract house that is also a crime scene. The disruption caused by the move—and the resentment felt by his wife and children—is again highlighted from the start by the visual prominence afforded boxes containing their belongings (his sleepwalking son Trevor even manages to climb into one of them during his nocturnal perambulations).

In *The Conjuring*, the Perron family moves into their historic new home in rural Rhode Island in order to make another fresh start. The fact that this move has placed extra financial strain upon blue-collar breadwinner Roger (Ron Livingston) is emphasized from the outset. He admonishes his five daughters to eat their pizza because, "It's expensive to feed you girls," and his wife Carolyn (Lili Taylor) later acknowledges that "I know it's a lot to pay off." The couple later explains to Ed and Lorraine—whose own large suburban home establishes them as probably comfortably middle class—that part of the reason why they have stayed in their increasingly dangerous new abode is that they can't afford to move. It's also worth noting that the film is set in 1971, just two years before the beginning of the oil crisis that would mark the point at which middle-class fortunes in the United States began their long decline. It could be argued then that the money problems affecting the precariously financed Perrons during their ordeal are perhaps merely a harbinger of the (nonsupernaturally influenced) financial worries to come. Roger is a truck driver, a professional category particularly hard hit by soon-to-come rise in fuel prices. By the end of the film, the family may have been saved from the forces of evil, but the bank and the bills will still need to be paid, and this time, presumably, no nice outsiders with large checkbooks in lieu of rosary beads will be coming to the rescue.

Of all the films discussed here, it is *Sinister* that most openly articulates the sense of shock and unfairness associated with massive realignment of financial and personal expectations caused by the recession. Just a few years previously, Ellison and his family lived in a mansion, and enjoyed the security and luxury provided by his success. Now, they've been forced to significantly downsize so that he can have one last chance at reviving his moribund career. No one is more aware than Ellison of how far they have fallen, but this doesn't stop him from repeatedly articulating a profound and ultimately fatal sense of entitlement. Having experienced fame and fortune, he is simply unable to come to terms with the fact that his own personal "Golden Age," like that of so many other middle-aged Americans, is in the past. When his wife Tracy (Juliet

Rylance) begs him to stop work on the project that is clearly causing him considerable psychological distress, he cries, "This is my shot, Tracy!" and claims that "Every minute we're here we're a little bit closer to that happy ending we've always dreamed about." It's a statement that evokes Noah's previously cited observation that the so-called American Dream is a lot more difficult to achieve than it once was. After all, happy endings, of course, are the very last thing that fate holds in store for the Oswalt family.

While the family units being terrorized in *The Exorcist*, *The Amityville Horror*, and *Poltergeist* were certainly physically and psychologically traumatized by their experiences, they all survived their ordeals, and were able to leave their homes behind at the end of the film. This is not the case in *Paranormal Activity, Insidious*, or *Sinister*. One could of course argue that, from a commercial perspective, the last minute twists and feel-bad endings of each film facilitate the creation of a franchise (which it did in all three cases), and, as such, provide another illustration of the canny production strategies that have helped Blumhouse become a major force in mainstream horror. However, the final moments also leave us with the disquieting sense that the fractured family cannot be put back together again, in part, because they have brought their terrible fate upon themselves.

Although Katie in *Paranormal Activity* was "singled out" as a child, Micah's insistence upon attempting to communicate with the entity severely exacerbates the situation. Furthermore, as the couple's relationship becomes increasingly strained, the demon's power increases. It is Josh Lambert's repressed talent for "travelling" in the astral ether that brings the demonic into two successive family homes in *Insidious*, while Ellison has brought Baghuul into contact with his family due to his insistence upon repeatedly viewing the 8mm footage, and upon investigating the ritual murders in the first place. This sense that victims have in part brought disaster upon their own heads is again further articulated in *The Conjuring*. "It as a big mistake acknowledging this doll. You gave it permission to enter your lives," Ed Warren tells terrified college students who unwittingly crossed paths with Annabelle. The Perron family also made the classic horror movie mistake of buying their home cheap (at a bank auction) without inquiring about its history.

The crawl with which *The Conjuring* ends reinforces this idea that individual culpability lies at the heart of every outbreak of supernatural unpleasantness by providing us with a mission statement from the real-life Ed Warren: "Diabolical forces are formidable. These forces are eternal, and they exist today. The fairy tale is true. The devil exists. God exists.

And for us, as people, our very destiny hinges upon which one we elect to follow."[25] It isn't difficult to see parallels between this notion of personal culpability and the kind of "you brought it upon yourselves" rhetoric that often accompanied commentary on the economic crash. For instance, a Rasmussen Poll conducted in December 2007 found that respondents overwhelmingly blamed "individuals who had borrowed more than they could afford to (54%) over Wall Street (25%)."[26] As Gretchen Morgenson noted in the *New York Times* in November 2007,

> It has become fashionable of late to say that America's sub-prime borrowers thoroughly deserve a good part of the blame for the current mortgage mess. They were either greedy (looking for easy money in a bubbly real estate market) or irresponsible (amassing a debt whose terms they did not understand). They should be punished for their behaviour, the argument goes—not rewarded with loan work outs.[27]

This perspective on the crisis explicitly castigates the vulnerable borrowers who had taken out subprime loans in order to try and secure their own piece of the much-vaunted "American Dream" while glossing over the predatory capitalism and fraudulent practices which facilitated these transactions in the first place. The situation brings to mind an argument made by Mike Wayne, when he notes that the basic template of many ghost stories in contemporary cinema is as follows:

> A dominant and often complacent social order repressing that which challenges its existence and values, marginalises opposition, kicking over the traces of violence which it has performed, and this in turn provokes some spirit crying out for past injustices to be recognised, for its memory to be redeemed, or for good old bloody vengeance to be wreaked.[28]

---

[25]Many of the beliefs espoused by the Warren's during the film—as well as, in particular, the "Annabelle" sequence—appear to come word-for-word from Gerald Daniel Brittle's *The Demonologist: The Extraordinary Career of Ed and Lorraine Warren* (first published in 1980).
[26]Starkman, Dean. "No, Americans Are Not All to Blame for the Financial Crisis: Exposing the Big Lie of the Post-Crash Economy." *The New Republic*, March 9, 2014, http://www.newrepublic.com/article/116919/big-lie-haunts-post-crash-economy (accessed June 17, 2014).
[27]Morgenson, Gretchen, "Blame the Borrowers? Not So Fast" *The New York Times*, November 25, 2007, http://www.nytimes.com/2007/11/25/business/25gret.html?pagewanted=all&_r=0 (accessed on June 17, 2014).
[28]Mike Wayne, "Spectres, Marx's Theory of Value, and the Horror Film" *Film International* 2.4 (2004), 5.

Yet the demonic entities which feature here all differ significantly from the displaced spirits who wreak havoc on suburbia in *Poltergeist*, the ghost of the murdered child seeking justice in *The Changeling* (1980), or the psychotically vengeful yet horribly mistreated in life ghosts of Sadako in *Ring* and the titular "Candyman" in Bernard Rose's film. They don't want to right past wrongs, terrorize those who have harmed them in life, or bring to light the crimes of the past. Although the protagonists in all four cases have done something to capture the attention of their demonic antagonists (just moving in to the wrong house is enough, it seems), their suffering takes place mainly in order to satisfy the entities' desire for pain and suffering—they represent evil of the very broadest, most unambiguous variety.

As we have seen, it is obvious that the films produced by the Blumhouse "assembly line" in the wake of *Paranormal Activity* have been carefully calibrated to resonate with the widest possible section of cinemagoers. They all feature competent, atmospheric camerawork, set design, and scoring. They make earnest use of clichéd signifiers of spookiness such as characters walking down dark hallways at night, haunted objects, mysterious footsteps, eerie children's drawings, and jarring musical cues. They star well-respected—if not quite A-List—actors such as Wilson, Farmiga, Hawke, and Byrne who can lend gravitas and a bit of name recognition to proceedings.[29] With the exception of the prominence afforded the possession trope and the preeminence of the demonic rather than the ghostly, the basic formula these films follow adheres fairly closely to that usefully outlined by Dale Bailey in his study of haunted house narratives in American popular fiction.[30] They also draw upon the plot templates and tone of earlier "classic" haunted house movies, in particular *Poltergeist* and *The Amityville Horror*, and, to a lesser extent, the likes of *The Changeling* and *The Entity* (1982).[31] Their very familiarity, in short, is part of their appeal.

However, in addition to utilizing a plot formula that clearly resonates with a mass audience and their undeniable on-screen and off-screen competency, as we have seen, the considerable box-office success of these films likely also owes much to the fact that they exploit a strain of anxiety that has proven particularly pertinent to modern American audiences. As George Packer observes, "If you were born around 1960 or afterward, you have spent your adult life in the vertigo of the unwinding. You have watched

---

[29]This is not the case in *Paranormal Activity* franchise because these films must cast unfamiliar faces in order to reinforce their supposed "reality" for the audience.
[30]Bailey, 56.
[31]*The Entity*'s star, Barbara Hershey, plays Josh's mother in both *Insidious* installments.

structures that had been in place before your birth collapse like pillars of salt across the vast visible landscape..."[32] The jolting realization that most present-day Americans will experience a much lower standard of living than their baby-boomer predecessors, for whom the economic problems that characterized the early 1970s had already provided an indication of the shocks to come, has (often literally) hit home. In the haunted house movies being produced by Blumhouse, this sense of profound uncertainty is effectively displaced on to the supernatural, and, in particular, on to reassuringly unambiguous demonic entities whose relentless persecution of ordinary families is always completely disproportionate to whatever these people may have done in order to attract such negative attention. There's a sense of sheer *unfairness* running through these films that very obviously resonates with an undercurrent that is running through society in general. The arrogance, incompetence, and sheer unbridled greed of major financial institutions across the world seems, to many ordinary citizens, to have gone almost entirely unpunished, while the consequences of their reckless decisions disproportionately impact upon those who are least equipped to cope. At a time when millions of Americans are wondering how they will gather together enough money to keep their home for another month, it is surely no coincidence then that, in major box-office hits such as *Insidious*, *The Conjuring*, and *Sinister*, the point when our protagonists achieve home ownership merely marks the onset of a series of horrific and seemingly inescapable supernatural complications.

---

[32]George Packer, *The Unwinding: Thirty Years of American Decline* (London: Faber and Faber, 2013), 4.

14

Glitch Gothic

Marc Olivier

A small crew of attractive twenty-somethings with an assortment of video cameras record themselves wandering around an abandoned building as one by one they fall victim to supernatural forces. That synopsis describes the found-footage horror film *Grave Encounters* (2011) as well as its sequel, *Grave Encounters 2* (2012), and also *8213 Gacy House* (2010), *Reel Evil* (2012), *Episode 50* (2011), *Paranormal Incident* (2011), *Paranormal Asylum: The Revenge of Typhoid Mary* (2013), *100 Ghost Street: The Return of Richard Speck* (2012), *The Crying Dead* (2011), *Greystone Park* (2012), and, with minor variations, perhaps a dozen more films released between 2010 and 2013. Apart from sharing a generic plot, these otherwise unremarkable found-footage horror films have in common a glitch aesthetic that exploits the shock of a digital noise event for the sake of gothic horror. Ghostly apparitions coincide with, and are increasingly incidental to, the presentation of violent disruptions to digital media. Visual glitches, or temporary disruptions to the flow of information such as unexpected pixilation, chromatic shifts, and other error-based distortions, now constitute essential tropes in the language of cinematic ghost stories. The jarring spectacle of data ruins is becoming to the twenty-first century what the crumbling mansion was to gothic literature of the nineteenth century: the privileged space for confrontations with incompatible systems, nostalgic remnants, and restless revenants. Re-contextualized within current media technologies, the return of the repressed relies not only on human psychology but also on the hidden logic of digital materiality, as found-footage horror films of the 2010s adopt what might best be described as a "Glitch Gothic" approach to the ghost.

Early gothic literature (or "Gothick" to specialists such as Victoria Nelson) temporally situates its characters in the period of pre-Reformation England, and physically places both the tormented living and the restless dead "in the suffocating embrace of an ancient abbey, castle, or ancestral home, the classic charged Gothick space linked to an oppressive past that generally goes up in flames by the story's end."[1] Once extracted from its literary roots, however, the term "gothic" becomes subject to increasingly unwieldy hybridized iterations. According to Maurice Lévy, the gothic has long outgrown its status as genre and may better be described as "a spreading process and imperialist conquest of the whole human experience."[2] Echoing Lévy, Fred Botting mentions at least eighteen examples of contemporary gothic hybrids (Queer Gothic, Imperial Gothic, Postcolonial Gothic, Postmodern Gothic, to name a few), which have nevertheless not dissuaded him from contributing his own neologisms, "Candygothic" and "Disneygothic," to the growing taxonomy, nor will it prevent this chapter from adding yet another sub-genre to the list.[3] Monstrous hybridism has always been the nature of the gothic beast, says Nelson, "The Gothick was and is the ultimate mongrel form."[4] Likewise, Lucie Armitt's *Twentieth-Century Gothic* embraces the broad scope of this "amorphous and ever-expanding 'monster'" by asserting that the gothic is less a cultural phenomenon than a "means of reading culture."[5] Untethered from any specific historical moment, the gothic becomes a lens, or, some would venture, the "dominant mode of the twenty-first century."[6]

The popularity of the gothic poses problems, however, if not to the work of literary critics, then to the ghosts whose function as Other relies on meaningful participation in a boundary war with normalizing forces. More than ever, Botting contends, "the monsters of and on technical screens are no different from the norms they once negatively defined."[7] And if ghosts and

---

[1] Victoria Nelson, *Gothicka: Vampire Heroes, Human Gods, and the New Supernatural* (Cambridge: Harvard University Press, 2012), 2.
[2] Maurice Lévy, "FAQ: What Is Gothic?" *Anglophonia: French Journal of English Studies* 15 (2004), 30.
[3] On "Disneygothic," see Fred Botting, *Limits of Horror: Technology, Bodies, Gothic* (Manchester: Manchester University Press, 2008), 2–4. For a discussion of "Candygothic," see Fred Botting, "Candygothic," in *The Gothic*, ed. Fred Botting (Cambridge: D.S. Brewer, 2001), 133–52.
[4] Nelson, 8.
[5] Lucie Armitt, *History of the Gothic: Twentieth-Century Gothic* (Cardiff: University of Wales Press, 2011), 2; 10.
[6] Catherine Spooner, "Preface," in *Twenty-First-Century Gothic*, eds. Brigid Cherry, Peter Howell, and Caroline Ruddell (Newcastle upon Tyne: Cambridge Scholars, 2010), xi.
[7] Botting, *Limits of Horror*, 9.

vampires are the new normal, where does that leave the uncanny? Inevitably, dispersed, according to what Jeffrey Sconce has labeled the "postmodern occult"—the narrative that human consciousness has been fractured by "the ghosts of fragmented, decentered, and increasingly schizophrenic subjectivities," and that history has evaporated into "a haunted landscape of vacant and shifting signifiers."[8] Typically, theorists such as Baudrillard and his "infinitely reversible" binaries fuel that train of thought by suggesting, for example, that the real has become unreal and the unreal has become real, until, through rapid oscillation, the two categories merge.[9] Botting's study of technology and horror adopts Baudrillard's rhetorical affection for role reversal, and proclaims that ghosts are no longer uncanny, but instead, the active "figures of a technological dimension from which human powers and autonomy seem increasingly alienated, video-synthesized and displaced by the machineries of post-modernity."[10] In this new spectral economy, humans and ghosts alike suffer from a loss of clearly defined roles. As a result, the gothic theorist roams through philosophical corridors such as the Žižekian "spectral frame" of virtuality, the Deleuzian void of "ab-sense," and the Lacanian "vacuole" of meaning and nonmeaning, only to end up in a phantasmal fantasy that lies "[i]n and beyond representation and signification."[11]

Even as categories break down, invert, or otherwise threaten meaning, a common theme in modern and postmodern discussions of the gothic is the supernatural affinity between technology and ghosts. Sconce has suggested that rather than view the "postmodern occult" as the radical point of rupture with the technological narratives of modernity, we might consider the supposed hyper-permeability of physical and spiritual realms via technology as a trope whose lineage can be traced back to the spiritual telegraph.[12] Ghosts, it seems, have always had a thing for gadgets. Ghosts were photobombing back in the 1860s, long before prank-happy teenagers made it a thing. Ghosts flit about in televisions (*Poltergeist*, 1982), VCRs (*Ringu*, 1998), the Internet (*Pulse*, 2001), voice mail (*One Missed Call*, 2003), and text messages (*Txt*, 2006). Think of a modern convenience, and chances are, a ghost has haunted it. Even toilets are not exempt (*Harry Potter and the Chamber of*

---

[8] Jeffrey Sconce, *Haunted Media: Electronic Presence from Telegraphy to Television* (Durham: Duke University Press, 2000), 170–71.
[9] Ibid., 180–81.
[10] Botting, *Limits of Horror*, 130.
[11] Botting, "Candygothic," 141.
[12] Sconce, 197.

Secrets, 2002).[13] In short, devices change, but the connection between the technological and the phantasmal does not.

In its current use, Glitch Gothic figures into the history of ghosts and technology as both a perpetuation of the enduring tradition that Sconce has explored, and as a material counterweight to the ghostly aspects of media. Insofar as glitches take place in digital media machines, they continue to assert a correspondence between machines and ghosts. Conversely, the glitch functions as a ghost-busting phenomenon because it interrupts rather than facilitates the transparency of media flow. In effect, the glitch draws attention away from ghosts, even if its affective shock, like a bolt of lightning, signals their presence. The glitch has its own binary concerns that are not steeped in the residue of humanity or the history of emerging modernity. The undergirding of digital media provides alternative temporal and formal structures that demand attention. Not surprisingly, the cultural fascination with the glitch aligns with media theory's turn away from the immateriality of "cyberspace" in favor of archaeological models of analysis. Media archaeology demystifies the great electronic beyond, and re-grounds information technology in the materiality of circuits, the ecological impact of machines, and the pre- or nonhuman temporalities of geological time and computational processes.[14] Object-Oriented Ontology also plays a strong role in the fight against the anthropocentric bias that imbues technology with uncanny humanity.[15] Likewise, the renewal of formalist modes of inquiry, even in the domain of affect theory, downplays the metaphysical and subjective tendencies of media analysis.[16] Viewed together, these various critical and philosophical positions foster the conditions that favor the glitch as a traveling companion to the twenty-first-century ghost.

The short, "Phase 1 Clinical Trials," from the found-footage horror anthology *V/H/S/2* (2013) offers an exemplary pairing of ghost and glitch grafted onto human vision through an experimental prosthetic mechanical eye. The film opens with the blurry point of view of a patient, Herman, as he emerges from postoperative stupor. Herman's one uninjured biological eye has just received a companion robotic eye thanks to a corporate donor, who, in exchange,

---

[13]Haunted toilets are, in fact, quite common in contemporary folklore. See Diane E. Goldstein, Silvia Ann Grider, and Jeannie Banks Thomas, *Haunting Experiences: Ghosts in Contemporary Folklore* (Logan: Utah State University Press, 2007), 32–3.

[14]On microtemporality, for example, see Wolfgang Ernst, "Let There Be Irony: Cultural History and Media Archaeology in Parallel Lines" *Art History* 28.5 (2005), 582–603. On the materiality of computer technology, see Garnet Hertz and Jussi Parikka, "Zombie Media: Circuit Bending Media Archaeology into an Art Method," *Leonardo* 45.5 (2012), 424–30.

[15]The best known popularization of object-oriented ontology is Ian Bogost's work *Alien Phenomenology, Or What It's like to Be a Thing* (Minneapolis: University of Minnesota Press, 2012).

[16]See Eugenie Brinkema, *The Forms of the Affects* (Durham: Duke University Press, 2014).

will receive all data coming through the device via an embedded recording chip—a compromise not unlike most end-user license agreements. In the age of Google Glass, the cyborgian premise barely enters the realm of science fiction. Herman is an early adopter. And even though the idea of no "private time" gives him pause, Herman's acceptance of terms does not register as a Faustian bargain any more than an "accept cookies" pop-up stops the average web user from proceeding to a page. The fusion of human and technological vision, and of public and private vision, typifies the ethos of the found-footage protagonist. In essence, Herman represents a more efficient version of the typical video camera-wielding protagonist in nearly every twenty-first-century found-footage horror film. He is the sinister corporate-manufactured counterpart to Dziga Vertov's kino-eye, the camera that is "more perfect than the human eye, for the exploration of the chaos that fills space."[17] But while Vertov's manifesto proclaims, "Long live the cinema-eye of the proletarian revolution!," Herman's generation opts in to corporatized mediation as a means of self-expression.[18] A more apt reworking of Vertov might read "Long—or until my next upgrade—live the revolutionary new iPhone that Instagrams my lunch, Facebooks my selfies, and Tweets my thoughts."

The premise of "Phase 1 Clinical Trials" exploits the fear that even the most emancipatory or empowering technological supplements to human biology are inherently riddled with adverse side effects. The surgeon warns Herman, "Because your prosthesis is attached directly to your visual cortex, your real eye is essentially battling with your camera eye to give you info right now. So when your brain gets used to having that chip in there, you should start to see more and more out of your uninjured eye again. Until then, you might see some glitches." Once Herman returns home, the gothic glitches begin to manifest. Herman enters his bedroom and notices that his bedsheets appear to be draped over a reclining human form. His vision warps with interfering lines and colors as he approaches to lift the sheets. Nothing. He turns and—*GLITCH!*—a white-faced man with sunken dark eyes appears amid jolts of visual interference (Figure 14.1). Our stunned everyman with the camera-eye moves to the hallway *GLITCH!*—another shocking visual distortion coincides with the appearance of a white-faced little girl, also with vacant, sunken eyes. The chaos subsides just long enough for Clarissa, the recipient of a cochlear implant from the same hospital, to show up on Herman's doorstep and explain that she, too, "picks up on certain frequencies" (the persistent technology-as-conduit trope). Another glitch,

---

[17]Dziga Vertov, *Kino-Eye: The Writings of Dziga Vertov*, ed. Annette Michelson, trans. Kevin O'Brien (Berkeley: University of California Press, 1984), 15.
[18]Ibid., 71.

and Clarissa's dead uncle appears behind her. "He wasn't a nice person," she says, undressing. And although Herman is more than happy to indulge Clarissa's belief that carnal distraction staves off ghost attacks, his new friend's short attempt at technological and psychological insight proves irrelevant. Herman's ghostly tormentors are not looking for closure. They are little more than gothic shells, emptied of the history one expects from the genre. There is no mystery of a past wrong to be solved, nothing to be put to rest, no meaningful vengeance to enact, just one glitch-ghost after another until barely a frame goes by without some form of digital disturbance. Soon, the visual violence culminates in Herman's desperate excision of his robotic eye with a straightedge razor—a wink to Luis Buñuel's surrealistic eye-slitting sequence in *Un Chien Andalou* (1929). Unabated by disembodiment, the spectacular fireworks of glitches continue to the bitter end, as a ghost retrieves the discarded camera-eye and interprets literally the concept of "video feed" by forcing the device down the esophagus of the mutilated victim.

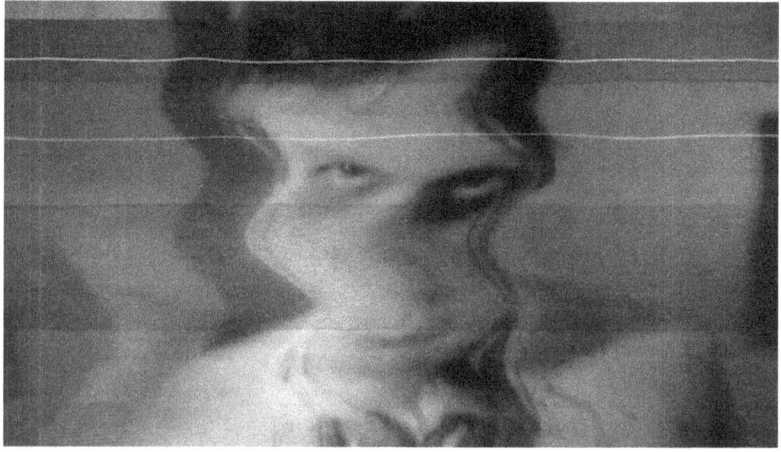

FIGURE 14.1 V/H/S *(2012, Adam Wingard et al., 8383 Productions).*

"Phase 1 Clinical Trials" strips Glitch Gothic to its bare essence: a relentless assault on vision, a clash of digital and biological spectral manifestations. Without detaching from the technology-as-conduit tradition, "Phase 1 Clinical Trials" couples the perceptual crisis of seeing a ghost with the technological crisis of the glitch. The source of terror in a ghost sighting, according to Tom Gunning, is "the transparency of vision."[19] The ghost resists close examination.

---

[19] Tom Gunning, "To Scan a Ghost: The Ontology of Mediated Vision," *Grey Room* 26 (2007), 119.

"Scanning a ghost is difficult because in some sense we cannot scrutinize them. They remain virtual, rather than embodied images."[20] Gunning explains that the uncanny power of ghostly transparency, as manifest, for example, in nineteenth-century spirit photography, results from the lingering "residue of a lost explanatory system," specifically, the predominantly phantasmal models of pre-modern vision influenced by Lucretius.[21] The Lucretian model created a "world thick with ghosts" because it proposed that objects were perpetually sending out their own simulacra, like thin layers of film, through the air and into direct contact with the eye.[22] In varying forms, ghosts shared an ontological kinship with the operations of sight until Johannes Kepler's revolutionary retinal theory discarded the notion of floating phantasmal images. Thereafter, modern visual systems had no place for pre-modern ghosts. Instead, posits Gunning, ghosts found a new home in optical media, whose function depends on the fabrication of simulacra of the objective world. "The virtual image becomes the modern phantom."[23]

The glitch is the semi-opaque counterpart to the terror of transparent vision. A digital glitch stuns the viewer through the sudden opacity of a medium designed for transparency. This is not to say that the twenty-first-century consumer is unaware of mediation, or does not enjoy navigating the world of multi-windowed, scalable screens. On the contrary, media theorists such as Anne Friedberg, Lev Manovich, Jay Bolter, and Richard Grusin have all identified a millennial turn to the multiplication of perspectives and screens corresponding to the rise of digital media. For Friedberg, the windows of the computer screen counteract single-point Albertian perspective.[24] For Manovich, media awareness represents an ideological restructuring, a "metarealism [...] based on oscillation between illusion and its destruction, between immersing a viewer in illusion and directly addressing her."[25] In a similar line of thought, Bolter and Grusin posit a contradictory "double logic of re-mediation" that makes the multiplication of media and its effacement part of the same process, as if transparency and immediacy can be recuperated through transmediative saturation.[26] Caution, if not ambivalence toward new media, nevertheless underscores all of these accounts of burgeoning media-awareness. Like the surgeon

---

[20] Ibid., 121.
[21] Ibid., 107.
[22] Ibid., 106.
[23] Ibid., 111.
[24] See Anne Friedberg's seminal work, *The Virtual Window: From Alberti to Microsoft* (Cambridge: The MIT Press, 2006).
[25] Lev Manovich, *The Language of New Media* (Cambridge: The MIT Press, 2001), 209.
[26] J. David Bolter and Richard A. Grusin, "Remediation," *Configurations* 4.3 (1996), 313.

in "Phase I Clinical Trials," theorists warn that our biological vision and mechanical vision are still not properly aligned, and that two systems are currently battling to give us information. Traditions of transparency and opacity compete for dominance in human perception. The newer, less transparent system dominates temporarily, but the promise of equilibrium reassures the anxious that a return to normality is forthcoming. Until then, there will be glitches.

Just as the visual crisis of transparency points to the residue of displaced optical theories, the crisis of glitch-born opacity hints at the coexistence of competing representational systems. The glitch opens even the most benign content to an occluded presence that is not spiritual and immaterial, but rather structural. In the flash of a glitch, data creaks open, like a hidden passageway, into the disquieting architecture of digital speech. In that instant when an image teeters on the brink of failure in its role as recognizable content, the viewer is thrust into an untenable state where looking *at* competes with looking *through*. Gunning's transparent optical crisis leads to the same foregrounding of the medium: "In these images, we no longer see *through* the photograph but become aware of the uncanny nature of the process of capturing an image itself. Our gaze is caught, suspended, stuck within the transparent film itself."[27] The paradox of the seen-unseen marks the nature of viewing both ghost and glitch, but Glitch Gothic does not and cannot echo Gunning's metaphor of the human gaze caught within transparent film, quite simply, because there is no film in which to be caught.

Too broadly defined, the visual crisis of glitch merely retreads the medium/message conundrum that precedes and exceeds the context of digital media. To understand the nature of Glitch Gothic, we must first distinguish glitch from error or noise. If a glitch were synonymous with every error, noise, malfunction, mistake, or accident, then the answer to the question "What is Glitch?" would be as problematically all encompassing as the response to the question "What is Gothic?" But a glitch is not noise. Or rather, a glitch is a *form* of noise, but not all noise is glitch. The graininess of the 16mm footage that contributes to the creepy credibility of *The Blair Witch Project* (1999), for example, is an inherent property of the film stock rather than a glitch. *The Blair Witch Project* is a noisy film, but not a "glitchy" one—although tellingly, the trailer for a recent Blu-ray edition of the film has been retrofitted with wildly spiking glitched transitional intertitles not present in the original 1999 theatrical trailers, as if to say that glitch is now

---

[27] Ibid., 112.

inseparable from all found-footage horror, whether digital or not.[28] Likewise, digital imitations of analog noise, such as Instagram filters, focus on medium-specific aesthetics rather than on transitory noise events. As glitch theorist and artist Rosa Menkman observes, the glitch is noise that lives on the brink of failure: "Noise turns to glitch when it passes a momentary *tipping point* at which it could tip away into a failure, or instead force new knowledge about a glitch's *techné*, and actual and presumed media flow, onto the viewer."[29] By definition, a glitch is an error that gets corrected. The glitch may reach a tipping point, but one where the user still has access to a representation of disrupted of flow through the machine's faithful rendering of corrupt data. Media professor Hugh S. Manon and glitch artist Daniel Temkin characterize the glitch as a resistance to breakdown: "When a software program opens a corrupt JPEG file, for example, and displays an image of unanticipated digital distortion, what we are witnessing is not failure, but rather the program's *failure to fully fail.*"[30]

Media theorist and artist Curt Cloninger defines glitch as "an affective event generated by a media machine (computer, projector, game console, LCD screen, etc.) running in real-time, an event which creates an artifact that colors and modulates any 'signal' or 'content' being sent via that machine."[31] For Cloninger, a glitch is enmeshed in an interaction between human and machine; it does not exist in an abstract or transcendent technological realm, but rather as lived affect experienced by humans during a media machine's utterance. Otherwise stated, "If a file corrupts on a server and no one is around to say 'oh shit,' it does not make a glitch."[32] Cloninger's insistence on affect as an ontological precondition of the glitch wrests the noise event from

---

[28]The trailer can be accessed in the preview section of the DVD *Knock Knock 2* (2011) released by Lion's Gate, August 7, 2012. The original trailer relied on an eerie glow and an occasional flash of pure white. Indeed, the glitch seems to be a requirement for found-footage horror advertisements, as seen in the trailer to *Afflicted* (2013), which features more than twenty glitches whereas the actual film has only one.

[29]Rosa Menkman, *The Glitch Moment(um)*, Network Notebook Series 04 (Amsterdam: Colophon, 2011), 31.

[30]Hugh S. Manon and Daniel Temkin, "Notes on Glitch," *World Picture* 6 (winter, 2011), 1, http://www.worldpicturejournal.com/WP_6/PDFs/Manon.pdf

[31]Curt Cloninger, "GlitchLnguistx: *The Machine in the Ghost/Static Trapped in Mouths*" in *GLI.TC/H READER[ROR] 20111*, eds. Nick Briz, Evan Meaney, Rosa Menkman, Willaim Robertson, Jon Satrom, Jessica Westbrook (Unsorted Books, 2011), 23, http://gli.tc/h/READERROR/GLITCH_READERROR_20111-v3BWs.pdf

[32]Curt Cloninger and Nick Briz, *Sabotage! glitch politix Man[ual/ifesto]*, http://booksfromthefuture.tumblr.com/post/86197395718/sabotage-glitch-politix-man-ual-ifesto (accessed on February 24, 2014).

whatever processes might otherwise be thought of as purely mechanical, and, in so doing, asserts that the glitch must first register with a human subject *as error* before it can be called a glitch. In short, horror precedes the glitch. For a moment, the viewer must attend to objects whose nature, codes, and languages are either obfuscated and repressed by design or simply foreign. Like a ghostly hand, the glitch points to something we do not (or dare not) understand. Once labeled a "glitch," however, the alterity that generated affect in the first place recedes into its status as a hiccup in the flow of meaning. A glitch does not exist until it withdraws into transparency. Like a ghost, it is always already dead. In that regard, the glitch is as much about the return of repression as it is about the return of the repressed.

If one agrees with Cloninger that the *pure* glitch, the glitch-in-the-wild, is experienced in real time, then the glitch-in-captivity is something *not quite* a glitch—a "glitch-alike," to use Iman Moradi's term.[33] A "pure glitch" is accidental and found, whereas a "glitch-alike" is deliberate and designed. Some glitch artists find Moradi's criteria for authenticity irksome because the binary schema demotes even real-time glitch performance art to "glitch-alike" status.[34] In cinema, however, the glitch-alike is the norm. Thanks to the availability of plug-ins, scripts, and after effects, most filmmakers forego the "real" glitch hunt altogether. Instead, they insert simulated glitch effects that take the glitch-alike to one more Platonic degree of remove from a personal encounter with machinic error. To be clear, a found-footage horror film does not show the viewer "real" glitches any more than it presents real ghosts or real found footage, but the glitch-alike must nevertheless achieve a degree of verisimilitude that matches the typical viewer's level of visual noise and error literacy. "Authentic" errors add believability, and more importantly, they open up the new gothic possibilities for media critique. As media consumers become more glitch-literate, they may one day learn the difference between a glitched jpg, gif, DV, or AVI file, as Menkman suggests by subjecting her own self-portrait to a taxonomy of glitch distortions in her "Vernacular of File Formats."[35] Likewise, Manon and Temkin note that one of the goals of glitch artistic

---

[33]Moradi's bachelor's honors thesis is one of the first academic studies on digital glitch art. I consulted Moradi's work on the now-defunct website oculasm.org (www.oculasm.org/glitch/download/Glitch_dissertation_print_with_pics.pdf). For an overview of Moradi's project, see Iman Moradi, "Seeking Perfect Imperfection. A personal retrospective on Glitch Art," *Vector* (e-zine) 6 (July, 2008), http://virose.pt/vector/x_06/moradi.html. See also, Iman Moradi, Ant Scott, Joe Gilmore, and Christopher Murphy, *Glitch: Designing Imperfection* (Brooklyn: Mark Batty Publisher, 2009), and Moradi's "Glitchbreak 11/11/11" in *GLI.TC/H READER[ROR] 20111*, 150–156.

[34]See, for example, Rosa Menkman, 36.

[35]Menkman, 17–25.

experimentation is to explore the materiality in the supposed immateriality of the digital image by exposing hidden differences in file formats:

> For example, when broken, a JPEG looks very different from a BMP. JPEGs are fragile and changes tend to be traumatic [...] BMPs are indexed color, with a compact color palette referenced by the pixel data throughout the file. If the palette gets scrambled, dreamy sherbet-coloured images result. Damaged PNG files, on the other hand, often appear as if an underlying reservoir of source-colors had been "wrung out" of the image, spilling from upper left to lower right. Likewise, TIFFs, DCS-formatted EPSs, and each of the other formats have their own characteristics. Once one becomes familiar with these material properties, it is hard to mistake a broken JPEG for a broken BMP, or even an 8-bit color BMP for a 24-bit one.[36]

One possible outcome of scrutinizing a glitch, then, is the realization that information, whether streaming in a video chat or recorded on a card or drive of some kind, resides within institutional spaces such as proprietary file formats. Glitch artists, more than filmmakers, have realized the potential to toy with those boundaries. Laimonas Zakas (aka "Glitchr"), for example, uses glitches in Twitter and Facebook to surprising, humorous, and unsettling effect. Glitchr's YouTube video "The Speech of Facebook" turns security check letters and numbers—the ghostly squiggles meant to prevent spamming by verifying that a user is human—into the a kind of garbled artificial speech one might imagine Siri to emit during an exorcism.[37] Glitch artist stAllio!, after months of experimentation with transcoding WTV (Window's Recorded TV Show) files, developed a formula for "summoning ghost frames" ("video frames which do not actually exist in a video file but which are sometimes revealed when using damaged data and/or glitch processes") by using the open-source video editing program, Avidemux.[38] Equally uncanny are the roadscapes of Google Street View, where the virtual *flâneur* encounters sidewalks peppered with human doppelgänger, or cars stretched and flattened into the asphalt. Errors related to the "nine-eyed" vision embedded in the orb of nine cameras that sits atop Google's Street View cars betray Google's efforts to stitch together a seamless double of the world. Google's

---

[36]Manon and Temkin, 9–10.
[37]Laimonas Zakas, "The speech of Facebook by Glitchr." Youtube video. Published Feb 27, 2013, https://www.youtube.com/watch/?v=7R0c9aPReyA
[38]stAllio!, "summoning ghost frames," *stAllio!s way* (blog), January 1, 2013, http://blog.animalswithinanimals.com/2013/01/summoning-ghost-frames.html

periodic updates lay those errors to rest, but unintentionally leave new errors for glitch hunters to pursue.[39]

A final digression from the world of found-footage horror and into the world of gaming illustrates a difference between playing with glitches and watching them at the movies. The identification and exploitation of gaming glitches is arguably the most widespread form of glitch practice. Gamers commonly share glitches and "cheats" that allow players to act within game space in ways not intended by the game's creators.[40] Thanks to glitches, gamers navigate "outside the map," arriving at times in liminal no-man's-land, walking through walls and objects, and jumping between levels, and defying the physics engines of a game. Like Neo in *The Matrix* (1999), the gamer achieves a level of supernatural power. Glitch-generated transcendence can either be read as a liberating poetic use of space, or simply as cheating.[41] Either way, the glitch operates counter to established norms, much like the classic gothic ghost. Also in gothic tradition, gamers experience uncanny phenomena. Cracked.com's list "The 8 Creepiest Glitches Hidden in Popular Video Games" includes human–animal hybrid "Manimals," driverless "ghost cars," "demon babies," boxers that "sink through the floor like ghosts," characters that rise from the dead, and floating disembodied heads.[42]

Compared to glitch art or gaming culture, Glitch Gothic horror is still in its infancy. In theory, Glitch Gothic horror opens the possibility of a dual institutional critique: the first, a Foucauldian-inflected reading of abandoned or decaying institutional spaces, and the second, a media-archaeological reading of abandoned formats or malfunctioning machinic speech. The *V/H/S* franchise, though not entirely devoted to ghosts, clearly skews to a media archaeological context. The nostalgic analog format featured in the trilogy's title modernizes the gothic literary tradition instigated by Horace Walpole's *The Castle of Otranto*, which favors antiquated architectural structures as titular characters. The wrap-around narratives of *V/H/S* ("Tape 56") and *V/H/S/2* ("Tape 49") combine traditional gothic elements, such as the haunted house, with dying media artifacts, such as the VHS

---

[39]See glitch artist, stAllio!, "Google Street View Glitches Revisited," *stAllio!s way* (blog), September 17, 2010, http://blog.animalswithinanimals.com/2010/09/google-street-view-glitches-revisited.html See also, Jon Rafeman's "9-Eyes" project, http://9-eyes.com/ which includes, but is not limited to, glitches in Street View.
[40]See "Glitch," on *Giant Bomb*, August 3, 2014, http://www.giantbomb.com/glitch/3015-511/
[41]Disney's *Wreck-It Ralph* (2012) personifies glitch in the character Vanellope Von Schweetz in order to explore the liberating and limiting effects of transgressing systemic norms.
[42]Maxwell Yezpitelock and M. Asher Cantrell, "The 8 Creepiest Glitches Hidden in Popular Video Games," October 25, 2011, http://www.cracked.com/article_19507_the-8-creepiest-glitches-hidden-in-popular-video-games.html

tapes and film reels. In generations measured by mechanical reproduction, copies of copies of VHS tapes—the media equivalent of corrupted, inbred aristocrats—lie about in houses that have been emptied of all function other than to serve them. In "Tape 56," a group of friends in search of a rare tape finds stacks of television sets aglow with static, perched in a formation one might expect from a Nam June Paik installation. A corpse slumped in an easy chair faces the televisions. Undeterred by the scene, one of the group positions himself between the La-Z-Boy and the televisions, and inserts a VHS tape into a VCR while the rest of his crew explores the house. The wraparound narrative for *V/H/S/2* ("Tape 49") only slightly modifies the scenario. "Tape 49" features two private investigators who break into a similar house in search of a missing student. For reasons unknown, the home is also equipped with the signature *V/H/S* shrine to cathode ray screens, now with the decidedly modern addition of a laptop. On the laptop sits one of the many VHS tapes from the student's grisly collection. Again, as in the first *V/H/S* anthology, the home invaders split up and perform two different modes of search. While one partner searches the house, the other searches the laptop and the tapes. In this way, the framework for both *V///H/S* films establishes a parallel between searching/viewing media and wandering through haunted architectural spaces.

Contrary to what the titles might suggest, the *V/H/S* films are more than exercises in hipster analog chic. At times, the films' fascination with retro media registers as forced and artificial, like the faux-ruins in vogue during the nineteenth century. However, within the tape lies a complex relation between new and old media. The cinematic homage to videotape culture that just happens to coincide with the real-life fall of the house of Blockbuster is not restricted to one format, neither is it limited to analog. The found videos in the *V/H/S* series come from of an array of analog and digital sources, culled from a seedy network of underground collectors, crudely edited and put on tape with the intention to re-digitize the work for eventual internet upload.[43] Digital technology is as omnipresent in the collection as analog. Among the devices that produce the "footage" in *V/H/S* and *V/H/S/2*, we see laptops running Skype, video spyglasses, smartphones, a nanny cam, VHS, Hi8, HD, Digital SLR, GoPro video cameras, and security cameras. Moreover, the wraparound narratives are themselves labeled "tapes." The *V/H/S* anthologies begin with the blue screen menu of a VCR and the insertion of a tape, signaling that the narratives that glue the short films together are themselves contained within a VHS tape. In other words, "Tape 56" *is*

---

[43]See the Bonus Feature interview of Brad Miska and Zac Zernan on *V/H/S*. DVD. Magnolia Home Entertainment, 2012.

the *V/H/S* anthology and "Tape 49" *is* the *V/H/S/2* anthology. Each group of films—wraparound included—is a complex remix of heavily remediated footage. Consider that in first 8 minutes of "Tape 49" alone—the discovery leading up to the insertion of the "Phase 1 Clinical Trials" VHS tape—the edit draws from five sources: a button spy camera worn by the male P.I., a camera mounted to the dashboard of the P.I.'s car, a handheld digital video camera carried by the male P.I., a Canon DSLR used in video mode by the female P.I., and a laptop webcam controlled by the (un)dead missing student.

Significantly, remediation gives another opportunity for noise to enter into play, and to compound the problem of deciphering information and error. The untrained eye fights to discern which noise elements belong to the original source and which the transfer of material to analog tape has added. Was that a glitch or a tracking error in the VCR? Are we seeing the wear and tear of videotape or the corruption of digital data? History or accident? Here, the answer is all of the above. In a noise-centered analysis, the *V/H/S* films reveal remediation as a process of resistance to the oversimplified either/or dichotomy of analog vs. digital media. The mysterious tapes constitute a form of burial rather than a media archaeological dig, given their tendency to conflate and compound layers of noise. As material objects, the VHS tapes represent an artifact of a particular analog form, but as archives, they express the logic and the noises of remix culture. Scan lines, tracking errors, seepage of over-recorded footage, pixelated obstructions, RGB distortion, and all manner of violence to information flow, both digital and analog, coexist in the tapes and assault the viewer with the viscera of media bodies.

Found-footage phantoms, like the intrepid young media addicts who film them, glide between formats and devices, not just in the *V/H/S* series, but also in Glitch Gothic films with less media-centric titles. Among the asylum-based generic paranormal fare mentioned at the beginning of this chapter, *Grave Encounters 2* merits attention for its portrayal of ghosts as obsessed with developing a media presence as any living human. Although every found-footage paranormal figure succumbs at one time or another to the urge of capturing a selfie when left alone with a surveillance camera, the ghosts of *Grave Encounters 2* seem hell-bent on producing their own sequel. In 2003, the ghosts killed off the crew of a fledgling reality series called "Grave Encounters." In 2010, the 76 hours of raw mini DV source footage for episode 6 ("The Haunted Asylum") was edited into *Grave Encounters*. Now, the evil spirits must contend with the film's less-than-stellar YouTube reviews. Film student Alex Wright, self-proclaimed genius and horror visionary, gives *Grave Encounters* a pathetic "one skull out of four" rating in a dismissive critique that will not go unpunished. Soon, a clip of "Grave Encounters" reality host, Lance Preston, arrives in Alex's inbox, courtesy of a YouTube user named "Death Awaits." A few messages later, and Alex has set aside his derivative student slasher project in favor of a horror-documentary about *Grave Encounters*. The tech-savvy occupants that haunt the asylum, however, have their own derivative slasher project in mind, one that will appropriate the footage of Alex and his crew.

Despite their adept use of messaging, YouTube, and Alex's printer, the spirits remain bound to the asylum. They do not leak from the spirit realm into the human via cyberspace as in *Pulse;* they do not crawl out of television sets as in *The Ring*, or pull humans into televisions as in *Poltergeist*. The ghosts of *Grave Encounters* are as subject to architectural structures as any classic gothic ghost, and as subject to technological structures as any human. Their use of electronic communication is no more nor less liberating or portal-like than a teenager's use of a cell phone. Like Alex, the ghosts suffer from certain material constraints. Both parties are desperate to make a film, and both must rely on borrowed equipment. Thanks to their online presence as "Death Awaits," the ghosts are able to lure the film crew to their location. The Internet, so often considered a virtualizing medium, serves the ghosts as proof of embodiment, an opportunity to set up a 3 a.m. rendezvous at the asylum as one user to another. When Alex and friends arrive in the designated room and find nothing but a table and Ouija board, they learn from the old-school ghost texting device the true nature of their Internet contact. Alex and his friend Jennifer place their hands on the cursor-like planchette and begin to ask questions: *Are there any spirits here with us now?*—Yes. *Who are we talking to?* D-E-A-T-H A-W-A-I-T-S. *What do you want us to do?* Alex and Jennifer lift their hands, but the planchette continues moving until it has spelled out the response: FILM EVERYTHING. The table flies to the ceiling, and as the students flee the room, the footage glitches with pixilation and waves of chromatic distortion.

As found-footage horror has no logical place for drama-heightening nondiegetic music, the glitch noise event fulfills the function of a score. Like the stabbing screech of strings that punctuate the bodily and cinematic cuts in the famous shower sequence of Hitchcock's *Psycho* (1960), found-footage glitches synthesize sonic and visual assaults to media(tized) bodies. Because the found-footage genre tends to downplay the editorial hand that has compiled and edited the source footage, an *auteur*-driven spectacle such as Hitchcock's celebrated fifty cuts and seventy-seven angles in 3 minutes is not an option. Glitches represent a method of media slashing that destabilizes and disorients the spectator without rapid-fire edits and virtuosic cinematography. Moreover, the visceral impact of the glitch heightens an anxiety that distinguishes twenty-first-century media horror from predecessors such as *Poltergeist*: not the fear that new media will absorb its user into an incorporeal digisphere, but the dreaded prospect that it cannot. The message of the glitch is that there is no escape from materiality.

Glitches are guts, some have argued.[44] "Just like when our inner systems break down and our many moving parts spill out for the world to see, glitches are the source of the same raw, abject, seduction."[45] We should not be surprised, then, that found-footage ghost stories so often take the form of slasher films. In *100 Ghost Street: The Return of Richard Speck*, paranormal investigators fall victim to the ghost of a mass murderer, each death surrounded by glitches. Two members of the team watch on their iPad as their friend tries to retrieve car keys from the pocket of a bisected body in the attic (Figure 14.2). Tell-tale glitches split the video feed horizontally as she approaches the lower half of the severed victim. The privileged eye of the camera picks up the ghost that lurks nearby, and, as the woman meets her demise, glitches in the video feed once again disrupt the picture. The fragmentation and horizontal lines of the glitch seem to decapitate the victim, who now slumps next to the guts of her dead friend. Meanwhile, the horror on the faces of the two men who watch the scene unfold on their iPad almost comically conflates the frustration of deciphering a bad feed with the helplessness of seeing a friend killed.

FIGURE 14.2 100 Ghost Street: The Return of Richard Speck *(2012, Martin Wichmann, The Asylum)*.

Death and media malfunction go hand in hand in Glitch Gothic horror. The most literal manifestation of that coupling, although not a ghost story, is the *V/H/S* short "Tuesday, the 17th." Originally conceived as a straightforward

---

[44]For a noise-centered (not uniquely glitch-centered) analysis of zombie films, see Allan Cameron, "Zombie Media: Transmission, Reproduction, and the Digital Dead," *Cinema Journal* 52.1 (2012), 66–89.
[45]Hannah Piper Burns and Evan Meaney, "Glitches Be Crazy: The Problem of Self-Identification through Noise," in *GLI.TC/H READER[ROR] 20111*: 73.

homage to *Friday The 13th* (1980), the director decided to modernize the slasher by featuring a killer who eludes video capture in human form and appears on camera only as a frenzy of jagged lines and colors. Although the footage is digital, the killer does not appear as a digital glitch, but rather as a tracking error normally associated with a misaligned playback head in a VCR. He is an apparition of mechanical, analog error in a digital film. Like a ghost, his presence is inherently anachronistic. As the killer slits the throat of one of his victims, the slashing effect imposed by his disruptive tracking noise eliminates the distinction between violence *in* footage and violence *to* footage (Figure 14.3). The killer simultaneously damages media and flesh. To his camera-carrying victim, Wendy, both threats are equally terrifying. As the killer approaches, Wendy cries out *"Why can't I film you?"* with the kind of desperation normally reserved for questions such as "Why are you doing this?" or "Why me?" For Wendy, terror and error are one and the same.

FIGURE 14.3 V/H/S *(2012, Adam Wingard, et al., 8383 Productions).*

To conclude, we must return to the asylum, the institutional container for malfunctioning minds. Reminders of the pre-Prozac era, abandoned mental hospitals represent an absence or failure of remedies. To encounter ghosts is to recognize that lack. "The ghost story," explains Colin Davis, "recounts a temporary interruption in the fabric of reality, a glitch in the matrix, in order that the proper moral and epistemological order of things can be put back to rights."[46] Glitch Gothic stories recount a temporary interruption in the fabric of

---

[46]Colin Davis, *Haunted Subjects: Deconstruction, Psychoanalysis, and the Return of the Dead* (Basingstoke: Palgrave Macmillan, 2007), 3.

virtuality or digitality in order that the spectral can become material. The ghosts of *Grave Encounters 2* do not attempt to evade digital capture; they demand it as a remedy to their diminished presence. "FINISH THE FILM," they scrawl in enormous letters onto the asylum wall. Alex accepts their demand, and fights with Sean Rogerson (aka Lance Preston, the host of "Grave Encounters" who has been trapped in the asylum since 2003) to finish the film and gain release from the asylum. In the course of the fight, five video cameras float into the air and capture the battle from all angles. Inexplicably, Sean gets swallowed up into a whirling vortex that closes immediately thereafter, leaving only Alex and his friend Jennifer. "The building wants an audience," he mumbles. "I'll finish your film, and those who see it will come," he yells, "I won't let you down!" Alex then strikes Jennifer repeatedly in the face with his camera, his lens cracking and further splitting the image with each blow. Within the context of a film so thoroughly pervaded by glitches, the visual language of noise events subsumes even the fractured picture of Jennifer's broken face (see Figure 14.4). Were this a shot from an earlier era—a Giallo film by Argento, for example—the fragmented image through the cracked lens would be a metaphor for a fractured psyche. Instead, the spectacle of physical violence is a metaphor for media breakdown. Jennifer's death becomes "footage" to be remixed, edited, and circulated within a genre that relies as much on the horror of digital guts as it does on the abject attraction of physical violence. The building and its ghosts get their audience thanks to the gothic space of digital structures, and like so many other twenty-first-century ghosts, they wait to be remediated by the next group of camera-wielding attractive twenty-somethings.

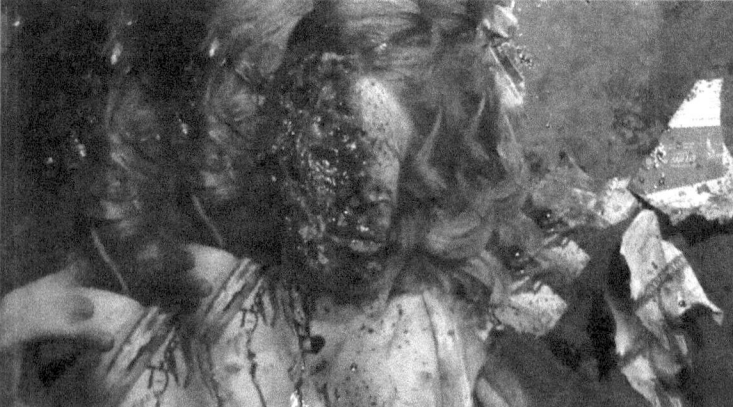

FIGURE 14.4 Grave Encounters 2 *(John Poliquin, 2012, Death Awaits Cinema)*.

15

Showing the Unknowable: *Uncle Boonmee Who Can Recall His Past Lives*

Mitsuyo Wada-Marciano

Introduction

The 2010 winner of Cannes' Palme d'Or *Uncle Boonmee Who Can Recall His Past Lives* (*Uncle Boonmee* from now on) transcends a number of boundaries of media (print, installation art, photography, and film), genre (art-house cinema, world cinema, human drama, political cinema, horror, fantasy, and slow cinema), and various conceptual dichotomies, such as "art" and "commodity," "past" and "present," "reality" and "fantasy," "human" and "animal," "man" and "woman," and "living thing" and "ghost." The film, moreover, crosses the cultural boundaries between the Eastern Buddhist philosophy of reincarnation (as expressed in the original Thai short story by Abbot Phra Sripariyattiweti) and the Euro-American audience, as the award signifies.

This chapter examines how the film accomplishes the transcendental, in a manner that goes beyond simple Orientalism. The filmmaker Apichatpong Weerasethakul states that *Uncle Boonmee* "reinforces a special association between cinema and reincarnation." He continues, "Cinema is man's way to create alternate universes, other lives,"[1] and

---

[1] Richard Lormand, *Uncle Boonmee Who Can Recall His Past Lives*, Film Press Plus http://filmpressplus.com/wp-content/uploads/dl_docs/UncleBOONMEE-Notes.pdf (accessed April 27, 2014).

indeed the film depicts the alternate worlds with parallel temporalities and cyclical time, instead of adopting the typical linear chronological development in European philosophical tradition. Weerasethakul's inventive deployment of cinematic time and soundscape uniquely expresses a narrative of reincarnation, which merges the original Buddhist idea of time and ghosts in diegetic space with the prevalent values in global culture, such as "slow cinema"—a type of cinema characterized by minimalism, austerity, and extended duration—and "deep ecology"—environmental philosophy advocated by the Norwegian philosopher Arne Naess since the 1970s. I would hypothesize that those universal qualities within the local qualities of the film have made *Uncle Boonmee* an alluring cultural commodity in the art cinema scene, namely international film festivals and critical discourses, and enabled the film to take the "glocal" position. The relationship between "the local" and "the global" has always been multifaceted, since "locality" is often chosen in global culture, and "the local" culture is increasingly concerned with "global" issues as sociologist Roland Robertson indicates.[2] This chapter attempts to uncover the film's uniqueness and attraction, which is not simply related with those cultural differences, but also with class differences in the cinematic cultural sphere.

Uncle Boonmee's polarized receptions

The film permeates with Buddhist supernaturalism—it borrows from a story of reincarnation, and a number of ghosts appear within the narrative space. In contrast with the familiar mainstream horrific or comedic ghosts (including Hong Kong horror-comedy *Encounters of the Spooky Kind* (1980) and Hollywood's *Ghostbusters* (1984)), *Uncle Boonmee* circumvents the stereotype by displaying the extraordinary in ordinary settings, as when ghosts appearing at a dinner table with family members nonplussed, demonstrating intimacy and tranquility toward their dead relatives.

The film starts from a dimly lit field in a Thai village near the border with Laos, where a water buffalo leads audiences further into the Nabua jungle. The buffalo is suggested as one of Uncle Boonmee's previous lives, and the film later implies that Boonmee was incarnated as an ugly, pebble-faced princess as well in a previous life. The protagonist Boonmee (Thanapat

---

[2]Roland Robertson, *Globalization: Social Theory and Global Culture* (London: SAGE Publications, 1992), 174.

Saisaymar) is dying from kidney failure and going through his last days with his loved ones: his sister-in-law, Jen (Jenjira Pongpas), and his nephew, Thong (Sakda Kaewbuadee). His deceased wife, Huay (Natthakarn Aphaiwong), and his long-lost son, Boonsong (Jeerasak Kulhong), later accompany Boonmee and his "family" at the dinner table. The film subsequently reveals that the ghosts of his wife and son have come back to guide Boonmee on his journey toward death. Huay, the ghost, has not changed a bit since she passed away nineteen years ago, and the son, Boonsong, is now incarnated in the form of the Monkey Ghost called "Ling-phi" in Thai. Boonsong explains his appearance: "There are many beings outside right now. So I had to come and see you, father ... [They are] spirits and hungry animals. They sense your sickness." His indirect ominous words foreshadow Boonmee's sudden death in the following day.

Uncle Boonmee is constructed with multiple stories and various filmic styles, and each part is not bound with narrative logic, other than the fact that the film is about Boonmee's reincarnation. Weerasethakul rationalizes his usage of the eclectic method as follows:

> I took a different approach to each of the six reels. The first reel, for example, follows my usual way of long-take filmmaking. The second reel, with the scene of the dinner with ghosts, is like old-fashioned cinema shot with a static camera, with an element also of Thai TV drama. Overall, the film is a tribute to all the cinemas I grew up with, whether Thai films, soap operas, or very classical horror movies. It was like, "OK, we're employing not a single film style, but using six different film styles."[3]

The fragmentation of the film is not only a result of Weerasethakul's artistic pursuit, but it also embodies his heterogeneous cultural memories from the public sphere (Thai novel, television, comic books, and cinema) and from the private one (memory of his father, who also died from kidney failure).

Due to this eclecticism, reception of the film varies. As I indicated earlier, while *Uncle Boonmee* won the Palme d'Or at the 2010 Cannes Film Festival and became the first Thai film to be draped in such glory, some film critics, on the other hand, simply dismissed the film as "unintelligible." For example, by comparing the previous winners of the Palme d'Or, such

---

[3] Ji-Hoon Kim, "Learning About Time: An Interview with Apichatpong Weerasethakul," *Film Quarterly* 64.4 (Summer 2011), 52.

as *4 Months, 3 Weeks and 2 Days* (2007), and *The White Ribbon* (2009), blogger Damon Wise in *Empire* writes:

> Compared to those films, the wilfully unintelligible *Uncle Boonmee Who Can Recall His Past Lives* (and hence must have seen you coming) is, to me, something of a PR disaster for the festival, a film that confirms the snobbish tastes of only an element of this year's Cannes attendees and bodes ill for an industry that has been driven into blockbusters and zero-budgeters by the recession, with little in between...I didn't like it, and I don't see why I have to.[4]

In contrast, film critic Peter Bradshaw in *The Guardian* praises the film without hesitation:

> This beautiful, mysterious and playful film by the Thai director Apichatpong Weerasethakul—winner of this year's Cannes Palme d'Or—is about ghosts, past lives and the fear of death, things that in another sort of movie would be presented as scary or sentimental, but are here accepted as alternative phenomena, existing alongside day-to-day normalities. The poetry is all in this calm and gentle equivalence. The film's sublimely spiritual quality induces a benign narcosis.[5]

What made Damon Wise associate the film with intellectual high-mindedness of Cannes, and why did film reviewer Peter Bradshaw elevate the film as otherworldly fantasy? I think they are indicating the same quality of the film, each in a different manner: a quality seemingly particular to Thai culture but at the same time something universal, able to touch a global audience. I will discuss the film's Buddhist temporality, and how the film connects this particularity to global cultural values in the following sections.

Concept of time

While one might find a number of peculiar aspects in *Uncle Boonmee*—after all the film belongs to "world cinema," a designation that readily distinguishes a film from Hollywood blockbusters—here I will focus on the

---

[4]Damon Wise, "Uncle Boonmee: An Explanation," *The Empire Blog in Empire*, http://www.empireonline.com/empireblogs/under-the-radar/post/p820 (accessed April 27, 2014).

[5]Peter Bradshaw, "Uncle Boonmee Who Can Recall His Past Lives—Review," The Guardian, November 18, 2010, http://www.theguardian.com/film/2010/nov/18/uncle-boonmee-who-can-recall-his-past-lives-review (accessed April 27, 2014).

film's usage of time as one of the most peculiar elements. As Bliss Cua Lim states, "Ghosts call our calendars into question."[6] She further suggests that "ghost films contain the seeds of such culturally resonant theories of temporal coevalness and inhabit the elusive, heterogeneous space posited by Bergsonism,"[7] here referring to Henri Bergson, who, in his *Matter and Memory*, explicates the tendency of our concept regarding space and time: "Homogeneous space and time are the mental diagrams of our eventual action upon matter; they are not the properties of things."[8] *Uncle Boonmee*, among other ghost films, makes the audience realize the possibility of non-homogenous space and time; that the homogeneous time can also be an abstraction or even simply an illusion. In the case of *Uncle Boonmee*, the film displays heterogeneous space and time, not only with the appearance of ghosts, but also with the cyclical time movement of Buddhism.

Boonmee talks about *karma* (how the effects of a person's action determine his destiny in his next incarnation or deed) and *samsara* (the repeating cycle of birth). After asking Jen to take over his bee farm, Boonmee assures her that he will find a way back to be able to help her even after he has died. Boonmee also expresses his strong belief that his terminal kidney failure is a result of his *karma*; he confesses that he killed many communists in the 1960s and moreover a lot of bugs through pesticides on his farm. Boonmee even asks Jen whether her deceased father has visited her after his death. Jen replies, "No, once he was dead, he was gone. He didn't become a ghost." Her pragmatic manner effectively works to anchor their conversation—and, further, the film—to the mundane facts of life (I will return to this aspect later).

The concept of time in *Uncle Boonmee* is neither linear nor following a specific logic beyond the film's vague explanation that Boonmee can recall his past lives as indicated in the title. Weerasethakul writes, "Originally, the script was more explicit in explaining which were the past lives, which were not. But in the film, I decided to respect the audience's imagination."[9] The film deploys cyclical time by following the logic of reincarnation or, more precisely, the accumulation of *ksana* (moments). His returned wife, Huay, for instance, refers to her ghostly time as, "I have no concept of time,"

---

[6]Bliss Cua Lim, *Translating Time: Cinema, the Fantastic, and Temporal Critique* (Durham and London: Duke University Press, 2009), 149.
[7]Ibid.
[8]Henri Bergson, *Matter and Memor*, Trans. Nancy Margaret Paul and W. Scott Palmer (London: George Allen and Unwin, 1911), 280.
[9]Richard Lormand, *Uncle Boonmee Who Can Recall His Past Lives*, Film Press Plus, http://filmpressplus.com/wp-content/uploads/dl_docs/UncleBOONMEE-Notes.pdf (accessed April 27, 2014).

and she has been unchanged since she died nineteen years ago. The film evokes a different sense of time than Western linear time and deploys a slower rhythm in its long takes. The film further intensifies the unfamiliar temporality by employing ghosts and/or spirits, which exist outside of normal temporality.

Historian Arnold J. Toynbee established the tie between cyclical time movement and Buddhism or post-Buddhaic Hinduism in the 1950s. He writes:

> The interpretation of the rhythm of the Universe as a cyclic movement governed by an Impersonal Law admits of an endless series of successive avatars of God, bringing revelation and salvation to His creatures in successive cycles; but the possibility of recurrence is incompatible with the dogma that there has been, or will be, an incarnation of God that has been, or will be, unique and final. The doctrine of avatars is characteristic of both Mahayanian Buddhism and post-Buddhaic Hinduism.[10]

Toynbee also associates a non-cyclical time with Judaism, Christianity, and Islam as follows: "The interpretation of the rhythm of the Universe as a non-recurrent movement governed by Intellect and Will is the most searching of all the challenges to the Judaic claim to uniqueness and finality."[11] Although given the facts that Toynbee's ideas are considered outdated (*An Historian's Approach to Religion* was first published in 1956), and his "mystical-religious worldview" and methodology of "forcing of facts to fit a preconceived theory"[12] have long been criticized, his extensive publications and numerous translations in many languages have had enormous influence on public opinion, not only in Anglophone cultures, but also on a global level. In this sense, *Uncle Boonmee*'s cyclical time movement neatly fits within the cognitive category of Buddhism as an exotic cultural Other.

The film's other-ness or exoticism is expressed on the level of filmic technique as well. The past is usually expressed through the flashback, which is frequently underlined by a change in hue, for instance, from color (present) to black and white (past). Although films often make clear whose "memory" or past the audience is following, the film *Uncle Boonmee* neglects the rule. For instance, in the afternoon when Jen and Thong arrive at Boonmee's house, she strolls around the tamarind farm with Boonmee.

---

[10] Arnold Toynbee, *An Historian's Approach to Religion* (London, New York and Toronto: Oxford University Press, 1956), 133.
[11] Toynbee, 134.
[12] M.P. "Books in Summary: *Arnold Toynbee and the Western Tradition.* By Marvin Perry. New York: Peter Lang, 1996. pp. xii, 145," *History and Theory* 36.1 (February 1997), 109.

SHOWING THE UNKNOWABLE

They later go under a shed for Boonmee's kidney treatment, where he lies down on the raised floor. After having a short conversation with Jen, he falls asleep (Figure 15.1). The camera cuts back to Jen observing Boonmee's sleeping face with a gentle smile (Figure 15.2). The empty shot of what is likely Boonmee's house's interior follows right after that (Figure 15.3). Then, the camera goes outside and captures Thong lying in a hammock on the veranda (Figure 15.4). Thong's shot is gradually accompanied by very low-volume acoustic music, which functions as a link between the previous shot (Figure 15.4) and the following sequence, in which an "ugly" princess is transported in a palanquin by her servants (Figure 15.5).

FIGURES 15.1–15.5 Uncle Boonmee Who Can Recall His Past Lives *(Apichatpong Weerasethakul, 2010, Kick the Machine)*.

Whose "memory" are we tracing here? If we follow our experience with cinematic language, the beginning of the sequence of the "ugly" princess (Figure 15.5) is easily identified as Thong's dream, or his memory that he is simply recalling while lying on the hammock. But this interpretation—that Thong is the subject of the "flashback"—is rather counterintuitive, because audiences have already been informed that the person who is supposedly recalling memories is not Thong, but Uncle Boonmee—again, as the title indicates. As I mentioned above, Boonmee is also asleep, though under a shed in a remote field; therefore, in theory, it is possible for us to associate the mythical "ugly" princess sequence with Uncle Boonmee, or even think that there is some spiritual connection between Boonmee, Thong, and the reincarnated subjects (the princess and/or the catfish, which makes love with the princess in the waterfall). The film's use of flashback does not follow convention because the subject (the princess) in the flashback does not meet with the one in the present, Thong taking a nap.

The film's soundscape plays a significant role in suspending the subjective uncertainty and in smoothing the stumbling disconnection between the shots of "present" and the "reincarnation" sequence. The insects' and birds' natural sounds in the pastoral field are inserted uninterruptedly throughout the five continuous shots and, as a result, audiences identify themselves as both being distant from the diegetic space (because they are always located on this side of the screen) and in proximity to the pastoral space (they concurrently experience the well-crafted soundscape while they view the film). While the audience in general may enjoy the naturalist expression on the screen, the uncertainty of the subject of the "memory," which is working, here, against the convention of flashback, has the potential to puzzle or frustrate certain audiences, as in Damon Wise's comment on the film's unintelligibility.

Uncle Boonmee displays double exoticism in the relationship between "memory" and "fantasy." The film indeed forces audiences to receive it as "foreign" on multiple levels. Through the narrative device of reincarnation, Boonmee could have been a water buffalo, an "ugly" princess and/or the catfish making love with the princess, a monkey ghost in the still-photo images, and also one of the Thai youth soldiers who is in those same photographs. The audience is urged to go through Boonmee's various past lives/personal memories, which are distantly tied to Thai's cultural and historic memory. While the film presents the "exotic" subjects in memories, the film itself also exists as the "exotic" in the film genre, fantasy.

The chairman of the Palme d'Or jury at the 2010 Cannes Film Festival, Tim Burton, stated about *Uncle Boonmee* that the world has become smaller, Westernized, and moreover Hollywoodized, but this film is a *fantasy* that he has never seen before.[13] The film genre of "fantasy" is indeed a category that can aptly include the film *Uncle Boonmee*. The uncertain tie with multiple memories makes the film trans-natural, magical, and imaginary. If the definition of a fantasy story is an imaginative fiction dependent for effect on the strangeness of setting and of characters, then we can assume it is not interchangeable with other "speculative fictions"—science fiction, for instance, which is set in the future and based on some aspect of science or technology. The fantasy genre is defined as being set in an imaginary world and features the magic of mythical beings. Something worth noting about this category, which originated in literature, is that in general the category is very much an English-language genre, as the name of the genre "fantasy" obviously indicates. Especially since J. R. R. Tolkien's *The Lord of the Rings*, published in the mid-1950s, became the most popular work in fantasy, the genre became predominantly set in medieval times. This trend in the fantasy literary genre indeed explains Tim Burton's comment on *Uncle Boonmee* well; the film brings to the European and/or American jurors a fantasy fiction, but it is a different type of fantasy from that of the Euro-centric medievalist narrative. The film is not simply the sharing of memories of "the exotic," but it also stands as "exotic" itself within the fantasy film genre and within the history of popular culture.

Slow cinema

Damon Wise's rejection of *Uncle Boonmee* as "unintelligible" is also related to the fact that the film shares many aspects with the so-called slow cinema. Slow cinema is usually defined as film that "highlights the viewing process itself as a real-time experience."[14] Tsai Ming-Liang's *Goodbye Dragon Inn* (2003)—especially the film's sequence set in an empty movie theater— is an often-cited example of the kind. In the case of *Uncle Boonmee*, we find more than a few shots in which the film resists linking an image to an explicit meaning. Weerasethakul effectively uses lighting and sound to make audiences engage with such scenes, which often lack a viewing subject in the diegetic space. The commonality between Tsai's sequence of the empty movie theater and Weerasethakul's scenes—besides being "slow"—is the moment of haunting, since both films present spectrality,that is, there is no

---

[13]*Uncle Boonmee Who Can Recall His Past Lives* official site in Japan, http://uncle-boonmee.com/review/(accessed May 4, 2014).
[14]Jonathan Romney, "In Search of Lost Time," *Sight & Sound* 20.2 (February 2010), 43–4.

one to see those scenes, but someone is seeing it, and we, the audience, share the spectral space and time through the "haunted" gaze.

The aforementioned water buffalo sequence, for instance, starts with only sounds of the field—voices of birds and insects—in pitch-black darkness. The gradual rise of dawn light opaquely projects the buffalo shifting around, unleashing itself, and then it soon leads us off-screen. The sound of water from the cow stepping into a creek makes us realize its movement from the field to the deep forest. The herder with aboriginal attire (half-naked wearing a straw skirt) finally comes into the screen/forest, searching for the buffalo, but it is difficult for us to establish a sense of time—of the day or historical period. Is the image in front of us happening now or a long time ago? We only view the image as it is presented to us, and then we hear the sound, "Keow"; the herder calls the cow's name. This sequence takes more than five minutes, and we are left alone to decide what it is about.

"Real-time experience" in slow cinema is not only expressed visibly but is also articulated aurally. The film intensely taps into our experience of hearing, "cinema as ear" in Thomas Elsaesser's and Malth Hegener's term. Damon Wise's rejection of *Uncle Boonmee* probably stems from the film's subversion of the hierarchical relationship between "image" and "sound." As Elsaesser and Hegener explicate the relationship between image and sound in classical cinema, the role of sound (three-dimensional) is to "give body, extension and shape to the image (two-dimensional)," and classical cinema often conforms "a hierarchical relationship between image and sound, whereby the latter is subordinated to the former."[15] In *Uncle Boonmee*, on the other hand, sound is pronounced over image, especially in the aforementioned dark opening sequence. While Elsaesser and Hegener characterize the subversion of the hierarchy between image and sound as occurring in the age of the blockbuster with new sound technologies (Dolby, Surround Sound, THX, Sound Design), I would argue that it is also the case in extreme art-house cinema such as *Uncle Boonmee*. The film's "primitive" look, or simplicity at a glance, leads audiences to assume that the film is principally naturalist in its reproduction of experience, but in contrast, the film's mythic narrative is expressed through the highly controlled soundscape of such advanced technologies.

The experience of sound/voice becomes crucial when the ghosts appear in the film. Uncle Boonmee's son, Boonson, for instance, enters onto the screen in the form of a Monkey Ghost, "Ling-phi." Weerasethakul directs

---

[15]Thomas Elsaesser and Malte Hagener, *Film Theory: An Introduction through the Senses* (New York and London: Routledge, 2010), 132.

the encounter of the other family members with the Monkey Ghost with a manipulation of light and sound, but not with elaborate digital imaging. Boonson ascends the stairs in the pitch-black darkness, and the family members at the dinner table (and of course the audience) can only recognize two moving dots of red light. Boonmee asks, "Jaai, is that you? Who are you?" and then we hear the voice of the ghost, "I'm Boonsong." The family members cannot recognize him from his appearance, but they do recognize his voice. Huay asks, "Boonsong, my son?" and then he replies "Mother." Jen, after a short silence, murmurs to Boonmee, "It's Boonson. I recognize his voice." Here again is another way of subverting the hierarchy between image and sound. Boonson's voice, reconnecting himself back to his family, becomes the single cue, not his new appearance with red eyes and black hair covering his whole body.

The unspectacular appearances of Boonson's and Huay's ghosts do not add much dramatic impact, but rather they create a sense of fantasy that makes audiences feel that it is possible to reunite with deceased loved ones and that ghosts can be our guardian angels. The film emphasizes the mundane-ness of the ghosts' actions: Huay helps Boonmee with his kidney treatment, and she keeps a bedside vigil next to a sleeping Jen. Even during Huay's crucial mission to lead Boonmee to the cave, where he ends his current life, her act of killing Boonmee by letting his body fluid out is depicted as an act of gentle assertiveness. There is neither dramatic struggle nor compelling murderous intent. All those dramatic actions seem rather intentionally restrained.

Slow cinema, according to Sukhdev Sandhu, can be seen as "an act of cultural resistance."[16] While for mainstream audiences, the cinema is nothing but films "downplaying drama, event, and action in favour of mood,"[17] it can also be interpreted as a challenge to audiences to contemplate the elusive qualities of cinema, or life in general, more specifically the humane quality of relationships among people. Jonathan Romney analyzes the reasons for the recent increase in this style of film, especially in the 1980s and early 1990s, from two aspects: first, commercial cinema has become so ossified, and therefore the joy of interpretation, in his term "filling the gap," has become totally lost; second, Romney thinks that slow cinema is a product of a specific contemporary social condition. He continues:

---

[16] Sukhdev Sandhu, "'Slow Cinema' Fights Back Again Bourne's Supremacy," *The Guardian* (March 9, 2012), http://www.theguardian.com/film/2012/mar/09/slow-cinema-fights-bournes-supremacy (accessed May 7, 2014).
[17] Ibid.

[T]he current Slow Cinema might be seen as a response to a bruisingly pragmatic decade in which, post-9/11, the oppressive everyday awareness of life as overwhelmingly political, economic and ecological would seem to preclude (in the West, at least) any spiritual dimension in art.[18]

Although his explanation lacks the cogent link between "time" (are we still in the same condition as of 2001?), "society" (if the slow cinema is a response to the specific social condition in the United States post-9/11, why have so many examples originated in Eastern Europe, Asia, and other non-Western regions?), and the genre itself, it is undeniable that critics among contemporary audiences have recognized the emergence of the cinema in global film markets over the last two decades. The recent linking of slow cinema with affirmative cultural values and as a challenge to the "ossified" blockbuster has given a sort of nominal value to the film *Uncle Boonmee* and provided a universal language for critics, or audiences in general, to further discuss the film.

Romney deploys the term "pragmatic" to frame the current social condition, an expression that is opposed to the "spiritual" quality of the so-called exotic art. In a certain way, *Uncle Boonmee* strategically plays with this dichotomy in cultural literacy, and, as I mentioned earlier, the film uses Jen, Boonmee's sister-in-law, as a "pragmatist" who embodies this viewpoint that connects with contemporary societies and their values. In one of the seemingly disconnected shots in the film, Jen is slaying insects flying to the light above the dining table with an electronic swatter. The sound of execution, a bursting noise like popping corn, is palpable and even comical. While Boonmee regrets that he has killed too many bugs on his farm and believes his kidney failure is a result of this *karma*, Jen, on the other hand, shows no hesitation in killing the bug intruders, an action which many audiences might have similarly performed. The subtle contrast created between Boonmee and Jen, "spiritual" and "pragmatic," reveals not only Weerasethakul's awareness of the reality that contemporary audiences share, but also of audience tastes and desires.

Deep ecology

Another crucial aspect that makes *Uncle Boonmee* universal, that is, appealing to a global audience, is that the film shares the concept of "bio-centric equality" with the contemporary environmental philosophy of "deep ecology." The film

---

[18]Jonathan Romney, "In Search of Lost Time: Part of a Special Section: Cinema of the 21st Century: 30 Key Films of the Last Decade," *Sight & Sound* 20.2 (February 2010), 43–4.

is about reincarnation, and Boonmee can allegedly recall his past lives as a variety of creatures: a water buffalo, a princess, a catfish, a bug, Monkey Ghost, or a soldier killing communists. The modern concept of reincarnation reflects a bio-spherical egalitarianism, which decentralizes human beings, placing them in an equal position with other beings. The founder of deep ecology, Norwegian philosopher Arne Naess (1912–2009), distinguishes his philosophy from other forms of ecology, which are more pragmatic in balancing economic interests in modernization and scientific developments, and Naess terms the latter as "shallow" or "reformist" ecology. His own view, instead, emphasizes the complex web of interrelationships in the natural world. He distinguishes between "the shallow ecology" and "the deep ecology" as follows:

> The *shallow ecology movement* is concerned with fighting pollution and resource depletion. Its central objective is the health and affluence of people in the developed countries.
> The *deep ecology movement* has deeper concerns, which touch upon principles of diversity, complexity, autonomy, decentralization, symbiosis, egalitarianism, and classlessness.[19]

Although Naess has written about deep ecology extensively, his core concept of deep ecology seemingly stems from two principles: the aforementioned "bio-centric equality" and "self-realization." Naess's eco-philosophy is eclectic, drawing from Spinoza's ethics and moreover Gandhian ethics on conflict resolution, namely *ahimsa* (nonviolence). The two principles of deep ecology, in Naess's mind, are bridged by Gandhi's teachings in the following manner:

> Paradoxically, it seems, [Gandhi] tried to reach self-realization through "selfless action"; that is, through a diminishment of the dominance of the narrow self or ego. Through the wider Self every living being is intimately connected, and from this intimacy follows the capacity of *identification* and, as a natural consequence, the practice of nonviolence. No moralizing is needed, just as we do not need morals to make us breathe. Rather, we need to cultivate our insight: "The rock bottom foundation of the technique for achieving the power of non-violence is belief in the essential oneness of all life."[20]

---

[19] Arne Naess, "The Shallow and the Deep, Long-Range Ecology Movement: A Summary," in *The Selected Works of Arne*, ed. Alan Drengson (Dordrecht: Springer, 2005), 7.

[20] Arne Naess, "Self-Realization: An Ecological Approach to Being in the World," in *The Selected Works of Arne*, ed. Alan Drengson (Dordrecht: Springer, 2005), 524.

Naess asserts that these core principles are realized in Gandhi: "Gandhi made manifest the internal relationship between self-realization, nonviolence, and what has sometimes been called biospherical egalitarianism."[21]

Let us go back to *Uncle Boonmee*. The conceptual link between the film and deep ecology (and Gandhian ethics, originally) adds further cultural value to the film, especially in the age of twenty-first-century postindustrial and eco-friendly movements. It is intriguing to think about the limitations of deep ecology and how an association with such limitations provides additional meaning to *Uncle Boonmee*. Philosopher Masahiro Morioka points out three drawbacks of deep ecology. First, he views deep ecology as an offspring of Romanticism and/or Utopianism, both of which criticize modern society and civilization, highlighting holistic harmony and spiritual world. In other words, deep ecology identifies with the limitation of Romanticism, which is to escape from reality toward interiority, spirituality, and totality at more theoretical level. Second, deep ecology was created as a counterargument to a nature-conservation movement. Therefore, it is useful to criticize current problematic social situations. However, the eco-philosophy lacks a pragmatic methodology or means for hands-on operation for changing society for the better. Third, deep ecology tends to ignore peoples' "desire"—either in material or emotional forms. Modern civilization has always been based on human beings' desires, such as having a variety of foods to eat and making money for a more comfortable life. Deep ecology, on the other hand, presents the concepts of "renewing oneself" or "self-realization" as a substitute goal for one's true desires, but it seems to Morioka that the ecological thinking treats material desires as insignificant. Finally, and the most relevant aspect for our discussion on *Uncle Boonmee*, deep ecology is basically constituted by a European middle class, especially by intellectual elites. Therefore, the ideas underpinning deep ecology reflect middle-class values; meanwhile these ideas have less impact on the people in still-developing countries. Morioka offers a more specific example: the inhabitants of a desert region cannot enjoy the life of the forest in reality. In other words, deep ecology often does not correspond with specific solutions to the problems facing real societies, such as racial discrimination and/or contradictions in democracy. The popularity of the film *Uncle Boonmee* among film festival judges and film critics indicates a parallel between the class specificity of deep ecology and the majority of the art cinema scene, middle-class intellectuals, whether in Europe, the United States, or other global cinema markets.

---

[21]Ibid.

Engaged Buddhism

The film *Uncle Boonmee* visually displays environmental issues such as "natural agriculture," and this aspect lets the film engage with those middle-class intellectuals on a deeper level. Uncle Boonmee has a tamarind orchard and runs a beekeeping business. He hires illegal immigrant workers from Laos and sometimes learns French from the Laotian workers. Jaai works as the chief worker and also helps with Boonmee's kidney treatment. The film offers a glance at the working environment on his farm, which seems peaceful and joyful. While the town dweller, Jen, shows her concern about hiring illegal immigrants because of the risk of crime, that is not Boonmee's worry. Instead, the film depicts how Boomee runs the ideal natural farm and treats his employees with trust and respect.

The representation of life on Boonmee's farm corresponds with the growing international movement of "engaged Buddhism." Anthropologist Susan M. Darlington reports on Thai environmental monks, known as "engaged Buddhists," with their three outstanding activities: (1) tree ordinations, (2) long-life ceremonies for rivers, and (3) integrated sustainable agriculture. The tree ordination is the best-known activity of environmentalist monks in Thailand, who make trees sacred, wrapping them in orange robes as an attempt to protect the forest. Phrakhru Manas Natheephitak of Phayao Province in northern Thailand, close to the location of the film *Uncle Boonmee*, arguably started promoting environmentalism in the late 1980s. People behave toward the trees covered in orange robes with the same respect they pay toward monks and, as a result, the monks can popularize the connection between Buddhists' responsibilities and nature via the movement.[22] Another monk, Phrakhru Pitak Nanthakhun of Nan Province in north Thailand, introduced "integrated agricultural methods by encouraging villagers not to plant cash crops, but instead to mix native crops and livestock that mutually support each other, negating the need for chemical fertilizers and pesticides."[23] Planting fruit trees beside the paddies is one of the recommended methods. The agricultural method encourages symbiotic relationships among the plants and animals, as we see in *Uncle Boonmee* as he runs the apiary and his bees make honey out of his tamarind orchard.

---

[22]Susan M. Darlington, "Translating Modernity: Buddhist Response to the Thai Environmental Crisis," *TransBuddhism: Transmission, Translation, Transformation*, eds. Nalini Bhushan, Jay L. Garfield, Abraham Zablocki (Amherst: University of Massachusetts Press, 2009), 192.
[23]Ibid., 200.

While Darlington states that "Thai environmental monks did not invent the idea of using Buddhism to deal with environmental issues,"[24] she highlights those three activities as innovations within Buddhist practice, which are also reactions against Thailand's environmental crisis, caused by the Thai government's promotion of economic development since the 1960s. She writes:

> The most visible—and debated—environmental impact of economic development is the loss of Thailand's forest. Statistics on deforestation between 1961 and 1998 vary, depending on the source. According to the Royal Forest Department (RFD), forestland decreased from 53.3 percent of the national's total land in 1961 to 25.6 percent in 1998.[25]

Within this social context in Thailand, the lifestyle that the film presents does not only seem to be progressive to local audiences, but it also evokes global audiences' sympathy, especially from people with ecological concerns.

Conclusion

I have discussed *Uncle Boonmee*'s strategy as art cinema, being a film having both local cultural influences and an attractiveness for global audiences, especially intellectuals concerned with issues of the environment and sustainability. While the film deploys a low-budget aesthetic in its supernatural elements, such as "Ling-phi" with red eyes and black hair all over the body and the appearance of the ghost wife, Huay (a visual technique inspired by Thai television horror programs), *Uncle Boonmee* conveys such contemporary cultural values as the recent cinematic trend of slow cinema, the eco-philosophy movement, and ecological Buddhism. Within cinematic culture, this strategy can best be explained through the concept of "glocalization."

Sociologist Roland Robertson defines "glocalization" as "trends of homogenization and heterogenization [that coexisting] throughout the modern age," and he writes:

> [The] movement for worldwide indigenization of a variety of social practices has been globally orchestrated, in the sense that that trend

---
[24]Ibid., 184.
[25]Ibid., 187.

has been encouraged by international organizations or by cross-national alliances between movements concerned with indigenization.[26]

The concept of "glocalization," according to Robertson, was invented for explaining the gap between greater homogeneity and the recognition that the world is more diversified culturally, and for describing how ideas or cultural products are distributed in both global and local markets. In his explanation, the global and the local coexist, but they are not located in any hierarchical high-low position.

In this light, *Uncle Boonmee*'s polarized receptions are further evidence of the film's "glocality." As I indicated earlier, the film won the Palme d'Or in 2010, but at the same time the film did not make the shortlist for the Best Foreign Language Film competition at the eighty-third Academy Awards. Although it is too simplistic to contrast the Cannes Film Festival and the Academy Awards as the former being for cutting-edge art cinema and the latter being for films-as-commodity, the differing receptions of *Uncle Boonmee* between these two events clearly indicate that the gap derives not simply from cultural differences (East vs. West), but rather that it is more closely related to multifaceted cultural values and literacy (pro-ecology vs. pro-modernization, slow cinema vs. blockbusters, and cinema as art vs. cinema as commodity) and that those opposing receptions are connected within a global–local cultural mobility. I think the aspects of "fantasy" and "amateurism" in *Uncle Boonmee* are at the heart of the film's challenge to contemporary audiences, and that the ghosts in the film symbolize those characteristics. While Katarzyna Ancuta indicates that a greater level of computer literacy among young directors caused technological improvement, or "professionalism" in Thai horror films, Weerasethakul instead intentionally chooses the other way, the amateurish representation of ghosts.[27] The aspect of refusing to use computerization can be understood as his nostalgia toward the Thai cinema from the past, but also the nostalgia itself can be seen as a signifier of the present valorizing the past as something meaningful.

Film critic Sukhdev Sandhu applauds *Uncle Boonmee* as slow cinema and as "an act of cultural resistance" by linking it to other examples of slow cinema: Jia Zhang-ke's *Still Life* (2006) and Carlos Reygadas' *Silent Light* (2007). Sandhu writes:

---

[26]Ibid., 171.

[27]Katarzyna Ancuta, "Global Spectrologies: Contemporary Thai Horror Films and the Globalization of the Supernatural," *Horror Studies* 2.1 (2011), 138.

[They] opt for ambient noises or field recordings rather than bombastic sound design, embrace subdued visual schemes that require the viewer's eye to do more work, and evoke a sense of mystery that springs from the landscapes and local customs they depict more than it does from generic convention.[28]

I, however, cannot view slow cinema, such as *Uncle Boonmee*, simply as "act of resistance." The film, tied to local culture and spirituality—including ghosts—functions as an "indigenous" and "communal" cultural representation, which then circulates and gains support through international organizations such as the Cannes Film Festival. While the enthusiasm toward the film is tied to the global demand for justification of local autonomy, at the same time one can find that there is a desire for the "indigenous" modern film to make a contribution to the global cinematic field. *Uncle Boonmee*, as a film, is not only showing ghosts—something unknowable—but also revealing how so-called cutting-edge festival films are produced and circulated within the expectations of the global middle-class intellectual community.

---

[28]Sandhu, "'Slow Cinema' Fights Back Again Bourne's Supremacy".

Afterword: Haunted Viewers

Jeffrey Sconce

Already entire days go by and no one thinks of *The Ghost of Dragstrip Hollow* (1959). A sequel of sorts to *Hot Rod Gang* (1958), the film contributed another hour's worth of footage to the growing reel of teenpics produced by American International Pictures in the 1950s and 1960s. It is a wisp of a movie, a 65-minute sampler of teenbait released as the undercard for *Diary of a High School Bride* (1959). Crazy hot-rod kids scheme to build a clubhouse where they can dance, eat pizza, and work on their jalopies. An eccentric aunt with a cantankerous parrot lends them an abandoned house to throw a dance party fundraiser. But the house is haunted! For the final twenty minutes of the movie, ghosts of all kinds haunt the hot-rodders: invisible spooks floating candles through the air; wispy emanations wafting through the hallways; living eyes searching from behind an oil portrait. Some kind of lizard man lives in a secret chamber behind the fireplace, prowling around when the kids are dozing to play pranks and scare them witless. But everything works out in the end, even after one of the gang violates the club charter by sneaking out for a quick drag race against her rival. In the end, we find the house isn't really haunted. The lizard man is behind it all. An unemployed actor once known for his monster roles, he has staged the evening's spooky festivities in the hopes of attracting attention (and thus work) from the Hollywood studios. In a poignant and rather unexpected moment of self-reflexivity, the beaten-down lizard man laments that even AIP no longer wants him.

Lizard man's unemployment is a target of comic derision in the film, even as it indexes the studio system's slow-motion death and decomposition—the majors divesting their theaters and pink-slipping their employees, exhibitors scrambling for product, television cementing its hold on the American psyche. Indeed, like so much of AIP's output, *The Ghost of Dragstrip Hollow* quickly moved from its brief moment on the big screen into its extended afterlife on the TV set. As part of a larger movie package, the film could pop up almost anywhere—late afternoon after school, Saturday morning matinee, late-night creature feature. There it served primarily as filler, a time-killer that allowed affiliates to insert a few more ads by local carpet magnates and used car kings while waiting for the network feed to resume. Did *The Ghost of Dragstrip Hollow* ever make it back to the big screen? It's not inconceivable. In the final days of the rep house, before the mass diffusion of the VCR and DVD, some curator might well have booked the film as emblematic of something—the AIP teenpic factory, hot rod madness, boomer camp. In the nineties, *The Ghost of Dragstrip Hollow* made its inevitable migration to VHS, paired with *The Ghost in the Invisible Bikini* (1966) in MGM's "Midnite Movies" series. A decade later, this double-bill found yet another repurposed life as a DVD release, serving that rarefied segment of the Boomer market looking to posses the highest-quality copies of their childhood obsessions.

Now, like so much of the cinema and the twentieth century generally, *The Ghost of Dragstrip Hollow* exists primarily as dematerialized data— the DVD deleted, the VHS copies warped and blurry, and the projection print—if one even still exists—languishing in storage. Digital access to the film is "free" with membership in Amazon Prime, a sign that the movie has finally hit rock bottom as a commodity. Now it slumbers in a computer somewhere, not so much a desirable "movie" as yet another obsolescent title included as bulk product to better market Amazon's vast library of "free" offerings. If a print does still exist, it sits on a shelf somewhere in Southern California hoping that a rogue programmer at LACMA or MoMA might grant it one final night on the big screen. But, as the film's teen-o slang, hot-rod fetishism, and dance-a-thon plot become increasingly incomprehensible to future generations, the chances of *The Ghost of Dragstrip Hollow* making it back to the silver screen grow ever slimmer with each passing year.

* * * * *

The "death of cinema" ends a long and productive alliance between ghosts and celluloid, a relationship bound by their shared mutual investment in the analog and the indexical. The "pastness" of the photographic image, an ontological feature central to both André Bazin's mummified "realism" and Roland Barthes' melancholy "death in person," ensures that the projected image is always a resurrection in light, a sliver of time and space inexorably receding into history.[1] The celluloid camera, meanwhile, has long been the privileged medium for capturing evidence of a *real* ghost. As Tom Gunning argues of photography's arrival, "the idea that people, places, and objects could somehow leave behind—cause, in fact—their own images gave photography a key role as evidence, in some sense apodictic." But even as "material support for a new positivism,"[2] photography evoked the uncanny, an eeriness that reaches its apotheosis in "spirit photography" and fleeting images of ghosts, specters that index the index of the person captured by photography's mecho-chemical realism. A ghost on film is the intersection of two analog worlds—a presence somehow materializing on the plain of physical reality and an "eye" mechanically rendering the full spectrum of visible light. Motion pictures, or perhaps pictures in motion, have certainly made the transition into the digital age, but not the cinema, a medium that in its transcription and projection of light always promised an analog window on its diegetic and profilmic worlds. Ghosts, meanwhile, are equally allergic to the digital era. As the index of analog beings, a phantom manifesting in the energetic fields that once held the body together, ghosts resist all efforts to be transformed into binary code and stored on a chip.[3]

One could argue that many popular arts (and audiences) are now extinct—stereoscopes locked away in attics; long dormant sheet music to tin-pan alley songs; hours of television broadcast into the ether (and beyond) without any material record left behind. And yet, of all the dead media, the cinema is *particularly dead*. After all, today's reader can encounter *Jane Eyre* in much the same way as the audience of 1848. And while there are twenty forgotten Victorian writers for every Charlotte Brontë, most of these authors can also, in theory at least, be resurrected by simply

---

[1] See André Bazin and Hugh Gray, "The Ontology of the Photographic Image," *Film Quarterly* 13.4 (1960), 4–9; Roland Barthes, *Camera Lucida: Reflections on Photography* (New York: Hill and Wang, 1981). Barthes' essay concentrates on still photography, making its use in cinema studies somewhat contentious. But, even if the celluloid print and still photograph do not share a common form of projection, they nevertheless remain bound as photo-chemical renderings of an absent presence, the past.
[2] Tom Gunning, "Phantom Images and Modern Manifestations: Spirit Photography, Magic Theater, Trick Films and Photography's Uncanny," in *Fugitive Images: From Photography to Video*, ed. Patrice Petro (Bloomington: University of Indiana Press, 1995), 42.
[3] A number of films have attempted to place ghosts in the digital realm, perhaps most notably Kiyoshi Kurosawa's *Pulse* (2001). While this seems a logical trajectory in terms of "haunted media," paranormal theorists have long maintained that the ghost, as a phantom of Being, is a manifestation of various analog spectrums and thus unlikely to survive in a digital environment. For a more detailed discussion of this issue, particularly in relation to recent efforts to digitize the brain, see Jeffrey Sconce, "The Ghostularity," *communication +1*, 4 (2015), http://scholarworks.umass.edu/cpo/

picking up a book. A Mozart recital—more rare now, perhaps—still has a few plausible venues that more or less recreate the basic context of the original performance. One could argue broadcast television is also a dead (or at least dying) medium, but even here a residual body clings to life. There is still a broadcast schedule, and programs from across the history of the medium can still be consumed on a television set. But screening a celluloid print in an actual movie theater is an increasingly impossible task, for a number of very material reasons.

The demise of the celluloid print, long predicted, is now a *fait accompli*. In 2013 Paramount announced that *Anchorman 2*, the belated sequel to 2004's *Anchorman*, would be the studio's final release in a 35mm format. The other majors either have or will soon be following Paramount into the all-digital age, a move that not only cuts distribution costs to theaters, but also acknowledges the ascendency of "secondary" markets to primary status. Even those entities that wish to screen celluloid find it an ever more challenging process. Prints are vanishing (and the studios, typically disinterested in their own history, have little incentive or desire to keep their libraries extant). Screening a celluloid print of a "classic" title is rarely profitable, its last vestiges living on in the highly subsidized "non-profit" venues of gallery, museum, and university. Many a struggling cine club, meanwhile, have discovered that the costs of insurance and HVAC maintenance alone make the seemingly simple act of renting a print, selling tickets, and screening a movie increasingly unfeasible. Unlike *Jane Eyre* or a Mozart concerto, a film screening requires access to a complement of cranky industrial-era technologies that no one has much (financial) interest in making or maintaining any longer. The celluloid print has become so obsolescent, in fact, that a generation of younger artists has adopted the convention of including both screen and projector in the space of a gallery installation—the unwinding reel of film noisily clacking through the film gate becomes part of the spectacle, a signifier of dated modernity more at home in "steampunk" than in the quotidian twenty-first century.

Most arguments concerning the "death of cinema" are fought on the terrain of ontology—a film coded into pixels and scanned onto a monitor (from behind no less!) is qualitatively different than light collected and projected. Truth be told, however, this obsession with ontology typically masks a more haunting absence—the death of the cinephile (and, in more extreme iterations, the film theorist). After all, most of the public has no real stake in the cinema's digital conversion. Vinyl records are more likely to stage a comeback than the celluloid print. There are no riots in the streets, no calls for boycotting, no burning imperatives to save the thousands of prints slowly decaying in storage. The only interested party, seemingly, are cinephiles, an audience that by definition already had an obsessive, even dysfunctional, relationship to the cinema. And though cinephile discourse on celluloid often hides behind aesthetics, lamenting the violence to the image that results from breaking its circuit of analog light, the real "victim" here is the gradual dissolution of an affective bond with something once known as "the cinema." Behind the many threnodies for celluloid as a medium is a melancholy nostalgia for the passing of film culture, an era when not only the "movies mattered," but so too did the critics and theorists of cinema who worshipped in the temple of the local art or rep house.[4]

Today's cinephile, an admittedly residual formation, remains perpetually baffled that the model established by the *Cinémathèque Française* has not survived into the new century. *How could people willingly choose to watch a movie on an iPad rather than spend the evening at the cinema? Why would a person want to debate the merits of a new film through an online flame war when they could do so over cappuccinos at the local cine bar? If kids today understood what they were missing by ignoring cinematic projection, they would put down their X-Boxes and iPhones and demand a new renaissance in the art of cinema.* A more esoteric version of the much-parodied "you kids get off my lawn" meme, such incredulity is less about "art" than age and affect. *How did the Seventh Art, this amazing hallucination of sound and light so central to my very being, end up on the scrapheap of history?* At the height of its influence in the academy, finally, film theory once held the promise that every movie, even something as lowly as *The Ghost of Dragstrip Hollow*, contained an occult secret of some kind—an ideological problematic to dissect, a psychoanalytic repression to unblock. As the cinema dies, so too does the possibility of bringing these secrets into the light of critical exegesis. Thousands of films, like *The Ghost of Dragstrip Hollow*, will survive as digital data (perhaps to the end of human time!)—but the spirit that animated such films as collectively significant and individually mysterious burns low.

Lamentations over the end of the cinema thus evoke yet another ghost—that of the cinephile spectator. Loving the cinema, the celluloid cinema, is an increasingly morbid affair—the aged and aging watching the dead or dying through a nineteenth-century contraption designed for the unlikely mechanical trick of stopping and starting a strip of images wrapped around

---

[4]For a cross-section of such discourse see David Denby, "The Moviegoers: Why Don't People Love the Right Movies Anymore?" in *The Best American Movie Writing, 1999*, ed. Peter Bogdanovich (New York: St. Martin's Griffin, 1999); Dave Kehr, *When Movies Mattered: Reviews from a Transformative Decade* (Chicago: University of Chicago Press, 2011); D.N. Rodowick, *The Virtual Life of Film* (Cambridge: Harvard University Press, 2009).

a cumbersome reel. The question for the future is just how the cinema, as "cinema," will haunt us. Ghost theory distinguishes between two very different manifestations: the poltergeist and the "haunting." For almost a century, parapsychologists have observed that poltergeists most often arrive suddenly and violently—disrupting a household by breaking plates, throwing objects, and generally making a paranormal ruckus. "Hauntings," on the other hand, involve more lingering and intermittent apparitions—the occasional shadow in the corner of the castle, inexplicable footfalls in the attic, a cold spot in the house with an attending bad vibe. While poltergeists seemingly erupt in relation to sexual and/or emotional conflict, "hauntings" focus more on a distant emotional trauma attached to a specific space. The classic haunting involves a ghost that does not know or cannot accept that it is dead, still drawn to the site of an unresolved conflict on the mortal plain. Given the historical affinity between ghosts and the cinema, it is only fitting that the cinema would itself follow this haunted trajectory. Once the brash poltergeist of the art world, celluloid exhibition is, a century after its arrival, a haunted space, charged with the affective energies of an audience that, for better or worse, resists walking into the digital light.

List of Contributors

Robert Alford is a PhD candidate in film and media at UC Berkeley. His research interests include gender and sexuality, sound, new media, critical geography, and sociolinguistics. His dissertation, "'To Know the Words to the Music': Spatial Circulation, Queer Discourse and the Musical" explores the relationship of popular song as an object for consumption and an affective medium to historic patterns of geographical circulation among queers, and the resulting linguistic association between homosexuals and the musical genre.

René Thoreau Bruckner writes and teaches about film history and theory, with particular attention to the related concepts of time, technology, and invention. His areas of interest include pre-cinematic visual culture and early film; early sound film and sound studies; experimental film, animation, and special effects; wildlife cinema and animal studies; and the time travel genre. He is currently building a research project on the history of time machines. His writing has appeared in publications such as *Cinema Journal*, *Discourse*, and *Estudios Visuales*.

Maurizio Cinquegrani is a lecturer in film studies at the University of Kent and has published widely on cinema and urban space. His first monograph, Of *Empire and the City: Remapping Early British Cinema*, was published by Peter Lang in 2014. He is now writing a book on documentary film and Holocaust landscapes for Edinburgh University Press. Swedish cinema is one of his main interests and his earlier scholarly work focused on Swedish pioneer filmmaker Victor Sjöström.

Dara Downey is a lecturer in American literature in the School of English, Drama, and Film in University College Dublin, and the author of *American Women's Ghost Stories in the Gilded Age* (Palgrave, 2014). She is coeditor of *The Irish Journal of Gothic and Horror Studies* and has written numerous articles and essays on gender and domesticity in American gothic fiction and film, from Charles Brockden Brown and Charlotte Perkins Gilman to Shirley Jackson and Stephen King. Her current research revolves broadly around Southern Gothic and religion.

Katherine A. Fowkes is Professor of Media and Popular Culture Studies in the Nido R. Qubein School of Communication at High Point University, where she teaches a wide variety of media courses. She specializes in fantasy films of all varieties, including those featuring comic and melodramatic ghosts. Her most recent book is *The Fantasy Film*.

Tom Gunning is the Edwin A. and Betty L. Bergman Distinguished Service Professor in the Department on Cinema and Media at the University of Chicago. He is the author of *D.W. Griffith and the Origins of American Narrative Film* (University of Illinois Press, 1993) and *The Films of Fritz Lang; Allegories of Vision and Modernity* (British Film Institute, 2000), as well as over hundred and fifty articles on early cinema, film history and theory, avant-garde film, film genre, and cinema and modernism.

Steffen Hantke has written on contemporary literature, film, and culture. He is author of *Conspiracy and Paranoia in Contemporary Literature* (1994), as well as editor of *Horror*, a special topics issue of *Paradoxa* (2002), *Horror: Creating and Marketing Fear* (2004), *Caligari's Heirs: The German Cinema of Fear after 1945* (2007), *American Horror Film: The Genre at the Turn of the Millennium* (2010), and, with Rudolphus Teeuwen, of *Gypsy Scholars, Migrant Teachers, and the Global Academic Proletariat: Adjunct Labor in Higher Education* (2007). He currently teaches at Sogang University in Seoul.

Mark Jancovich is Professor of Film and Television Studies at the University of East Anglia, UK. He is the author of several books: *Horror* (Batsford, 1992); *The Cultural Politics of the New Criticism* (CUP, 1993); *Rational Fears: American Horror in the 1950s* (MUP, 1996); and *The Place of the Audience: Cultural Geographies of Film Consumption* (with Lucy Faire and Sarah Stubbings, BFI, 2003), and the editor of several collections. He is currently writing a history of horror in the 1940s.

Murray Leeder currently teaches film studies at the University of Calgary and holds a PhD (2011) in cultural mediations from Carleton University. He is the author of *Halloween* (Auteur, 2014) and has authored more than a dozen articles, including studies of such ghost films like *The Legend of Hell House*

(1973), *The Fog* (1980), *Poltergeist* (1982), *Ghostwatch* (1992), *Stir of Echoes* (1999), and *Masked and Anonymous* (2003).

Jay McRoy is Professor of English and Cinema Studies at the University of Wisconsin—Parkside. He is the author of *Nightmare Japan: Contemporary Japanese Horror Cinema* (Rodopi, 2008), the editor of *Japanese Horror Cinema* (Edinburgh University Press, 2005), and the coeditor, with Richard Hand, of *Monstrous Adaptations: Generic and Thematic Mutations in Horror Cinema* (Manchester University Press, 2007).

Bernice M. Murphy is a lecturer in popular literature at the School of English, Trinity College, Dublin, and director of the school's MPhil in Popular Literature. She is the author of *The Suburban Gothic in American Popular Culture* (2009), *The Rural Gothic: Backwoods Horror and Terror in the Wilderness* (2013), and *The Highway Horror Film* (2014). She has also edited *Shirley Jackson: Essays on the Literary Legacy* (2005) and coedited *IT Came From the 1950s! Popular Culture, Popular Anxieties* (2011). Along with Elizabeth McCarthy, she is cofounder of the online *Irish Journal of Gothic and Horror Studies*.

Simone Natale is a research associate at Humboldt University Berlin, Germany. He is the author of *The Spectacular Supernatural: Spiritualism and the Rise of the Media Entertainment Industry* (forthcoming in 2016 with Pennsylvania State University Press) and of numerous articles published in journals such as *Media, Culture & Society*, *Media History*, *Early Popular Visual Culture*, *Celebrity Studies*, the *Journal of Radio and Audio Media*, and the *Canadian Journal of Communication*. He has been a research fellow of the Italian Academy at Columbia University, New York City, and a postdoctoral fellow of the Humboldt Foundation at the University of Cologne.

Marc Olivier is Associate Professor of French Studies at Brigham Young University, where he teaches critical theory, European cinema, and French literature. His research on how emerging technologies interact with visual media has led to publications on topics as varied as microscopy, entomology, photography, and horror film. He is currently working on a book about domestic objects and horror.

Jeffrey Sconce is Associate Professor in the Screen Cultures Program at Northwestern University. He is the author of *Haunted Media: Electronic Presence from Telegraphy to Television* (Duke 2000). His forthcoming book, *The Technical Delusion*, examines the historical relationship between electronic media and the boundaries of delusional thinking.

Mitsuyo Wada-Marciano is Professor of Film Studies at Carleton University (Canada). Her research interests are Japanese cinema and East Asian cinema in global culture. She is the author of *Nippon Modern: Japanese Cinema of the 1920s and 1930s* (2008) and the coeditor of *Horror to the Extreme: Changing Boundaries in Asian Cinema* (2009). Her latest publications are *Japanese Cinema in the Digital Age* (2012) and the edited book *Viewing "Postwar" in the 1950s Japanese Cinema* (in Japanese, 2012). She is currently finalizing a book manuscript on the cinema in post-Occupation Japan.

Li Zeng is an associate professor of cinema studies in the School of Theatre and Dance at Illinois State University. She gained her doctoral degree in Radio/Television/Film at Northwestern University in 2008. She has published book chapters, film reviews, and articles on Chinese television and contemporary Chinese cinema in journals including *Jump Cut, Visual Anthropology, Critical Arts*, and the *Journal of American-East Asian Relations.* Her research interests include film history, film genre studies, East Asian cinema, feminist theory, cultural memory, and gender studies.

Index

Abbott, Stacey 181
abjection 172, 187–97, 202, 210
Abraham, Nicholas 131–3
Advise and Consent (1962) 127
Afflicted (2013) 261
AIP. *See* American International Pictures
Alcott, Louisa May 147
Always (1986) 167
American Independent Pictures 123, 126
Amicus Productions 116
Amityville Horror, The (1979) 147, 237, 241–4, 246, 248, 250
Anchorman (2004) 293
Anchorman 2 (2013) 293
Ancuta, Katarzyna 288
Anderson, Jeffrey M. 114
Annabelle (2014) 236
Anthony, Susan B. 17
Argento, Dario 270
Armitt, Lucie 254
L'Armoire des frères Davenport (1902) 34
art cinema, ghosts in 129–42, 271–89
Aspern Paper, The (1947) 125 n.25
Auden, W.H. 163
Audition (1999) 209
Avenging Conscience, The (1914) 41
Awakening, The (2011) 198

Bailey, Dale 244
Baise-moi (2000) 207
Balázs, Béla 6–7, 87
Balmain, Colette 207, 211
Balzac, Honoré de: *Cousin Pons* 18, 22, 38

Banquet, The (*Ye yan*, 2006) 231
Baraduc, Hippolyte 51 n.38
Barthes, Roland 181, 188, 193, 291
Baudrillard, Jean 38, 255
Baudry, Jean-Louis 8, 40
Bazin, André 70 n.26, 291
Bedknobs and Broomsticks (171) 82, 92–3
Beetlejuice (1988) 12, 159, 160, 166–75
Belafonte, Harry 174
Bell, Alexander Graham 22
Belton, John 106
Benjamin, Walter 38
Ben-Hur (1959) 127
Bergman, Ingmar 129–42
Bergson, Henri 105, 163, 168–70, 174, 275
Berserk (1967) 124 n.21
Besant, Annie 51 n.38
Bishop of the Ozarks, The (1923) 6
Black Cat Mansion (1958) 206
Black Narcissus (1947) 125
Blair Witch Project, The (1999) 260–1
Blake, Linnie 202
Blavatsky, Helena 42
Bloom, Claire 120–1, 126
Blumhouse Productions 13, 235–51
Body Snatcher, The (1945) 128
Bolter, Jay 259
Booth, Edwin R. 4
Botting Fred 254–5
Bottomore, Stephen 6
Boucicault, Dion 31
Boulton, Davis 121
Boy with Green Hair, The (1948) 126 n.28
Bradshaw, Peter 274

Brainscan (1997) 196 n.20
Brewster, David 23–4
Briefel, Aviva 10 n.39, 180–1
Brontë, Charlotte: *Jane Eyre* 147, 292–3
Brummett, Barry 6
Buddhism 200, 203, 271–2, 286–7
Bulwer-Lytton, Edward: "The Haunted and the Haunters" 10, 42–6
Bunny Lake is Missing (1965) 124, 127
Buñuel, Luis 114
Burnt Offerings (1976) 12, 124 n.21, 143–58
Burton, Tim 159, 173, 279–80
Butler, Ivan 115

Cabinet of Dr. Caligari, The (1920) 67, 87
Canudo, Ricciotto 6
Capote, Truman 119
Cardinal, The (1963) 127
Carpenter, William Benjamin 63
Carrie (1976) 147
Castle, Terry 11, 40, 54, 66, 70
Castle, William 124
Cat and the Canary, The (1927) 10–11, 60–75
Cat People (1942) 125
Cellphone (*Shouji*, 2003) 230
CGI. *See* computer generated imagery
Chaney, Lon 125
Changeling, The (1980) 250
Charge of the Light Brigade, The (1968) 124
Un Chien Andalou (1929) 258
China, ghost films in 219–33
Chion, Michel 97, 100
Cinephilia 292–3
Citizen Kane (1941) 128
Clarens, Carlos 116
Clayton, Jack 116, 118, 120, 123–6
Cloninger, Curt 261–2
Clover, Carol 214
Coates, Paul 36–7
College Chums (1907) 84
comic ghost films 159–75
computer generated imagery (CGI) 182, 192–8, 220

Conjuring, The (2013) 13, 235–40, 242
Connor, Steven 71, 85
Cook, Florence 28–30
Cowan, Ruth Schwartz 157
Crary, Jonathan 18, 38
Craven, Wes 192
Creed, Barbara 172, 214, 220, 225
Cries and Whispers (*Viskningar och rop*, 1972) 135–6, 139
Cronenberg, David 191–2
Crookes, William 28–9
Crowther, Bosley 110 n.36, 117, 119–20, 122–3
Crying Dead, The (2011) 253
Cui, Shuqing 227
Cure (1997) 209
Curse of the Cat People (1944) 116, 127
Curtis, Barry 8, 10, 246

Daguerre, Louis 18–19, 22
Dark Mirror, The (1946) 125
Dark Secret of Harvest Home, The (1978) 124 n.21
Dark Skies (2013) 236, 237
Dark Water (2002) 209
Dark Waters (1944) 147
Darlington, Susan M. 286–7
Darnton, Robert 23
Davenport Brothers 26, 30, 31, 32–3
Davies, Owen 160, 170
Dead of Night (1945) 125
Dead Ringer (1964) 124 n.21
Dead Silence (2007) 236
Death Sentence (2007) 236
deep ecology 272, 283–5
Defending Your Life (1991) 167
de Havilland, Olivia 124
de Manasseine, Marie 52, 54
de Maupassant, Guy 202
Demon Seed (1977) 107
Derrida, Jacques 7–9, 99, 131, 200, 216
Devant, David 64
Diaboliques, Les (1955) 123
Diary of a High School Bride (1959) 290
digital, the ghost and 195–8, 253–70, 290–5

Doane, Mary Ann 105–6, 148
Dogma (1999) 93 n.22
domesticity, the ghost and 143–58
Dr. No (1962) 127
double exposures. *See*
    superimpositions
Dragonwyck (1946) 125 n.25
draugr 11, 130, 134, 138, 140, 141
du Chomón, Segundo 4

Earthbound (1920) 6
ectoplasm 7, 26, 29–30, 162
Efter repetitionen (*After the Rehearsal*, 1984) 134, 138, 139
8213 Gacy House (2010) 253
Elsaesser, Thomas 281
Encounters of the Spooky Kind (1980) 272
Entity, The (1982) 250
Episode 50 (2011) 253
Epstein, Jean 87
Exodus (1960) 127
Exorcist, The (1973) 107, 144, 172–3, 179, 242, 248
Experiment Perilous (1944) 126

Fanny and Alexander (*Fanny och Alexander*, 1982) 139, 141
Faraday, Michael 63
femme fatale 220–6
financial crisis 235–51
Fog, The (1982) 3 n.10
Fontaine, Joan 124
Forbidden Planet (1956) 122 n.16
found-footage horror 12, 13, 197–8, 253–70
4 Months, 3 Weeks and 2 Days (2007) 274
Fowkes, Katherine A. 9, 159–75
Fox sisters, the 22, 84–5, 182 n.7
Francis, Freddie 119
Freer, Ada Goodrich 50
Freeze Out (2000) 206
Freud, Sigmund: *The Psychopathology of Everyday Life* 54; "The Uncanny" 19–22, 40, 53
Friday the 13th (1980) 213, 214, 269
Friedberg, Anne 259

Frighteners, The (1996) 179
From Russia with Love (1963) 127
Frostbiten (2006) 142 n.21
Fukurai, Tomokichi 49
Funny Girl (1968) 127

Gabo, Frank 131
Gallagher, Leigh 248
Game of Death (1945) 128
Gandhi, Mohandas 284–5
German Expressionism 80–4
Ghost (1990) 167, 168
Ghost and Mrs. Muir, The (1947) 1, 3, 159
Ghost Breakers, The (1940) 59
Ghostbusters (1984) 179, 272
Ghost Dad (1990) 159
Ghost Dance (1983) 7, 200
Ghost Hunters (2004–) 2
Ghost in the Invisible Bikini, The (1966) 291
Ghost in the Machine (1993) 196 n.20
Ghost of Dragstrip Hollow, The (1959) 290–1, 295
Ghost of Otama Pond, The (1960) 206
Ghost Sisters (*Gui mei*, 1985) 226, 229
Ghostwatch (1992) 189, 196
Gillman, Charlotte Perkins: "The Yellow Wallpaper" 54
glitches 253–70
Glitre, Kathrina 161
glocalization 277, 287–8
Goethe, Johann Wolfgang von 87
Goldstein, Alvin G. 55
Golem, wie er in die Welt kam, Der (1920) 77–93
Gonzalez, Ed 113–14
Goodbye Dragon Inn (2003) 280
Gordon, Avery 1 n.1, 201
Gorky, Maxim 5–6, 42, 43
gothic 126, 144–51, 254–5; glitch gothic 253–70; marital gothic 147–8
Gothika (2003) 147
Grave Encounters 2 (2012) 253, 266–7, 270
Greene, Graham 4
Greystone Park (2012) 253

Grusin, Richard 259
Gunning, Tom 10, 17–34, 83–4, 248–50, 292
Guy Named Joe, A (1943) 169

Hagener, Malte 281
Halloween (1978) 184, 185, 213, 214
Hammer Film Productions 116, 123, 126
Hangover Square (1945) 126
Hanke, Ken 114
Harlow, Jean 4
Harris, Julie 120–1, 122, 126–7
Harry Potter (series) 89
Harry Potter and the Chamber of Secrets (2002) 255–6
Hatty, Suzanne E. 148–9
haugbúi 11, 131
haunted house narrative 59–75, 143–58, 160–75, 184, 235–51, 264
Haunting, The (1963) 11, 115–28, 144, 150, 154, 184, 185
Heaven Can Wait (1977) 168
Here Comes Mr. Jordan (1941) 168
Holland, Norman 148
Holt, Victoria 147
Horsfield, Margaret 157
Hot Rod Gang (1958) 290
Houdini, Harry 32–3, 65
Hour of the Wolf (*Vargtimmen*, 1968) 136–7, 139
House Next Door, The (1978) 243
housework 143–58
Hush ... Hush Sweet Charlotte (1964) 124 n.21
Hutchings, Peter 126

I Saw What You Did (1969) 124 n.21
I Spit On Your Grave (1978) 206
Ichi the Killer (2001) 209
Innocents, The (1961) 11, 60, 115–28, 144, 182 n.8, 186–7
Inside an Old Grave (Gu mu huang zhai, 1991) 227
Insidious (2001) 13, 235–41, 243, 246, 248
Insidious: Chapter 2 (2013) 236

Invisible Woman, The (1940) 164
Iron Claw, The (1916) 84
Irving, Henry 31

Jackson, Michael: "Black or White" 193 n.18
Jackson, Shirley: *The Haunting of Hill House*: 144, 154, 239–40
Jacobs, Ken 13
James, Henry: "Turn of the Screw, The" 54, 116, 124, 144
Jancovich, Mark 115–28, 145–8
Jane Eyre (1944) 125 n.25
Japan, ghost films in 199–217
J-Horror 196–7, 209–16
Johnson, Richard 126
Jordan, David Starr 10, 47–9
Journey into the Unknown (1969) 124 n.21
Joyce, James: *The Dead* 134
Ju-on: The Grudge (2002) 209, 213–16
Ju-on (series, 2002–2006) 13, 200, 206

Kafka, Franz 2
kaidan 200–2
Kellar, Harry 65
Kepler, Johannes 259
Kerr, Deborah 118, 119, 120, 124–5
King, Katie 28–30
King, Stephen: *Danse Macabre* 115–16, 244; *The Shining* 144, 148–9
Kliner, Barbara 128
Knock Knock 2 (2011) 261
Kovacs, Lee 9
Kristeva, Julia 172, 187–90
Kuroneko (1968) 200, 206–9, 209

Lady in a Cage (1964) 124 n.21
Laemmle, Carl 61
Lailai wangwang (1998) 230
Last Exorcism, The (2010) 197
Laura (1944) 183–4
Let the Right One In (*Låt den rätte komma in*, 2008) 142
Leadbetter, C.W. 52
Le Fanu, J. Sheridan 145

Legend of Hell House, The (1973) 107, 184
Leiber, Fritz: *Conjure Wife* 125
Leni, Paul 60
Lévy, Maurice 254
Lewton, Val 116, 128
Liaozhai (1986) 227
Lightfoot, Gordon: "If You Could Read My Mind" 10, 39–40, 56
Lim, Bliss Cua 2, 102, 275
Limelight (1952) 126 n.28
Lindqvist, Ajdvide: *Handling the Undead* (*Hanteringen av odöda*) 141–2
logos 87–8
Longest Night in Shanghai, The (*Ye Shanghai*, 2007) 231
Look Back in Anger (1959) 124
Lord of the Rings, The (series) 89, 280
Luciano, Dana 84
Luckhurst, Roger 9
Lucretius 259
Lundemo, Trond 3

Magic. *See* stage magic
Magician, The (*Ansiktet*, 1958) 136, 137–8, 139
Manon, Hugh S. 261–3
Manovich, Lev 259
Marasco, Robert: *Burnt Offerings* 144, 149, 152–4, 158
Martini, Simone 88
Maskelyne, John Neville 31, 33, 36, 37, 65
Maskelyne, Neville 65
Massé, Michelle 147
Matheson, Richard: *Hell House* 240; *A Stir of Echoes* 56
Matrimony (*Xingzhong yougui*, 2007) 221, 230–2
Matrix, The (1999) 264
Matter of Life and Death, A (1946) 169
Mayerling, The (1968) 127
McCorristine, Shane 50
mediumship. *See* names of particular individuals
Medusa 225
Méliès, Georges 4, 22, 33–5, 37, 65

Mendeleev, Dmitri 63
Menkman, Rosa 261
Merleau-Ponty, Maurice 99–100
Metropolis (1927) 80
Metz, Christian 104–5
Midnight Lace (1960) 124
Mierendorff, Carlo 86–7
Milbank, Alison 42
Miller, Daniel 151
Morgenson, Gretchen 249
Morioka, Masahiro 285
Most Dangerous Game, The (1932) 128
Most Haunted (2002–2010) 2
Mozart, Wolfgang Amadeus 293
Ms. 45 (1971) 207
Müller, Robert 86–7
Mulvey, Laura 6
Mumler, William H. 24–5, 27
Münsterberg, Hugo 54, 63
My Amityville Horror (2012) 242
Myers, Frederick W.H. 50

Nadar 19
Naess, Arne 272, 284–5
Nanny, The (1965) 124 n.22
Nanthakhun, Phrakhru Pitak 286
Napier, Susan 214
Nathan, Robert: *Portrait of Jennie* 98
Natheephitak, Phrakhru Manas 286
Nead, Lynda 4, 51–2, 61
Nelson, Victoria 254
nensha 49
Night Must Fall (1964) 123
Night of the Eagle (1962) 124
Night Walker, The (1964) 124
Nightmare on Elm Street (1984) 213, 214
Noah, Timothy 244–5
noise 70–3, 253–70
Noriko's Dinner Table (2005) 209
Nosferatu (1922) 80, 181
Nowell, Richard 146–7

Ogier, Pascale 7–8
Oh God! (1977) 93 n.22
Old Dark House, The (1932) 59
Omen, The (1976) 146

INDEX

100 Ghost Street: The Return of Richard Speck (2012) 253, 268
One Missed Call (2008) 196, 255
onryō 199–216
Orphanage, The (2007) 240
Others, The (2001) 192, 240
Ozu, Yasujirō 184, 215

Packer, George 244, 250–1
Paik, Nam June 265
Painted Skin (Hua pi, 2008) 13, 219–33
Painted Skin: The Resurrection (2012) 233
Palladino, Eusapia 63
Pan, Laikwan 222
Paranormal Activity (2009) 13, 197, 235–41, 248–50
Paranormal Asylum: The Revenge of Typhoid Mary (2013) 253
Paranormal Incident (2011) 253
Paul, Robert W. 64
Paul, William 173
Peeping Tom (1960) 146
Peirce, Charles Sanders 13
Pepper's Ghost 5, 41
Peters, John Durham 3
Phantasmagoria 40, 66
Phantom Carriage, The (Körkarlen, 1921) 6
Photography. *See* nensha; spirit photography; thoughtograph
Pizzotto, Mark 10
Place, Janey 225
Plato's Cave 40
Pliny the Younger 40
Poltergeist (1982) 189, 196, 237–43, 248, 250, 255, 267
poltergeists 295
Portrait of Jennie (1948) 11, 97–114
Preminger, Otto 127
Psycho (1960) 123, 144, 146, 167, 267
Pu Songling: *Strange Tales from Liaozhai* 219, 220–1, 224, 226, 231
Pulse (2001) 209, 255, 267, 292 n.3
Pulse (2006) 196
Purge, The (2013) 236, 7
Purge: Anarchy, The (2014) 236

Qian shou (1999) 230
quality horror 115–28

Rabuzzi, Kathryn Allen 156
Radcliffe, Ann 144
Rank, Otto 22
Rashomon (1950) 108
Rayner, Alice 9–10, 56
Rebecca (1940) 124, 144, 183, 184–5
Redgrave, Michael 125
Reel Evil (2012) 253
Reisz, Karel 123
Return from Witch Mountain (1978) 124 n.21
Rice, Anne: *Interview with the Vampire* 192 n.16
Richardson, Tony 123–4
Richet, Charles 29–30
Ring/Ringu (1998) 4, 209, 210–12, 240, 250, 255
Ringu (series 1998–2005) 13, 200, 206, 210
Ringu 2 (1999) 210
Ringu 0: Bāsudei (2000) 210
Ring, The (2002) 196, 210, 267
Ring Virus, The (1998) 210
Robert-Houdin, Jean Eugène 32
Robertson, Roland 287–8
romance, the ghost and 97–114, 219–34
Romance with a Fox (Hu yuan, 1986) 226
Romero, George 192
Romney, Jonathan 282–3
Room at the Top (1959) 118, 119, 124
Rosemary's Baby (1968) 124, 146
Ruffles, Tom 9

Sandhu, Sukhdev 282, 288–9
Saturday Night and Sunday Morning (1960) 123
Savini, Tom 192
Scared Stiff (1953) 59
Scary Movie series 193
Sconce, Jeffrey 2, 3, 13, 53 n.45, 99, 107, 255, 290–5
Scream (1996) 209
Screaming Woman, The (1972) 124 n.21
séances 22–3, 28–32, 62, 85
Secret Beyond the Door (1947) 124, 144

Selznick, David O. 98–9, 100, 103, 104, 110–14
Serios, Ted 49
Seven Brides for Seven Brothers (1954) 126 n.28
Shannon, Claude 72
Shaolin Soccer (2001) 231
Sherlock Jr. (1924) 41
Sherman, Leona 148
Shiller, Robert J. 245
Shining, The (1980) 144, 147–9, 154–5, 184, 185–6, 190–2, 194
Shinto 200
Siddons, Anne Rivers 143, 150
Sigh, A (*Yisheng tanxi*, 2000) 230
Sikov, Ed 161
Silent Light (2007) 288
Silverman, Kaja 108
Sinister (2012) 13, 235–41, 246–8, 251
Sir Arne's Treasure (*Herr Arnes pengar*, 1919) 129, 140
Sixth Sense, The (1999) 12, 168, 179–81, 192
Sjöström, Victor 129, 130, 132–3
sjunde inseglet, Det (*The Seventh Seal*, 1957) 130
slow cinema 272, 280–3
Smith, George Albert 4, 65
Sobchack, Vivian 73
Society for Psychical Research, the 49
Sommerlek (*Summer Interlude*, 1951) 133, 134, 136
Sons of Ingmar (1919, *Ingmarssönerna*) 129
sound 11, 70–3, 77–93, 97–114. *See also* noise
Sound of Music, The (1965) 127
Spadoni, Robert 71
Spinoza, Baruch 132, 284
Spiral (1998) 210
Spiral Staircase, The (1945) 122, 123
Spirit, A (*Jing bian*, 1983) 226
spirit photography 2, 24–38, 67–70. *See also* Mumler, William
spiritualism 22–38, 41, 50–4, 59–75, 84–7. *See also* ectoplasm; séances; spirit photography; spiritualist exposures

spiritualist exposures 59–75
Spiritualist Photographer, The (1903) 34–5
Sripariyattiweti, Abbot Phra 271
stage magic 31–5, 64–5, 67, 74. *See also* names of particular individuals
stAllio! 263
Stanwyck, Barbara 124
Stead, W.T. 6, 10, 50–3
Still Life (2006) 288
Stiller, Mauritz 129
Stir of Echoes (1999) 10, 55–6, 192
Stone Tape, The (1972) 3 n.10
Stott, Andrew 163, 164, 172
Straight-Jacket (1974) n.21
Strindberg, August 134, 138–9
Student of Prague, The (1913) 22
suburbia 235–51
Suicide Club (2001) 209
Sunday's Children (*Söndagsbarn*, 1992) 138
superimpositions 5, 24, 34, 67–70, 130. *See also* spirit photography
Suzhou he (*Suzhou River*, 2000) 231
Suzuki, Koji: *Ringu* 210

Temken, Daniel 261–3
Ten Commandments, The (1923) 78–93
Ten Commandments, The (1956) 91–2, 93
Teo, Stephen 219–20
Terminator 2: Judgment Day (1991) 193 n.18
Tetsuo, the Iron Man (1989) 209
Thailand, ghosts films in 271–89
These Amazing Shadows (2011) 44
Thief of Bagdad, The (1924) 83
Thompson, Silvanus 47
thoughtography 48–9
Three Men and a Baby (1987) 4
Through a Glass Darkly (*Såsom i en spegel*, 1961) 131
Thunderball (1965) 127
Tibbett, John C. 186
time, the ghost and 97–114, 274–80
Todorov, Tzvetan 11, 43, 60

Tokyo Fist (1995) 209
Tolkien, J.R.R.: *The Lord of the Rings* 280
Tom Jones (1963) 123–4
Tom Thumb (1958) 216
Tomie: Re-Birth (2001) 209
Toop, David 73
Topper (1937) 12, 159–66, 168, 169, 171–2, 174–5
Torok, Maria 131–3
Toynbee, Arnold J. 276
Trip to the Moon, A (1903) 34
Trog (1970) 124 n.22
Truly, Madly, Deeply (1991) 167
Turvey, Malcolm 87 n.15
Twilight series 147
Twin Peaks (1990–1) 126 n.28
Txt (2006) 255
Tyler, Parker 7

Ueda, Akinari 202
Ugetsu Monogatari (1953) 200, 202–6
uncanny 19–22, 40, 51–2, 74, 99, 107–8, 131–2, 140, 181, 189, 202, 211, 255–6, 259–60, 263
 technological uncanny 6
Uncle Boonmee Who Can Recall His Past Lives (2010) 10, 13, 271–89
Uninvited, The (1944) 186–7

Vampyrer (2010) 142 n.21
Vertov, Dziga 87, 257
V/H/S (2012) 197, 264–6, 268
V/H/S/2 (2013) 256–260, 264–6
Villiers de L'Isle-Adam: "The Very Image" 20–1
Virgin Spring, The (*Jungfrukällan*, 1960) 206
Virtuosity (1995) 196 n.20
vision/visibility 31–57, 179–98, 256–60
von Reichenbach force 49
von Uchatius, Franz 51

Wait Until Dark (1967) 124, 127
Walas, Chris 192

Wallace, Alfred Russell 36
Walpore, Horace: *The Castle of Otranto* 264
Washington Square (1949) 125 n.25
Watcher in the Woods (1980) 124 n.21
Watson, Thomas 22
Wayne, Mike 10 n.39, 250
Wei, Xiao 225–6
Weird Woman (1944) 124
Welles, Orson 128
West Side Story (1961) 126 n.28, 127
Wharton, Edith 147
What Lies Beneath (2000) 147, 192–5
Whatever Happened to Baby Jane? (1962) 124
Wheatley, Helen 116
Whissel, Kristen 89, 197 n.21
White Noise (2005) 3 n.10
White Ribbon, The (2009) 274
Wild Strawberries (*Smultronstället*, 1957) 132, 134
Willard, John 60
Wilson, Sloane: *The Man in the Gray Flannel Suit* 151
Winston, Stan 192
Winter Lights (*Nattvardsgästerna*, 1962) 133
Wise, Damon 274, 279, 281
Wise, Robert 116, 120–1, 127–8
Witches, The (1966) 134
Wizard of Oz, The (1939) 67
Woman in Black, The (1989) 184
Woman in Black, The (2012) 184, 198
Wonderful World of the Brothers Grimm, The (1962) 126 n.28
Wood, Nancy 106
Wyler, William 127

Xianchu, Wan 225
X-rays (Röntgen rays) 44, 47, 49–50

Young, Terence 127

Zakas, Laimonas (Glitchr) 263
Žižek, Slavoj 131–2, 141

www.ingramcontent.com/pod-product-compliance
Lightning Source LLC
Chambersburg PA
CBHW070750020526
44115CB00032B/1603